"In this volume Bruce Waltke, James Houston, and Erika Moore cover a selection of psalms that strikingly combine sadness and sorrow with faith and hope. . . . Masterful exegesis here blends with luminous theological perspectives and pastoral insights."

— J. I. PACKER
Regent College

"If you plan to preach on these hymns of hurt and confusion, this book is a good place to begin. Each psalm is translated in a helpful way, which is vital for preaching these psalms well."

— HADDON ROBINSON
*Gordon-Conwell
Theological Seminary*

"Here is the finest of guides to laments in the book of Psalms. The authors recover a cogent interpretation of personal sin that forms the basis of the need for God's redemption. The cry of lament begins in the heart of the psalmist — and of his readers — and proceeds to express complete dependence on God. Journey on this ancient path of laments that bring us into God's presence as no other texts of Scripture do."

— RICHARD S. HESS
Denver Seminary

The Psalms as Christian Lament

A Historical Commentary

Bruce K. Waltke, James M. Houston, and Erika Moore

WILLIAM B. EERDMANS PUBLISHING COMPANY
GRAND RAPIDS, MICHIGAN

Published 2014 by
Wm. B. Eerdmans Publishing Co.
2140 Oak Industrial Drive N.E., Grand Rapids, Michigan

Library of Congress Cataloging-in-Publication Data

Waltke, Bruce K.
The Psalms as Christian lament: a historical commentary /
Bruce K. Waltke, James M. Houston, and Erika Moore. pages
cm
Includes bibliographical references and index.
ISBN 978-0-8028-6809-1 (pbk.: alk. paper)

1. Bible. Psalms — Criticism, interpretation, etc.
2. Laments in the Bible.
I. Title.

BS1445.L3W35   2014
223'.206 — dc23

2013048119

www.eerdmans.com

Contents

Contents

Contents

PROLOGUE

Biblical lament is too mysterious to equate cheaply with psychological complaint. Nor can it be comprehended exhaustively for a seminary textbook. It certainly reflects upon the human condition, but it also reflects upon the character of God. It is a vital aspect, then, of theological anthropology, itself an increasingly central concern for Christianity in the twenty-first century. Our study of lament psalms will hopefully provide a basis for a theology of lament.

Our motive is not that of previous scholarship that identified one genre or category of the Psalter as "lament psalms," in contrast to other genres, such as praise.[1] Our selection of psalms would then be debatable, for other psalms could have been chosen as more expressive of the genre identified as "lament." We have, in fact, in our collaborate effort to combine the history of the interpretation with contemporary exegesis of selected psalms, simply taken the traditional "seven penitential psalms," of which Psalm 51 was already selected in our previous work,[2] together with Psalms 5 to 7 as a cluster, together with special pleas for Psalms 44 and 49.

As we shall see, the early Church Fathers did not take their "penitential" character with the same literal emphasis as the medieval culture was to do later. Our sample, then, is in no sense comprehensive, but more contextual of a basic human posture of our finitude, of our sinful nature, of our need of redemption, of our trust and communion with God, all in the light of God's purpose for humanity to be created and destined in the *imago dei*.

As for finitude, the problem of being persecuted for righteousness' sake was more vexing for the psalmist in the old dispensation than for Christians in the new dispensation. The old dispensation promised blessings to those who

---

1. Bruce K. Waltke and James M. Houston with Erika Moore, *The Psalms as Christian Worship: A Historical Commentary* (Grand Rapids/Cambridge, UK: Eerdmans, 2010), pp. 93-95.
2. *The Psalms as Christian Worship*, pp. 446-83.

were faithful and obedient to God's law and threatened his punishment against the unfaithful and disobedient (cf. Leviticus 26; Deuteronomy 28). Though the first prophecy in the Bible — "he [the offspring of the woman] will crush your [the Serpent's] head and you will strike his heel" (Gen. 3:15) — hints at the persecution of the righteous, the Book of the Law by Moses, the human founder of Israel, did not express that inevitability. In the old dispensation, many saints (e.g., Abel, Job, Moses, Jeremiah) suffered, like the psalmists, for being faithful. Several Old Testament stories recognize the spiritually formative value of suffering. In the wilderness, Israel learned what living with the LORD meant. Through causing Israel to hunger and then feeding them, the LORD taught them to be teachable (Exod. 16:4; Deut. 8:2-4). By allowing the Canaanites to remain in the land he taught holy warfare to the descendants of Joshua's generation (Judg. 3:1-2). But mostly the old dispensation kept saints in the dark about the necessity of the righteous to suffer the buffeting of the wicked. By contrast, the Lord Jesus Christ, confiding in his followers as friends, teaches them clearly that they will be persecuted. "Servants," he said, "are not greater than their master. If they [the world] persecuted me, they will persecute you also" (John 15:20). Because of their finitude, Christians are still perplexed about undeserved sufferings (2 Cor. 4:8-9), but, because they have been forewarned, they do not protest them but expect them (cf. 2 Tim. 2:3, 12), unlike the innocent psalmists, who protest their sufferings.[3] In short, as a result of Christ's forewarning, one cannot speak of "the psalms as Christian complaint."

To be sure, Christians, like the psalmists, mourn their sufferings, and they hunger and thirst for righteousness (cf. Matt. 5:3-11). The Lord Jesus with the psalmist said "my soul is troubled" (John 12:27; Ps. 6:2-3[3-4]), and "into your hands I commit my spirit" (Luke 23:46; Ps. 31:5[6]). Like the lamenting psalmist, he was "hated without reason" (John 15:25; Ps. 35:19) and a "close friend lifted his heel against [him]" (John 13:18; Ps. 41:9[10]). Paul also identified with the psalmist when he wrote: "For your sake we face death all day long; we are considered as sheep to be slaughtered" (Rom. 8:36; Ps. 44:22[23]). But, unlike the psalmist, Christians rejoice in their suffering, and this for two reasons. First, Christians, more so than the psalmists, know that undeserved sufferings produce virtues (Rom. 5:3-5; Jas. 1:2-3; 1 Pet. 1:7). And second, because Jesus Christ "has brought life and immortality to light" through his death for sin, burial, and authenticated resurrection (2 Tim. 1:10; 1 Cor. 15:3-8), they know better than the psalmist that great is the reward in heaven of those who are persecuted because of righteousness and faith in Jesus Christ (Matt. 5:10-12; 1 Pet. 4:13). Francis Bacon said well: "Prosperity is the blessing of the

---

3. *The Psalms as Christian Worship*, pp. 95-97.

Old Testament; adversity is the blessing of the New, which carries the greater benediction, and the clearer revelation of God's favor."[4] Moberly comments on this opposition and persecution: "The Christian vision can contextualize such things within the life of discipleship."[5] In short, one cannot speak of "the psalms as Christian joy in suffering."

Being "poor" and being in "lament" are linked in the Psalter: in seeking righteousness in the law court as a plaintiff; in crying out for help in danger, oppression, and the threat of death; in need of health and cure in the presence of sickness and disease; and, in the truly penitential psalms, in seeking forgiveness, redemption, and restoration of communion with God.[6] Lament is then both individual and national; and this is especially true in the psalms, for they are often the lament of Israel's king, who is in corporate solidarity with his people.[7]

Mysteriously, Jesus Christ himself, as the God-Man, fed his inner life in communion with his Father, at the significant stages of his life and death, on the Hebrew Psalms. He probably first learned them at his mother's knee as a small child (cf. Ps. 22:9-10[10-11]; 2 Tim. 1:5; 3:14-15). When he was baptized in solidarity with all humanity, the recitation of a psalm gave clarity to his earthly mission. In his nakedness and cruel suffering on the cross, it was with a psalm that he died.[8] As the epistle to the Hebrews comments, "in the days of his flesh, Jesus offered up prayers and supplications with loud cries and tears, to him who was able to save him from death, and he was heard because of his reverence" (Heb. 5:7). Likewise in the persecution and suffering of his followers, Paul and Silas, who chanted psalms at midnight while they were imprisoned (Acts 16:25).

As the Fathers of the fourth century struggled to sustain both the humanity and the deity of Christ, within the Greek culture of the immutability of the divine, the Nicene Christianity that was shaped through these struggles inserted a critical article: "for us . . . he was made man." This we may paraphrase as "who for the sake of human persons was made a human person." The incarnation is *for* a specifiable objective.[9] Biblical lament is subsumed within this divine

---

4. Francis Bacon, "Essays or Counsels Civil and Moral," Essay V, in *Harvard Classics,* vol. 3, ed. Charles W. Eliot (New York: P. F. Collier & Son, 1937), p. 16.

5. R. W. L. Moberly, *Old Testament Theology: Reading the Hebrew Bible as Christian Scripture* (Grand Rapids: Baker Academic, 2013), p. 236.

6. Steven J. L. Croft, *The Individual in the Psalms* (Sheffield: JSOT Press, 1987), pp. 49-72.

7. *The Psalms as Christian Worship*, pp. 91, 106.

8. Samuel Terrien, *The Psalms and Their Meaning for Today* (Indianapolis: Bobbs-Merrill, 1952), p. viii.

9. Robert W. Jenson, "For Us . . . He Was Made Man," in *Nicene Christianity: The Future for a New Ecumenism,* ed. Christopher R. Seitz (Grand Rapids: Brazos, 2001), pp. 75-83.

purpose. For to have a genuine human existence as God intended us to enjoy is to exercise lament before him. This is expressive of his sovereign grace, of our trust in his good purposes, and of our final destiny, to be transformed to the image of his Son.

Our historical commentaries are not comprehensive; rather, they are selected vignettes showing how lament was exercised for particular concerns and personal issues at differing periods of church history. Each of the early Fathers has his own style of pastoral theology that expresses his own personhood. Only from the time of Bede and Alcuin do the numerical "seven Penitential psalms" begin to have social force, as the penitential culture from the thirteenth century until the Reformation dominated the use of the Psalter.[10] As Michael P. Kuczynski observes so well: "The psalms came to shape late medieval moral discourse so dramatically because writers who knew the Psalms intimately . . . argued that the ethical principles latent in the Psalms could and must be applied to the daily everyday behavior of late medieval people."[11]

In the England of Henry VIII, the penitential psalms might subtly have been used as a political protest against his marital affairs.[12] Lament psalms were also appropriated in the ways rivalry operated even among the reformers.

Such historical insights should caution our use and perhaps misuse of the lament psalms for our own cultural contexts and individual agendas. For as we face the aging of a large segment of the population, we are beginning to reinterpret the Baby Boomers' culture of professional "success" into "a disability culture" of caring for an excessive population of the aged.[13] Lament, then, will take on new significance.

Such shifting perspectives make it all the more important that "lament" be based on its biblical expressions. Crucial in this century is the need of a deepening understanding of theological anthropology. Just as the mystery of *creatio ex nihilo* is linked with the call of Abraham, so too human personhood cannot be

10. Clare Costley King'oo, *Miserere Mei: The Penitential Psalms in Late Medieval and Early Modern England* (Notre Dame, IN: University of Notre Dame Press, 2012). While comprehensive as a literary study, it reveals the Catholic bias toward a "penitential culture" that is still interpreted as "Augustinian" in origin. It ignores the Carolingian reform as being the strong precursor of medieval penitential culture.

11. Michael P. Kuczynski, "The Psalms and Social Action in Late Medieval England," in *The Place of the Psalms in the Intellectual Culture of the Middle Ages,* ed. Nancy van Dusen (Albany, NY: State University of New York Press, 1999), pp. 191-214.

12. Clare Costley King'oo, "Rightful Penitence and the Publication of Wyatt's *Certayne Psalmes,*" in *Psalms in the Early Modern World,* ed. Linda Phyllis Austern, Kari Boyd McBride, and David L. Orvis (Burlington, VT: Ashgate, 2011), pp. 155-74.

13. Hans S. Reinders, *Receiving the Gift of Friendship: Profound Disability, Theological Anthropology, and Ethics* (Grand Rapids /Cambridge, UK: Eerdmans, 2008).

understood without the doctrine of the *imago dei*.[14] Both are metaphysical categories that do not contradict human sciences, but add a dimension unavailable to human understanding. "Lament-before-God" is a similar category, transcending human complaint when only viewed in terms of secular psychology.[15] No one scholarly discipline can be independent of the other, as we are trying to express in this work. For we are standing at a new door of perception, a new specialty that may become for the next generation of scholars "a theology of lament."

Our biblical exegete, Dr. Bruce Waltke, professor emeritus of biblical studies, Regent College, has devoted much of his academic life to the textual study of the Psalms, to give us, like Calvin before him, "the plain meaning of the text."[16] His exegetical studies comprise the central substance of our book. Dr. James Houston, founding principal of Regent College and professor emeritus of spiritual theology, has provided the history of commentary and the personal profiles of its selected contributors. Dr. Erika Moore, professor of Old Testament at Trinity School for Ministry in Ambridge, Pennsylvania, wrote the exegetical portion for Psalm 39, did valuable editing, and prepared the glossary and indices.

---

14. David B. Burrell, Carlo Cogliati, Janet M. Soskice, and William R. Stoeger, eds., *Creation and the God of Abraham* (Cambridge: Cambridge University Press, 2010).

15. We can be sympathetic to attempts to relate the Psalms to human dependency and suffering, such as proposed by Dennis Sylva, *Psalms and the Transformation of Stress: Poetic-Communal Interpretation and the Family* (Louvain: Peeters, 1996), but such attempts do not interpret biblical lament.

16. See Bruce K. Waltke, "Biblical Theology of the Psalms Today: A Personal Perspective," in *The Psalms: Language for All Seasons of the Soul,* ed. Andrew J. Schmutzer and David M. Howard Jr. (Chicago: Moody Publishers, 2013), pp. 19-28.

CHAPTER 1

The Psalms as the Christian's Lament

I. The Importance of Lament in the Psalter

If, as John Calvin asserted, "the Psalms are the mirror of the soul," then lament is a major element. For more than a third of the Psalter consists of "lament psalms." Some forty-two are individual laments, and another sixteen are corporate laments. Ten of these lament psalms echo the wisdom psalms in their focus on the Torah. R. W. L. Moberly notes that "the predominance of laments at the very heart of Israel's prayers means that the problems that give rise to lament are not something marginal or unusual but rather are central to the life of faith. . . . Moreover they show that the experience of anguish and puzzlement in the life of faith is not a sign of deficient faith, something to be outgrown or put behind one, but rather is intrinsic to the very nature of faith."[1]

In iconography the helplessness of outstretched arms, the postures of kneeling in supplication, or of abandonment in lying upon the dust of the ground, how both body and spirit are poured out in grief, express the most intimate feelings of grief in a very public way.[2] Such lament follows the theme that once everything was good, but now all is lost. In a dirge like 2 Samuel 1:17-27 or 3:33, the "lostness" is expressed "in a long series of very specific gestures and postures: one crouched on the ground, threw dust on the head, rent the clothes, donned coarse apparel, abstained from nourishment" (Pss. 35:13-14; 69:10-11[11-12]). Thus the inwardly chaotic emotions are expressed outwardly in these differing bodily actions.[3]

Yet this intense — almost violent — embodied form of prayer, while still in the Christian liturgy, is not practiced today with the intensity that the Psalms

---

1. R. W. L. Moberly, "Lament," *NIDOTTE*, IV, 879.
2. Othmar Keel, *The Symbolism of the Biblical World: Ancient Near Eastern Iconography and the Book of Psalms,* trans. Timothy J. Hallett (Winona Lake, IN: Eisenbrauns, 1997), pp. 318-23.
3. Keel, *Symbolism,* pp. 318-19.

seem to convey. Erich Zenger in his study on the psalms of divine wrath articulates the protest of other German scholars, such as Otto Bayer and Ottmar Fuchs, that our liturgical prayer culture suffers great depletion when lament is absent.[4] Without it we cannot express our solidarity with the sick, the disabled, the persecuted, the tortured, the dying — that is, with those in the depths of despair and darkest desolation. Terrorism, the increasing violence of our times, medical advances in which the escalation of disabilities accompanies the prolonged ageing of our population, as well as the effects of global warming in environmental disasters, are all deepening causes for general lament today.

Depression is becoming a pandemic condition, which along with stress-related diseases is promoting much lament.[5] If "Pain — is missed — in Praise," as Emily Dickinson suggested, then as some pastoral theologians are now arguing, it is time we began to make more use of lament as a renewed focus for hope.[6]

II. The Loss and Gain of Lament in Our Western Society

It is obvious that "lament" and "confession" are not central features of our Western Christian life today. Rather a "programmatic" and pragmatic view of Christian action prevails, reflecting the secular attitude around us. The pursuit of knowledge, rather than the desire to be "known of God," does not encourage a confessional posture. The autonomous agent, who in self-sufficiency excels in all the gadgetry of the "Electronic Revolution," is reluctant to see him or herself as "despairing in absolute need." Lament and confession as expressed in the psalms both require that one stand in the presence of God as Sovereign and Holy Lord, implying accountability, openness to the Other, awareness of sin, of personal shortcoming, and of attribution of the whole cosmos to the Creator. Public lament is no longer practiced in our culture when we no longer review the past as "open to a God-directed history," as expressed in the Old Testament. On occasion, we may confess "sins," but "sin" as the universal human condition of humanity before God is not an inducement for confession as expressive of Christian identity today.

The strong Roman Catholic tradition of priestly confession was reexamined by the Synod of Bishops in 1983 in order to study the contemporary "crisis of confession." Since, traditionally, Catholics profess to having a confessional

---

4. Erich Zenger, *A God of Vengeance*, trans. Linda L. Maloney (Louisville: Westminster John Knox, 1996), pp. 88-89.

5. Teresa S. Smith, *Through the Darkest Valley: The Lament Psalms and One Woman's Life-long Battle Against Depression* (Eugene, OR: Resource Publications, 2009).

6. This is the argument of Kathleen D. Billman and Daniel L. Migliore, *Rachel's Cry: Prayer of Lament and Rebirth of Hope* (Eugene, OR: Wipf & Stock, 2006).

self-identity, this "crisis" is critical indeed. For many today the human agenda for social justice/injustice over confession has eclipsed any deep sense of personal "sin-before-God." Confession is interpreted radically as being appropriate for simpler societies in bygone times, but now human limitations are being identified as "sins" with each other, as defined by human sciences, rather than by biblical theology.

Against this, we may admit that "ritualized confession" can become meaningless, while the replacement of theological "sin" with social "sins" is indeed anti-Christian. Is not the mark of truly social action in recognizing "sin" as self-isolation that separates us from both God and our fellow humans? Likewise, should we not interpret a confessional way of life as expressive of the dynamic of conversion, not only in the past tense, but as ongoing in daily renewal, healing, and reconciliation? The recovery of the Psalter as the Christian's lament and repentance may thus help us to become more "open" with God, within ourselves, as well as with each other in progressive relational growth.

III. Lament in a Post-Critical Culture

Ironically, lament has been neglected by the church only to be revived in distorting ways. Since 9/11, together with the ease with which the electronic revolution is conveying global news — much of it violent and tragic — lament is taking center-stage in our culture. In a famous remark, Clemenceau once stated that "war is too dangerous to leave to the generals." Now we have to add, "and the interpretation of lament is too subversive to leave to liberal theologians." It reduces "I AM" to a god whose sense of social justice is being questioned like an accused criminal in the dock! It pushes the limits of what it is to be human to being as gods. It legitimizes the voice of blasphemy, all in the name of "scholarship." Walter Brueggemann calls lament "a wake-up call," "a reconfiguration of power in a dialogic mode." This reconfiguration of power is "the antithesis of praise," which, in Brueggemann's opinion, only legitimizes the status quo of orthodox Christianity.[7] Several scholarly essays by his students are being published, following his anti-trust argument that "conventional formulations are of little help for the primal reality and primal speech of Jews and Christians, pain is open to more than one 'explanation.' "[8]

---

7. Walter Brueggemann, "Lament as a Wake-Up Call," in *Lamentations in Ancient and Contemporary Cultural Contexts,* ed. Nancy C. Lee and Carleen Mandolfo (Atlanta: SBL no. 43, 2008), pp. 221-36.

8. Brueggemann, "Lament as a Wake-Up Call," p. 229.

Postmodernist thinking has the historical defect of creating a rhetoric of collage effects.[9] Brueggemann's fixation with the lament form, summarized in his theme of "orientation-disorientation-reorientation," is a revolt against biblical orthodoxy in that it provides a psychological alternative, and then suggests a new approach to biblical interpretation.[10] This psychological lament becomes a new tool for subversion, to destroy covenantal faith between God and humankind. On the contrary, Westermann has pointed out how lament is a central theme of the Old Testament,[11] acting between sin and mercy, in a relational series of events where humanity cries out to God, and yet also where God himself bemoans his judgment against his covenant people (Hos. 6:4; Jer. 12:7-13).

The element of contingency (i.e., the dependence of the human upon God) in lament is now deeply ambivalent in contemporary scholarship. It can refer to the mystery of God, "whose ways are not our ways." It can refer to the false absolutism of rationalism, to which postmodernists now react legitimately. It can reflect on distrust of an ordered universe, and on disbelief in the sovereignty of the Creator. It can reflect the amount of pain and suffering humans can endure, collapse under, or transcend, resulting in post-traumatic nervous stress or in post-traumatic spiritual growth. Ultimately, lament can express the deepest trust in God, or it can wholly reject God; lament then becomes the spiritual experience of trustful humility, or the defiance of God in pride. Biblical lament is prayer; secular complaint collapses into the meaningless.[12]

Biblically, lament is a transition, like the Exodus, a tempted environment of murmurings and distrust, or a joyful anticipation of the Promised Land.[13] As Oswald Bayer has observed: "Systematic theology in general tends to refer to a happy ending all too hastily and fails to take seriously the fruitless disorientations

---

9. In the 1960s, avant-garde architecture first experimented with differing designs in the same building that expressed a collage effect of perhaps "classical," "gothic" and other periods all mixed together. Similarly, post-critical scholars freely quote Locke, Kant, Kierkegaard, Freud, Ricoeur, etc., as Brueggemann does, with no sense of context, presuppositions, and history; it is "the quote" that in itself is quotable. In place of biblical evidence or theological context, the modern disciplines of psychology and sociology become the guiding authorities for what is culturally and historically intrusive of another world.

10. See Walter Brueggemann, "The Costly Loss of Lament," *JSOT* 36 (1986): 57-71; Peter W. Flint and Patrick D. Miller, *The Psalms in Theological Use: On Incommensurability and Mutuality* (Leiden/Boston: Brill, 2005), pp. 581-602; "The Psalms as Limit Expressions," in *Performing the Psalms*, ed. Dave Bland and David Fleer (St. Louis: Chalice, 2005), pp. 31-50.

11. Claus Westermann, *Elements of Old Testament Theology*, trans. Douglas W. Scott (Atlanta: John Knox, 1982), pp. 167-74.

12. G. K. Beale and D. A. Carson, eds., *Commentary of the New Testament on the Old Testament* (Grand Rapids: Baker Academic, 2007), p. 638.

13. Eg. Psalms 10, 13, 22, 60, 102.

of the journey in all its uncertainties."[14] Joy is the last word, but lament may fill much of a Christian's earthly sufferings. Søren Kierkegaard, who reflected much upon Job, left his mark in a corner of Copenhagen's cathedral — Vor Frue Kirke — dedicated to Job and to all lamenters, in a creedal statement: "We believe that God is great enough to harbour our little lives with all their grievances, and that he can lead us from darkness through to the other side." Then through the semi-darkness, the eye can begin to see dimly pinned to a picture of a cross, the words of the apostle Peter: "Cast all your anxiety upon him because he cares for you" (1 Pet. 5:7).

IV. Biblical Causes for Lament

Real as cultural causes for renewed lament may be today, they do not explain the fundamental causes of biblical lament. In our first volume we argued for the pivotal importance of Psalm 1, as the prelude to all the psalms, with its key significance of "the way of the righteous." Lament is a corollary of right-relatedness, since "to lament" is to express impaired or disrupted relationships. Its intensity is greatest when it is "before" and "about" God. In this sense a secular culture cannot "lament," for when truth is relative, contingent, meaningless, and "anything goes," then there is no basis for "biblical lament." Rather righteousness/order and lament are set antithetically, as are light and darkness.

Lament may be accusatory of God, often in a passionate reaching out to God, when everything seems to speak against God. Psalms such as Psalm 44 exacerbate lament into protest. Protest is understandable in the old dispensation, for undeserved suffering for the sake of righteousness does not fit the paradigm of covenant blessings for keeping covenant and covenant curses for violating covenant (Leviticus 26; Deuteronomy 28). In the new dispensation, however, Christians are Christ's friends and he makes it clear to them that suffering is constitutive of the Christian faith. As he suffered innocently, so must they, for they are not greater than their master (John 15:14-21; Rom. 5:1-5; 8:34-39). Consequently, a voiced protest is not heard in Christ's or the apostles' teaching.

Nevertheless, the problem of theodicy has been reawakened in the nightmare of the *Holocaust,* which continues to haunt us. Is that why it is German pastors who are urging the church to recover the role of lament in our liturgy, not Americans? Yet there is a converse to lament in confession in the Psalter. Here it is a focus, not on the wrath of God but on the holiness of God, before whom the

---

14. Quoted by Claudia Welz, "Trust and Lament," in *Evoking Lament: A Theological Discussion,* ed. Eva Harasta and Brian Brock (London: T. & T. Clark, 2009), p. 135.

suppliant acknowledges the reality of being a sinner. Here the bodily expression is one of prostration, *proskynesis,* of feigning to be dead before the holy presence of "I AM." The Psalms prohibit any such posture except to God alone, for true confession and repentance is only valid in the presence of the God above all gods (Pss. 81:9[10]; 106:9).

Shame is a diminution of honor, or failed relationships (Ps. 22:2, 8-9[3, 9-10], 12[13], 14[15]), especially before God (Ps. 22:7[8]). It may express the sense of wrongdoing in which the whole self is involved (Ps. 51:6[8]); or most frequently as the shame felt from ridicule by others (Psalms 6, 44). These causes for shame leave the identity of the psalmist diminished, primarily before God, but also from the hostility of others (Ps. 35:16), to become vulnerable (Ps. 31:12[13]), ostracized (Ps. 102:6[7]), and socially powerless (Ps. 38:12[13]); he is left alone like a bird on the roof (Ps. 102:7[8]). It is the enemy's boast, "by our tongues we will be strong; with our lips who can be our master?" (Ps. 12:4[5]). Yet Psalm 12 speaks of "another speech," when God speaks in verses 6-7(7-8), to provide security. Where a corporate identity is strongly developed as it was in biblical times, social diminishment is a strong motive for lament.[15]

The prominence given to lament in the Psalms thus arises from Israelite identity as a covenanted community before God, surrounded by pagan nations and set in a hostile world. Evil threats abound from innumerable "enemies," "the wicked," national "foes," even one's own negative emotions. All of these present threats to the psalmist's identity and well-being, even from within one's own family or community. Patrick Miller has argued that the vagueness of identity of "the hostile other" affords flexibility to the complainant for a multitude of threats.[16] Gerald Sheppard goes further, identifying "the enemy" not historically, but from a socio-rhetorical context in which the prayer was expressed in the presence of one's enemies, as an accusatory public function of prayer.[17]

Ever since Gunkel broadly classified the Psalter as expressing petition/ lament, thanksgiving, and praise, these genres have been generally acceptable to scholars. Indeed, this is the Chronicler's own verdict in 1 Chronicles 16:4, where he states: "[David] appointed some of the Levites . . . to make petition, to give thanks, and to praise the Lord." Having reflected upon the Psalms as the church's worship in our first volume, we now focus upon a further selection of Psalms of lament,

---

15. Amy C. Cottrill, *Language, Power, and Identity in the Lament Psalms of the Individual* (New York and London: T. & T. Clark, 2008), pp. 6-64.

16. Patrick D. Miller, "Trouble and Woe: Interpreting the Biblical Laments," *Interpretation* 37 (1983): 34-35.

17. Gerald T. Sheppard, "Enemies and the Politics of Prayer in the Book of Psalms," in *The Bible and the Politics of Exegesis,* ed. David Jobling, Peggy I. Day, and Gerald T. Sheppard (Cleveland: Pilgrim, 1991), p. 70.

which reflect upon the limitations, sufferings, fears, protestations, aspirations, as well as confession and penitence of the worshiper before God. Lament begins so soon in the Psalter, as we have already reflected upon Psalms 3, 4; to these we added the great penitential psalm, Psalm 51. But it is misleading when so many scholars assume "lament" is only an Old Testament category, not found in the New Testament, or that lament was discontinued with the shift from Judaism to Christianity. Instead, we shall argue that lament still remained formative for the deepening of Christian devotion in early Christianity, and it needs today to be strongly recovered.

Apart from Psalm 51, included in our first volume, the other six Penitential Psalms are our basis for this book (Psalms 6, 32, 38, 102, 130, 143), together with Psalms 5, 7, 39, 44. In our historical surveys, we shall also distinguish differing pastoral theologies of "lament," both among the early Christian commentators, as well as in later leaders of the church. The individual lament psalms illustrate the dictum, "tell me how you lament, and I will tell you who you are." For in "lament" the figured world and the identity of the one in distress are both more deeply revealed. While we are emphasizing "lament" and "confession" in these psalms, we recognize that "prayer" and "petition" are broader traits of the Psalter, as expressing the covenantal life of Israel with "I AM."[18]

V. The Old Testament Context for Lament

Biblical "lament" is not then an isolated emotion, but it is set within its own religious context. Just as an ecological environment has its own context, so Old Testament "lament" can only be appreciated distinctively within its biblical mindset. Complaints and dirges may be expressive of literary genres, but in their distinctive usage in the Psalms the sufferer seeks to share his suffering with God and with hope of deliverance. It is anticipatory of what the Resurrection would later reveal.[19] This context we may summarize under seven characteristics.

A. The Humanity of the Psalms

A broad introduction to the Psalter has already been given by one of the authors.[20] However, a further introduction to the theological context for biblical

---

18. Bruce K. Waltke and Charles Yu, *An Old Testament Theology* (Grand Rapids: Zondervan, 2005), pp. 10-12, 875-80.

19. Geoffrey W. Grogan, *Psalms* (Grand Rapids: Eerdmans, 2008), p. 395.

20. Waltke and Yu, *OT Theology*, pp. 870-90.

lament and confession is appropriate. Hebrew faith and culture have always been richly human, in the sense that cultural practices including rites of passage, festivities, feasting, fasting, and mourning allowed for the expression of all their emotions and passions before God, on the national, familial, and individual level. It is as if the robust Hebraic expression of being "human" was itself a preparation for when God himself would become fully human in the incarnation. The Old Testament characters are human beings like ourselves, who expressed themselves in poetry and narrative, as we do. All their emotions were communicated with the flow of their lives, as they danced, sang, laughed, shouted, complained, cried, became angry, confessed, lamented, and mourned.[21] Perhaps few have equaled Martin Luther in his personal appreciation of the Psalms in this regard, when he asks:

> What is the greatest thing in the Psalter but this earnest speaking amid the storm winds of every kind? Where does one find finer words of joy than in the psalms of praise and thanksgiving? There you look into the hearts of all the saints. . . . On the other hand, where do you find deeper, more sorrowful, more pitiful words of sadness than in the psalms of lamentation? There again you look into the hearts of the saints, as into death, yes, as into hell itself. . . . When they speak of fear and hope, they use such words that no painter could so depict for your fear or hope, and no Cicero or other orator has so portrayed them. And that they speak these words to God and with God, this I repeat, is the best thing of all. This gives the words double earnestness and life.[22]

B. Responsibility before God

If "humanness" is one trait of the Psalter, another is *individual* consciousness of responsibility. Among the ancient civilizations surrounding Israel, corporate responsibility was legalized early, so that their kings or pharaohs were considered guardians of their constitutions. In contrast to these pagan laws that incriminated a whole family, city, or clan, the Book of the Covenant (Exod. 20:22-23; 33) and the Book of the Law (Deut. 29:18-21) emphasized the claim of the Law upon an individual as well.[23] As Eichrodt states, "guilt, from being an objective fate which

---

21. Marvin R. Wilson, *Our Father Abraham: Jewish Roots of the Christian Faith* (Grand Rapids: Eerdmans, 1989), pp. 139-41.

22. Martin Luther, *Word and Sacrament,* Luther's Works, vol. 1, ed. E. T. Bachmann (Philadelphia: Fortress, 1960), pp. 255-56.

23. For example, the sons of Saul to the Canaanite city of Gibeon, 2 Samuel 21.

drags the wrongdoer with it, irrespective of his inner relation to his deed, becomes a matter of personal and conscious responsibility."[24]

While the legal presupposition "Thou shalt not" still frames the Ten Commandments, the *ḥeseḏ* love of the Lord remains the underlying and strongest appeal for being a moral agent. Motivation based on relationships is more effective than brute legal power. All of Israel's history was to be interpreted as undeserved "gift": from the gift of life first breathed upon Adam, to the "call" of Abram, to entry into the Promised Land, and to the kingly anointing of David.[25] The Psalms thus express that the *ḥeseḏ love* of "I AM" endures forever (Psalm 136).

C. Faith in the Creator

A third distinctive of the psalmist is that Israelite faith reflects faith in the Creator. It is conceivable that a Babylonian or an Egyptian could escape from the suzerainty of their country, but none can ever escape the sovereignty of the Creator. Nor is he a world-principle contributing to some cosmogony that may be conceived abstractly, nor an explanation of some theodicy, as Job's friends argued. Mysterious as God's ways in creation may appear to humans, or conversely, however humans are placed within his created realm (Psalms 8, 19, 29, 104, 135, and 147), humans can yet live realistically. Eichrodt observes: "It is only when a lively sense of the living rule of the godhead in the mighty course of natural forces is obscured by later rational reflection, which attempts in its own strength to illuminate the relation between the life of man and of nature, that the autonomy of nature's laws is raised to alien and uncanny power."[26] For the Israelite, "I AM," who created all things, is also the Lord of history, who has chosen his people. The will of "I AM" as Creator is at one with the will of the Redeemer to save his people, individually as well as collectively.

D. God as Author of Suffering

A fourth element is that while God is the infinite Giver, he is also the Author of suffering, both of deserved and undeserved pain. He understandably inflicts condign punishment, but he also incomprehensibly rejects in his wrath. Other religions can

24. Walther Eichrodt, *Man in the Old Testament* (London: SCM, 1966), p. 11.

25. Bruce Waltke, in his *Old Testament Theology*, interprets all its essential premises as "gift" from "I AM," whether it is creation, humankind, or his covenant relationship.

26. Waltke and Yu, *OT Theology*, pp. 31-32.

explain human calamity and destruction as the work of demons and evil powers, but in Israel the sufferings of human life lie ultimately under the sovereignty of God. This is why the laments of the psalmist are always God-directed, never in complaint to other sources, even when the psalmist can complain like a crime detective, "Who-did-it?" Even when the character of God seems to be in contradiction to the evil inflicted upon the complainant, the end result is a deeper trust and more perceptive knowledge gained of God. This is why, also, the voices of lament and even of protest are at one and the same time the voice of praise. The first three stanzas of Psalm 44 end with "all day long" (vv. 8[9], 15[16], 22[23]),[27] yielding the amazing paradox that Israel praises God all day long, while they are reviled all day long and are being put to death all day long. This is so because they place themselves in the overarching story of the LORD's calling and preserving through his mighty acts of salvation a people for himself, and through whom he will bring blessing to the nations. Israel also mixes lament with praise, because they know beyond doubting that in God's unchanging, unfailing love they will be saved in the end.

Often we learn as Christians only through suffering what we could not otherwise have gained without the pain endured (Rom. 5:1-5). Repeatedly, the Old Testament prophets affirm the educative value of suffering, without which God's true love, patience, and forgiveness could not have been experienced. With the prophets, it seems as if failure was their calling, suffering it bitterly when their message was unheard, disobeyed, and rejected. As Maria Boulding has observed: "Many a prophet was not merely a failure but a programmed failure. Only by failing could he do the Lord's work, yet his failure was no less painful for that,"[28] as evidenced in Hosea's experience with his wife, spoken by Isaiah of the Suffering Servant, or in the lamentations of Jeremiah. Again, this is anticipatory of Jesus, "the failed Messiah," "a little Lamb looking as if it had been slain, standing in the centre of the throne . . . who reigns forever and ever" (Rev. 5:6, 13).

E. The Reality of Sin before God

A fifth element of lament and confession in the Old Testament is the reality of sin, as sin against God. Prominent in the priestly role of offering sacrifices is the expiation for sin that God himself provides. Yet as readily as sacrifices could degenerate into cultic practices with no true repentance, the divine prerogative of

27. So also, independently, Martin Kessler ("Ps. 44," in *Unless Some One Guide Me . . . Festschrift for Kaarel A. Deurlood*, ed. Janet W. Dyk et al. [Maastricht: Shaker, 2001], pp. 193-204, esp. 198).

28. Maria Boulding, *Gateway to Hope: An Exploration of Failure* (Petersham, MA: St. Bede's, 1985), pp. 37-38.

forgiveness, not bounded by any sacrificial system, is celebrated in such psalms as 40, 51, and 69, to ensure pardon as the immediate gift of God. "Sin" and "grace" are never separated, as the apostle later states with such assurance: "where sin abounded, grace did much more abound" (Rom. 5:20).

A model of penitential prayer for divine forgiveness is portrayed in Nehemiah 9:1-37. It marks the renewal of the covenant on the people's return from captivity in Babylon. As mourners, they fasted, put on sackcloth, and threw dust on their heads — all expressive of the presence of death among them. For separation from God is "death." They then confessed their own sins, as well as the wickedness of their fathers. Spending part of the day reading the Law, they then confessed *and* worshiped, accompanied by the Levites and their choral leaders. The penitential prayer/psalm that follows is a recitation of God's history with Israel, since he chose Abram, and made a covenant with Israel. There follow the redemptive Exodus from Egypt, his preservation of the people in the wilderness, the Law given in Sinai, and their relapses later, from keeping the covenant. Thus two stories are interwoven: the faithlessness of Israel, but the faithfulness of God. Such confession is both petition and worship, personal confession of sin with the contrasted *ḥesed* love and mercy of the Lord. God's intervention in human history is thus the ground for God's continuing relationship with Israel, personally and collectively.

This model prayer on the twenty-fourth day of the seventh month, however, is part of Israel's renewal during that month. On the first day of that month Ezra read the Law and the people mourned their sin. But Ezra and Nehemiah commanded the people not to weep but to rejoice, for God's holy day is a time for joy, and "the joy of the LORD is their strength" (Neh. 8:1-12). On the second day they celebrated the feast of booths and for seven days "there was very great rejoicing" (vv. 8:13-18). In short, the penitential prayer on the twenty-fourth day is in the context of great joy. Neither they nor the psalmists are disoriented; they know and trust their God and their relationship to him.

F. Facing Death

A critical distinctive of how an Israelite might "lament" lies in the shadowy presence of *Sheol,* as the realm of the dead. The term is used sixty-six times in the Old Testament, mostly in poetry with rich images of the grave.[29] As poetic expres-

29. See Bruce K. Waltke and James M. Houston with Erika Moore, *The Psalms as Christian Worship* (hereafter *PACW*) (Grand Rapids: Eerdmans, 2010), p. 335; R. Laird Harris, Gleason L. Archer, and Bruce K. Waltke, eds., *Theological Wordbook of the Old Testament*, vol. 2 (Chicago: Moody, 1980), pp. 891-93.

sions, no further speculations are implied; it is a terminus of clinical life. As the psalmist faces *Sheol,* he depicts it as "depth," "darkness," "decay," and "dust." But the worst aspect of *Sheol* as the place of nonlife was the absence of "I AM": "For in death there is no remembrance of you, in *Sheol* who can give you praise?" (Ps. 6:5[6]; cf. 88:3-6[4-7]). It is "the land of silence" (Ps. 94:17), and thus the antithesis of praise. Even for the living *Sheol* is never far away, since sickness, persecution, and sin remain threats to life before God.

But for the psalmist *Sheol* is not beyond God's reach (Ps. 139:8) and does not have the final word. In the first stanza of Psalm 49, by the sons of Korah, the psalmist states what all can see: "No one can redeem the life of another or give to God a ransom for them — the ransom for a life is costly, no payment is ever enough — so that they should live on forever and not see decay. For all can see that the wise die, that the foolish and the senseless also perish, leaving their wealth to others" (vv. 7-10[8-11]). But in the second stanza of that psalm he confesses what eyes of flesh cannot see: death and decay are not the final end of the upright: "But the upright will prevail over them [those who trust and boast of their wealth] in the morning . . . God will redeem me from the realm of the dead [Heb. *Sheol*]; he will surely take me to himself" (vv. 14-15[15-16]). Likewise Asaph, after his complaint about the prosperity of the wicked and the suffering of the righteous, confesses: "When my heart was grieved and my spirit embittered, I was senseless and ignorant; I was a brute beast before you. Yet I am always with you; you hold me by my right hand. You guide me with your counsel, and afterward you will take me into glory. Whom have I in heaven but you? And earth has nothing I desire besides you. My flesh and my heart may fail, but God is the strength of my heart and my portion forever" (Ps. 73:21-26). Amazingly, David, giving voice to his greater son, prophesied: "Therefore my heart is glad and my tongue rejoices; my body also will rest secure, because you will not abandon me to the realm of the dead, nor will you let your faithful one see decay. You make known to me the path of life; you will fill me with joy in your presence, with eternal pleasures at your right hand" (Ps. 16:9-11).[30]

Nevertheless, in spite of this hope for the eternal presence of God and for realizing justice beyond its miscarriage in this life, Israel never created its culture in the attempt to penetrate through death into the afterlife, as Egypt so conspicuously tried. Rather everything living is expressive of the continual dependent presence of God; in life man is but dust which is "God-breathed," as in the creation of Adam.

Israel had no *specific* understanding of immortality, for, as Paul says: "This grace [to be saved and called to a holy life] was given us in Christ Jesus before the

---

30. See Waltke and Houston, *PACW,* pp. 33-38.

beginning of time, but it has now been revealed through the appearing of our Savior, Christ Jesus, who has destroyed death and has brought life and immortality to light through the gospel (2 Tim. 1:9-10; Titus 1:1-3). Since Israel did not have this specific understanding of immortality, the unity of the Israelite family is such that life and death are united, so that we are told Samuel was buried in his own house in Ramah (1 Sam. 25:1). Significantly then, burial grounds were family properties over many generations. In *Sheol* the body has gone to be with the ancestors, but the memory of the deceased is still a blessing to their successors. The genealogies reflect upon this continuity between life and death. As long as the deceased's memory is preserved, they live on among their heirs. For it is the transcendence of God that still rules over life or death. Again this Hebraic historical continuity prepared the birth of Christianity to receive the resurrection of Christ from the dead, as a present reality of living "in Christ" whether dead or alive. Christian lament for those "asleep in Jesus" is profoundly different from those "who have no hope," for now "death has been swallowed up in victory" (1 Cor. 15:54).

G. Living by God's Word

A uniqueness of Israel is that unlike the hydraulic civilizations, which lived by their massive exercise of irrigation, by state authority, and by human despotism, Israel's identity — past, present, and future — is wholly dependent upon God, "I AM," as source and sustainer:

> The land you are entering to take over is not like the land of Egypt, from which you have come, where you planted your seed and irrigated it by foot as in a vegetable garden. But the land you are crossing the Jordan to take possession of is a land . . . the Lord your God takes care of; the eyes of the Lord are continually on it from the beginning of the year to the end of it. (Deut. 11:11-12)

To live in "the Promised Land" is not just a military victory but an ethical injunction. As baptism is now for the Christian, Israel had a rebirth to live entirely dependent upon God, "in whom we live, and move, and have our being; and without whom we can do nothing." Living by God's word expresses this way of *being*. This sums up how wholly countercultural was "the way of Israel" in contrast to the pagan nations around it. God and his Word ruled their lives and destiny. "Entering the Promised Land" is then undertaking to serve God ethically, to become docile to the Torah, the catechetical teaching of the Covenant to love the Lord and to serve him "with all your soul" (Deut. 11:13). Psalm 1 stands then as the entry into

God's territory, so that all the psalms that follow are to be treated as expressed by God's covenant keepers. They are not to be treated just as relics of previous literary legacies, of pagan peoples before the existence of Israel. Petition, lament, confession, penitence, as indeed praise and thanksgiving in the Psalter, bear the distinctive of coming from "God's people." The writer to the Hebrews reminds us that "during the days of Jesus' life on earth, he offered up prayers and petitions with loud cries and tears to the one who could save him from death, and he was heard because of his reverent submission. Although he was a son he learned obedience from what he suffered, and once made perfect he became the source of eternal salvation for all who obey him . . ." (Heb. 5:7-10). Was it in his use of the Psalms that Jesus as a human being gained insight into his mission and identity? Do then the same psalms have continued relevance for our own identity as Christ's followers?

VI. The Penitential Psalms

As far as we can trace, Augustine (354-430) followed by Cassiodorus (c. 485-585) are the first commentators to group the penitential psalms together as psalms of confession (6, 32, 38, 51, 102, 130, 143). Alcuin (735-804) also adopted this grouping, and by the eleventh century onwards commentaries on these seven psalms (both lay and clerical) began to appear. From our perspective today, at least four of these psalms scarcely reflect confession and repentance (Psalms 6, 38, 102, 143).[31] But as we shall see, the Fathers read much more of God's judgment and our need of repentance into these psalms than we may now appreciate. Augustine translated the Hebrew term in the title "according to the *sheminith*" (Psalms 6, 12) as "the eighth," which he with previous commentators interpreted as reference to the final day of judgment, thus suggesting this psalm warns the unrepentant of the ensuing wrath of God. For this reason it had become church practice to baptize on Sunday, both the day of new creation, the symbol of eternity, and also the day of God's judgment. Baptisteries were often designed in octagonal form to symbolize "the eighth day," since it celebrated too the resurrection of Christ. We do not know the process by which Augustine chose these "Seven Psalms." Earlier than Augustine, Athanasius in advising Marcellinus about appropriate psalms for various circumstances states: "In confession of sins, Psalm 51 . . . ; if you wish to remember the mercy and judgment of God, Psalm 102." He makes no reference to the other "Seven."[32] While

31. This is the perspective of Susan Gillingham, *Psalms through the Centuries* (Oxford: Blackwell, 2008), p. 114.

32. See list collated by J. M. Neale and Richard Frederick Littledale, *A Commentary on the Psalms: From Primitive and Mediaeval Writers* (London: Joseph Masters, 1874), pp. 16-17.

Cassiodorus follows the Psalm homilies of Augustine quite closely, Cassiodorus is distinctive in identifying each of the penitential psalms. He follows Origen in suggesting that there are "seven ways of being forgiven: by baptism, suffering martyrdom, almsgiving, forgiving the sins of the brethren, diverting a sinner from the error of his ways, abundance of charity and by repentance."[33] Fortunately, Cassidorus does not allow this unorthodox suggestion of "the seven ways of penance" to control his commentaries on the penitential psalms; rather, with Augustine's guidance, he comments on each psalm's own context. But it anticipates the whole doctrinal confusion on penance that was to develop later.

Bede and then Alcuin summarized each psalm to elicit memorization of the Psalter and to make distinctive each psalm. By the fourteenth century, in selecting a single verse from each of the "Seven Psalms," a tradition arose in personal devotion to link each psalm appropriately against a cardinal sin. Psalm 6 was used against Anger; Psalm 32, against Pride; Psalm 38, against Gluttony; Psalm 51, against Lechery; Psalm 102, against Greed; Psalm 130, against Envy; and Psalm 143, against Sloth. The conciliar Reformer, Jean Gerson, used this tradition in his writings. Martin Luther's early treatise on "The Seven Penitential Psalms" (composed in 1517) protests against the abuse of indulgences, and suggests that four of them are "Pauline Psalms" (Psalms 32, 51, 130, and 143). Psalm 130 is his favorite.[34]

The seven cardinal sins (first adopted by the Desert Fathers in Egypt) trace their origins to Hellenistic astrology. Many Hellenistic sects believed that the soul, after death, had to journey through the seven zones of heaven, while the evil spirits, sometimes seven, hindered their passage. This may have originated in Persia, been passed on by Babylon, and adopted by Gnostic sects in Egypt.[35] The *Testament of Reuben* (part of the pseudepigraphic work, *Testament of the Patriarchs*, c. 109-106 BCE) lists seven evil spirits: deceit; lust or fornication; gluttony; vainglory; pride; lying; and injustice.[36] In the *Corpus Hermeticum*, possibly in the first century CE, Poimandres states: ". . . thereupon the man mounts upwards through the structure of the heavens. And to the first zone of heaven (Moon) he gives up the force which works increase . . . [i.e. *acedie*]; to the second zone (Mercury), the machinations of evil cunning; to the third zone (Venus) the lust

33. O. D. Watkins, *A History of Penance* (London, 1920), 136f., as cited in *Cassiodorus: Explanation of the Psalms*, trans. and annotated by P. G. Walsh, vol. 1 (New York/Mahwah, N.J.: Paulist Press, 1990), p. 534.

34. Robert Charles Hill, trans., *St. John Chrysostom: Commentary on the Psalms*, vol. 2 (Brookline, MA: Holy Cross Orthodox Press, 1998), p. 185.

35. Morton W. Bloomfield, "The Origin of the Seven Cardinal Sins," *Harvard Theological Review* 34, no. 2 (1991): 121-28.

36. R. H. Charles, *Apocrypha and Pseudepigrapha of the Old Testament in English*, vol. 2 (Oxford: Oxford University Press, 1913), pp. 282ff.

whereby men are deceived; to the fourth zone (Sun), domineering arrogance; to the fifth zone (Mars), unholy daring and rash audacity; to the sixth zone (Jupiter), evil striving after wealth; and to the seventh zone (Saturn), the falsehood which lies in wait to work harm."[37] The apostle Paul's allusions "to the powers in heavenly places"[38] may reflect this mindset without conceding to astrology.

Evagrius Ponticus (c. 345-399), mentored by Makarios, used simple short sentences of prayer for his mode of teaching. "There is no need to speak at great length; it is enough to stretch out one's hands and say, 'Lord, as you will and as you know, have mercy on me' (Ps. 41:4[5]). And if the warfare grows pressing, say, 'Lord, help me!' (Ps. 94:17).[39] He knows very well what we need and he acts mercifully towards us." These Desert Fathers were simply reciting the short petitions, like "arrow prayers" shot into the heavens. Evagrius also cites Makarios as recognizing anger as the great obstacle to prayer. Indeed it is likely that all the eight vices were catalogued by Evagrius as generic evil thoughts *(logismoi)* that hinder the monk's prayer life. These he ordered as gluttony, fornication, avarice, sadness, anger (sometimes reversed as anger-sadness), acedia, vainglory, and pride. Evagrius' manual and guide for the daily life of the monks *(Praktikos)*, which was influenced by the book of Proverbs, begins by describing these vices, which he categorizes in groups. Gluttony, lust, and avarice are bodily temptations, while sadness stands alone as a frustration of desire, what we might now call depression. Anger is directed to others socially, acedia is the discouragement to be tempted to give up the life of a monk, while the spiritual temptation of vainglory in one's spiritual progress leads to pride, by which Satan fell. Later all these vices became interwoven into the Christian practices of psalmody and prayer.

Later, at the end of the sixth century, Gregory the Great reduced the cardinal vices to seven, in a revised sequence: pride, anger, envy, sloth, avarice, gluttony, and lust.[40] J. M. Neale describes the Seven Penitential Psalms as "the seven weapons wherewith to oppose the seven deadly sins: the seven prayers inspired by the sevenfold Spirit to the repenting sinner: the seven guardians for the seven days of the week: the seven companions for the seven Canonical Hours of the day."[41] There developed the medieval tradition of interpreting "the Seven"

---

37. W. Scott, *Corpus Hermeticum,* vol. 1 (Oxford: Oxford University Press, 1924), pp. 123ff.

38. 2 Corinthians 12:2ff. and Ephesians 6:11-17; 4:8 have no allusions to astrology, while speaking within this culture.

39. Robert E. Sinkewicz, *Evagrius of Pontus: The Greek Ascetic Corpus* (Oxford: Oxford University Press, 2003), pp. viii-xix.

40. A full history of how the seven deadly sins evolved in the history of the church is discussed thoroughly by Morton W. Bloomfield in *The Seven Deadly Sins* (East Lansing: Michigan State University Press, 1967).

41. Neale and Littledale, *A Commentary on the Psalms,* p. 124.

as seven steps on the ladder of repentance. The first step is fear of punishment (Ps. 6:1[2]). The second step is sorrow for sin (Ps. 32:5). The third step is hope of pardon (Ps. 38:15[16]). The fourth step is the love of a cleansed soul (Ps. 51:7[9]). The fifth step is longing for heaven (Ps. 102:16). The sixth step is having distrust of self (Ps. 130:6) by looking only to the Lord. The seventh step is prayer against the final judgment (Ps. 143:2): "enter not into judgment with thy servant."[42]

42. Cited by Norman Snaith, *The Seven Psalms* (London: Epworth, 1964), p. 10.

CHAPTER 2

Psalm 5: A Royal Petition for Protection from Malicious Liars

PART I. VOICE OF THE CHURCH

I. Introduction

As we saw in our previous volume, the first commentaries on the Psalms were probably motivated against mindless singing and liturgical chants, where the words were not being understood by the congregation. This was a serious issue, as the defense of early Christianity was grounded upon the Christological use of the Psalms, that is, of Christ "as great David's greater Son."

There were three basic exegetical presuppositions that help us understand the mindset of the earliest commentators.[1] First, there was the idea of corporate solidarity, best expressed in Augustine's *corpus Christi,* that the corporate Israel, as the "I" of the Psalms, has become the "I" of Christ and his church. Second, in the correspondences of history, the history of God's people is a continuous one, later events echoing previous ones. Knowing God as the Lord of history, the early Christians could relate the events of the Old Testament to their own situation. Third, in eschatological fulfillment, Peter in his first sermon could affirm that "the last days" are being actualized now.[2]

In addition to these three basic exegetical presuppositions, early commentators were also concerned to defend the faith by a threefold polemic against heresy. A primitive fragment of a psalm attributed to a Hippolytus of Rome (early third century CE) is the earliest evidence of this threefold polemic against the heretics, whether Gnostics or Marcionites.[3] This work is referred to by both Jerome and

---

1. Richard N. Longenecker, *Biblical Exegesis in the Apostolic Period,* 2nd ed. (Vancouver: Regent College Publishing, 1999), pp. 76-80.

2. Acts 2:14-21.

3. Marie-Josephe Rondeau, *Les Commentaires Patristiques du Psautier,* vol. 1 (Rome: Pont.

Theodoret of Cyrus.[4] Against the Gnostics, there are historicity and real events being reflected in the Psalms. Against the Marcionites, the Psalms are the bridge between the two biblical testaments. It is from this tradition, defending a Christological use of the Psalms, that Jerome's translation of Origen's commentaries on the Psalms was based, though it is difficult to determine what is from Origen and what is original to Jerome.[5]

II. Lament of the Scholar Monk, Jerome

Jerome (342-420) lived in an age of great cultural and religious turbulence, when Arianism (the predecessor of Islam) dominated the eastern Mediterranean. He fled from Rome in 385 to Palestine, establishing his humble abode in Bethlehem, where his outstanding literary output for the next thirty-five years earned him fame as the leading biblical scholar of his day. Contemporary scholars are beginning to identify various personae throughout Jerome's life: adulating Origen in his youth; later, seeking to become more original as his own fame grew; separating himself from Origen when the political climate against the latter worsened; and finally taking shelter behind his own device, the primacy of the *Hebraica veritas* ("Hebrew verity").[6] Jerome took advantage of his new Hebrew habitat to study the language, seek out Jewish scholars, learn the topography of the Holy Land, and use the rich library resources that Eusebius had built up in Caesarea. Ordained as a priest by bishop Paulinus of Antioch, Jerome sought rather to be an ascetic under the influence of Evagrius, Pachomius, Cassian, and other Desert Fathers. Jerome's own *Life of Paulus the First Hermit* (c. 375) was the archetype that he interpreted lay behind Anthony's asceticism. Later, Jerome sought to dwell beneath the shadow of the biblical prophets themselves.

Until now, it was popularly accepted by the Church Fathers that the Septuagint version was inspired by God as the basis for the Christian use of the Old Testament. Jerome, however, relied on rabbinical sources for Old Testament texts and their meanings. It was a dangerous balancing act that he claimed made him *vir trilinguis,* "the man of three languages," for he was working independently of

---

Institutum Studiorum Orientalium, 1982), pp. 27-63; Pierre Nautin, *Le Dossier d'Hippolyte et de Méliton* (Paris: Cerf, 1953), pp. 15-32, 99-107.

4. J. A. Cerrato, *Hippolytus between East and West* (Oxford: Oxford University Press, 2002), p. 55.

5. Rondeau, *Les Commentaires Patristiques,* pp. 53-55.

6. Megan Hale Williams, *The Monk and the Book: Jerome and the Making of Christian Scholarship* (Chicago and London: University of Chicago Press, 2006), pp. 81-95.

the scholarship of his earlier mentors in their use of allegory to search for the hidden/spiritual meaning of the text.[7]

Jerome's first serious study of the Psalms was his translation of the Psalms commentary of Hilary of Poitiers (300-368). In 387 he composed *Commentariola in Psalmos,* focusing primarily on philological issues. About the same time he wrote his *Tractatus in Psalmos,* to expand on the spiritual meanings of the Psalms. In his revision of the Old Latin version of the Septuagint he began with the Psalms *(Psalterium Gallicanum).* As in all monastic communities, the Psalms shaped the daily liturgy. Likewise, Jerome preached from the Psalms, and lived in a community that had all the psalms in its consciousness. This he described in a letter to Marcella: "In Christ's humble cottage there is only rustic simplicity; except for the chanting of the psalms, silence is perfect. Whenever you go, the husbandman sings the alleluia over his plough; the toiling harvester refreshes himself with the psalms; the vine dresser prunes his vine in a song of David. These are the popular songs of this country; the love songs of the shepherd's whistle; the lyrics of the farmer as he tills the soil with devotion."[8] Thus, for Jerome, the Psalms themselves echoed not only the daily liturgical start to the monk's day and its regular "hours," but filled the consciousness of the Bethlehem community.

Under his canopy of independent scholarship ("Hebrew Verity"), he distanced himself from his earlier Greek teachers, such as Origen, who was shortly to be denounced as a heretic (the turn of the fifth century was to become a time of political denunciations).[9] The Psalter became the springboard for his later serious scholarship, his commentaries on the Prophets (c. 392, his magnum opus), for the Psalms were already "prophetic." Jerome defined the purpose of a commentary: "To explain what has been said by others and make clear in plain language what has been written obscurely."[10] But he does not always follow his own definition, nor does he acknowledge all his sources; he sometimes leaves the reader to decide on varied interpretations, and sometimes the text is handled hurriedly without an adequate conclusion.[11] He balanced the literal interpretation (basically textual

---

7. Williams, *The Monk and the Book,* pp. 81-95.

8. *The Fathers of the Church: The Homilies of St. Jerome,* vol. 1 (Washington, DC: Catholic University of America Press, 1964), pp. xi-xii.

9. An old acquaintance, Epiphanius of Salamis initiated the condemnation of Origen in 393. Behind the polemics was the right claimed by monks to be scholars, and thus outside the domain of the city clergy. See Elizabeth A. Clark, *The Origenist Controversy. The Cultural Construction of an Early Christian Debate* (Princeton: Princeton University Press, 1992), p. 150.

10. Williams, *The Monk and the Book,* p. 102.

11. René Kieffer, "Jerome: His Exegesis and Hermeneutics," in *Hebrew Bible Old Testament: The History of Its Interpretation,* ed. Magne Saebo, vol. 1/1 (Göttingen: Vandenhoeck & Ruprecht, 1996), p. 677.

criticism) with a historical (usually citing Jewish sources) critique. Yet he granted the "spiritual/tropological" interpretation to be the climax of biblical exegesis, not because it is "spiritual" *per se,* but because it is Christological.[12]

Jerome's critical study of the Psalter probably took place in 393-94, at the beginning of his exhaustive study of the Prophets. But he already viewed the Psalms prophetically as anticipating Christ and the church. Later, about the turn of the century, he preached a large number of homilies on the Psalms near the Basilica of the Nativity in Bethlehem.[13] His intensely ascetic life of radical renunciation, combined with his own scholarly ambitions, resulted in fervent arguments with friends and foes alike.[14] In his scholarly study of Jerome, J. N. D. Kelly confesses: "[T]he deeper springs of his psychology elude us, and, for all his readiness to talk about himself, there is an unsolved enigma about the real Jerome. . . . There is no doubt about the reality of his conversion, or of his passionate devotion to Christ and the world-renouncing asceticism he believed to be inculcated by the gospel; but if this burning commitment was the driving force of his life, the forms in which it found an outlet were often strange, sometimes repellent."[15] Fighting others whom he assumed were heretics makes him a suitable polemicist to comment on Psalm 5!

III. Jerome's Interpretation of Psalm 5

His theme for Psalm 5 is that "David sings at the beginning that the Church wins the inheritance at the end." This notion he takes from the Psalm's superscription, which he translates as: "Unto the end, for her that obtains the inheritance. A psalm of David." He interprets this "inheritance" to be the Christian church, for Israel was its "beginning"; now, he argues, "the fifth psalm sings in the name of the Church."[16]

Following this trajectory, he further argues that only the church can be bold

---

12. Henri de Lubac, S.J., *Scripture in the Tradition*, trans. Luke O'Neill (New York: Herder & Herder/Crossroad, 2000), p. 67.

13. James C. Howell, "Jerome's Homilies on the Psalter in Bethlehem" in *The Listening Heart: Essays in Wisdom and the Psalms in Honor of Roland E. Murphy*, ed. O. Carm, Kenneth G. Hoglund, Elizabeth F. Huwiler, Jonathan T. Glass, and Roger W. Lee (Sheffield: JSOT Press/Sheffield Academic Press, 1987), p. 181.

14. Williams, *The Monk and the Book*, pp. 262-63.

15. J. N. D. Kelly, *Jerome: His Life, Writings, and Controversies* (New York: Harper & Row, 1975), p. 336.

16. *The Fathers of the Church*, vol. 48, *The Homilies of St. Jerome*, trans. Sister Marie Liguori Ewald, I.H.M. (Washington, DC: Catholic University of America Press, 1964), pp. 15-16.

enough to claim it is seeking virtue and truth, in praying, "Hearken to my words, O Lord. . . . At dawn you hear my voice." This is not the liturgical "third" or "sixth" hour or indeed full morning. It is at "dawn," when in imitating Moses, the church "stands before God." Jerome implies that the church from its very beginning was resolute for the truth of God. No arrogant sinner can "stand" in the presence of God. It is only the church that can fight against heretics with the hatred with which God himself would destroy his enemies, for "You destroy those who tell lies" (v. 6[7]). (Having professed this, Jerome himself was a ruthless fighter!) They are "bloodthirsty" and "deceitful" "whom the Lord abhors" (v. 6b[7b]). These are heretics because they both deceive by their false teaching, and destroy the souls of those who believe such heresies.[17]

The true Christian is kept safe by frequenting the house of the Lord, his temple (v. 7[8]), and by following in the Way of the Lord, i.e., by his word (v. 8[9]). The heretics are deceitful, since "they mean one thing in the heart; they promise another with their lips . . . they speak Christ and hide the anti-Christ."[18] As Jerome comments on verse 10[11], "Heretics do not have Christ, the Truth, on their lips, for they do not have Him in their hearts."[19]

For Jerome then, Psalm 5 is a polemic against the heretics of his day. From this psalm he derives the authority to declare them false and to call for them to be cast out of the church (v. 10[11]). Behind his commentary he is thinking of the Arians, who deny the deity of Christ; of the Montanists, who think revelation is self-induced ecstasy; of the Pelagians, who think they can achieve their own defense; and even turning against old friends more from political squabbles and false rumors than from honest investigation. We might well lament the state of the church at the turn of the fifth century, which embroiled and tarnished the names of even true witnesses. It appears that Jerome himself in his lament died a brokenhearted old man.

IV. The Continuing Influence of Jerome

Ironically, as anti-traditionalist as Jerome was in exploring versions other than the Septuagint, he became the father of the Latin Bible, the Vulgate. His influence continued for the whole church even well after the Reformation, more than a millennium after his work. The Reformed artist Albrecht Dürer depicts him at

---

17. Jerome follows the LXX, "I was destroying," instead of the Hebrew, "I shall destroy," as cited by J. N. D. Kelly, *Jerome,* p. 330.

18. *Fathers of the Church,* p. 21.

19. *Fathers of the Church,* p. 20.

his desk as a scholar, with a lion at his feet. The lion symbolizes his defense of the truth, while the desk reflects his critical study of the Word of God.

In his own day he mediated between the churches of the East and West, and he continues to be authoritative later for both Catholic and Protestant churches. Moreover, irascible he might be, but as an ascetic he modeled the monastic life for generations after him. Psalm 5 was his *cri de coeur*.

PART II. VOICE OF THE PSALMIST: TRANSLATION

A psalm by David[20]

1   Give ear to my words, "I AM,"
     Understand my burning meditation.
2   Pay attention[21] to my cry for help, my King and my God,[22]
     for to you I pray.[23]
3   "I AM," in the morning you hear my voice;
     in the morning I arrange [my words] for you and watch vigilantly.
4   For you are not a God who delights in wickedness;
     evil cannot sojourn with you.
5   Arrogant boasters cannot stand before your eyes;
     You hate all who do wrong.
6   You destroy those who tell lies;
     the bloodthirsty and deceitful "I AM" detests.
7   But I, by your great loyalty, can come to your house;
     I bow down toward your holy palace in fear of you.
8   "I AM," lead me in your righteousness because of my enemies —
     make your way straight[24] before me.
9   For there is nothing in their mouths[25] that is steadfast;

---

20. "For the director of music. For flutes" is a postscript to Psalm 4. See Bruce K. Waltke and James M. Houston with Erika Moore, *The Psalms as Christian Worship (PACW)* (Grand Rapids/Cambridge, UK: Eerdmans, 2010), p. 88.

21. לְקוֹל ("out loud"; Aquil., lit., "to the sound of") is omitted as tautological.

22. The plural form designates "I AM" as so thoroughly characterized by the qualities of the noun, God-ness; only a plural is appropriate for this designation (*IBHS*, p. 122, P. 7.4.3a,b).

23. The Hebrew syntax of verses 1-2[2-3] is chiastic:
Object + verb (2 words) + Vocative (1 word) + verb + object (2 words)
Verb + object (3 words) + Vocative (2 words) + object + verb (3 words).

In this way "he surrounds God with petitions" (John Goldingay, *Psalms*, vol. 1: *Psalms 1–41* [Grand Rapids: Baker Academic, 2006], p. 127).

24. הַיְשַׁר (Kethiv) and הוֹשַׁר (Qere) are alternative forms of *hiphil* imperative יָשַׁר.

25. Literally, "in his mouth." Ancient Near Eastern literature, as in the Tell Fekherye In-

their heart is filled with violence.
Their throat is an open grave;
    They make their tongues smooth.
10   Make them liable, God!
    Let them fall from their intrigues.
Banish them for their many obstinate rebellions,
    for they are obstinate against you.
11   And so,[26] all who take refuge in you will be exuberant;
    They will shout for joy forever.
Place yourself as a shield around them,
    that those who love your name may exult in you.
12   For you, "I AM," bless the righteous;
    you surround them[27] with favor like a shield.

For the director of music. With stringed instruments. According to sheminith. (Psalm 6:1a)

Part III. Commentary

I. Introduction

A. Literary Context: Psalms 1–5

Psalm 1 restricts God's blessing to those who lovingly keep the Law. Psalm 2 commissions "I AM's" anointed king/son to destroy the wicked through prayer. Psalms 3–5 are royal petitions, asking God to protect David, his chosen king, from stiff-necked rebels within his own kingdom. In Psalm 3 his enemies are numerous; in Psalm 4, in high positions; and in Psalm 5, malicious liars. Psalms 4 and 5 draw to a close with "for you" (4:8[9]; 5:12[13]).

As noted above, the earliest commentators rightly interpreted the corporate solidarity of King David and Israel in continuum with the corporate solidarity of

---

scription, shifts pronouns between first, second, and third persons without formally signaling the change of perspectives (A. Abou-Assaf, P. Bordreuil, and Alan Millard, *La Statue del Tell Fekherye et Son Inscription Bilingue Assyro-Arménienne,* Recherche sur les Civilisations 7 [Paris: ADPF], p. 198).

26. After an imperative a verbal form not preceded by its subject or a negative particle is normally either a jussive or a cohortative. This second volitional form signifies purpose or result (*IBHS,* P. 34.6a, p. 577).

27. Form is singular; see n. 25.

Christ and his church, and that which Augustine called the *corpus Christi* is an echo of King David and Israel's holy assembly. In Psalm 5 corporate Israel typifies the corporate solidarity of the Lord Jesus Christ and his church whose life is threatened by fraud and deceit.[28] Christ comforts his church, warning: "Slaves are not greater than their master. If they persecuted me, they will persecute you also" (John 15:20). In the alchemy of grace, God uses nefarious enemies to drive the church to prayer and so to know him better and to participate more fully in redemptive history.

The superscript of Psalm 3 and the content of Psalms 4 and 5 show the rebels in these psalms come from within nominal Israel. Jerome rightly applies the psalm to heretics within the church. Inferentially, in Psalm 5 nominal Israel comes to the temple to pray (5:4-5[5-6]). All three psalms fit the context of Absalom's rebellion (Psalm 3: superscript). These royal petitions alternate between morning prayers (Psalms 3 and 5) and an evening prayer (Psalm 4).

Psalm 5 argues the case why God should save his king, punish the king's enemies, and protect the faithful. He paints his enemies as black as they really are. Absalom and his council plotted the death of God's anointed king and implicitly the death of those loyal to God's anointed (2 Sam. 16:21-23).

B. Form Criticism

The psalm exhibits the typical motifs of a lament/petition psalm: (1) address with introductory petitions to be heard (1-2[2-3]); (2) confidence with lament (3-6[4-7]); (3) petitions with lament (7-10[8-11]); and (4) petition with praise (11-12[12-13]).[29] Psalms 3 (v. 7[8]) and 5 (v. 10[11]) move beyond petitions to be delivered to a petition to punish the enemy. Elsewhere we defended the theology of these so-called imprecatory psalms that make Christians wince.[30]

C. Rhetorical Criticism

David's characterization of his enemies is unsparing, piling on six terms for their malicious speech: "arrogant boasters" (5[6]); "tell lies" (6a[7a]); "bloodthirsty and deceitful" (6b[7b]); "nothing in their mouth . . . is steadfast" (9[10]); "their throat is an open grave", and "they make their tongues smooth" (10[11]). The tongue is

---

28. Cf. Naboth, Jeremiah, and Stephen, who are not kings.
29. Verse 12[13] also functions as a benediction.
30. Waltke and Houston, *PACW*, pp. 95-98.

a deadly spiritual sword (Pss. 12; 52:2[3]; 55:21[22]; 57:4[5]; 59:7[8]; 64:3-4[4-5]; cf. Prov. 18:21; 25:18; Jer. 9:8). C. S. Lewis (1898-1963) comments on this emphasis:

> I think that when I began to read [the Psalter], the ability of words to inflict immense harm surprised me a little; I had half expected that in a simpler and more violent age when more evil was done with the knife, the big stick, and the firebrand, less would be done by talk. But in reality the Psalmists mention hardly any kind of evil more often than this one, which the most civilised societies share.[31]

By their insidious machinations the arrogant boasters hope to discredit the king and topple him (cf. the fate of Naboth, 1 Kgs. 21).

The psalm consists of two stanzas of equal length: the bases of the petitions (vv. 1-6[2-7]) and the petitions themselves (vv. 7-12[8-13]). The first stanza consists of two strophes of three verses (2 + 1 and 1 + 2) each: an invocation (vv. 1-3[2-4]) and confidence (vv. 4-6[5-7]). The second stanza consists of three strophes of equal length (vv. 7-8[8-9], 9-10[10-11], 11-12[12-13]). The stanzas' strophes are arranged in an alternating structure. Their first strophes escalate from petitions to be heard (vv. 1-3[2-4]) to petitions to be delivered (vv. 7-8[8-9]), and their second strophes, which pertain to the enemies, escalate from an unsparing vilification of them (vv. 4-6[5-7]) to an even more disparaging characterization of them (vv. 9-10[10-11]). The psalm concludes with a benedictory petition for the people (vv. 11-12[12-13]). The exegesis below uses the following outline to trace the psalm's argument:

Superscript

I. Bases for petitions	1-6[2-7]
A. Invocation: "The Watchtower"	1-3[2-4]
1. Introductory petitions	1-2[2-3]
2. Introduction: arranges words	3[4]
B. Confidence: "I AM" abhors the wicked: "The Sacred Tent"	4-6[5-7]
1. "I AM" has no delight in evil; wicked cannot stand in his presence	4[5]
2. "I AM" detests bloodthirsty and deceitful	5-6[6-7]
II. Petitions	7-12[8-13]
A. Save me for the sake of my enemies: "The Highway"	7-8[8-9]
B. Banish the liars for the sake of your people: "The Sepulcher"	9-10[10-11]

---

31. C. S. Lewis, *Reflections on the Psalms* (New York: Harcourt, Brace, 1958), p. 75.

          C. Protect your faithful ones for the sake of your Name:
             "The Shield"   11-12[12-13]

Subscript   *(Psalm 6: superscript a)*

Beside this analysis of the psalm's structure, based on form criticism, the poet possibly also intends a chiastic structure to contrast the devout and the depraved.

   I. Devout (singular): introductory petitions (escalation from
      words > cry for help)   1-3[2-4]
      II. Depraved: God abhors them (escalation in distance:
         abhor > banish)   9[10]; 4-6[5-7]
         X. Devout: enters holy place: extreme closeness   7-8[8-9]
      II'. Depraved: (Escalation: nothing in mouth steadfast >
         tongues flatter)   9-10[10-11]
   I'. Devout (plural): Praise (God himself their shield [extreme
      closeness])   11-12[12-13][32]

Within the above structure of II. X. II' there may be yet another chiasm:

   A. Evil cannot dwell with you   4[5]
      B. Boastful cannot stand in your presence   5a[6a]
         C. "I AM" abhors bloodthirsty and deceitful   6b[7b]
           X. "I AM" shows unfailing kindness to king
               and saves him   7-8[8-9]
         C'. Rebels' throats are open tombs and tongues flatter   9[10]
      B'. Let them fall by their own schemes   10a[11a]
   A'. Banish them for their abundant transgressions   10b[11b][33]

---

32. Adapted from paper to Bruce Waltke by Gregory Salazar (Reformed Theological Seminary, 2009).

33. Adapted from paper to Bruce Waltke by David Jenkins (Regent College, 2008).

II. Exegesis

A. Superscript

1. Genre: A Psalm

In the extant Hebrew text the postscript of the preceding psalm has been united with the superscript of the following psalms.[34]

A *psalm* refers to a song that is sung to the pizzicato of a stringed instrument. The psalmist puts the cacophony of his situation into harmony with music and song. Psalm 5 vibrates with fervency. Fervent prayer is effective (James 5:16); it is the fire and the incense; without fervency it is no prayer.

2. Author: "Of David"

Elsewhere, against a scholarly consensus, we defended both that לְדָוִד *(ldvd)* meant "by David" and that superscripts were historically reliable.[35] In that connection we also argued for an extensive royal interpretation of the Psalter. The internal evidence of this psalm validates both theses: (1) Treachery against anointed is viewed as treachery against God; (2) all psalms regarding treachery/liars are "by David"; (3) salvation of the faithful depends on the salvation of psalmist. These arguments are buttressed by (4) his use of martial language (cf. "shield"); and (5) his right to enter temple.

B. Bases for Petitions (5:1-3[2-4])

1. Invocation (5:1-3[2-4])

Rabbi Morganesque notes several unifying features of the first strophe: (1) subject-matter: "I AM" and David versus "I AM" and wicked in second strophe; (2) framed by "I AM" (1A, 3A[2A, 4A]); (3) dynamic escalation: threefold plea to be heard and threefold development: "words" > burning "meditation" > arranging words; (4) reason God should listen: "pray to you [alone]"; and (5) at center and as apex God's titles: "my King and my God." Those names turn the cry of distress into calm confidence.[36]

---

34. See note 20.
35. Waltke and Houston, *PACW,* pp. 89-92.
36. Rabbi Morganesque, personal correspondence.

a. Introductory Petitions (5:1-2[2-3])

David's threefold terse command to God shocks us. In fact, however, this invocation is one of the three longest in personal invocations (Pss. 22:2-3[3-4]; 88:2[3]). A comparison with Akkadian prayers is instructive. The invocations of *shuilla*-prayers in Mesopotamia, the prayers to which the Hebrew laments of the individual are most frequently albeit wrongly compared, typically have a very deferential tone and an extended hymn, a protocol befitting a person when addressing an authority.[37] A. Lenzi helpfully distinguishes between Akkadian *shuillas,* which are addressed to cosmic high gods like Shamash ("Sun"), and *dingir.sha,dib.ba,* prayers in which the suppliant prays to one's personal god, who on occasion is also a high god. These invocations were much shorter, for they are addressed to "a deity who is presumably much closer to the supplicant than the high gods."[38] Thorkild Jacobsen envisions the personal god as a kind of parent figure.[39] We do not address our mother in the same way we address a mayor, governor, or president.[40] Lenzi notes a general claim made by Catherine Bell: "the greater the social distance experienced or desired between persons, the more their activities abide by those conventions that acknowledge social distance."[41] David models for us a right relationship to God: a recognition of God's sublimities and of his intimate presence with us.[42]

The invoking imperatives must be nuanced by the social relationship between the psalmist and God. "Through the volitional forms a speaker aims to impose his or her will on some other person . . . the force with which that will is exerted depends on various factors, including the speaker's social standing *vis-à-vis* the addressee, the social context of the discourse, and the meaning of the verb."[43] The epithets, "my King and my God," give them a deferential tone and texture. In short, the three imperatives assert our intimacy with God and the three epithets assert our respect for him. In verse 7[8] David expresses his bold access to God, but he bows in worship.

37. E. Gerstenberg, *Der bittende Mensch: Bittritual und Klagelied des Einzelnen im Alten Testament* (WMANT 51; Neukirchen-Vluyn: Neukirchener Verlag, 1980), p. 87.

38. Alan Lenzi, "Mesopotamian Prayers and Biblical Laments," *Journal of Biblical Literature* 129, no. 2 (2010): 312.

39. Thorkild Jacobsen, *Treasures of Darkness: A History of Mesopotamian Religion* (New Haven: Yale University Press, 1976), pp. 175-80.

40. The German language distinguishes *Sie* from *du*; French, *Vous* from *tu*; and Spanish, *Usted* from *tú*

41. C. Bell, *Ritual: Perspective and Dimensions* (New York: Oxford University Press, 1997), p. 143.

42. Communal laments in the Psalter (Psalms 44, 60, 74, 79; 80, 83, and 89), as might be expected, have more extended invocations.

43. *IBHS*, P. 341c, p. 565.

29

1[2] *Give ear to* implies that "I AM" will be sympathetic to him. What we give ear to gives us away; for example, the political pundits we prefer to listen to reveal our political preferences. *My words* refers to the verses that follow the invocation. "I AM" *(yhwh)* translates and abbreviates God's personal sentence name, "I Am Who I Am" (Exod. 3:14).[44] His name signifies that God is eternal and that he must define his mystery by revealing himself in interpreted historical acts and by propositional statements.[45] *Understand* means to see insightfully through the senses (1 Sam. 3:8; 2 Sam. 12:19) and appropriate after "give ear." *Burning meditation* occurs in Psalm 39:3[4]: "my heart grew hot within me. While I *meditated*, the fire burned; then I spoke with my tongue." Arabic and Akkadian cognates mean "to crackle (of a flame)," and "grow angry, flare up in anger" respectively, matching the association of "heart" with heat and of "meditation" with burning fire (1 Sam. 1:13; Rom. 8:26f.). Charles Haddon Spurgeon (1834-1892) comments: "Words are not the essence but the garments of prayer."[46]

2[3] *Pay attention* denotes being willfully and consciously attentive (Isa. 32:3). *My cry for help* glosses this unique occurrence of the noun *šwʿ*. The verb in *piel* means "cry out for help" in distress (Ps. 18:6[7]) and anticipates a savior (Pss. 18:41[42]; 30:2[3]; 72:12; cf. Job 30:28). *My King* assumes that "I AM" is the central symbol of Israel's social systems. Vast literary deposits throughout the ancient Near East from Mesopotamia, through Syria-Palestine, to Egypt over many centuries document that the king established and maintained all aspects of order throughout the kingdom (Psalms 72, 101, and 146). Keith Whitelam comments on the king's functions: "The true exercise of his duty as warrior was to protect and defend the state against internal and external military threat; as judge, to guarantee order through the establishment of justice" (1 Sam. 8:5, 20; 2 Sam. 12:1-15; 14:2-4; 15:1-6).[47] An attack on God's anointed, who was the earthly occupant of what was the equivalent of the heavenly throne, was an attack against "I AM's" kingship.[48] *My God* designates David's commitment of his life to "I AM"

---

44. Waltke and Houston, *PACW*, pp. 136-38.

45. In the progress of revelation God revealed himself as a triunity. The Trinity may be likened to the triadic chord: C, E, G. Each note has the same substance, but each functions differently, yet together they constitute a unity. After God's incarnation in the Second Person, God wishes to be invoked in the name of his Son, the Lord Jesus Christ (cf. John 15:16).

46. Charles Haddon Spurgeon, *The Treasury of David: Spurgeon's Great Commentary on Psalms.* An updated edition in today's language, updated by Roy H. Clarke (Nashville: Thomas Nelson, 1997), p. 45.

47. Keith W. Whitelam, *Anchor Bible Dictionary,* vol. 4 (New York, London, Toronto, Sydney, Auckland: Doubleday, 1992), p. 44.

48. Waltke and Houston, *PACW*, pp. 164-79.

as the quintessence of all divine, transcendent, heavenly powers.[49] Commenting on "my," A. A. Anderson writes that "[it] seems to bridge the gulf between the almighty sovereign and the humble petitioner."[50] Etymologically, the root of *I pray to you* has a juridical background, and probably carries the connotation of "to ask for a favorable estimation/decision,"[51] for another (i.e., "to intercede") or for ourselves (i.e., "to petition," "to pray"). The petition is brought to God in his temple (Isa. 37:14). The king has no higher court or other place to petition a judge for enacting a favorable verdict than God in his temple (1 Sam. 2:25). We identify our god by the person and place to whom and to which we turn in distress. Spurgeon eloquently expressed the truth of this verse: "Prayer without fervency is like hunting with a dead dog. Prayer without preparation is like hawking with a blind falcon. . . . The Holy Spirit is the author of prayer, but He uses thoughts of a fervent soul to fashion a golden vessel. Let our prayers and praises be the steady burning of a well-kindled fire, not the flashes of a hot and hasty brain."[52]

b. Arranges Words (5:3[4])

A chiastic structure segues the imperative mood into the indicative:

A.	Pay attention to my words, "I AM"	1[2]
	B. Hear my voiced *(qôl)* cry for help	2a[3a]
	X. For to you I pray	2b[3b]
	B'. "I AM," you hear my voice *(qôl)*	3ab[4ab]
A'.	I arrange [my words] before you	3b[4b][53]

The segue is strengthened by gapping "words" (1a[2a]) as the object of "I arrange" (3b[4b]). Verse 3[4] is a janus. "Hear my voice" looks back to "I AM" as Judge, and "arrange my words" looks ahead to plaintiff's case (4-6[5-7]).

In the morning, as Jerome rightly discerned, denotes "daybreak," the coming of sunrise, from the time when the stars that presage the new day are still visible (Job 38:7) and people and things are scarcely visible (Gen. 29:25; Ruth 3:14; 1 Kgs. 3:21) to the breaking of the sun over the horizon (Judg. 9:33; 2 Sam 23:4; 2 Kgs. 3:22). It is an appointed time of worship (Exod. 29:39; 36:3; Num. 28:4, 8, 23; 2 Kgs.

---

49. F. M. Cross, *TDOT*, 1.247, s.v. *'el.*

50. A. A. Anderson, *The Book of Psalms,* vol. 1: *Psalms 1–72* (Grand Rapids: Eerdmans, 1972; reprinted 1989), p. 82.

51. H. P. Stähli, *TLOT,* 2.991, s.v. *pll.*

52. Spurgeon, *Treasury of David,* pp. 25f.

53. Adopted from a paper to Bruce Waltke from R. T. Griffith (Reformed Theological Seminary, 2009).

3:20; Ezek. 46:15) and the principal one of the three times for prayer in the Psalter (5:3[4]; 55:17[18]; 59:16[17]; Ps. 88:13[14]). Court was convened in the morning and justice dispensed (Exod. 18:13-14; Ps. 88:13[14]; Mic. 2:1; Zeph. 3:5; cf. Job 7:18; Ps. 73:14).[54] The rays of the rising sun chase away the darkness of the night, which is the light for the wicked (Job 38:12-13). Exposed in the light of truth, the wicked stand condemned (Gen. 19:27; 20:8; Judg. 9:33; 19:25-27; 2 Kgs. 3:22; Ruth 3:14). In Mesopotamia *Shamash* ("Sun") was the god of justice. In Egypt it was thought the sun-god dispelled all evil.[55] The repetition of "in the morning" connotes the urgency of his case; it is first on the docket; it cannot be delayed. He arranges his case to convince the Judge and then vigilantly awaits the verdict, confident of a favorable verdict. *You hear* signifies that outwardly God gives his ear to the speaker's words (cf. "give ear," verse 1a[2a]) and inwardly he consents to them ("understand," verse 1b[2b]). *I arrange (my words)* means to arrange felicitously to argue his case.[56] He eagerly anticipates the verdict: *and I watch.* The Hebrew root of "watch" "carries the implicit meaning of alert and active watching rather than simply gazing . . . (1 Sam. 4:13)."[57]

C. Confidence: "I AM" Abhors the Wicked (5:4-6[5-7])

As a sentinel on a watchtower, the psalmist watches vigilantly for an answer to his petition (Hab. 2:1), because he knows evil cannot coexist with God. "As fire and water resist each other, as light and darkness are utterly diverse, so God resists wickedness."[58] His case rests on God's unique holiness (v. 7[8]). In the religions surrounding Israel, "holiness" was devoid of a moral element.[59]

---

54. Barth (*TDOT,* 2.226-28), while appreciating the contribution of J. Ziegler ("Die Hilfe Gottes 'am Morgen,'" Festschrift F. Nötscher, *BBB,* 1 [1950], pp. 281-88), does not find convincing the data that the morning is the "suitable time for divine help."

55. O. Keel, *The Symbolism of the Biblical World: Ancient Near Eastern Iconography and the Book of Psalms,* trans. T. J. Hallet (New York: Seabury, 1978), pp. 288-90.

56. Wood is set in order on an altar for a fire (Gen. 22:9), a table is arranged for a meal (Ps. 23:5), troops draw up in battle order for engaging the enemy (Gen. 14:8), and words and arguments are drawn up in preparation for the presentation of a persuasive argument (Job 13:18). The last use best fits this context that features words. V. Hamilton (*NIDOTTE,* 3, 536, s.v. 'rk) documents this forensic use in Job 32:14; 37:19; Psalm 5:3[4]; 50:21; Isa. 44:7.

57. Keith N. Schoville, *NIDOTTE,* 3, 831, s.v. *ṣph.*

58. Cf. William S. Plumer, *Psalms: A Critical and Expository Commentary with Doctrinal and Practical Remarks* (Edinburgh: Banner of Truth Trust, 1975), p. 80.

59. Mitchell Dahood (*Psalms 1-50* [AB; Garden City, NY: Doubleday, 1966-70], p. 31) notes an unpublished Ugaritic text. It "describes the excesses of El, the head of the Canaanite pantheon, while he is at table. As a result of his intemperance, El ends up wallowing . . . 'in his excrement

Several felicitous features unify the second strophe. (1) Rabbi Morganesque notes that verbs pertaining to God's emotions — [not] delights (4[5]) and detests (6[7]) — frame the strophe.[60] (2) Six terms in escalating darker tones bring the wicked into ever-sharper focus. (3) These are matched by six terms in ever-darker tones that bring God's reaction to the wicked into ever-sharper focus. Three pertain to his emotional responses: from "who does not delight" (4[5]), to "hate" (5[6]), to "detest" (6[7]); and three escalate his divine actions from "cannot find asylum" (4[5]), to "cannot stand before him" (5[6]), to "you destroy" (6[7]). (4) An ABB'A' pattern interfaces God's spiritual aversion to wickedness and wrongdoers (AA') and his refusal to admit them into his presence (BB'):

A. For you are not a God who delights in wickedness;
   B. Evil cannot sojourn with you.
   B'. Arrogant boasters cannot stand before your presence;
A'. You hate all who do wrong.[61]

1. "I AM" has no delight in evil; wicked cannot stand in his presence (5:4[5])

Verses 4[5] and 7[8] pertain to rights of asylum at God's sanctuary. Terrien notes: "[A]ccording to ancient customs of hospitality, a stranger might sojourn in a Bedouin tent and elude his pursuers for three days."[62] There are barriers, however, inherent in true religion that take ethics into account (Ps. 15:1). Only those who fear "I AM," in whom he delights, find asylum in his tent (Psalm 15). He banishes from his presence the likes of David's enemies and hands them over to the persistent death that pervades the world apart from his grace (Ps. 1:5; cf. Prov. 2:22; 2 Thess. 1:5-10). *Not a god who delights in wickedness* is a litotes: an understatement to emphasize its opposite. "Delight" denotes a psychic feeling of pleasure and expresses a person's affection for another. R. Van Leeuwen defines *in wickedness* thus: "in contrast to positive root ('righteous') ('wicked') expresses negative behavior — evil thoughts, words and deeds — antisocial behavior that

---

and his urine.' " The gods in the Canaanite pantheon were like the gods of Homer's world: full of lust, carried grudges, bent on revenge, and motivated by personal gain. By common grace Xenophanes (c. 565-470 BCE) hurled darts of derision against Homer and Hesiod for perpetuating the scandalous tales about the gods.

60. Rabbi Morganesque, personal communication.

61. Verses 5-6[6-7] are also linked by the assonance of *yityaṣṣᵉbû* and *yᵉtāʿēḇ*, the words second from the beginning of 5a[6a] and from the end of 6b[7b] respectively.

62. Samuel Terrien, *The Psalms: Strophic Structure and Theological Commentary* (Grand Rapids: Eerdmans, 2003), p. 105.

simultaneously betrays a person's inner disharmony and unrest."[63] *Evil* conveys the factual judgment that something is bad, whether it be a concrete physical state (e.g., "ugly" cows, Gen. 41:3; "poor/bad" figs, Jer. 24:2), an abstraction, "calamity/disaster," or, as here, moral behavior that injures others (Ps. 15:3). Stoebe suggests that the basic meaning of "evil" is what harms life, not what benefits it.[64] The plaintiff, personifying "evil" as a resident alien, asserts it *cannot sojourn with you.* "Sojourn" signifies to leave one's homeland for political, economic, religious, or other circumstances and to dwell as a newcomer and resident alien without the original rights of the host community for a definite or indefinite (Ps. 61:4[5]) time in order to find protection, a resting place, and a home in another community (Gen. 12:10; 19:29; 20:1; Ruth 1:2; Judg. 19:16; Jer. 42–50, 12×).

2. *"I AM" versus Wrongdoers (5:5-6[6-7])*

5[6] The three occurrences of *arrogant boasters* show they are "arrogant God-defying boasters who work wickedness" (Pss. 75:4[5]; 73:3ff.). In Dante's *Purgatorio* pride, love of self, is the first of seven terraces on the mount of root sins.[65] All the uses of the Hebrew root for "they cannot stand" pertain to presenting oneself firmly to engage in a mission, such as a fight, or in a commission. The collocation *before your eyes* "tends toward the metonymic abstract conception of 'presence'" (Pss. 18:25[26]; 101:3, 7; Joel 1:16).[66] M. Dahood defends a forensic interpretation of "stand before you" on the bases of "the term 'arrange' in v. 3[4] and the collocation of both these verbs in legal context of Job xxxiii 5: 'if you are able, refute me; draw up your case and *stand before me.'"*[67] *You hate* is the most general term to express "intense and passionate dislike, a feeling of extreme aversion for and/or extreme hostility toward someone or something." Its nearest verbal parallel is "to abhor/detest" (cf. v. 6[7]). *All* [without exception] *do* (i.e., execute, put into action the necessary means to secure the success of their enterprise) *malevolence* (אָוֶן).

6[7] The Hebrew root of *you destroy* originally meant "to be lost, to wander about, run away"; from this it expanded to "to destroy." Its antonym is "to remain." *Those who speak lies* refers to those whose statements do not accord with actuality. Lies are absolutely denied in God's nature (Num. 23:19); the wicked by nature are burdened with it (Ps. 58:3[4]). Truth, whether according to correspondence, coherence, or relational theory of truth, is founded in the character of God. All

---

63. C. van Leeuwen, *TLOT*, 3.1262, s.v. *rš*ʿ.
64. Stoebe, *TLOT*, 2.491, s.v. *ṭôb*.
65. Canto XII.
66. E. Jenni, *TLOT*, 2.878, s.v. *ʿayin*.
67. Dahood, *Psalms 1–50*, p. 31.

that does not conform to his communicable attributes is surreal "and . . . will be consigned to the fiery lake of burning sulfur. This is the second death" (Rev. 21[8]).

Abhors denotes having sensibilities offended. Sensibilities are relative to a person's character and values. The Truth, the Lover of Righteousness and Justice, abhors *the bloodthirsty*. "Blood," according to Gerleman, "has become an ethically qualified concept: 'bloody deed' and (in accordance with Hebrew thought almost synonymously) 'bloodguilt.'"[68] The Hebrew grammatical construction *and deceitful* identifies the bloodthirsty as also deceitful. *Mirmâ* denotes an evil design to deceive a victim in order to harm them.

D. Petitions and Praise (5:7-12[8-13])

The following outline sketches the segue from first to second stanza by means of mood changes:

Strophe 1	1-3[2-4]
Imperatives	1-2[2-3]
Janus: Indicative	3[4]
Strophe 2: Indicative	4-6[5-7]
Strophe 3	7-8[8-9]
Janus: Indicative	7[8]
Imperative	8[9]

In contrast to the wicked who cannot come into God's presence (4-5[5-6]), the anointed king now enters boldly but reverently into God's holy — and so dangerous — presence (7[8]). The stanzas are united in a concentric structure:

A.	For the faithful king:	vv. 7-8[8-9]
B.	Against the wicked	v. 9[10]
B′.	Against the wicked	vv. 10[11]
A′.	For the faithful nation	vv. 11-12[12-13]

1. Save Me for the Sake of My Enemies (5:7-8[8-9])

7[8] David maintains a subtle equilibrium between his right of access, which is based on his covenant relationship with "I AM," and his reverent fear of God. *But I* contrasts David's privileged position to enter God's presence, not a contrast

---

68. G. Gerleman, *TLOT*, 1.337. s.v. *dam*.

between his character with theirs (Ps. 66:18-19). *By your . . . kindness* refers to "I AM's" eternal nature to deliver or protect "as a responsible keeping of faith with another with whom one is in a relationship."[69] God's "presence is indissolubly linked to a love that forgives [the trusting] as much as it requires."[70] *Great* signifies that God's kindness exceeds human kindness.[71] Within the developing canon, *to your house* was reinterpreted from David's tent sanctuary to Solomon's temple and finally to the church triumphant, secure in the bosom of the resurrected Jesus Christ (John 1:14; 2:12-23; 1 Cor. 3:16-17; 6:14-20; 1 Pet. 2:4-10).[72]

The verb *qdd* ("kneel down in homage") is always linked as preparatory action to *I bow down* with nose to the ground (Gen. 19:1). The genuflection symbolizes reverence, homage, high respect of a person to an exalted superior. *Your holy palace* signifies a royal residence (cf. "my King," v. 2[3]; Ps. 45:8[9], 15[16]), probably a synonym for "your house" (1 Sam. 1:9; 3:3), although it could also indicate the main hall of the temple, in contradistinction to the foyer and the most holy place. The tent David pitched for the ark-of-the-covenant (1 Chron. 15:1) may be called a palace, because of its solemn dedication, not for its magnificence, although nothing is known about its structure.[73] *Your holy* qualifies the royal residence as sanctified by God's presence.[74] "Holy" refers to the sacred in contrast to the common, to the clean in contrast to the unclean (Lev. 10:10).[75] Moreover, God's holiness is often associated with his power. After seventy men were smitten by "I AM" in Beth-shemesh, the grieving inhabitants ask: "Who can stand before (withstand) 'I AM,' the holy God?" (1 Sam. 6:20; cf. 2 Samuel 6). No wonder David prostrates himself in homage before his awesome, holy God, and adds: *in fear of you.*[76]

8[9] *Lead me* originated in the shepherd's life and is commonly used in situations of leading one safely through snares and triumphantly to a desired and promised destiny (Exod. 15:13; 32:34; Deut. 32:12; Pss. 5:8[9]; 23:3; 78:14, 53; 139:23[24];

---

69. K. D. Sakenfeld, *The Meaning of Ḥesed in the Hebrew Bible* (Harvard Semitic Museum 17; Missoula, MT: Scholars, 1978), p. 233.

70. Terrien, *The Psalms*, p. 106.

71. A. F. Kirkpatrick (*The Book of Psalms* [Grand Rapids: Baker from the 1902 edition of the University Press, Cambridge, 1982], p. 23) notes the contrast between the "great" (רב, literally "multitude of"/ "abundant") kindness and their "abundant" (רב) "transgressions" (v. 10[11]).

72. "Cannot sojourn" and "can come" suggest that "with you" and "before you" in verses 4[5] and 5[6] refer to God's presence in his royal tent-shrine.

73. J. J. Stewart Perowne, *The Book of Psalms* (Grand Rapids: Zondervan, 1966; reprinted from George Bell & Sons, 1878), p. 133.

74. James L. Mays, *Micah: A Commentary* (Philadelphia: Westminster, 1976), p. 40.

75. Jackie A. Naude, *NIDOTTE*, 3.878.

76. B. Waltke, "The Fear of the LORD," in *Alive to God* (Downers Grove, IL: InterVarsity, 1992), pp. 17-33.

Isa. 40:11; 49:10; Rev. 7:17).[77] The juxtaposition of the verb of motion, "lead," with an abstraction *in your righteousness* [*ṣdq*] suggests that the parallel "way" is elided, yielding "your righteous way." *Righteousness* values the divine and human modes of behavior as doing what is communally faithful and beneficial as defined by the Lawgiver. In some social contexts, the word is used of the king whose task is to create a selflessly favorable order for the whole people (2 Sam. 8:15; Jer. 22:3, 15; 33:15; Ezek. 45:9). A. A. Anderson glosses the term: "by means of your righteous acts of salvation."[78] K. Koch says: "*ṣedeq* never encompasses merely an ethical behavior but . . . a circumstance of sound, unassailed success."[79] "As good shepherd and conqueror of evil, the Lord is implored to lead the way, driving out the lurking evil and clearing away the dangerous obstacles"[80] (Ps. 23:3). H. A. Brongers shows that a paraphrase is necessary for the often elliptical particle *for the sake of*,[81] such as, "and as a consequence I will be delivered from their venom and triumph over *my enemies* (Pss. 27:11-12; 59:9-10[10-11]). We should also add something like: "so that my enemies will be frustrated and not succeed." The geometric term *make straight* on a vertical axis means "upright" and on a horizontal axis either straight or smooth/level. On the metaphorical straight, smooth, divine highway with "I AM" leading him, the king can run freely and not be tripped up by a rough surface or a stumbling block (i.e., by his enemies who are ready to pounce on him). Woodenly *your way* denotes a traversable road. In its figurative sense "way" is four notions: 1) "character"; 2) "social context"; 3) "conduct" (i.e., specific choices and behavior); and 4) "consequences of that conduct" (i.e., the inevitable destiny of such a lifestyle). The character and context of God's life is his sublime holiness as expressed in his covenant; his conduct is righteous, for without fail he delivers his covenant partner in need; and the consequence of such a way is eternal life.

2. Banish My Enemies for the Sake of Your People (5:9-10[10-11])

A concentric structure links the wicked in the king's presentation of his case with his petition that "I AM" punish them:

A.	Wicked cannot sojourn with "I AM"	4[5]
B.	Wicked cannot stand before "I AM"	5[6]

77. Jenni, *TLOT*, 2.730, s.v. *nḥh*.

78. Anderson, *Psalms*, p. 84.

79. K. Koch, *TLOT*, 2.1052, s.v. *ṣdq*.

80. John Eaton, *The Psalms: A Historical and Spiritual Commentary with an Introduction and New Translation* (New York and London: Continuum, 2005), p. 73.

81. H. A. Brongers, "Die Particle לְמַעַן in der biblisch-hebraischen Sprache," *Oudtestamentische Studien* 18 (1973): 84-96.

C. "I AM" hates and destroys liars	6[7]
C'. Wicked lie and are destructive	9[10]
B'. Declare wicked guilty	10a[11a]
A'. Banish wicked	10b[11b]⁸²

In this strophe the king first accuses his enemies of being deceitful murderers (9[10]) and then petitions God for the verdict to find them guilty and banish them (10[11]).

9[10]   God's chosen king asks God to lead him to safety, *for* he traverses the dark valley of malicious liars who seek to discredit him and so topple him (cf. Psalms 17; 25; 27-28; 31; 35; 41; 52; 54-57; 59; 63-64; 71; 86; 109; 140-41). A concentric structure puts their murderous intent at the center (B/B') of their deceptive speech (A/A').

A. "Not a word from their mouth can be trusted"	9aa[10aa]
B. "Their inward part is filled with malice"	9ab[10ab]
B'. "Their throat is an open grave"	9ba[10ba]
A'. "With their tongues they tell lies"	9bb[10bb]

There is nothing excludes the exception of even one single statement, and *in their mouth* (see n. 25), a metonym for words, excludes the exception of any one of his adversaries. The Hebrew root of *that is steadfast* means: intransitively, "to stand firm"; transitively, "to establish, found, anchor"; and passively, as here, "to be firm, true, certain." The metaphor pictures the words in the mouth as something anchored in truth (6[7]). *Their inner part* refers to the inner organs of the upper half of the human torso, especially the heart (1 Sam. 25:37).[83] *Are filled with violence* glosses the literal: "[their inner part] is violence" — that is to say, "totally filled with violence."[84] "Violence" denotes destructive forces that bring ruin.[85] The destructive forces, always plural in this use, are usually evil speech (Ps. 38:12[13]), which in many instances is also associated with lies and treachery (Job 6:30; Pss. 52:2[4]; 7[9]; 55:11[12]; 57:1[2]; 59:11[12]; 94:20). *Their throat,* which gives their heart voice, may refer to the outer part of the throat, i.e., neck (Isa.

82. Adapted from a paper by Sean McKenna presented to Bruce Waltke (Reformed Theological Seminary, 2009).

83. The figure probably aims to match as an anagram *qirbān* "their inner part" with *qeḇer* "tomb" in the parallel.

84. "I am prayer" means "I am totally given to prayer" (Ps. 109:4), and "I am peace" means "I am wholly given to peace" (Ps. 120:7; cf. Prov. 8:30; 10:1).

85. *HALOT,* 1:242 s.v. *hawwâ.*

3:16; Ezek. 16:11) or, as here, to its inner part, "throat," a metonymy for the act of speaking (Pss. 115:7; 149:6; Isa. 58:1). *Is an open* grave, as T. D. Alexander notes, "is always related to the burial of people, never of animals or lifeless objects. Among the ancient Israelites it was customary to bury their dead in either a natural cave or a chamber hewn out of soft rock, with each family having their own burial tomb for the interment of deceased relatives." He further notes: "Because of their association with death, graves are viewed as unclean (Isa. 65:4). Even touching a grave defiled an individual, so as to render him unclean for seven days."[86] To judge from Jeremiah 5:16 — "Their quivers are an open grave; all of them are mighty warriors" — the metaphor, "open grave," symbolizes insatiability, destruction, and death (Prov. 30:15b-16). *They make . . . smooth*, whose nominal derivative is used of David's five smooth stones, is used literally only of making metal smooth (Isa. 41:7). Once (Hos. 10:2) it is used metaphorically of a heart that is "smooth" (i.e., deceitful). Its seven other occurrences (Pss. 5:9[10]; 36:2[3]; 55:21[22]; Prov. 2:16; 7:5; 28:23; 29:5) metaphorically refer to "flatter in order to deceive." Paul appropriates this condemnation of David's enemies within nominal Israel to the whole human race, because humankind untouched by God's grace is depraved, obstinately rebelling against God (Rom. 3:13).

10[11]   Like a prosecuting attorney David summarizes the case and calls upon the heavenly jury, which cannot fail, for a favorable verdict. The Hebrew root of *make them liable* denotes "a situation in which someone is or becomes obligated to discharge guilt by giving something."[87] In other words, David asks: "Declare them guilty and so liable to pay the damage they inflicted on the anointed king." The metaphor *let them fall* occurs ninety-six times for violent death.[88] *From their intrigues* means that the vitriolic propaganda through which the enemies plotted to trap and topple the king will boomerang and topple them, as happened to Haman who was hanged on the gallows he constructed for Mordecai (Esth. 7:10). *Banish them* means "forcibly to drive or push his enemies away,"[89] presumably from "I AM's" protective presence. Outside of the protection and provision of God's presence lies cosmic, elementary death. *For the abundance of their obstinate rebellions* marks their rebellion as the originating force of their being pushed away. "To rebel" designates "an open and brazen defiance of God by humans."[90] *Obstinate against you* implies that plotting against the king is rebellion against

86. T. Desmond Alexander, *NIDOTTE*, 3.865, 67, s.v. *qbr*.
87. R. Knierim, *TLOT*, 1.192, s.v. *'asam*.
88. Allan M. Harman, *NIDOTTE*, 3.130, s.v. *npl*.
89. L. C. Coppes, *TWOT*, 2.556, s.v. *ndḥ*.
90. Alex Luc, *NIDOTTE*, 3.706, s.v. *pšʿ*.

God.[91] "Obstinate" consistently implies a conscious and willful attitude and an active, subjective participation (cf. Deut. 21:18, 20; Isa. 30:9; Ps. 78:8).

3. Protect Your Faithful Ones for the Sake of Your Name (5:11-12[12-13])

The petitions to banish the wicked and to protect the righteous are bound together by the theme of praise. Punishing the wicked will result in the praise of "I AM" by the faithful (11[12a]) and so will protecting the faithful (11b[12b]). God's protection of them is certain, for he shields them (12[13]). Thus verse 12[13] also serves as a benediction for the faithful.

These petitions against the wicked and for the righteous are also linked by three striking contrasts: (1) The wicked fall to their own demise (v. 10[11]), but the righteous find a refuge in God (v. 11[12]). (2) The speech of the wicked is deadly and deceitful (9[10]), but the righteous sing for joy (11[12]). (3) The wicked are banished from God (10[11]), but God shelters the righteous.[92]

11[12]   Verse 11[12] coheres in a chiastic structure:

A. All who seek refuge in you rejoice forever	11aa[12aa]
B. Make yourself a shelter over them	11ab[12ab]
A'. Lovers of your name exult in you	11b[12b]

God's rejection and punishment of the obstinate rebels will elicit shouts of victory from the faithful. *And so* (n. 26) *all* [without exception] *who take refuge (ḥsh) in you rejoice (śmḥ).* Ḥsh occurs thirty-seven times, always with the meaning "to seek/take refuge in God,"[93] and śmḥ denotes elementary spontaneous, outward joy.[94] In festivals this Dionysian joy manifests itself in joyful frolicking (Jer. 50:11), in stamping the feet and clapping the hands (Isa. 55:12; Ezek. 25:6), and in dancing, music, and shouts of joy (1 Sam. 18:6; 2 Sam. 6:12, 14; 1 Kgs. 1:40, 45; Neh. 12:27). T. Longman notes that *they will shout for joy (rnn)* signifies a loud, enthusiastic shout, "to yell"; the tone has to be determined by the context, although it usually expresses happiness, joy, relief.[95] R. Ficker adds: "*rnn* does not solely mean a loud, in some circumstances inarticulate, unoriented [sic!] cry; in Proverbs 8:3,

---

91. A. Cohen, *The Psalms* (London: Soncino Press, 1950), p. 12.

92. Jonathan G. Smith in a paper presented to Bruce Waltke (Reformed Theological Seminary, 2009).

93. For apparent exceptions see Bruce Waltke, *The Book of Proverbs: Chapters 1–15* (Grand Rapids: Eerdmans, 2004), p. 582, n. 52.

94. E. Ruprecht, *TLOT*, 3.1, 273-74, s.v. *brk*.

95. Tremper Longman III, *NIDOTTE*, 3.1127, s.v. *rnn*.

rnn indicates wisdom's wooing, inviting cry."[96] *Forever,* according to E. Jenni,[97] means "the most distant time," either in the past (about twenty times) or the future (about three hundred times). Such distant time is relative: a lifespan (Exod. 21:6) or the furthest conceivable time (15:18).[98] In the canon of Holy Scripture it refers to an unending future that outlasts clinical death.

The faithful's praise for the destruction of the king's enemies segues into a petition that God protect them with the purpose that they praise God's name. The root of *place yourself as a shield,* according to *HALOT,* means "to shut off as a protection." The sense seems to be like that of a soldier who takes cover. *Around them* construes *ʿal* to have its comprehensive locational sense ("around, about").[99] The root of *that . . . may exult* pertains to the jubilant gladness in the cult that accompanies the triumph over enemies (Pss. 9:2-3[3-4]; 68:2-3[3-4]; Prov. 11:10; 28:12; 1 Chron. 16:31-32). *Those who love* designates their emotional feeling of strongly desiring something that flows out of their perceptions and as a result causes them to go after (Jer. 2:25b), seek (Prov. 8:17 [Q]), run after (Isa. 1:23), cleave to (Deut. 11:22; 30:20; Prov. 18:24) *your Name.* In the world of the Bible a name, beyond being an identification mark, often pertains to one's existence (compare God's naming of the objects of the cosmos [Genesis 1] and Adam's naming of the animals and his wife [Genesis 2]). To have one's name cut off was to cease to exist. A name also described the character and sometimes the destiny of a person or thing. For the significance of God's name see verse 1. "I AM's" presence, symbolized by the Glory cloud and by his Name being located there, made the temple and Mount Zion "holy."

12[13] *Bless* means to fill something with potency for life (vitality, prosperity, abundance, fertility), enabling them to succeed (Gen. 22:17). The living, eternal God is the source of all blessing, which is usually mediated through humans, including through their prayers. His blessing on the righteous mediates his life to them, including both its provisioning and its protection (Jer. 31:23-26). *The righteous* refers to those who love to bring about right and harmony for all by submitting themselves to the Law/Word *(Logos)* of God. The only other occurrence of *surround* refers to Saul's army surrounding/closing in upon David and his men. The meaning of *with favor* is two-sided, namely *will* and *pleasure* (Isa. 60:10). Here his favor assumes the concrete form of saving help by placing a shield around them (Ps. 106:4). *Like a shield,* says T. Longman, refers to "a special kind of shield used to protect the entire body.[100] The word likely refers to the shield used during the siege of cities,

96. R. Ficker, *TLOT,* 3.1,240, s.v. *rnn.*
97. E. Jenni, *THAT,* 2.230, s.v. *ʿôlām.*
98. Anthony Tomasino, *NIDOTTE,* 3.346, s.v. *ʿôlām.*
99. *IBHS,* P. 11.2.13, p. 216.
100. The *māgēn* is a round, light shield that is made of wood or wicker and covered with

particularly when warriors are trying to undermine the walls. Often a shield bearer will have sole responsibility of moving the shield in order to protect himself and an archer who accompanies him. These shields often have a little overhang that protects the warrior from arrows shot from an elevation, like the top of a city wall."[101]

E. Subscript (6:6:1a)

The meaning of *lam^enaṣṣēaḥ* is uncertain but probably means "for the director of music."[102] The Hebrew root means "to inspect," often with the connotation "to supervise" and is used in the context of temple work and activities and, more specifically, sometimes in contexts of its music (Ezra 3:8; 1 Chron. 15:21; 23:4; 2 Chron. 2:1-17; 34:12-13; see above).[103]

PART IV. CONCLUSION

David Dickson (1583-1662), one-time professor of divinity at Edinburgh University, summarizes the psalm thus:

> David, as a type of Christ, and one of the number of afflicted followers, as an example of exercise to others in after ages, doth pray for himself, and against his enemies, raising sundry arguments to strengthen himself in his hope to be heard. Firstly, from the grace of God bestowed on himself to use the means, vv. 1, 2, 3. Secondly, from the justice of God against his wicked enemies, vv. 4, 5, 6. Thirdly, from his own steadfast purpose and desire to continue in God's service, as to walk uprightly [sic! by God's kindness to do right by him], as the enemy shall not have advantage of him by his miscarriage, vv. 7-8. Fourthly, from the ripeness of sin in his adversaries which prepared them for sudden destruction, vv. 9, 10. Fifthly, from the certain hope and defence and spiritual blessings to be bestowed on himself and on all believers, out of the free love and favour of God toward them, vv. 11, 12.[104]

---

thick leather rubbed with oil (cf. Isa. 21:5) to preserve it and to make it glisten, and is carried by the light infantry to ward off the enemy's sword, spear, or arrows (see Ps. 3:3[4]).

101. T. Longman, *NIDOTTE*, 3.819-20, s.v. ṣinnâ (see Y. Yadin, *The Art of Warfare in Biblical Lands* [New York: McGraw-Hill, 1963], pp. 406, 418, 462).

102. Waltke and Houston, *PACW*, pp. 207-8.

103. J. Wheeler, "Music of the Temple," *Archaeology and Biblical Research* 2 (1989): 12-20.

104. David Dickson, *Commentary on the Psalms* (London: Banner of Truth Trust, 1959), p. 19.

CHAPTER 3

Psalm 6: Pursuit of Moral Excellence

Part I. Voice of the Church

I. Gregory of Nyssa

Gregory of Nyssa (c. 335-394), who lived in the generation before Jerome, has long been eclipsed by his elder brother Basil the Great, as a secondary father of the church. Contemporary scholars rate him far more importantly, as one of the greatest Christian minds of his times.[1] Probably earlier married, he was a rhetorician, and only later appointed a bishop by his elder brother Basil in an obscure small district of Cappadocia, within the greater diocese of Caesarea. Only later, at the Council of Constantinople in 381, was he recognized as a foremost theologian. He is now being more fully understood and praised.[2] As Swiss theologian Hans Urs von Balthasar appraises him: "Less brilliant and prolific than his great master Origen, less cultivated than his friend Gregory Nazianzen, less practical than his brother Basil, he nonetheless outstrips them all in profundity of his thought, for he knew better than anyone how to transpose ideas inwardly from the spiritual heritage of ancient Greece into a Christian mode."[3]

Gregory wrote a homily on Psalm 6 and also discusses the psalm in two passages in his treatise "On the Inscriptions of the Psalms." Gregory identifies

---

1. A pioneer scholar in this regard is Jean Daniélou, *La Platonisme et la Théologie Mystique: Essai sur la doctrine spirituelle de Saint Grégoire de Nysse* (Paris: Aubier/Éditions Montaigne, 1944); and "Gregory of Nyssa" in *Spirituality through the Centuries: Ascetics and Mystics of the Western Church,* ed. James Walsh (New York: Kennedy & Sons, 1964), pp. 31-42).

2. Robert L. Wilken, "Liturgy, Bible and Theology in the Eastern Homilies of Gregory of Nyssa," in *Écriture et culture philosophique dans la pensée de Grégoire de Nysse: Actes du Colloque de Chevetogne (22-26 Septembre 1969),* ed. Marguerite Harl (Leiden: Brill, 1971), pp. 127-43.

3. Hans Urs von Balthasar, *Presence and Thought: Essay on the Religious Philosophy of Gregory of Nyssa,* trans. Mark Sebanc (San Francisco: Ignatius, 1995), p. 15.

Psalm 6 as a psalm of confession and penitence in the context of David's repentance for his sin with Bathsheba and for the death of Uriah her husband (2 Sam. 11:1–12:25). But he is distinct with his pastoral theology of spiritual progress, most fully expressed in his later work, the *Life of Moses*. In his treatise on the psalms' titles, he had already interpreted the spiritual meaning of the psalms to be a series of five steps and challenges in the Christian's growth in virtue, knowledge, and holiness.[4] He sees these stages in the spiritual progress of the Christian's restoration to "the image and likeness of God," as our creation mandate. He identifies these five steps with the five books of the Psalter: (1) turning from evil to good; (2) a continual thirst for virtue; (3) attainment of union with God in sharing the divine perspective, as well as (4) in purity of life; and (5) in deeper understanding and experience of the unsurpassable grace of God.[5]

It is likely that Gregory's homily on Psalm 6 is one of his early, youthful works,[6] yet it is already germinal to what he developed maturely in his *Life of Moses* and in his homilies on the Beatitudes. With his classical education, he embraced the pursuit of excellence *(aretē)* (now interpreted as godliness) as the quest for the blessed life. This is set within the anagogical (from the Greek *anagōgē*, "upward descent") parameter of the awareness of living between time and eternity, Gregory's basic theme. From Origen onwards, the anagogical mode had become one of four ways the patristic commentators began to read Scripture: the letter, allegory, morality, and anagogy. These were later summarized in the fourteenth century as follows: "The letter teaches events, allegory what you should believe, morality teaches what you should do, anagogy what mark you should be striving for."[7]

We need forbearance with Gregory's commentary, for he devotes the first half of it to outlining his pastoral mindset, before he deals with the text proper. He writes his commentary within the bookends of the superscript, *sheminith,* and the moral virtue of *epektasis* (Gk., "extension").

II. The Anagogy of "the Eighth Day"

We also need patience with Gregory's commentary on the title *sheminith* (used in Psalms 6 and 12), for his is a textual and philological misinterpretation. But

---

4. Ronald E. Heine, *Gregory of Nyssa's Treatise on the Inscriptions of the Psalms* (Oxford: Clarendon, 1995), pp. 50-80.

5. Heine, *Gregory of Nyssa's Treatise,* p. 68.

6. Jean Daniélou, "La chronologie des sermons de Grégoire de Nysse," *Recherches de science religieuse* 29 (1955): 368-71, suggests all Gregory's writings on the Psalms are dated to 387-88.

7. Jean Leclercq, *The Love of Learning and the Desire for God* (New York: Fordham University Press, 1982).

Gregory was theologically much closer to the spiritual intent of the psalm than contemporary literal exegesis often provides. First, his theme of "the eighth day" reflects upon "new creation," the eternal breaking into time by the resurrection. A favorite text is Philippians 3:12-14, which he interpreted as conjoining "the eighth day" with *epektasis* (the perpetual upward striving of the soul): "Not that I have already obtained this [i.e., resurrection life] or have already reached the goal; but I press on to make it my own because Christ Jesus has made me his own. Beloved, I do not consider that I have made it my own; but this one thing I do, forgetting what lies behind, and straining forward to what lies ahead, I press on toward the goal for the prize of the heavenly call of God in Christ Jesus."

Second, his emphasis upon the pursuit of moral excellence transforms classical *aretē* as a basic passion of the Greeks, of being "heroic," to becoming godly. Gregory references Isaiah 2:3, "Come now, let us ascend the mountain of the Lord," for which he uses Moses' ascent of Mount Sinai as his exemplar for the pursuit of spiritual progress. His *Life of Moses* and *The Beatitudes* (examples of his mature works) both elaborate on this basic Christian quest of moral excellence. But even in his youth when he comments on Psalm 6, he is already engaged in this pursuit. What matters for Gregory is that we read this psalm, as indeed all Scripture, anagogically, that is, with an eternal destiny, a view to heaven, in mind. But his anagogical reading of Psalm 6 is based on the mistaken notion that the Hebrew word *sheminith* is part of the superscription to Psalms 6 and 12. He rightly thinks the Hebrew word was probably a musical direction, but its meaning, "according to the eighth octave," is fanciful. He compounds the error of this etymological fallacy by suggesting the feminine ending *(-th)* of *sheminith* modifies the elided Hebrew word for "day," mistakenly thinking this *masculine* noun is a feminine word!

"The eighth day" for the early church was the resurrection, and behind that, it pointed to the Levitical day of circumcision and purification. After the seven days of creation, there is now the "new day" of redemption, pointing to the eternal state, in contrast with the cyclical view of the material world, where each seven-day period follows week after week. From Irenaeus, Origen, Eusebius, Athanasius, Didymus, to his older brother Basil and close friend Gregory Nazianzen, there was this consensus about "the octave" of the temporal, making way for the eternal.[8] Gregory connects the "eighth day" with "this is the day the Lord has made" of Psalm 118:24. Anagogically, the eschaton has broken into temporal time, to give humanity a new goal and purpose in life. Gregory associates "the octave" also with what the prophet Malachi calls "the day of the Lord" (Mal. 4:5[3:23]).

---

8. Casimir McCambley, OCSO, "On the Sixth Psalm: Concerning the Octave by Gregory of Nyssa," *Greek Orthodox Theological Review* 32, no. 1 (1987): 39-50.

The celebration of circumcision and of cleansing on the eighth day again reflects upon "the day" of radical transformation of the human status and destiny. His older brother Basil summarizes the issue: ". . . it is the day that the Psalmist calls the eighth because it is outside this time of weeks. Thus whether you call it 'day,' or whether you call it 'eternity,' you express the same idea."[9]

This patristic emphasis on allegorical language is rightly censured by literary critics as fanciful imagination. But in reading the Scripture "spiritually," the patristic exegetes were rightly attempting to interpret the Psalms, as all the other Scriptures, theologically; they were mindful of the whole biblical content of revelation. So while the literal interpretation of the Hebrew *sheminith* is indeed textually and philologically a misinterpretation, Gregory was theologically much closer to the spiritual intent of the psalm than much contemporary literal exegesis often provides. Although Gregory's work is not to be commended for his intellectual apprehension of the biblical text, his hermeneutical intent of pursuing moral conformity with God is praiseworthy. What matters for Gregory is that we use this psalm, as all Scripture, for our moral growth, quoting 2 Timothy 3:16, ". . . for our instruction and . . . training in righteousness" (an important text for his understanding of the holy purpose of Scripture). As authors of *The Psalms as Christian Worship* and *The Psalms as Christian Lament,* we aim to recover the spiritual ends of the patristic commentators through the plain sense of Scripture.

III. The Pursuit of Excellence

As the other bookend to embrace the Psalm, Gregory emphasized the need of *epektasis,* meaning for him the soul's continual stretching toward God. For Gregory, the way to reach "the eighth day" was by living earnestly a godly life. It is not just scholarly skill that is required to be transformed by God's word, but faith, humility, confession, repentance, perseverance, to know and love God, in the endless pursuit of the virtuous life. Thus Gregory gave special attention to *epektasis.*[10] This was not just an intellectual quest of virtue as it was for the Greek philosophers, but now for the Church Fathers, it was the pursuit of never-ending love, permeating all of the Christian life. This is how Gregory interprets the Greek ideal of *aretē,* as one of the basic passions of the ancient Greeks. *Aretē* is translatable as excellence, whether in cultivating a healthy body in the gymnasium for competing in the Olympic games, or disciplining an educated mind to pursue ethics

---

9. Basil the Great, *The Hexaemeron,* PG 29.52A.

10. Martin Laird, *Gregory of Nyssa and the Grasp of Faith: Union, Knowledge and Divine Presence* (Oxford: Oxford University Press, 2004), pp. 38-39, 179, 180.

in the academy, or mentoring for civil leadership in the life of the city-state. All these contributed toward the rewards of a happy life, of *eudaimonia,* i.e., "being-at-work-in-accordance-with-virtue." How then can I make my life a success, asks Aristotle, in the pursuit of happiness? Gregory's response is that the Christian should continually make spiritual progress in godliness, in seeking God himself. But for the Greeks, as for secular humanists today, there is no theological notion of "sin," whereas for the Christian this must be the starting point of the "ascent to God" just as Moses in ascending the mount began with the expiation of sacrifices.

IV. Gregory's Interpretation of Psalm 6

Within these two bookends of "the eighth day" — as the eternal in time — and of the ascending quest of *epektasis,* Gregory now interprets the psalm. With surprising unanimity, he is at one with the other early Fathers in interpreting this as a penitential psalm of David reflecting the events recorded in 2 Samuel 11:1–12:25. However, the logic of his interpretation is personal.

A. *The Awareness of the Need of Confession*

To become aware of the eternal is for Gregory the awareness of God's judgment upon sin. The primary need of confession and repentance is then the central message of Psalm 6. Later Church Fathers considered Psalm 6 to be the first of the "seven penitential psalms." The first verse (second in the Hebrew text), "O Lord, do not rebuke me in your anger, or discipline me in your wrath," teaches that forgiveness must occur first of all, before we can ever begin to enter "the eighth day." God's "anger" (v. 1[2]) is not an irrational emotion, but the appropriate judgment against sin. Some of the most primitive Christian inscriptions on burial tombs (c. 120) depict the crowing cock, associated with Peter's denial of Jesus. It reflected the time of Peter's great sin, but it also heralded the dawn of "the eighth day" of the resurrection. Gregory does not make this connection of earlier Christians, but he is emphatic that the psalmist is saying: "I do not wait for the correction of my hidden faults to take place in me through the dreadful scourges that proceed from that divine anger; but I choose to experience beforehand, by my confession."[11] This then is the first step of the ascent: to see oneself as a sinner, in need of forgiveness and divine mercy.

11. For an English translation of Gregory's commentary on Psalm 6 see Brian E. Daley, S.J., "Training for 'The Good Ascent': Gregory of Nyssa's Homily on the Sixth Psalm," in *In Dominicio*

B. The Awareness of Our Sickly Mortality

For Gregory, the next step of the ascent is to see how morally sick one is, "languishing" in great weakness (v. 2[3]). The literal text might imply physical disability, but Gregory asserts this is also the moral condition of being a sinner before God. Like other early commentators, Gregory interprets "my bones are troubled" (v. 2b[3b]) as referring to his natural moral strength as moral virtues. But they too are "troubled," as is his soul (v. 3[4]). Gregory challenges God, "So why, Lord, are you taking so long to cure me?" implying that if confession and penitence will give healing to his sick soul, how prolonged must this process be? He is arguing with God: "Do you not see how quickly human life fades away; so might I not die physically before the moral treatment is completed?" Or again, it might be wise to anticipate the crisis of your life by correcting the moral condition of your soul (v. 4[5]), lest death come first, and all thought of healing come to nothing. For only the living penitent can experience the gracious healing of their soul by God. In death this is no longer possible (v. 5a[6a]). "Such confession has the power on earth but it no longer exists in Hades" (v. 5b[6b]).

C. The Necessary Expressions of Repentance

In some Chinese house churches today, it has become a practice for new converts to weep continuously for a whole week long as a mark of their conversion. In Gregory's Christian culture it was customary for converts to be excluded from the main body of the church, as a distinct class of penitents. Publicly assigned to particular parts of the building, they prostrated themselves, or knelt, or stood openly weeping in repentance. The terms "confession" and "penance" were interchangeable, as being the same reality of contrition. Literally, the bed of the penitent is soaked with tears, and every night he becomes weary of his moaning. "My eye is troubled with anger" (v. 7[8]) implies one's mind and soul — synonymous with "the eye" — are wasting away in the presence of the anger of God. In remarks on Psalm 101, Gregory notes that the terms "confession" and "praise," while linguistically distinct, were morally in conjunction. By confession we depart and separate from evil things, and by praise we embrace the grace of God to receive all his benefits. The same double sense of "confessing" may be in Gregory's mind as he discusses Psalm 6, between voluntary penance and a grateful sense of God's healing forgiveness.

Eloquio, In Lordly Eloquence, Essays on Patristic Exegesis in Honour of Robert Louis Wilken, ed. Paul M. Blowers et al. (Grand Rapids: Eerdmans, 2002), pp. 190-92.

D. The Exposure of Our Own Inward Dark Passions

The fourth element recognized by Gregory in Psalm 6 in addition to the fear of God's judgment, the awareness of our sinfulness, and the act of confession, is the disclosure of our own secret thoughts *(logismoi)*. This is similar to the teaching of Evagrius Ponticus (345-399), an earlier Father who dealt most discerningly with the heart's hidden thoughts. Likewise, for later fathers like Gregory, the "enemies" or "foes" or "workers of iniquity" of the psalmist are not external threats. They are one's own negative emotions buried within oneself. So "the workers of iniquity" in verse 8[9] and "all my enemies" in verse 10[11] Gregory interprets as being one's own emotional/spiritual inwardly destructive habits. As Diogenes is reputed to have told his pupil Alexander the Great, "You are your own worst enemy." Alexander, in fact, did not die on the battlefield but on his bed, due to excessive drinking and sexual orgies. Significantly, on his bed at night, the psalmist's inner thoughts are "put to shame" by their exposure and confession. But the psalmist affirms that in the intimacy of God's knowledge of us, he has "heard the voice of the one who turns to him in tears" (v. 8b[9b]). "When that has happened," comments Gregory, "in order that the Good might remain uninterruptedly with us for the rest of time, the Prophet [i.e., David] asks that the thoughts hostile to it might be vanquished through shame." "For it is not possible for a hostile, lawless thought to be vanquished in any other way, if shame over it does not cause it to vanish," observes Gregory. This is his comment on the last verse of the Psalm, "all my enemies shall be ashamed and utterly turned back" (v. 10[11]). Gregory adds: "Now our enemies clearly are 'those of our own household,' which 'come forth from the heart and defile a person.' Yet when they are turned away quickly by shame (v. 10b), the hope of a glory that will never end in shame will take its place in us, by the grace of the Lord, to whom be glory for the ages. Amen."[12]

V. Conclusion

In this brief commentary on a psalm of only ten (Hebrew eleven) verses, Gregory has given us a summary of his pastoral theology. In turn, it provides also the basic character of the whole book of psalms, as seen through the lens of a highly educated Greek mind. Yet it converts all the terminology valued by the classical world into Christian ideals. It illustrates what the writer to the Hebrews states, "the word of God is living and active, sharper than any two-edged

---

12. Translation by Brian E. Daley, S.J., "Training for 'The Good Ascent,' " p. 217.

sword, piercing until it divides soul from spirit, joints from marrow; it is able to judge the thoughts and the intentions of the heart" (Heb. 4:12). As Paul asserts in 2 Corinthians 10:5: "We destroy arguments and every proud obstacle raised up against the knowledge of God, and we take every thought captive to obey Christ" — for the intimacy of God penetrates our inmost thoughts. We may call Gregory of Nyssa "the C. S. Lewis of his day." Both of them highly educated in classical education, both have also been misunderstood as "neo-Platonists" due in part to the use they made of Plato and later admirers such as Plotinus. With his friend Charles Williams, Lewis seemed more aware of the realism of the spiritual life than of the earthly, and with his friend Tolkien, of myth enlarging the imagination more than factual realism.

In Raphael's fresco of the academy of Plato, he shows Plato and Aristotle walking hand-in-hand, with Plato pointing his finger upwards in pursuit of "the Eternal ideas" as "the Good," while Aristotle is pointing forward to the concrete and the realizable of human thought and action. Any true Christian should be in pursuit of what is holistic, "that your whole spirit, soul and body be kept blameless at the coming of our Lord Jesus Christ" (1 Thess. 5:23). This, then, is what Gregory and Lewis have in common, seeing all of human life holistically, under the eternal light of God's sovereignty. As Lewis once told me (Houston),[13] the central message of all his writings was to protest against all forms of reductionism. That was why he used so many different genres to describe the Christian life. Gregory in his time would have made the same protest, in embracing the Christian life as the incessant pursuit of becoming "embodied" Christians, in the conjunction of flesh and spirit, of being earthly and yet having a heavenly ascent. This is the message of the Incarnation, of God becoming manifest in human flesh.[14] The hermeneutics to describe this embodiment must inevitably be figural, as transcending a literal meaning.

---

13. It was in 1955, when he was leaving Oxford to teach in Cambridge. I had known him for seven years and I asked him what was the central message of all his works. "Against reductionism of the Christian faith" was his response, citing the importance of his educational lectures on "The Abolition of Man."

14. See the excellent study of Hans Boersma, *Embodiment and Virtue in Gregory of Nyssa: An Anagogical Approach* (Oxford: Oxford University Press, 2013).

PART II. VOICE OF THE PSALMIST: TRANSLATION
A ROYAL PETITION FOR VINDICATION BY SALVATION FROM DEATH

A psalm by[15] David

1   "I AM," stop rebuking me in your anger;
       and stop disciplining me in your wrath.
2   Be gracious to me, "I AM," for I am fainting away;
       heal me, "I AM,"[16] for my bones tremble in fright;
3   and my soul is exceedingly dismayed.
       And as for you, "I AM," how long?
4   Turn, "I AM"; deliver me;
       Rescue me for the sake of your unfailing love.
5   For none proclaim your name in the land of the dead.
       Who gives praise to you in the Grave?
6   I am worn out[17] from[18] my sobbing;
       All night long[19] I cause my bed to float.
       I dissolve my couch with my tears.
7   My eyes[20] waste away from vexation;
       They fail because of[21] all my foes.
8   Get away from me, all you who do evil,
       for "I AM" has heard my weeping.
9   "I AM" has heard my cry for mercy;
       "I AM" accepts my prayer.
10   All my enemies will be ashamed and exceedingly dismayed;
       they will turn and suddenly be put to shame.

---

15. For the meaning of *ldwd,* credibility of superscripts, and extensive royal interpretation see Bruce K. Waltke and James M. Houston with Erika Moore, *The Psalms as Christian Worship (PACW)* (Grand Rapids: Eerdmans, 2010), pp. 89-91.

16. A few medieval mss. omit its first occurrence in 2Aa[3Aa] and a few + LXX[B] (Vaticanus) omit the second. Both the external and internal evidence favor retaining MT. Perhaps some scribes deleted one or the other in an attempt to reduce the eight occurrences of "I AM" *(YHWH)* to the sacred number of seven. Also, the double occurrence in verse 2[3] matches its double occurrence in the penultimate verse 9[10]. Finally, the psalm's symmetry favors its retention (see "Literary Context").

17. See *IBHS,* P. 30.3.3a, p. 491 for the perfective form of stative verbs.

18. Causal *b*ᵉ marks the originating force of his exhaustion (*IBHS,* P. 11.2.5e, p. 198).

19. If the phrase is intentionally indefinite, it means "each"/"every" night (GKC, P. 127b, c). However, Hebrew poetry often omits the article, allowing the gloss "all night long."

20. Construed as a collective singular.

21. Construed as causal *b*ᵉ (see n. 18).

PART III. COMMENTARY

I. Introduction

A. *Literary Context*

See Psalm 5 for fuller literary context. Psalm 6, like Psalms 3–5, is another royal petition that "I AM" rescue his king, giving courage to the faithful.[22] As in Psalms 3–5, the king to whom "I AM" had promised the ends of the earth (Ps. 2:7-9) pours out his lament; this time for a sickness so severe and so long-continued that he totters on the brink of the grave. He intuits that his sickness is the providential "golden rod that enriches us by its blows."[23] His enemies interpret it as God's curse that validates their rejection of him as "I AM's" chosen king. Psalm 38 echoes and clarifies this psalm. God's anointed, though in extreme physical and mental anguish, overcomes his malicious enemies through God-given defiant faith.

An alternating pattern of morning psalms (3 and 5) and night psalms (4 and 6) binds these royal petitions together. The night psalms escalate from a prayer before lying down to sleep (4:8[9]) to his doleful appeals all night long (6:7[8]). Moreover, in them, the king's enemies escalate from highborn poltroons who are losing confidence in him but have not yet rejected him, to evildoers who celebrate his imminent death. Psalms 3–5 assume or assert David's innocence; Psalm 6 implies his guilt.

B. *Rhetoric and Structure*

The number three universally symbolizes completeness.[24] The numerical value of the name *YHWH* is twenty-six (y = 10; h = 5 [2×]; w = 6); when multiplied by three its value is seventy-eight. Remarkably, there are seventy-eight words in the psalm. Moreover, on form-critical and rhetorical grounds I (Waltke) had divided

22. This petition psalm has the typical motifs of lament/petition psalms: direct address (v. 1[2]), introductory petition to be gracious (v. 2[3]), petition to be saved (vv. 4-5[5-6]), lament (vv. 6-7[7-8]), confidence and praise (vv. 8-10[9-11]). "The theme of Answer to Prayer belongs to this genre (10:17[16]; 22:24[25]; 28:6; 31:22[23]; 34:6[7]; 66:19[20])." Samuel Terrien, *The Psalms: Strophic Structure and Theological Commentary* (Cambridge and Grand Rapids: Eerdmans, 2003), p. 114, n. 7l.

23. Charles Haddon Spurgeon, *The Treasury of David: Spurgeon's Great Commentary on Psalms*. An updated edition in today's language, updated by Roy H. Clarke (Nashville: Thomas Nelson, 1997), p. 31.

24. See http://www.greatdreams.com/three/three.htm.

the psalm into two equal stanzas of five verses each: verses 1-5[2-6] and 6-10[7-11]; each of these consists of two strophes (1-3[2-4], 4-5[5-6]; 6-7[7-8], 8-10[9-11]). After observing the coincidence of three times twenty-six and of the number of words, I counted the number of words in each of the two stanzas and to my astonishment found thirty-nine words, half of seventy-eight, in each stanza. That led me to consider the length of the previously identified strophes and, remarkably, they are structured in the concentric pattern of three verses (twenty-four words) and two verses (fifteen words) and two verses (fifteen words) and three verses (twenty-four words). Hebrew poetry is given to symmetry and to gematria in the sense that numbers, such as three, have symbolic and spiritual values. If this structure is intentional, we can infer that even *in extremis* — bones trembling in fright and his consciousness slipping away — the psalmist's triumphant faith enables him to regain his rationality.

Three of the four strophes begin with an imperative (vv. 1, 4, 8[2, 5, 9]) and both strophes of the first stanza end in a question. The psalmist's frame of being "exceedingly dismayed," first of himself (vv. 2b, 3[3b, 4]) and then of his enemies (v. 10[11]), dramatically profiles how his petitions reverse his situation. The exegesis follows this outline:

Superscript
I. Petitions and lament   1-5[2-6]
    A. Introductory petitions and lament   1-3[2-4]
        1. Petitions
            a. To cease discipline   1[2]
            b. For grace and healing   2A-Ba[3A-Ba]
        2. Reason for petition: lament   2Bb-3[3Bb-4]
    B. Petitions for salvation   4-5[5-6]
        1. Petitions for salvation   4[5]
        2. Reason for petition: praise   5[6]
II. Lament and confession of trust   6-10[7-11]
    A. Lament   6-7[7-8]
        1. Extreme sorrow   6[7]
        2. Vexation caused by enemy   7[8]
    B. Confidence   8-10[9-11]
        1. Address to enemies: depart; "I AM" hears lament   8-9[9-10]
            a. "I AM" hears weeping   8[9]
            b. "I AM" accepts prayer   9[10]
        2. Enemies will be dismayed   10[11]

C. Message

Since Pope Innocent III (1160-1216), the church has officially numbered Psalm 6 as the first of Seven Penitential Psalms (Psalms 6, 32, 38, 51, 102, 130, and 143) to be sung or recited during Lent.[25] The nomenclature of Penitential Psalm is fully appropriate for Psalms 32, 38, and 51 but only somewhat appropriate for the others, because the others express no remorse, regret, or compunction for sin. In Psalm 6 David implicitly admits his guilt, asking God to stop disciplining him *in his anger* and that his discipline not exceed the measure of loving correction. Should God's royal slave die, virtue will be crucified.

The psalm teaches that God is moved to stop disciplining his erring saint by a fervent, not stoical, and a well-argued, not a hasty-brain, petition. God can be moved to act by spiritual fervency and by rational arguments. Specifically, David argues: (1) God has disciplined him so long and so severely, the blows of his chastening rod are transmogrifying into a fatal sword thrust; he swoons in grief (vv. 1, 3[2, 4]); (2) God displays his glory by his grace and unfailing love to his covenant partner (v. 2[3]; cf. Exod. 34:6); (3) God will promote his glory and praise by rescuing his chosen king from the grave (vv. 4-5[5-6]); (4) His bed-drenching tears display his extreme suffering and fervency (v. 6[7]); (5) his malicious and malignant enemies taunt him that he is under God's curse and so justify their reason to reject God's chosen king (vv. 8-9[9-10]); (5) God's heaping shame on the fleeing foe will fortify the faith of the faithful (v. 10[11]). In other words, it is unthinkable that "I AM" would not show David compassion; would not extend his sublime glories to his chosen king; would not save him, obscuring his glory; would be impervious to his tears; would vindicate evildoers in their rejection of God's chosen king; and would cast a millstone around the necks of his trusting people.

As death takes God's anointed king into its decisive grip, the king's faith grasps the eternal verity: God hears and accepts his prayer. Confident that God hears his prayer, he routs by faith the horde of assailants taunting him: "Get away from me," the king shouts, while assuring the faithful that the routed evildoers will be put to shame.

The psalm's general and universal language makes it easier to apply the psalm to the contemporary reader's "own situation."[26]

---

25. *New Catholic Encyclopedia*, vol. 11, pp. 85-86.

26. Mark D. Futato and David M. Howard, *Interpreting the Psalms: An Exegetical Handbook* (Grand Rapids: Kregel, 2007), p. 123.

II. Exegesis

A. Superscript

For the exegesis of the postscript to Psalm 5 "for the director of music; with string instruments; according to sheminith," see Psalm 5: subscript. For the exegesis of the superscript to Psalm 6, *a psalm by David* (מִזְמוֹר לְדָוִד), see Psalm 5: Superscript.

B. Petitions and Lament (6:1-5[2-6])

Unlike Psalms 3–5, wherein the psalmist petitions "I AM" for salvation after a confession of trust, in Psalm 6 he places his seven petitions for salvation up front (vv. 1-5[2-6]).

1. Introductory Petitions and Lament (6:1-3[2-4])

Two parallel negative petitions not to discipline the psalmist any longer in anger are matched by two positive petitions to be gracious to him and restore his life (vv. 1-2[2-3]). He needs restoration because he is losing his physical and psychic vigor, making him appear unfit to be king (v. 3[4]).

a. Petitions to Cease Discipline in Anger (6:1[2])

Like Psalms 3–5, David's prayer is blunt and terse, not grandiloquent (Ps. 6:1[2]). His first word, as he slips into death, is God's name, "I AM" (יְהוָֹה, Ps. 6:1[2]). *Stop* (-אַל) could be glossed "do not," but since the rest of the psalm shows he is under discipline, the negative particle for urgent petition is better glossed "stop." In an unusual grammar to mark strong emphasis, *in your anger* (בְּאַפְּךָ) interrupts the negative proclitic ("do not") from its verb.[27] *'Ap* ("anger," literally, "nose") points to the physically visible state of excitement of an individual breathing heavily as a consequence of anger, an obvious anthropomorphism. God's anger flares up against those who assail his righteous character and exalted lordship, and his wrath issues from his zeal to affirm before the whole creation his lordship and holiness (Exod. 32:10-14; Num. 25:3f.; Deut. 6:15; 7:4; passim). None can stand before his fierce anger, and unless he relents, none survive (Exod. 32:11-14; Ps.

---

27. Bruce K. Waltke with M. P. O'Connor, *Introduction to Biblical Hebrew Syntax* (Winona Lake, IN: Eisenbrauns, 1989), P. 34.2.1.e, p. 567.

90:7-11). Fortunately, God is slow to anger (Exod. 34:6; Pss. 103:8; 145:8), tempers his anger with his benevolent attributes of grace and mercy, and gives vent to it only for a moment (Pss. 27:8f.; 30:5[6]; 85:3[4]f.). The lexeme rendered *rebuke me* (תוֹכִיחֵנִי) belongs in the sphere of legal proceedings (Isa. 29:21; Amos 5:10) and the form used here means "to establish what is right." Its subject is usually an authority initiating and enacting to bring about what is right. If the authority does not act to bring about what is right, it is party with the wrongdoer. A rebuke can be penal or remedial. Its pedagogical intention here can be seen in its parallel "discipline me" and in its use in the Davidic covenant, which lies behind the psalm (2 Sam. 7:14). A rebuke may be verbal ("instruction"), or, as here, some sort of affliction. "I AM's" remedial rebuke is a severe mercy (Prov. 3:12; Job 5:17).[28] In David's case, however, the discipline must stop now; the king is passing through the gates of death into the land of the dead.

Since the synonymous parallel, *and stop disciplining me in your wrath* (וְאַל-בַּחֲמָתְךָ) adds nothing significantly new, it functions to escalate the urgency of the king's plea. The phrase, "in your wrath," shares the same emphatic syntax as its parallel, "in your anger" (v. 1a[2a]). "Wrath" (*ḥēmâ*) is derived from the root *ḥmh* "to be hot," "be ardent," from which developed the specific meaning "excitement," "anger," "wrath" against someone from a sense of having been wronged. Schunck says: "*ḥēmâ* probably lent expression to the hot inward excitement accompanying anger."[29] Etymologically, *'aph* refers to an individual's outward physiognomy, "a snorting nose," and *ḥēmâ* to the inner emotional state he feels, the inner glow of anger. With fallen humankind wrath may be cruel and merciless but not with God, who by nature is full of grace and in full control of his emotions. Although the lexeme יָסַר (*yāsar*) may have simply an essential meaning "to communicate knowledge in order to shape specific conduct," it also often connotes "to chasten" either by words or, as here, the metaphorical rod (Prov. 9:7).[30] N. Shupak says: "The Hebrew noun *mûsar* and the verb *yāsar*, [like their Egyptian equivalents], have the double meaning of 'instruct-reprove' and 'chastise-beat.'"[31] M. Saebo finds its synonyms are instructive with regard to chastisement: *lmd pi*, "to teach," *hi*, "to rebuke,"

---

28. C. S. Lewis, *The Problem of Pain* (London: Geoffrey Bles, 1940), pp. 30-33. Lewis illustrates the truth by noting that an artist may not take much trouble over a picture drawn to amuse a child, but he takes endless effort in a great work of art that he loves. Lewis argues that were the magnum opus sentient, as "the artist rubbed and scraped off and recommenced for the tenth time," it would cry out in pain. Lewis drew the conclusion that when we complain of our sufferings we are not asking for more love, but for less.

29. K. D. Schunck, *TDOT*, 4.463, s.v. *ḥēmâ*.

30. B. Waltke, *The Book of Proverbs: Chapters 1–15* (Grand Rapids: Eerdmans, 2004), pp. 175-76.

31. N. Shupak, "Egyptian Terms and Features in Biblical Hebrew," *Tarbiz* 54 (1984-85): 107.

ykḥ and *sûb*, "to turn around."[32] W. E. Lane observes that the lexeme *yāsar* always presupposes an educational purpose and is never used to refer to the correction of animals or to the divine discipline of foreign nations.[33] David marginalizes the immediate causes, his sickness and his enemies, because when God the Ultimate Cause turns away from his wrath, the immediate cause will disappear.[34]

b. Petitions for Grace and Healing (6:2A-Ba[3A-Ba])

2A[3A]: for grace   The psalmist throws himself through the black visage of God's anger and directly unto his gracious heart. He wants God to release him from his left hand of justice and raise him up with his right hand of mercy. *Be gracious to me* (חָנֵּנִי) entails four notions about God at one and the same time: (1) his covenant relationship to his king; (2) his condescension to take note of his need (Ruth 2:10; 1 Sam. 20:3), (3) his feeling of goodwill (Gen. 19:19; 32:5–33:10) and (4) his capacity to meet the need of the favored beneficiary.[35] Grace "is entirely free and wholly undeserved."[36] *I am fading away* (אֻמְלָל) is used of wasted ramparts and walls (Lam. 2:8); inhabitants in a parched land (Hos. 4:3); mothers who become infertile (1 Sam. 2:5; Jer. 15:9); fishermen whose trade fails (Isa. 19:8); and the exalted of the earth along with their lands that fade and wither (Isa. 24:4). "Weakness is indeed the first and best argument for God's mercy."[37]

2Ba[3Ba]: for healing   Heal me, רְפָאֵנִי — that is, "to restore a former state of well-being" — specifies the favor to be bestowed. The derivatives of *rp'* mostly re-

---

32. M. Saebo, *TLOT*, 2.549, s.v. *ysr* "to chastise."

33. W. E. Lane, "Discipline," in *ISBE* 1 (1979): 948-50.

34. Elizabeth Achtemeier rightly takes Norman Snaith to task for arguing that it is improper to speak of God as "angry." In his view the sinner should first feel that God is angry with him, but when he grows up spiritually and knows "more about the tender mercies of God," he will give up such language. Achtemeier responds: "Such a view is nonsense in light of the biblical revelation, not only of the Old Testament, but also of the New; and it is such views which have led to the popular belief that the God and Father of Jesus Christ is a sentimental little godlet of love who winks at our wrong-doing and loves us no matter what we may do. Throughout the Bible God destroys Israel and mankind as a whole for its lack of reliance on his lordship and for its rebellion against his sovereign commands. Such is surely part of the meaning of the cross of Christ — that we die for our sin against God! Else why was it necessary that Jesus undergo that torturous crucifixion? But the mercy of the story is that Jesus dies in our place, taking our deserved death upon himself, and it is to the same God who later sent Jesus Christ that the author of Psalm 6 appeals." Elizabeth Achtemeier, "Overcoming the World: An Exposition of Psalm 6," *Interpretation* 28 (1974): 80. Citation of Norman Snaith, *The Seven Psalms* (London: Epworth, 1964), pp. 15f.

35. L. Reed, *JBL* 73 (1954): 58f.

36. N. Snaith, *TWBOB*, p. 101.

37. Theopylact. IV. 1, 363.

fer to physical healing of the injured (2 Kgs. 8:29) and from all sorts of sicknesses (Gen. 20:17; Lev. 13:18, 37; 14:3; Deut. 28:27). Without healing one dies (Eccles. 3:3; Jer. 14:19). Throughout the ancient Near East sickness was traced back to the influence of the divine and/or demonic power, but in Israel "I AM" is the ultimate source of sickness and healing (Exod. 15:26; Deut. 32:39; 1 Sam. 2:6; 2 Kgs. 20:5, 8; Pss. 103:3; 147:3).[38] Sufferers often petition "I AM" for healing, knowing that their sin caused their affliction from him (Num. 12:13; 2 Chron. 21:18).[39] Thus *rp'* is filled with a deeper content, for healing is associated with requisite forgiveness at the time of restoration to material well-being (Jer. 3:22; 2 Chron. 7:14; cf. 2 Chron. 36:16). Where forgiveness is no longer possible, there is no longer the prospect of healing (2 Chron. 36:16). "I AM" heals people on the condition of their obedience (Exod. 15:26), repentance (Isa. 6:10; Jer. 3:22; Hos. 6:1), and/or prayer (Isa. 19:22; Ps. 30:3[4]; 2 Chron. 7:15). These virtues of piety and ethics are assumed in Psalm 6:2[3] (Prov. 3:7-8). Outward healing, therefore, is the external verifiable indicator of spiritual healing.

c. Reason for Petitions: Lament (6:2Bb-3[3Bb-4])

2Bb[3Bb]: Skeletal frame trembles   He backs up his plea to be healed by three laments: his bones tremble in fear (v. 2B[3B]), his psyche is dismayed (v. 3A[4A]), and "I AM" is unrelenting (v. 3B[4B]). My *bones* (עֲצָמָי) refer to the inner and firmest part of the body (i.e., skeleton, bodily frame; Ps. 109:18)[40] or to the psyche. Its basic notion is physical, but, as Dalglish notes, it moves largely in the psychical or metaphoric category.[41] Both senses occur here, as signified by the gloss *tremble in fright* (נִבְהָלוּ). As for "fright," the term never denotes merely a physical malady, but always denotes a psychological state of extreme fright at imminent threat (Gen. 45:3; Judg. 20:41; 1 Sam. 28:21). *Bāhal (niphal)* means his whole skeleton is racked and shaken (Ezek. 7:27). At the brink of the Abyss, he trembles from the

---

38. The Book of Job and the psalms of innocence (i.e., Psalms 22, 26) teach that all afflictions, including sickness, are not due to sin. The Israelites were well aware that wounds, injuries, and fractures had natural causes and were subject to medical treatment (Isa. 38:21), but never divorced from "I AM's" activity (e.g., Exodus 21; Numbers 35). The Code of Hammurabi (Paragraphs 215-25) also reckoned with injuries from natural causes; see *Ancient Near Eastern Texts Relating to the Old Testament*, ed. James B. Pritchard (Princeton: Princeton University Press, 1955), p. 175. There is also a very modest start toward something like hygiene in Leviticus 13–15 (E. Neufeld, *Biblical Archaeologist* 34 [1971]: 42-46).

39. J. J. Stamm, *Erlösen und vergeben im Alten Testament* (Bern: A. Francke, 1940), pp. 48-84.

40. So Gesenius-Buhl with Aquila, Syriac, Jerome iuxta hebraeos.

41. E. Dalglish, *Psalm Fifty-One in the Light of Ancient Near Eastern Patternism* (Leiden: E. J. Brill, 1962), p. 142.

prospect of a divinely inflicted, premature death, not from a normal malady that creeps silently through the windows in old age (Eccles. 12:1-8).

3[4]: Soul dismayed   *And my soul is dismayed* (וְנַפְשִׁי נִבְהֲלָה) implies the reason for his urgent appeals. *Nepheš* is glossed "soul" reluctantly, because the English idiom demands it here. Unlike "bones," *nepheš* does not refer to a part of his body but to his whole psychic being. Its traditional gloss "soul" may mislead an English-speaking audience into thinking of "soul" in the New Testament sense of Greek *psychē*, "the seat and center of life that transcends the earthly."[42] Hebrew *nepheš*, however, refers to the passionate drives and appetites of *all* breathing creatures, both animal and human. In the New Testament a person has a "soul"; in the Old Testament a breathing mammal is a *nepheš*.[43] With his very being as subject, *bāhal (niphal)* has its usual sense of "dismay" due to the fright of imminent death (v. 2[3]). To underscore the extremely high degree of his dismay, he adds *exceedingly* (מְאֹד).

He begins and ends the first strophe with the divine Name. *And as for you, "I AM,"* focuses on God as the ultimate cause of his affliction (v. 1[2]). The gripping aposiopesis expresses his extreme agitation. The elided predicate of *how long* (עַד-מָתָי, lit., "until how long") can be supplied from the imperative that opens the second strophe: "How long until you turn around and save me?" (Ps. 13:2-3[3-4]). The phrase is rich in meaning: (1) it posits a historical past between "I AM," the psalmist, and his unstated affliction. (2) It expresses his submission as he humbles himself under God's mighty hand (Ps. 130:5-6; Luke 22:42; James 4:10). (3) It expresses hope: God does not keep his anger forever. "I AM" punishes to the third and fourth generations, but his unfailing love extends to a thousand generations. Plumer contrasts David's response to that of Quintilian on the death of wife and children, especially the recent death of a promising son. Quintilian complained: "Who would not detest my insensibility, if I made any other use of my voice, than to vent complaint against the injustice of the gods, who made me survive all that was dearest to me? . . . There reigns a secret envy, jealous of our happiness, which pleases itself in nipping the bud of our hope."[44] "All God's delays are maturing." If God delays to be gracious, it is not that he is without love, but that he wants to incite us to more fervent prayer, to make us more vigilant against sin, to try our faith, and to make us realize how much more grievous is the lot of the impenitent.

42. W. Bauer, *A Greek-English Lexicon of the New Testament and Other Early Christian Literature*, trans. William F. Arndt and F. Wilbur Gingrich; 2nd ed. rev. F. Wilbur Gingrich and Frederick W. Danker (Chicago: University of Chicago, 1979), p. 893.

43. B. Waltke, *TWOT*, 2:587-91, s.v. *nepheš*.

44. William S. Plumer, *Psalms* (Edinburgh: Banner of Truth Trust, first published in 1867; reprinted in 1978), p. 9.

C. Petitions for Salvation (6:4-5[5-6])

In the second strophe (vv. 4-5[5-6]) the petitions for salvation (v. 4[5]) are linked with the motivation (v. 5[6]) by the medial logical particle *kî* ("because").

4[5]: First, God must change his posture toward his king. *Turn* (שׁוּבָה) has the central meaning of "having moved in a particular direction to move thereupon in the opposite direction. . . ." Here, its original physical notion gives way metaphorically to the psychic-spiritual turning from anger to grace, from beating to healing. "I AM" is repeated for the fifth time in four consecutive verses, emphasizing the king's privileged access to him. *Deliver me* (חַלְּצָה) has the original idea of "to escape, withdraw," but it cannot be proved that this etymology distinguishes it from other verbs in the semantic field of deliverance. Its parallels are, among others, *nṣl* "save," originally "pull out," and, as here, *yāšaʿ (hiphil)*, originally "make room for someone." *Ḥālaṣ* is used exclusively with "I AM" as the deliverer. The passive forms are divine passives, although they do not mention any agent.[45] The English idiom here allows the more accurate gloss for *nepheš, my life* (נַפְשִׁי), which adds an intensely personal element to the notion of self. *Rescue me* (הוֹשִׁיעֵנִי) plays a large role in the book of Psalms.[46] Although the etymology of *yāšaʿ* is uncertain,[47] it clearly denotes deliverance in both the military (Judg. 12:2; 1 Sam. 11:3) and juridical spheres (2 Sam. 14:4). The two ideas coalesce, for the word denotes military or physical intervention because it is one's due or right (Deut. 28:29, 31). Sawyer notes that in the Old Testament salvation and deliverance seldom, if ever, express a spiritual state exclusively: their common theological sense is that of a material deliverance attended by spiritual blessings.[48] The psalmist knows

---

45. C. Barth, *TDOT*, 4.438, s.v. *ḥālaṣ*.

46. In Psalm 3 the root appears in three different forms (*yᵉšûʿātâ* v. 2[3]; *hôšîaʿ*, v. 7[8]; *yᵉšûʿâ*, v. 8[9]).

47. The customary etymology, which sees the basic meaning in Arabic *wasiʾa* "to be wide, spacious," is now called into question because it meets with difficulties in the discrepancies in expected consonantal correspondences in South Arabic. Nevertheless, the etymology is enticing because its antonym is *ṣrr* "to be narrow" (Isa. 63:8f.; Jer. 14:8) (cf. F. Stolz, *TLOT*, 2.584). The nominal form *ṣar* is glossed "foe" in verse 7.

48. J. Sawyer, "What Was a *Môšiaʿ*?" *VT* 15 (1965): 479. He summarizes his argument that *môšiaʿ*, the *nomen opificum* of the root *yšʿ*, has a forensic sense: Negatively, (1) there are no cases in the Old Testament where a forensic meaning is impossible, and (2) there is no other word used so consistently in similar contexts; and positively, (1) three quarters of its occurrences suggest . . . the language of the law court, (2) the most probably [sic!] etymology . . . suggests a forensic origin for the root *yšʿ*, (3) there are other examples of forensic words appearing in wider and more general contexts, but still retaining forensic overtones, (4) the *môšiaʿ* was always on the side of justice, (5) his activity seems to have been verbal rather than physical in many contexts, unlike

that he has been under God's wrath justly and makes no protest of innocence, but he has been amply punished (Isa. 40:2), and, should God's anointed die, the severity of the punishment would be unjust. God must act now, for the king is at the point of death. Moreover, toward God he is guilty, but toward his malicious and malignant enemies he is innocent. The responsibility to deliver for the cause of justice fell particularly upon the king (1 Sam. 10:27; 2 Kgs. 6:26) and, above all, upon "I AM." The afflicted party has the responsibility to cry out, as in the case of rape (Deut. 22:23-27). This is why the psalmists frequently emphasize that they have raised their voice, presumably in public (v. 3:4[5]). Parallels show that God's righteousness (Ps. 71:15), strength (Pss. 21:1[2]; 28:8), blessing (Ps. 3:8[9]), and unfailing love (Ps. 119:41) are bound up with his salvation. Accordingly, the human role is to trust God *alone,* as well as to ask (Pss. 33:1; 60:11, 12[13, 14]; 146:3), but trusting God alone does not exclude using human means (Psalm 3). *For the sake of* (לְמַעַן) abbreviates the full thought "your unfailing love/kindness demands it" (Ps. 5:8[9]).

1. Reason for Petition

5[6]: No Public Praise to "I AM"   The medial logical particle *for* (כִּי) asserts the reason God should deliver him: the praise of God's name is at stake. *None* (אֵין) glosses the particle of expressing negativity in verbless clauses, literally, "there is not." The verbal noun with objective genitive זִכְרֶךָ, traditionally "remembrance of you," is glossed for clarity by *proclaim your name. Zākar* denotes the active cognitive occupation with persons or situations by retaining and reviving impressions of them and *proclaiming* them to others.[49] Achtemeier, presumably building on Brevard Childs's study,[50] insightfully notes: "But not to know what Yahweh has done means not to know who he is, for it was in the remembrance of his activity that Israel learned the character of its Lord."[51] "I AM" eradicates the wicked from history by erasing the mention of them (Exod. 17:14; Deut. 25:19; Job 18:17; Pss. 9:6[7]; 34:16[17]; 109:15; Prov. 10:7). God, in the silence of those who have no remembrance of being delivered from death, does not exist. Achtemeier comments: "In our present-day ignorance of the biblical record of what Yahweh has done, we share the dead's lack of remembrance. We do not know our God

---

its synonyms, and (6) there was a place in ancient Israel for an "advocate" or a "witness for the defense," as also for a "witness for the prosecution."

49. H. Eising, *TDOT*, 4.66, s.v. *zākar.*

50. Brevard S. Childs, *Memory and Tradition in Israel* (London: SCM Press, 1962), especially p. 71.

51. Achtemeier, "Overcoming the World," p. 84.

because we do not remember his acts."[52] The tragedy of Joshua's generation that stormed the land was their failure to teach their children the mighty acts of God (Judg. 2:10). It is the tragedy of America after the Supreme Court decision to take the Bible and prayer out of the public schools in 1963. *In the realm of death* (בְּמָוֶת) invests the term that otherwise means "death," with its rarer use, "the place of the dead." G. Gerleman says: "a few expressions relate death to a spatial realm: 'gates of death' . . . 'ways of death' and 'chambers of the realm of the dead' (Ps. 6:6[7]), where *māwet* equals *šeʾôl*. . . ."[53]

The question *who* (מִי) finds its answer in the parallel, "there is no one." The answer is so obvious that the question functions as an exclamation and as a rhetorical question, for it does not aim to gain information but to give information with passion. *Gives credit* (יוֹדֶה) glosses *yādâ (hiphil)*. This term occurs one hundred times, always with the meaning "to respond to another's action or behavior with public praise." Here the public praise, were there one, would be in response *to you* (לָךְ), whose antecedent is "I AM," for delivering a person from death. Implicitly, "I AM" should save the psalmist from death so that the psalmist can publicly confess that "I AM" saved him. *In the grave* (מִשְּׁאוֹל) glosses *šeʾôl* (LXX Hades). This noun occurs sixty-six times in the Old Testament, fifty-eight times in poetry. The frequent prepositions with it show that it is the grave below the earth. The biblical poets use rich and varied figures to depict it. *Sheol* has a "mouth" (Ps. 141:7), which it "enlarges" (Isa. 5:14), and it is "never satisfied" (Prov. 27:20; 30:16). It is so powerful that no one escapes its "grip" (Ps. 89:48[49]; Song 8:6), but some are redeemed from it (Ps. 49:15[16]; Prov. 23:14; Hos. 13:14). It is like a prison with "cords" (2 Sam. 22:6) and a land that has "gates" (Isa. 38:10) with "bars" (Job 17:16). Here corruption is "the father," and the worm "the mother and sister" (Job 17:13ff.). It is "a land" of no return to this life (Job 7:9); an abode where socioeconomic distinctions cease. Rich and poor (Job 3:18-19), righteous and wicked (Eccles. 9:2-3) lie down together. It is a land of silence (Ps. 94:17), darkness (13:3[4]), weakness, and oblivion (Ps. 88:11-18[12-19]). The destructive nature of this realm is intensified by the addition of "Abaddon" (Prov. 15:11; 27:20). One errs in using this figurative language to build a doctrine of the intermediate state. On the other hand, these vivid and powerful figures transform the grave from a six-foot pit to a metaphorical and transcendent realm distinct from life on top of the earth inhabited by living mortals and from heaven inhabited by the immortal God and his court. Those who descend there will never again participate in salvation history or join the holy throne at the earthly temple (Ps. 6:5[6]; Isa. 38:18). Like the Jordan River and Mount Zion, the grave symbolizes eternal realities that transcend their physical space.

---

52. Achtemeier, "Overcoming the World," pp. 84-85.
53. G. Gerleman, *TLOT*, 2.663, s.v. *mût*.

D. Lament and Confidence (6:6-10[7-11])

The first strophe of the second stanza picks up and escalates the psalmist's extreme psychic disturbance (v. 3[4]) to the pouring out of his sorrow in an incredible flow of tears (vv. 6-7[7-8]). His tears reinforce his appeals for God's compassion; they are not tears of self-pity. In its second strophe, abruptly, as though rising from the dead, his psyche changes from fear to faith as he commands his enemies to decamp and depart from him in shame (vv. 8-10[9-11]). This shift occurs in connection with a threefold repetition of "I AM," suggesting that his recalling of Israel's and his covenant-keeping God shifts his psyche from distress to confidence. The first strophe of the second stanza backs up his appeals for compassion by pointing to the flow of tears that accompany them (vv. 6-7[7-8]). The reference to his anguish and vexation caused by his enemies in verse 7B[8B] segues into the final strophe (vv. 8-10[9-11]). Here he confesses by faith, while he still pictures himself on his bed floating in his tears, that God hears his prayer, whereby he routs his enemies (vv. 8-9[9-10]) and predicts they will be put to shame (v. 10[11]).

1. Lament (6:6-7[7-8])

6[7]: Extreme Sorrow   *I am worn out* (יָגַעְתִּי) shifts the movement of his lament from severe psychic disturbance to extreme physical exhaustion. The verb *yāga'* and its various derivatives have the abstract meaning of "be/become weary" in the sense of bodily fatigue, of exhaustion. "Extended semantic fields arise from the effort exerted while being or becoming weary, so that one 'toils' or 'labors.'"[54] His fatigue, as from hard labor, is *from my sobbing* (בְּאַנְחָתִי); see note 18. David Thompson defines *'nḥ* as "an intense, negative response to terrible circumstances, actual or anticipated."[55] The response is normally glossed by "to groan" or "to sigh," but no text is definitive. Its parallels in Psalm 6:6[7] suggest the response is sobbing, and that notion fits all other contexts (Job 3:24; 23:2; Ps. 38:10; Isa. 21:2; 35:10; Lam. 1:22). The psalmist's terrible circumstance is both actual and anticipated. He is about to die (vv. 2-3a[3-4a]), for "I AM's" anger until now has been unrelenting (vv. 1-3b[2-4b]). By placing the adverbial phrase *every night* (-בְּכָל לַיְלָה), "in[56] each/every night") between verb and its object the poet emphasizes the duration and extremity of his anguish.[57] *I cause . . . to float* (אַשְׂחֶה) glosses *śḥh*, a root that occurs only three times. The verb can refer to physical swimming

---

54. G. Hasel, *TDOT*, 5.387-88, s.v. *yg'*.

55. D. Thompson, *NIDOTTE*, 1.455, s.v. *'nḥ*.

56. Temporal *b* (*IBHS*, P. 11.2.5c, p. 196).

57. The parallel by contrast is chiastically constructed (object-verb), without separating them by the adverbial phrase "with my tears."

[in a manure pile] (Isa. 25:11). However, the poet probably does not picture his bed as having spread-out hands, and if not, "float" would be the better gloss. *My bed* (מִטָּתִי) refers to a stationary or portable piece of furniture — not a sleeping mat — spread with covers, cloth, and pillow for reclining, more specifically for sleeping (Exod. 8:3[7:28]), for the sick (Gen. 47:31), for resting (1 Sam. 28:23), for the dead (2 Sam. 3:31), or for feasting or carousing (Ezek. 23:41). The parallel "in my tears" is gapped. The extreme hyperbole of his bed floating in his tears strikingly enables us to feel his extreme physical and mental anguish as he pleads for salvation from death.

The verb of *I dissolve* (אָמְסֶה) refers to the melting of ice (Ps. 147:18) and to the consuming by a moth וַתֶּמֶס כָּעָשׁ (Ps. 39:11[12]). The noun *my couch* (עַרְשִׂי) occurs eight times in poetry, once in prose (Deut. 3:11), and three times in parallel with *miṭṭāṭî*. It was definitely used for reclining in sleep (Ps. 132:3) and possibly for reclining during a meal, since no distinction can be made between *miṭṭāṭî* and *'ereś* in Psalm 6:6[7]; Amos 3:12; 6:4. *With my tears* (בְּדִמְעָתִי) are not tears of self-pity but appeals to God for compassion (Pss. 39:13[14]; 56:8[9]; Jer. 31:16). "I AM" reassures a sick Hezekiah: שָׁמַעְתִּי אֶת-תְּפִלָּתֶךָ רָאִיתִי אֶת-דִּמְעָתֶךָ ("I have heard your prayer and seen your tears," Isa. 38:5). Tears result from the physiological deterioration of the body caused by distressful circumstances: "Tears . . . are nothing less than the oozing out of the body's vital substance. The immediate consequence is that the subject is left weak and exhausted, in particular his eyes are considered to be wasting away through tears which are part of their substance flowing out and sapping their strength."[58]

7[8]: Vexation Caused by Enemy   Verse 7A[8A] continues the psalmist's appeal through his tears, and verse 7B[8B] functions as a janus to the final stanza of his confidence in the face of his enemies. *My eyes* (עֵינִי, lit., "my eye") continues the motif of sobbing as can be seen in Jeremiah's lament: "My eyes fail from weeping" (כָּלוּ בַדְּמָעוֹת עֵינַי, Lam. 2:11). A denominative of עָשֵׁשׁ, glossed *waste away* (עָשְׁשָׁה), may more literally mean "moth-eaten." Instructively, Psalm 39:11[12] combines *msh*, "dissolve"/"melt," with עָשׁ, "You consume [their wealth] like a moth" (וַתֶּמֶס כָּעָשׁ). Psalm 6:6-7[7-8] puts the two words back to back. A contemporary equivalent is: "he wept his eyes out." *From vexation* (כָּעַס, 1 Sam. 1:6, 16; Prov. 12:16; passim) is also used of "I AM's" vexation and anger caused by sin.[59] The parallel identifies his adversaries as his provocateurs.

58. Thomas W. Overhalt, "The Psychology of Tears in the Old Testament: Part I," *Catholic Biblical Quarterly* 33 (1971): 18.

59. Some versions gloss the noun by "grief" (Ps. 6:7[8] = Ps. 31:9[10]) and "sorrow" in Ecclesiastes (1:18; 2:23; 7:3; 11:10). But Ecclesiastes is probably the latest book in the Old Testament canon and even in that book the meaning is uncertain; it certainly means "vexation" in 11:10.

They fail (עָתְקָה) glosses a root whose abstract meaning is "move on."[60] In Job 32:15 it means "to fail": "words have failed them" (הֶעְתִּיקוּ מֵהֶם מִלִּים), literally, "words move from them." *Because of all* (בְּכָל, n. 21) is definite in construct with *my foes* (צוֹרְרִי); it refers to the aggregate and not to the distributive individual. *Ṣōrĕrî* denotes an assailant who opposes and attacks in a conflict or dispute (Ps. 129:1f.). The harassment may be physical as in battle (Num. 10:9) or verbal ("provoke," 1 Sam. 1:6). The Canaanites that remain in the land persecute Israel as "pricks in the eye" and "thorns in the side" (Num. 33:55).

2. Confidence (6:8-10[9-11])

As suddenly and miraculously as a resurrection from the dead, David's psyche rises out of the depths to heavenly heights, from anguish to courage, from sorrow to joy, from sobbing to laughter (Isa. 35:10; 51:11). What happened to change defeat into victory? The text mentions neither a high priest's oracle, such as changed Hannah's face from sadness to happiness (1 Sam. 1:17-18), nor a prophet's words, such as roused Zerubbabel, the royal scion, and Joshua, the high priest, to rebuild the house of God in Jerusalem (Ezra 5:1). In connection with his threefold repetition of "I AM," God's covenant-keeping name, the Holy Spirit in David reawakens his voice of faith: "The sure knowledge that his prayer has been answered is not something which man can work out for himself, but is a gift from God."[61] The true David emerges. "Lament has done its work. In voicing all the tensions of his soul, the poet moves through his anguish to new insights, a firmer faith and unrivaled confidence."[62] By faith he routs his provocateurs. The anticipated anguish that evildoers would triumph over the Just, that the spiritually blind would pluck out the eyes of all who see Reality, that the unfailing loyal One would fail, that Love would remain angry forever, that death with its silence and forgetfulness would forever separate the elect from Life, were all unthinkable.

God's regenerating spirit of faith never worked in Saul. When pressed to extremity by his troops deserting as the Philistines gathered against him, Saul disobeyed his prophet and in unbelief began battle without him. David, by contrast, though staring death in the face, by faith knows his salvation must be close at hand. If God does not intervene now, all that is lovely, noble, excel-

---

60. The root occurs seven times: four times in *qal* and thrice in *hiphil*. In *qal* it is used of mountain cliffs that move (i.e., "erode," Job 14:18; cf. 18:4) and once of moving ("to advance" [in years and strength"], Job 21:7). Twice as a one-place (i.e., internal) *hiphil* (i.e., "to cause oneself to move") it means to "move on" in a journey (Gen. 12:8; 26:22). Twice it occurs as a two-place *hiphil* with reference to "erode" of mountains (Job 9:5) and to copying proverbs (Prov. 25:1).

61. Artur Weiser, *The Psalms: A Commentary* (Philadelphia: Westminster, 1962), p. 133.

62. Personal correspondence from Rabbi Morganescu.

lent, pure will die an eternal death. He cannot bring eternal life from his own resources.

a. Address to Foes: (6:8-9[9-10])

8[9]: "I AM" Hears Weeping   The David who composed the songs of trust that have sustained God's people for three millennia (Pss. 23:1-6; 27:1-6) and emerges with faith's confidence in almost every psalm (Pss. 3:3-6[4-7]; 4:3-5[4-6]; 5:3-7[4-8]), by faith spiritually routs his horde of assailants, as our Lord routed Satan (Matt. 4:10), with the command: *Get away from me* (סוּרוּ מִמֶּנִּי). In a figure of speech known as apostrophe, the psalmist redirects his sobbing voice to God and his commanding voice to the malicious horde surrounding him. D. Kidner comments: "This is not merely a hard-pressed sufferer rounding on his tormentors, but a sovereign asserting his power to purge his realm of mischief-makers, as his kingly vow demands; cf. Psalm 101."[63] *Sûr* — the first word of verse 8[9] — sounds like *ṣôrĕrî*, the last word of verse 7[8]; it essentially means "to turn aside from the direction one has set out on" (1 Sam. 6:12). The parallel psalm, Psalm 38:1[2], 10-22[11-23], suggests they taunted the failing king with the insinuation that he was under God's curse; they depart spiritually defeated — *all you who do evil* (כָּל-פֹּעֲלֵי אָוֶן Ps. 5:5[6]). Not one of those who use their hurtful and deceptive power against God can stand before God, who responds to faith's voice.[64] Logical particle *for* (כִּי) introduces the reason: If God be for the king, who can be against him (Rom. 8:31)? "I AM" *has heard* (שָׁמַע יְהוָה) means the Eternal God outwardly gives his ear to the speaker's words and inwardly consents to them. The parallels to hears *my weeping* (קוֹל בִּכְיִי, lit., "sound of my weeping"), hears my petitions and prayers (v. 9[10]), validate the interpretation that his tears were appeals to God's compassion and covenant faithfulness, not tears of self-pity. The enemy's gazing at the king's misfortune with satisfaction derogates the God who chooses and loves him. The enemy's implied rejoicing reflects spiritual blindness, for universal salvation flows from God's king. The root *bkh* ("to cry, bewail") occurs with *dm'* ("tears"); his weeping refers to the flood of tears his eyes shed in his appeal

---

63. Derek Kidner, *Psalms 1-72: An Introduction and Commentary on Books I and II of the Psalms* (Leicester: InterVarsity, 1973), p. 62.

64. Terrien, *The Psalms* (p. 114), misinterprets the psalm because he bases it on S. Mowinckel's early *Psalmenstudien* [PIW, II. 11] that the "workers of evil" were sorcerers thought to have cast spells on the sufferer, because of the association of *"awen"* with power. This interpretation rests on the dubious assumption that "evildoers" always means the same thing and that the psalmist held pagan mythological convictions. Accepting the Bible's own witness to itself, David followed the Mosaic Torah, which rejected pagan mythological convictions (Deut. 18:14). Later Mowinckel conceded that the term could have a general reference (*PIW* II, 250).

to God to save him (vv. 1-7[2-8]). His sweet tears to God contrast sharply with Israel's sour tears before God when they murmured against him in the wilderness (Num. 11:4, 10, 13, 18, 20; 14:1; Deut. 1:45).

9[10]: "I AM" Accepts Prayer His repeating "I AM" *has heard* (שָׁמַע יְהוָה) binds his weeping (v. 8[9]) with his prayers (v. 9[10]). The object of hearing now is *my cry for mercy* (תְּחִנָּתִי, traditionally "supplications," "pity," a correlative word for the preceding object, "weeping"). T*eḥinnâ*, a semantic equivalent of *taḥᵃnû/nîm*, derives from the root *ḥnn*, linking verses 9[10] and 2[3] together. Stoebe comments: "The theological background of the concept strongly underscores grace in the word's conceptual scope."[65] T*eḥinnâ* and *taḥᵃnû/nîm* "are expressions of a mind beset with terror which does not have established formulations."[66] תַּחֲנוּן elsewhere denotes the appeal of a poor man to the rich (Prov. 18:23), and, ironically, of a captured Leviathan begging his human captor for mercy (Job 41:3[40:27]). "I AM" *accepts my prayer* (יְהוָה תְּפִלָּתִי יִקָּח), an addition that clarifies that "hear" does not mean merely that God outwardly gives ear to his prayer but that he also inwardly consents to it. T*epillâ* means "a request for an assessment, a consideration" either for others (= "intercession," Pss. 35:13; 84:8[9]; 109:4) or for self ("prayer," "petition"). Almost half of the usages of *tepillâ* occur in petition psalms, either in introductory petitions, imploring God to be favorable (17:1; passim), or in the praise section, rejoicing that God heard his prayer (65:2[3]; passim). In short, his address to his adversaries, which is based on faith, has tones of confidence and praise.

b. Address to Faithful: Enemies Will Be Dismayed (6:10[11])

The psalmist now addresses the congregation of the faithful who surround the king, who with him descended into the depths of despair and by faith reemerged in triumph. Instead of pronouncing a benediction on them, he fills them with courage and praise by pronouncing a malediction on his enemies. Having routed his enemies by spiritual words, by faith he predicts their shame in defeat. The evildoers of verse 8[9] are equated with *all my enemies* (כָּל־אֹיְבָי). "Enemies" refers to wicked persons who oppose the one God favors. They can be defined by the noun's descriptive predicates: "oppress" (Deut. 28:53), "persecute" (1 Kgs. 8:37), "smite" (Lev. 26:17; Jer. 30:14), "pursue, persecute" (Hos. 8:3), "deal treacherously with, deceive" (Lam. 1:2). Their proud behavior is often mentioned: "They make

65. H. J. Stoebe, *TLOT*, 3.444, s.v. *Ḥnn*; תְּחִנָּתוֹ in 1 Kings 8:28 is replaced by תַּחֲנוּן in 2 Chronicles 6:21.

66. *HALOT*, 4.1719, s.v. *taḥᵃnûnîm tahnûnîm*.

themselves great (Lam. 1:9), scoff and revile (Ps. 74:10, 18; Lam. 1:21; Ezek. 36:2), rejoice at misfortune (Lam. 2:17), open wide their mouths, i.e., rail (Lam. 2:16), gnash with their teeth (Lam. 2:16), etc."[67] So profiled, *they will be ashamed* (יֵבֹשׁוּ) registers their reversed psychology from pride to humiliation. *Bôš* expresses the notion that they risked their fortune on the king's death, hoping that the evil and/or foreign god on which they depended would advance their honor, but as it turned out it proved false and so brought them to ridicule.[68] The fortunes of the king and his enemies will be so reversed *they* [now] *will be exceedingly dismayed* (6:3[4]).

The enemies will *turn* (יָשֻׁבוּ) from their gloating over the dying king, when "I AM" turns from his wrath against him (6:4[5]). To underscore their total defeat David repeats *they will be ashamed* (יֵבֹשׁוּ). Plumer comments: "mercies, obtained by weeping and prayer, are well suited to give courage. They are like armor won in battle to hang up as trophies to show what can be done."[69] This will happen *in an instant* (רָגַע). When "I AM" ceases his wrath, as certainly he must, he will pop the enemies' arrogance like a pricked balloon. In this way "I AM" decisively shows his allegiance to his restored S/son and also his supreme power over the wicked. He also shows that he cannot abide the presence of the wicked a second longer.

PART IV. CONCLUSION

It is worthy of note that by the conclusion of the psalm nothing outwardly has changed. Nevertheless by faith he routs his spiritual enemies, assures the faithful that the enemy, not the godly elect, will be put to shame. He leaves the house of God a transformed man. And as a barren Hannah returned home, assured that God heard her prayer, gave birth to Israel's savior in its darkest hour, so David returned to his palace and did not die a premature death.

Elizabeth Achtemeier, in a fine discussion on the use of the psalm in the history of the synagogue and the church during the first millennium, sounds a sour note when she comments: "And *strangely* [italics mine] enough, the psalm came to be used in both synagogue and church for funerals or for memorial masses and offices for the dead."[70] Yet few psalms are more reassuring to the dying and those whom the dead leave behind than this psalm. It generates faith

---

67. H. Ringgren, *TDOT*, 1.215, s.v. *'āyabh*.

68. Cf. H. Seebass, *bosh*, *TDOT*, 2.252. In Akkadian literature from the earliest to the latest stages of the language we encounter prayer in the style, "Let me/us not be put to shame"; e.g., "O Sink, let me not be put to shame"; "I trusted in her and was not put to shame."

69. Plumer, *Psalms*, p. 100.

70. Achtemeier, "Overcoming the World," p. 77, citing Eric Werner, "The Sacred Bridge,"

that God hears the prayers of his loved ones while they still have life and delivers them from implacable death. By saving his king from death in the prime of life, the king serves as an example to young and old alike that God saves his chosen loved ones from death. Even in clinical death the righteous seek refuge in "I AM," the God and Father of our Lord Jesus, and they will not be put to shame (Prov. 14:32). To judge from the paucity of evidence, God's covenant people in the old dispensation only dimly perceived that clinical death could not separate them from God (Pss. 49:15[16]; 73:23ff.; Isa. 26:19). That hope was validated and brought to the full light of day by the resurrection of Jesus Christ from the dead: "Christ Jesus . . . has destroyed death and has brought life and immortality to light through the gospel" (2 Tim. 1:10).

More importantly, the psalm is appropriately used at funerals because David is a type of Christ Jesus' death and resurrection. Before noting the typology, it is worth noting that Jesus knew this psalm by heart. During the time of the primitive church, Psalm 6 was in the Jewish liturgy just before the concluding Kiddish. It may well be that our Lord participated in that weekday recitation. In any case, he echoes "My soul is dismayed [LXX *tarassō*]" (v. 3[4]) in John 12:27. He quotes exactly "Get away from me" (v. 8[9], so too LXX) to evildoers (Luke 13:27; cf. Matt. 7:22-23; Luke 6:46).

With that background, now consider the typology. Eaton comments: "The psalm has continued to be associated with Christ's weeping, pleading, loss of strength and beauty, and at last victory over the evil one."[71] The psalm was appropriately used on Ash Wednesday. Both David and the Lord Jesus Christ suffered under God's wrath; both humbly accepted God's discipline; both were in anguish at the prospect of death and separation from God; both prayed earnestly to be delivered; both committed themselves to God alone; both tasted the grave; both were reckoned by the malicious and malignant enemies as under a curse; both were heard by God when they prayed; both rose victorious from the sphere of death; and in so doing routed their enemies; both praised God for their salvation, discomforting the damned and comforting the faithful.

But the Antitype is so much greater than the type: David suffered justly for his sin, our Lord suffered justly for our sins, not for his own, and because he himself was without sin satisfied God's wrath against sin and removed sin and its wages from all who trust him. David was slipping away into the grave, but our Lord was buried in the grave and descended into Hades. David was deliv-

---

The Interdependence of Liturgy and Music in Synagogue and Church during the First Millennium (New York: Columbia University Press, 1959), pp. 6, 156, 159.

71. John Eaton, *The Psalms: A Historical and Spiritual Commentary with an Introduction and New Translation* (New York and London: Continuum, 2005), p. 76.

ered from a premature death but eventually died a normal death in his old age; Christ rose from the dead and lives forever. This is the story the church gives to the terrified sick and dying: "We tell our 'old, old story,' or we literally have nothing to tell."[72] Until our Lord's return all the elect must clinically die, but David's psalm will always assure them that the God of life, and not death, will have the last word in their narrative. And if the type gives us that assurance, how much more will the Antitype?

72. Achtemeier, "Overcoming the World," p. 87.

CHAPTER 4

Psalm 7: A Royal Petition for Cosmic Justice

Part I. Voice of the Church

I. Introduction

In this chapter we consider: 1) the misinterpretations of the psalm's superscript; 2) the commentary on Psalm 7 by John Chrysostom (349-407), who saw David as an exemplar for godly living; and 3) two Christian monarchs in the eighth and ninth centuries who used David's kingship as an exemplar for their monarchies: Charlemagne (742-812) with his advisor Alcuin (735-804), and Alfred the Great (849-899). Early commentators misinterpreted the superscript's identification of the psalm's historical background, and contemporary scholars misrepresent David.

II. The Words of Cush the Benjamite

The Targum superscription of Psalm 7 rightly (see exegesis) refers to the time when Saul was trying to kill David; the Vulgate version identifies the context as Absalom's revolt to kill his father, David. Whatever occasion provides the source of this lament, the psalmist feared assassination. Since the early commentators followed the Vulgate, they all referred to Absalom's revolt (2 Samuel 15–17). They identify Cush with Hushai, David's friend, who functioned as a mole in Absalom's camp to sabotage the plot to destroy David and his loyal supporters. "Hushai's words," according to this interpretation, informed David of Absalom's accusations against him.[1] The motive is the same: to destroy his good name as a righteous king and so eliminate him.

---

1. *St. John Chrysostom: Commentary on the Psalms,* trans. Robert Charles Hill (Brookline, MA: Holy Cross Orthodox Press, 1998), vol. 1, pp. 102-3.

III. Literary and Contemporary Assassinations of David

It is an old story still being played out, for contemporary scholars are more divided than ever about the character of David. For some, David is a literary fiction like Hamlet, never historically validated. Contemporary historical literary criticism has subjected the "death of his reality" to what Paul Ricoeur calls the "hermeneutics of suspicion." In each literary age, selective elements of "the David story" have been highlighted, whether in Carolingian, Anglo-Saxon, late Medieval, Renaissance, or Stuart cultures. For it is basically a "human story,"[2] belonging to all times. The late Renaissance was particularly fascinated with the David story. Between 1500 and 1700 over a hundred plays, poems, and prose works with David as subject were published in English alone![3] The revival of Stoicism set the mood then, identifying Hamlet with David on such issues as the tragedy of revenge.[4]

Other scholars interpret David's laments for Saul and Jonathan (2 Sam. 1:17-27), Abner (2 Sam. 3:31-39), Amnon (2 Sam. 13:31-36), and for Absalom (2 Sam. 19:1-8), as public mourning out of political necessity. After all, David stands to gain from each death.

Nevertheless, David's biographer in the Book of Samuel aims to refute this skepticism. He recounts that in Abner's funeral procession, David commanded Joab and the people to tear their clothes and walk in front of the bier while he brought up the rear of the procession; thereby he symbolically distanced himself from Joab's murderous actions and "all the people and all Israel knew that day that the king had no part in the killing of Abner" (2 Sam. 3:37). As Bruce puts it: "in their collective judgment they acquit him of wrongdoing."[5] Let Scripture interpret Scripture is the basis of our reflections. So when in the Psalms David illustrates "the way of the righteous" as Psalm 1 depicts, then we see David very differently from our cultural perspectives. In David's dealings with his sons, he constantly avers: "Will not the Judge of all the earth do right?" The apostle Paul echoes the two incidents when David could have killed Saul, as his troops and Abishai wanted him to do: first, while Saul was relieving himself in a cave (1 Samuel 24) and second, while Saul was in a deep sleep (1 Samuel 26). With theological perspicacity David recognized that God had anointed Saul as king, making Saul God's property to dispose of according to his sovereign will (1 Sam. 24:6; 26:9).

---

2. Raymond-Jean Frontain and Jan Wojcik, eds., *The David Myth in Western Literature* (West Lafayette, IN: Purdue University Press, 1980), pp. 1-10.

3. Frontain and Wojcik, *The David Myth*, p. 97.

4. Eleanor Prosser, *Hamlet and Revenge* (Stanford, CA: Stanford University Press, 1967), pp. 36-73.

5. Bruce Waltke with Charles Yu, *An Old Testament Theology* (Grand Rapids: Zondervan, 2007), p. 658.

For David, the word of the Lord was "justice (vengeance) is mine, says the Lord" (Rom. 12:19; cf. 1 Sam. 26:10). His response to Saul's jealous spirit was simply: "May the Lord judge between you and me. And may the Lord avenge the wrongs you have done to me" (1 Sam. 24:12). Apart from his sin with Bathsheba, David acted in accordance with God's law, whereas the story of his unrighteous rivals, be it Saul or Absalom, is illustrative of the principle that "the way of the wicked" was always to take the law into his own hands.

IV. The Exemplary Pastoral Theology of John Chrysostom

Among the early fathers, the pastoral theology of **John Chrysostom** is distinctively exemplary. It is based on the text of the apostle Paul's injunction, "be imitators of me [Paul], as I am of Christ" (1 Cor. 11:1). He sees David in the Old Testament functioning as a role model similar to the apostle Paul in the New Testament.

John Chrysostom was a monk, preacher, and bishop, a rare combination even in his day.[6] Scarcely a decade after his ordination he was already listed in Jerome's *Lives of Illustrious Men* (c. 392) as being the author of many books, but since Jerome had not read them, his praise might have been ironic.[7] Yet as a preacher, rather than as a scholar, John was rapidly promoted to Archbishop of Constantinople (c. 397), where at first he was acclaimed for his sweeping reforms. Palladius of Galatia (c. 363-430) reports that "because of all these reforms [by Chrysostom] the church was flourishing more excellently from day to day. The very color of the city was changed to piety; everyone looked bright and fresh with soberness and Psalm-singing."[8] Did John bring this new liturgy of "psalm-singing" from his own desert practice?

Chrysostom, whose name means "The Golden Mouth," is known best, not as a bishop, but as one of the greatest preachers of his day, trained and influenced as a classical rhetorician and moralist, whose exemplary hermeneutics dominate all his writings.[9] No doubt his preaching was already influenced by the Cappadocian Fathers who preceded him, Basil and his brother Gregory of Nyssa. Writing

6. J. N. D. Kelly, *Golden Mouth: The Story of John Chrysostom — Ascetic, Preacher, Bishop* (Princeton: Princeton University Press, 1994).

7. Stefan Rebenich, *Jerome* (London and New York: Routledge, 2002), p. 98.

8. Palladius, Homily, 5 in *Palladius: Dialogue on the Life of St. John Chrysostom*, trans. Robert T. Meyer, Ancient Christian Writers 45 (New York: Newman, 1985), p. 40.

9. See Mary Albania Burns, *Saint John Chrysostom's Homilies on the Statues: A Study of the Rhetorical Qualities and Form* (Washington, DC: Catholic University of America Press, 1930); also Robert Louis Wilken, *John Chrysostom and the Jews: Rhetoric and Reality in the Late 4th Century* (Berkeley: University of California Press, 1983).

to his younger brother Gregory (c. 358), Basil advises, "The great way to find our duty is to the attentive practice of the God-inspired Scriptures, for in these we find both the practical counsel and the lives of blessed men handed down in writing, as some living icons of life according to God, for the imitation of good works . . . just as painters, when they are painting other pictures, constantly look at the example, doing their best to transfer its lineaments to their own work; so also it is necessary for him who desires to make himself perfect in all branches of virtue, to look at the lives of the saints as though living and moving statues and to make their good his own through imitation" (Ephesians 2).[10]

Our classical museums today are full of Greco-Roman marble busts of their philosophers. Writing to his wealthy banker friend, the Epicurean Atticus, Cicero reminds us of this role of "the sculpted word" in portraiture: "I am not at liberty to forget Epicurus, even if I want to, since we have his image not only in our paintings, but also on our cups and rings."[11] As Bernard Frischer has argued, such sculptured heads were much more than a portrait; they provided advertisement for recruitment of students, of what to expect in the teachings of those immortalized by such a portrait. Asklepios, with his healing qualities, is thus conjoined in the same bust with Hercules with his powerful abilities.[12]

Is then Basil's preaching a reaction against this mythical classical iconology, replacing it with the historical and living deeds of biblical heroes? Was Chrysostom doing an analogous synthesis, this time of David and Paul, in his idealized archetype of morals drawn from both the Old and the New Covenants? Both are needed by Chrysostom as exemplars of the excellence (*aretē*) of godly lives. He interprets David to exemplify a wide range of *aretai*: faith, repentance, humility, gentleness, and clemency. His favorite stories to substantiate this living ethical portraiture are: David's duel with Goliath (1 Samuel 17–18); his adultery with Bathsheba (2 Samuel 11–12); the punishment chosen by David in the census account (2 Samuel 24); his responses to Absalom's rebellion (2 Samuel 15–18); and his sparing of Saul's life (1 Samuel 24, 26). Chrysostom also contrasted the divine origin of Greek heroes with the lowly origins of David as king. Indeed, Chrysostom even argues that despite living within the Old Covenant, David was already bearing the fruits of the New Covenant in being Christ-like.[13] While Chrysostom preached about David even in his homilies on New Testament books such as Matthew and Romans, he did write three homilies specifically on David

---

10. Quoted by Pak-Wah Lai, *John Chrysostom and the Hermeneutics of Exemplar Portraits*, unpublished Ph.D. dissertation, University of Durham, UK, 2010, p. 1.

11. Bernard Frischer, *The Sculpted Word: Epicureanism and Philosophical Recruitment in Ancient Greece* (Berkeley: University of California Press, 1982), p. 87.

12. Frischer, *The Sculpted Word*, pp. 209-31.

13. Pak-Wah Lai, *John Chrysostom*, pp. 99, 103.

and Saul.[14] They detail David's moral qualities, and how wholly dependent he was upon the grace of God for these virtues.

V. Chrysostom's Commentary on Psalm 7

Modern exegetes might become impatient with Chrysostom's thirty-six-page homily on the seventeen verses of Psalm 7. His is not really "exegesis" but a hermeneutic for "character-shaping" in exemplary ethics. He begins by lamenting that his audience — like many today — do not know the heroes of the Old Testament. He spends five pages recounting the story about Absalom's rebellion, which he believes lies behind the psalm. Archetypal ethical teaching requires counterpoint in the role played by the "enemy." David's stories are well suited for this contrastive approach, which Chrysostom uses to full advantage. He sketches a vivid picture of how Absalom breaks all bounds of convention, in order to highlight David's virtues. Chrysostom then focuses on David's friend Hushai, who in penetrating Absalom's camp in order to counter the advice being given by Ahithophel, proved to be craftier and more dangerous than "the angry young man," Absalom. This contrast gives Chrysostom the opportunity to eulogize the virtues of true friendship as another source of edification for the audience. Also "taking risks for virtue's sake, keeping hope alive," and having "eyes on one thing alone, God's unassailable assistance and his favor" — these become the lesson of the story.[15] As Hushai succeeds in winning the ear of Absalom, he does so, argues Chrysostom, because "when God is in control, difficulties become easy."[16] After the defeat and death of Absalom, Chrysostom explains, "he [David] wrote the psalm, offering songs of thanksgiving to God, attributing the whole strategy to him: 'Lord, my God, I take refuge in you'" (v. 1[2]).[17]

Chrysostom then emphasizes how prayer should be made to God: first, it is "in worthiness to receive something; then praying according to God's laws; third, persistence; fourth, asking nothing earthy; fifth, seeking things to our real benefit; sixth, contributing everything of our own."[18]

Using exemplars of each type, Chrysostom returns to David's prayer, "Lord, if I have done this" (v. 3[4]), i.e., been the agent of Absalom's downfall, then David

---

14. Robert Charles Hill, trans., *St. John Chrysostom: Commentary on the Psalms* (Brookline, MA: Holy Cross Orthodox Press, 1998).

15. *St. John Chrysostom: Commentary on the Psalms*, p. 113.

16. *St. John Chrysostom: Commentary on the Psalms*, p. 114.

17. *St. John Chrysostom: Commentary on the Psalms*, p. 115.

18. *St. John Chrysostom: Old Testament Homilies* (Brookline, MA: Holy Cross Orthodox Press, 2003), p. 117.

has no cause for responding to evil with evil. If David, living within the context of the Old Covenant, realized he could not be so vindictive, what excuse could we possibly have to be revengeful after the coming of Christ, when a higher level of morality is expected of us?[19]

Chrysostom recounts David's similar attitude toward Saul, sparing Saul's life more than once in response to the latter's wickedness toward David. "Loving one's enemies, as Jesus commanded us" means that "we are responsible for not making them our enemies." This we can control, as Paul said: "As far as possible for you, be at peace with everyone" (Rom. 12:18). It should be the vices themselves that make them our enemies, not our reactive wounded passions that promote them. Speaking of David, he exhorts: "Note the righteous man's loving spirit, how in every situation he has an eye to what is of common advantage, the removal of evil, not for him to settle scores with his enemies but for his enemies to abstain from wickedness. Let this in every case be our concern."[20]

Chrysostom uses Paul's epistles to comment on the text of the psalm. Whereas the bias of the Western churches favored the Book of Romans, in the East Paul's Corinthian letters were preferred. Within this Pauline context, Chrysostom is vividly applying the psalm to the sufferings of his present audience, as if they were playing out David's role and situation. He points out the self-condemning and self-destructive logic of evil, as the psalm itself concludes (v. 16[17]).

Pivotal to Chrysostom's exemplary hermeneutic is the notion that David exemplifies the righteous character of "I AM," as later the apostle Paul is the imitator of Christ.[21] "The wicked, you see," argues Chrysostom, are in the habit of hating without reason or cause. Christ, too, remember, was hated for no good reason; as he says, "they hated me without a cause" (Ps. 69: 4[5]). He likens David to Christ and Paul, not making enemies, though enemies surrounded them. In this exemplification of David's, Christ's, and Paul's travails, Chrysostom exegetes from the Scriptures that "the way of the wicked" brings its own destruction, while "the way of the righteous is protected by 'I AM,' the righteous God" (v. 9[10]), who is "a righteous judge" (v. 11[12]).[22]

The psalmist concludes with thanksgiving to "I AM" because of his "righteousness" (v. 17[18]). So Chrysostom concludes: "This is the very reason why we too should undergo all suffering: not in expectation of the kingdom, nor of some other hope of future goods, but for God himself. . . . Love God not for what he

19. *St. John Chrysostom: Old Testament Homilies*, p. 119.

20. *St. John Chrysostom: Old Testament Homilies*, p. 130.

21. For an in-depth study of John Chrysostom's archetypal use of Paul, see Margaret M. Mitchell, "The Archetypal Image: John Chrysostom's Portraits of Paul," *The Journal of Religion* 75, no. 1 (1995): 15-43.

22. *St. John Chrysostom: Old Testament Homilies*, p. 132.

gives but for who he is."[23] Unlike the association of David with literary tragedies, such as King Lear, David is depicted by Chrysostom as expressing the moral resilience we identify with the character of Christ himself. Later commentators, such as Augustine, will associate Judas' betrayal of Jesus with Absalom's treachery toward David.[24]

Chrysostom used Psalm 7 to preach David as an exemplar; we now turn to two Christian kings in the eighth and ninth centuries who used David's monarchy as their exemplar: Charlemagne in France and Alfred the Great in England.

VI. Charlemagne (c. 742-812)

As "the new David," who was consecrated with holy oil at his coronation, and who acted as both priest and king *(rex et sacerdos)*, **Charlemagne** sought to be a true Davidic shepherd. Charlemagne's predecessors, the Merovingian kings, were despots, deriving their power from blood descent, their high-mindedness being limited only by civil war, assassination, and superstitious fears. But Charlemagne, his advisors, and especially his successors in the later reform synod of Aachen (816/17) sought to have biblical legitimacy of faith and doctrine for "sacred kingship." Appeal was made to the biblical commentaries of the early Church Fathers. It was an attempt to remove the schism of the Western and the Eastern churches by restored respect for the major church councils. Saintly simplicity was conjoined to sacred learning. This was attempted not just at the clerical level, but with the laity also, in introducing Christian morals within marriage and family life.[25]

VII. Alcuin (735-804)

Most influential as a theological advisor to Charlemagne was **Alcuin**, who, between 797 and 800, used the scholarly resources of Northumbria to produce a definitive text of the Vulgate Bible. Seeking also uniformity of liturgy in worship throughout the empire, Alcuin recognized the uniqueness of the psalms for both public and personal devotion. With remarkable insight, Alcuin admonishes: "Let us pay careful heed to how we sing the Psalms, and we shall see how they can achieve more in prayer than human words can ever express. They contain the

23. *St. John Chrysostom: Old Testament Homilies,* pp. 146-47.

24. *Saint Augustine: Expositions of the Psalms, 1–32,* trans. Maria Boulding (Hyde Park, NY: New City Press, 2000), p. 113.

25. Andre Vauchez, *The Spirituality of the Medieval West: The Eighth to the Twelfth Century,* trans. Colette Friedlander (Kalamazoo, MI: Cistercian Publications, 1993), pp. 19-28.

sweetest love of the divine law; they arm the soul with courage in spiritual warfare, and are also a formidable stronghold in times of tribulation. They expel the fear and sadness of this passing age, and gladden our minds with spiritual joy and happiness."[26] Again Alcuin affirms: "If you are afflicted by various trials . . . greater than you can bear, sing within your innermost heart the Psalms. Immediately the merciful God will help you and enable you to bear the temptation that is upon you. If the present life seems disdainful to you, and your spirit loves to contemplate the eternal homeland, and you seek Almighty God with an ardent desire, chant psalms single-mindedly, and the merciful God will swiftly console your mind. If you think that God has abandoned you in the midst of tribulations, sing psalms with compunction of heart and God will immediately gladden you in the midst of all your sufferings. In times of quiet, and in periods of prosperity, use the Psalms."[27]

Alcuin had definite ideas about Christian kingship derived from the Old Testament model of David. For the next two centuries this Davidic ideology was to influence the monarchy in England as well as on the continent.

VIII. Alfred the Great (c. 849-899)

King of Wessex in southeast England, **Alfred the Great** is a later exemplar of this Davidic monarchy. His fights and diplomacy against the Danes, by which he saved England from conquest, were inspired by David's fight with Goliath. He illustrates the role of the Psalter in his commentary on Psalm 7. His preface reads: "David sang this seventh Psalm when he complained of his misfortune to God (that was when Absalom his son had driven him from the kingdom) — when Chus[28] son of Gemini abused and cursed him, he lamented that to God; and so does each man who sings this Psalm complain of[29] his suffering[30] to God; and so

26. Douglas Dales, *A Mind Intent on God: The Prayers and Spiritual Writings of Alcuin: An Anthology* (Norwich, UK: Canterbury Press, 2004), pp. 45-46.

27. Dales, *A Mind Intent on God,* pp. 68-69.

28. I am not quite sure how Shimei becomes the proper name Chus here, but the correlation comes from Arnobius and Augustine.

29. The word "complain of" here is different from that used in the first sentence. While this word — *mænan* — does mean "complain of," it can also mean something like "signify," or "denote" — I presume this to be the progenitor of the modern word "mean," as in the sentence, "A red traffic light means [signifies] stop." This is how the Augustinian system of signs and sacraments operated.

30. The Old English word here for suffering — *eorfoðe* — is important in Old English literature of exile and lament; e.g., The Wanderer, a wisdom figure who discovers God through his experience of exile, is described as "mindful of eaorfoðe." It would also seem that this word is used frequently in the penitential psalms. What this tells us is that in the Old English social

did Christ when he was on earth."[31] The king was the exemplary model for Christian conduct, demanding exceptional self-control. Like David in his openness to the prophet Nathan's rebuke, the king was open to the rebukes of his bishops; as Charlemagne was to Alcuin, the king accepted them as his advisors and friends.

Alfred was unique in cultivating his own devotional scholarship, for he personally translated the *Soliloquia* of Augustine, the *Regula pastoralis* of Gregory the Great, the *Consolatio philosophiae* of Boethius, as well as presented the text and commentary of the first fifty psalms in the Vulgate.[32] Although it was translated into the vernacular, the purpose was for the pastoral instruction of the royal household, which was to be in turn the exemplar of a Christian household for the whole kingdom. It seems Alfred possessed two Carolingian Psalters, both annotated by him for his own private devotions. He recognized Gregory the Great as archetype of humble obedience, and hence lament and repentance marked his response to the Davidic model of kingship.

PART II. VOICE OF THE PSALMIST: TRANSLATION

A lament[33] by David, which he sang to the LORD concerning the accusations[34] of Cush, a Benjamite.

1   "I AM," my God, I seek refuge in you;
      save me from all who pursue me, and rescue me,
2   otherwise he will tear me apart like a lion
      that snatches me away with no one to rescue me.
3   "I AM," my God, if I have done this:
      if there is guilt on my hands;
4   if I have repaid my ally[35] with evil;

---

imaginary, these Psalms might have been read in terms of a certain genre of wisdom poetry. E. G. Stanley has argued that a number of these wisdom poems are penitential.

31. David Pratt, *The Political Thought of King Alfred the Great* (Cambridge: Cambridge University Press, 2007), p. 122.

32. D. Whitelock, *Bede to Alfred: Studies in Early Anglo-Saxon Literature and History* (London: Variorum reprints, 1980), p. 89.

33. *Shiggāyôn* is probably related to Akkadian *schigu*, a term used in ritual texts to denote a psalm of lamentation. Dalglish notes that such psalms were normally employed by the king and that the Sumerian *erschaschunga* lament psalms, from which Akkadian *schigu* is a direct derivate, originated c. 1600-1450 BCE and were included in the Sumerian canon formed about 1300 BCE (E. Dalglish, *Psalm 51 in Light of Ancient Near Eastern Patternism* [Leiden: Brill, 1962], p. 34).

34. The psalm's content favors gloss "accusation" (*BDB*, 1.1.g, p. 182, s.v. *dbr*).

35. Gloss *to my ally* (שׁוֹלְמִי) is uncertain. Can mean "be at/keep peace" (Job 22:21); "to be

and rescued his foe[36] without cause,[37]

5   then let[38] my enemy pursue me and overtake me;
    let him trample my life to the ground
    and cause my glory to dwell in the dust.   Selah[39]

6   Arise, "I AM," in your anger;
    rise up against the rage of my enemies.
    Awake, my God; decree[40] justice.

---

complete/whole/sound" (Job 9:4), "to complete" (1 Kgs. 7:51; Isa. 60:20; Neh. 6:15; 2 Chron. 5:1). Most English versions gloss this denominative of *šālōm* as "be at peace" (ASV, CSB, DBU, ERV, GNV, KJV, NIV, NJB, RSV). *HALOT* glosses it "friend" (so also ESV, NAB, NAS, NLT, TNK; YLT uniquely "well-wisher"). *BDB* thinks it means "to complete a covenant of peace" and so glosses it as "ally" (NET, NJB, NRSV, and NIV). This nuance best suits the treaty context of verse 4B[5B]). Mitchell Dahood (*Psalms 1–50* [Garden City, NY: Doubleday, 1966], p. 43), citing Jean Nougayrol (*Iraq* 25 [1963]: 110), notes Hittite *sulummū* had the double value of "peace" and "treaty."

36. MT reads: "And I have rescued my foe without reason," which is a semantically impertinent accusation. LXX, Syr. and Tg. probably read וָאֲלֹחֲצָה (*wāʾēlihiṣâ*, "and I oppressed," not *wāʾᵃhalᵉṣâ* and I rescued"), albeit in Syriac, not in Hebrew, *ḥlṣ* can mean "plunder." Metathesis (i.e., reading *lḥṣ* ["to oppress"] for *ḥlṣ* ["to rescue"]) is a well-attested scribal error. Many English versions, however, questionably gloss this retroversion by "plunder" (so CSB, ESV, NKJ, NLT, and NRSV; with more finesse by "robbed" [NIV]), but the semantic leap from "oppress" to "plunder" is questionable and finds no analogy in the Hebrew Bible. Some translations (KJV, ASV, DBY, ERV, NAB, TNK) salvage MT by the *pilpul* "even I who rescued one who without cause is my enemy." But in that case one expects conjunctive *waw* — used either as a disjunctive (i.e., "now I") or an ascensive (i.e., "even I") — not a narrative *waw* ("and so"). Also, one would expect "I" to be expressed. If that is David's intended thought, he could not have expressed himself more unclearly. Robert G. Bratcher ("A Translator's Note on Psalm 7:4b," *The Bible Translator* 23 [1972]: 241f.) interprets MT to mean that David is guilty of not exacting the law of *lex talionis* (to punish in kind for an evil act) as demanded in Exod. 21:25, Lev. 24:19-20, Deut. 19:21. But to show mercy to an enemy is not in itself a capital offense. Edward J. Kissane (*The Book of Psalms*, vol. 1, *Psalms 1–72* [Dublin: Browne & Nolan, 1952], pp. 28f.) interprets MT to mean that David freed his enemy who had injured his ally. Had David done so, he would be guilty of high treason. However, this interpretation demands a reading between the lines that no translator suspected. "My enemy" more naturally refers to the parallel "my ally" than to an unknown third party. Jeffrey H. Tigay ("Psalm 7:5 and Ancient Near Eastern Treaties," *JBL* 89 [1970]: 178-86) achieves a more cogent, similar sense by emending *ṣôrᵉrî* ("my enemy") to *ṣôrᵉrô* ("his enemy"): "if I rescued his foe without cause." This reading is preferred because: (1) Scribes commonly confuse *î* and *ô* — in the DSS they may be indistinguishable; (2) the parallel "my adversary" abets this confusion and so does the reference to "my enemies" in verse 6[7]; (3) the introduction of "his enemy" is unexpected and so more difficult; (4) yet this emendation "clarifies" Cush's accusation against David in their historical context (see exegesis).

37. The parallel "evil" favors construing וְרָקִם as an accusative of state modifying the subject, not the object as in KJV, ASV, et al. (*IBHS*, P. 10.2.2d, pp. 171f.).

38. יִרְדֹּף mixes Qal (*yirdōp*) and Piel (*yᵉraddēp*).

39. The meaning of *selah* is uncertain (see A. A. Anderson, *Psalm 1–72* [The New Century Bible Commentary; Grand Rapids: Eerdmans, 1972], p. 49).

40. Precative perfective (*IBHS*, P. 30.5.4c, p. 494).

7   Let the assembled peoples gather around you,
         and return[41] on high over them.
8   Let "I AM" judge the peoples.
         Vindicate me, "I AM,"
         according to my righteousness, according to my integrity, O Most
             High.[42]
9   Let a disaster,[43] I pray, bring the wicked to an end,[44]
         but establish the righteous;
         for[45] the One who tests hearts and emotions is a righteous God.[46]
10   God takes it upon himself to be[47] my shield,
         the one who saves the upright of heart.
11   God is a righteous judge,
         a God who is indignant every day.[48]

---

41. שׁוּבָה is commonly emended to *šᵉbâ* ("sit enthroned"; LXX, ASV, ERS, ESV, NAS, NET, NJB, YLT). The received text, however, is both sensible (see exegesis) and more difficult. Why would a scribe insert a medial *waw* and introduce an unexpected reading?

42. The gloss construes עָלָי, *'ālāy* (traditionally "that is in me"; LXX, ASV, DBY, DRA, ERV, ESV, JPS, KJV, NASB, RSV, NRSV) as an alternative or shortened form for *'elyôn*. The Ugaritic counterpart of *'elyôn* is *'ly*, a form attested also in Psalm 57:5[6]. First suggested by Dahood ("The divine name 'Êlî in the Psalms," *Theological Studies* 14 [1953]: 452-57), this interpretation has been accepted by Cyrus Gordon (*Ugaritic Textbook* [Analecta Orientalia 38; Rome: Pontificium Institutum Biblicum, 1965], p. 456, entry 1855); G. Wehmeier (*TLOT*, 2.893, s.v. *'lh*); tentatively by *HALOT*, and some English versions (NET, NIV, NLT). The epithet may have been chosen for its assonance with עָלֶיהָ ("over it").

43. All the English versions, except JPS, against the MT accents read רַע רְשָׁעִים; *ra' rᵉšā'îm* as a grammatical construct, yielding, "evil of the wicked." The MT accentuation yields a perfect sense and is the more difficult reading as shown by the consensus of the English version (William Wickes, *Two Treatises on the Accentuation of the Old Testament* [New York: Ktav, 1972], 1.43).

44. Probably an intentional pun between גְּמָלְתִּי שׁוֹלְמִי רָע (verse 4[5]) and יִגְמָר-נָא רַע.

45. For the logical use of paratactic *waw* see G. B. Caird, *The Language and Imagery of the Bible* (Philadelphia: Westminster, 1980), esp. p. 118.

46. The syntax of this verset is uncertain. Another option is "for [you], O righteous God, are the one who tests. . . ." But in that case one would expect "you" to be expressed in the text. The preferred translation, however, has the disadvantage of shifting addressees from God to the congregation. Probably the shift segues to the next stanza addressed to the congregation (see Introduction: Form and Rhetorical Criticism).

47. The circumlocution, *God takes it upon himself to be* (עַל-אֱלֹהִים, lit., "is upon God") aims to unravel a terse use of the preposition עַל ("upon"), which has no one-word equivalent in English — "with" in many English versions misses the thought. *'al* here signifies that God feels the burden or duty to be David's shield (*IBHS*, P. 11.2.13c, p. 217). Some English versions emend the text to *'ālî* ("O most high God"), but the final *yodh* is missing, unlike *'ālî* in v. 8[9].

48. See GKC, 127b.

12   If a sinner does not repent,[49]
          he will sharpen his sword;[50]
          he will bend and string his bow.
13   And[51] he will prepare his deadly weapons;
          he will make ready his flaming arrows.
14   Observe: whoever[52] is pregnant[53] with evil
          conceives malice and gives birth to deception.
15   Whoever digs a pit and hews it out
          falls into the trap he has made.
16   The trouble he causes recoils on him;
          his violence comes down on his own head.
17   I will give thanks to "I AM" because of his righteousness;
          I will sing the praises of the name of "I AM" Most High.

To the director of music. Upon the *gittith.*

49. Lit., "if he does not turn." Almost all the English versions think the antecedent if "he" is a reference to the human turning back [from sin]. Only the KJV ("he turns not back") and NIV ("does not relent") retain the only stated antecedent, namely, God (v. 11[12]). Although nothing in the Hebrew text indicates a change of subject from God to a human being, semantic pertinence demands the psalmist refer to a human turning back from sin (i.e., repenting). The point of the psalm is that God is righteous and judges according to his character. If God relented from exacting justice, he would not be righteous. Deuteronomy 32:36 speaks of God relenting from exterminating Israel so that his enemies would not misunderstand and gloat. That notion, however, is foreign to this context. God may relent from his engaging in divine warfare when a person repents (Exod. 34:6; Psalm 51; Prov. 28:13). The probably indefinite pronoun (i.e., "if one does not repent") is glossed "sinner" for clarity.

50. Following Aquila, Jerome, and some rabbinic commentators, A. A. Macintosh ("Notes and Studies: A Consideration of Ps 7:12f.," *Journal of Theological Studies* 33 [1987]: 481-90) translates 11B-12A[12B-13A]: "God utterly condemns the unrepentant. Every day he whets his sword . . ." But this translation unnecessarily runs roughshod over the *soph passuq* at the end of verse 11[12] and stumbles over *'im* at the beginning of verse 12[13]. MT makes good sense if *zāʻam* is interpreted as intransitive.

51. An initial וְלוֹ (lit., "to him/it") in the Hebrew text is ambiguous. It may mean "for him[-self]" (so ASV, BBE, DBY, ERV, ESV, JPS, KJV, YLT, NAS, NJB, NKJ), or "against him [the foe]" (so NET) or be an untranslatable, centripetal *lamedh* (text; so also NIV, CSB, NAB, NLT, NRSV; see T. Muraoka, "On the So-called *Dativus Ethicus* in Hebrew," *Journal of Theological Studies* 29 [1978]: 497). The LXX reading is attractive (καὶ ἐν αὐτῷ, "and on it [the string]") but grammatically unlikely because *qšt* is feminine and the pronoun of *lô'* is masculine.

52. Since the pronoun lacks an antecedent, it is probably indefinite, whoever (*IBHS*, P. 4.4.2, pp. 70f.).

53. The rare lexeme *ḥbl* may be glossed by "be pregnant" (*HALOT*, p. 285f. s.v. IV *ḥbl*) or "to writhe in childbirth" (*BDB*, p. 287 s.v. I. *ḥbl).* Song 8:5 favors "to go into labor," but the parallel of Ps. 7:14[15] favors "be pregnant."

PART III. COMMENTARY

I. Introduction

A. Literary Context

Psalm 7 draws to a close the series of royal petitions (see "Literary Context" of Psalms 5 and 6). Cush's libelous accusation against David provokes the righteous king to confess in this public prayer God's cosmic rule of righteousness and justice. He draws his prayer and confession to conclusion with a promise: "I will sing the praises of *the name* of 'I AM' Most High." The praise of the Most High's *name* ties together Psalms 7–9. Psalm 8 begins and ends with the refrain "I AM," our Lord, how majestic is *your name* in all the earth," and Psalm 9:1-2[2-3] begins: "I will sing the praise of *your name, O* Most High."

B. Legal Context and Argument

Israel has one king too many; God anointed righteous David before he eliminated wicked Saul. The conflict on earth between David's good and Saul's evil displays on the stage of salvation history God's righteousness as cosmic Judge. The innocent king lives by faith in God's righteousness, and the wicked king and his army live by faith in human might and cunning. The innocent king's faith expresses itself in petitions to "I AM" as the cosmic Judge to rescue him from the jaws of his ravishing foes. His formidable adversaries accuse David of high treason, a capital offense. In Psalm 7 we learn: "no weapon forged against you will prevail, and you will refute every tongue that accuses you. This is the heritage of the slaves of 'I AM,' and this is their vindication from me, declares 'I AM'" (Isa. 54:17).

The righteous king seeks his refuge in God against *all* his foes (vv. 1-2[2-3]) and thereupon presents his petitions in the form of a legal brief. His brief consists of a purgatory oath of his innocence (vv. 3-5[4-6]; cf. Exod. 22:10f.), and of a counterplea for poetic justice (vv. 6-12[7-13]).

The purgatory oath is based on the principle of ban-innocence: a person is innocent unless proved guilty (Deut. 17:4). Job made a similar defense in Job 31, "one of the moral peaks of the Old Testament."[54] Two stipulations of God's covenant with Israel necessitated his oath. First, "do not blaspheme God or curse the ruler of your people" (Exod. 22:28). *A minore* ("curse") *ad maius* ("treason")

---

54. D. Kidner, *Psalms 1–72: An Introduction and Commentary on Books I and II* (Leicester, UK/Downers Grove, IL: InterVarsity, 1973), p. 63.

the stipulation regards blasphemy and treason as correlatives; this is so because the king is sacred by prophetic anointing. Both Shimei and Naboth were put to death for violating this law (1 Kgs. 2:9; 21:8-14). Second, God's covenant protects the innocent: "One witness is not enough to convict anyone accused of any crime or offense they may have committed. A matter must be established by the testimony of two or three witnesses" (Deut. 19:15; cf. 17:6). David's pure conscience does not condemn him (vv. 9-11[10-12]), and neither do priest, judge, or prophet (Deut. 17:8-9). Even Saul's own son, Jonathan, risks his life in defense of David (1 Samuel 20). David's counterplea also finds its basis in Israel's covenant; namely a false witness is to be punished as that witness intended to do to the other party (Deut. 19:16-21).

Since the wicked king functions as Israel's highest court on earth, the righteous king appeals to the higher court of God's throne. At the dedication of the temple, Solomon prayed for poetic justice from this high court: "Judge between your servants, condemning the guilty by bringing down on their heads what they have done, and vindicating the innocent by treating them in accordance with their innocence" (1 Kgs. 8:31-32).

C. Form and Rhetorical Criticism

Psalm 7 is a lament of the innocent king. H. Schmidt labeled it a prayer of the accused,[55] confirming inductively the credibility of the psalm's superscript.

The psalm falls into two stanzas, as can be discerned by the change of addressees: petitions to God to show himself righteous (vv. 1-9[2-10]) and confessions to the congregation that the Most High is righteous (vv. 10-16[11-17]).[56] According to Gerald Sheppard, prayers were meant to be overheard by the congregation.[57] Moreover, according to G. Morson and C. Emerson, "there [is] a tendency to 'depersonalize' and 'disembody' the speech of the authoritative figure so that it is not perceived as merely one person's opinion."[58]

Each stanza has two strophes and each strophe has two units. The two strophes of the petition stanza (vv. 1-9[2-10]) consist both of fervid pleas to rescue the innocent (vv. 1-5[2-6]) and of a counterplea that the Most High vindicate the

---

55. Cited by Tigay, "Psalm 7:5 and Ancient Near Eastern Treaties," p. 178.

56. Carleen Mondolfo, "Finding Their Voices," *Horizons in Biblical Theology* 24 (2002): 27-52.

57. Gerald T. Sheppard, "Enemies and the Politics of Prayer in the Book of Psalms," in *The Bible and the Politics of Exegesis*, ed. P. Day et al. (Cleveland: Pilgrim, 1991).

58. Gary S. Morson and Caryl Emerson, *Mikhail Bakhtin: Creation of a Prosaics* (Stanford, CA: Stanford University Press, 1990), p. 164.

innocent by bringing disaster on the wicked (vv. 6-9[7-10]). The two strophes of the confidence stanza (vv. 10-17[11-18]) confess that God is righteous (vv. 10-13[11-14]) and praises the Most High's righteousness in upholding proverbs of poetic justice (vv. 14-17[15-18]). The last three strophes are each four verses. The psalm pivots on verse 9B[10B]. The confession that God is righteous segues the agitated petitions for God to display his righteousness into the serene confessions that he is righteous. The four petition strophes reflect an alternating structure:

A. For Self: Petition to rescue righteous	1-5[2-6]
B. For Enemy: Petition to let disaster bring wicked to an end	6-9A [7-10A]
Transition: The Tester of thoughts and emotions is righteous	9B [10B]
A'. For Self: Righteous judge is my warrior	10-13[11-14]
B'. For Enemy: Praise that malice of wicked is repaid in kind	14-17[15-18]

The two key words of the psalm are the titles and descriptions of "I AM"[59] and words related to the concept of righteousness (e.g., justice, upright, integrity, vv. 6, 8[7, 9] [4×], 9[10] [2×], 10[11], 11[12], 17[18]).[60] The two combine in: "righteous judge," "decree justice" (vv. 6, 11[7, 12]); "judge the peoples," "vindicate me" (v. 8[9]); "righteous God" (vv. 9[10], 17[18]); "saves the upright" (v. 10[11]); "I will give thanks to 'I AM' because of his righteousness" (v. 17[18]).

The exegesis follows:

Superscript	
I. Petitions:	1[2-10]
A. Petition for deliverance	1-5[2-6]
1. *Affirmation of trust and petition*	1-2[2-3]
a. Trust	1[2]
b. Petition	2[3]
2. *Purgatory oath*	3-5[4-6]
a. Threefold conditions	3-4[4-5]
b. Threefold curse	5[6]
B. Petitions for justice	6-9[7-9]

59. "I AM's" titles are: "my God" (vv. 1, 3, 6[2, 4, 7]), "enthroned over assembled peoples on high" (v. 7[8]), "Most High" (v. 8[9]), "God Most High" (v. 10[11]), "'I AM' Most High" (v. 17[18]).

60. See also N. H. Ridderbos, *Die Psalmen, Stilistische Verfahren und Aufbau; Mit Besonderer Berücksichtigung von Ps 1–41*, Beiheft zur Zeitschrift für die alttestamentliche Wissenschaft, 117 (New York/Berlin: De Gruyter, 1972).

D. Message

Psalm 7 reminds persecuted and defamed saints that they are elected to engage in a holy war occasioned by the persistence of evil within the cosmic and social orders (1 Kgs. 8:31f.). Humans, apart from God's saving grace, are pregnant with evil, plan trouble, and bring forth deception (v. 14[15]; Ps. 5:9[10]; Rom. 3:10-17). Malice, deceit, and murder ever war against righteousness, justice, and truth. There can be no truce, for evil loves company (cf. Gen. 3:1-5; Prov. 1:10-15). So God's persecuted elect must fight the good fight (1 Tim. 6:12) — that is to say, as trusting lambs against ferocious lions. Saints win in this holy war both by seeking refuge in God[61] and by their zeal for the honor of his name. Sluggards, the apathetic, idolaters, and the self-confident go down in defeat in this spiritual warfare. As the psalms cited in footnote 61 show, seeking refuge in God is not a retreat into passivity but an advance into spiritual warfare in the name of "I AM." The warrior's faith in God's righteousness as cosmic ruler of all and as the examiner of every hidden, human thought and emotion attenuates their

---

61. The verb occurs in Pss. 5:11[12]; 7:1[2]; 11:1; 16:1; 25:20; 31:1[2], 19[20]; 37:40; 57:1[2]; 64:10[11]; 71:1; 118:8, 9; 141:8; 144:2; the noun in Pss. 14:6; 27:1; 31:2[3], 4[5]; 61:4; 62:7-8[8-9]; 71:7; 73:28; 94:22; 142:4.

fervid pleas into calm confidence, purging them of cowardly fear, of showing inappropriate pity and of "stupid humility" (Luther).[62] The Lord Jesus Christ exemplifies this ideal warrior, of whom David was a type, and is the Christian's sword and shield.

II. Exegesis

A. Superscript

Uniquely, the superscript labels the psalm as "Lament" (see note 33). Internal evidence supports interpreting *leōāwiḏ* as *by David* (Psalm 5: Superscript). John Eaton makes the case that this is a royal petition:

> He summons God "to arise" in judgment over the peoples (vv. 6f.) and so resolve the crisis he is facing. Only Yahweh's anointed could appropriately invoke the world-dominating epiphany to bring his personal salvation. But this royal element should not be insulated from the rest of the psalm, where in fact there are indications of threatening war (vv. 11 and 13f.) and of the psalmist's military capacity (vv. 5, 11) and "glory" (v. 6). There is nothing to clash with this interpretation.[63]

The psalmist's petition matches the historical period when a determined Saul pursued David. David's lament matches David's narrative in the following ways: being pursued to death (vv. 1-2[2-3]; 1 Samuel 20-26); is an ally of the enemy (v. 4[5]; 1 Samuel 17-19); is slandered (v. 4[5]; 1 Sam. 24:9; 26:19); is innocent (vv. 3-6[4-7]; 1 Sam. 24:10); appeals to God as judge (vv. 6-13[7-14]; 1 Sam. 24:12, 15); depends upon God to bring disaster on the wicked (v. 9[10]; 1 Sam. 24:15; 26:10); cites Proverbs on evil (v. 14[15]; 1 Sam. 24:13); and speaks of evil/guilt as in his hands (v. 3[4]; 1 Sam. 26:18). Finally, the accusation that he rescued Saul's enemy (v. 7:4B[5B]) fits the treaty stipulations in that historical epoch.

The historical incident *which he sang to "I AM" concerning the accusations of Cush, a Benjamite,* is unknown in other sources, suggesting the psalm reflects an early, independent, authentic witness to the life of David. As a

---

62. Cited by Hans-Joachim Kraus, *Psalms 1–59: A Continental Commentary,* trans. Hilton C. Oswald (Minneapolis: Fortress Press, 1993), p. 176.

63. John H. Eaton, *Kingship and the Psalms* (SBT, second series, 32; Naperville, IL: Allenson, 1976), p. 30f.

Benjamite, Cush was probably a supporter of Saul.[64] A Jewish tradition identifies Cush with Saul.[65] The content of the psalm suggests that Cush accused David during the time of Saul's determined attempt to kill David (see above). The incident involving the accusation of Doeg the Edomite, a mercenary of Saul, provides an analogous background to this psalm. In that case, however, David took responsibility for exposing the priests of Nob to Saul's vengeance (1 Sam. 22:22).

B. Petitions (7:1-9[2-10])

1. Petition for Deliverance (7:1-5[2-6])

The victimized king, after stating, *I seek refuge in you* (Ps. 5:11[12]) — not in his own wit or strength — pleads to be delivered from all his foes (vv. 1-2[2-3]). He approaches God as a Judge and protests his innocence (vv. 3-5[4-6]). These two units are linked by identical introductory vocatives: *"'I AM' my God"* (vv. 1 and 2[3 and 4]).

a. Affirmation of Trust and Petition (7:1-2[2-3])

As in Psalms 5 and 6, the psalmist forgoes flummery and addresses God directly; his need is urgent. His enemies like a pack of lions chase him down, and if their leader catches his holy prey, he will tear him apart and carry him off to devour him, leaving his bones ignominiously without proper burial. Unlike David who rescued his sheep from the mouths of lions and bears, there is no one to rescue the shepherd king. The quatrain (four lines) is linked by the logical particle "otherwise" and by the lexeme "rescue" — in the Hebrew text the last word of each verse.

1[2]: Affirmation of Trust "I AM" (*yhwh*, 5:1[2]), *my God* (5:2[3]), combines God's intimate covenant relationship with Israel with his incommunicable attributes of infinite wisdom and power. *Save me* (6:4[5]) *from all* (6:10[11]), so that none remain to harass me. *Who pursue* likens his enemies to lions in a chase or hunt (v. 2[3]). Lions symbolized power, cruelty, and ruthlessness (Isa. 5:29; Nah. 2:11-12).

---

64. Superscripts to the period in which David was persecuted by Saul are found in Pss. 7, 34, 52, 54, 56, 57, 59, 142.

65. Saul's father, a Benjamite, was named Kish.

2[3]: Petition for Salvation   Otherwise *he will tear . . . apart* has the full thought
of "to seize a creature predatorily and tear its flesh violently." *Me* (נַפְשִׁי, *naphšî;*
6:4[5]) *like a lion* (v. 1[2]). As a shepherd, David was very familiar with the ferocious African lion (1 Sam. 17:34-35; see below on v. 5[6]). The shift from many
enemies to *one who snatches me away* also occurs in Psalms 5:9[10]; 17:6-7[7-8];
35:7-8; 55:19-20[20-21]; 109:4-5[5-6].

b. Purgatory Oath (7:3-5[4-6])

In verses 3-5[4-6] David presents exculpatory evidence to defend himself. In the
conditional protasis ("if") he lists three accusations pertaining to treason (vv.
3-4[4-5]), and in the apodosis he defends himself by invoking on himself three
dire consequences pertaining to his being mauled by a lion if proved guilty of
treason.

i. Threefold Conditions (7:3-4[4-5])

3[4]   *If I have done* means deliberately to perform an act that affects someone
favorably or, as here, unfavorably. *This* refers to Cush's accusation (superscript),
specified in verse 3[4] as treachery. *Guilt* refers vaguely to crimes of a social,
property, or commercial nature.[66] *On my hands* shows that "guilt" is a metonym
for a crime that he committed. He may not have done the crime himself, but if
he instigated it, he is guilty, as witnessed in the Nuremberg trials.

4[5]   Verse 4[5] specifies the abstract accusations of verse 3[4]. The glosses *to my
ally* (n. 35) and *treachery* (lit., "evil")[67] are necessary to clarify that a breach of an
ancient Near Eastern treaty is in view. Several ancient Near Eastern treaties and
other texts relating to them call upon allies to treat the other's enemy as their own
enemy. One text from ancient Ugarit reads: "To my lord's enemy I am an enemy,
and to my lord's ally I am an ally."[68] Assuming the former ally is Saul, according
to this interpretation David is guilty of high treason for rescuing Saul's enemy to

---

66. R. Knierim, *TLOT*, 2.8950, s.v. *ʿāwel.*

67. Masculine רַע and its feminine doublet *rāʿâ*, with no difference in meaning, denotes *evil*
(ill-disposed and sin), "wickedness," "injustice," "wrong," "calamity," "distress," "disaster," "deprivation," "misfortune." Stoebe (*TLOT*, 2.491, s.v. *ṭôḇ*) suggests that the basic meaning of *rāʿâ* is what
harms life, not what benefits it. More fundamentally its root, *r*, conveys the factual judgment that
something is bad, whether it be a concrete physical state (e.g., "ugly" cows, Gen. 41:3; "poor/bad"
figs, Jer. 24:2), an abstraction, "calamity/disaster," or moral behavior that injures others (Ps. 15:3).
The value judgment that something is bad depends on the taste of the one making the evaluation,
so "in one's eyes" is often added to the word.

68. See "Treaty Between Mursilis and Duppi-Tessub of Amuru," Para. 9, *ANET*, p. 204.

do David's dirty work against Saul. *Without cause* (n. 37) is necessarily added, for many fled to David for good reason (1 Sam. 22:1, 20). Cush's accusation implied that David gave sanctuary to the wicked king's enemies without good reason. David could be open to this accusation, because he accepted into his ragtag army "all those who were in distress or in debt or discontented . . . about four hundred men were with him" (1 Sam. 22:2). If David had accepted into his army any guilty of high treason, he could be accused of disloyalty to his king. According to our historical sources, however, David was always loyal to Saul, except when he cut off the hem of Saul's garment; and then he confessed his wrong against God's anointed king (1 Sam. 24:4-15). So we should assume David did not accept any guilty of high treason into his army.

ii. Threefold Curse (7:5[6])

5[6] In his quest for justice and his protestation of innocence, David implicitly likens his pursuers to a lion on the hunt and himself to the prey, in a crescendo of three wishes. The climactic third, *and let him [fatally] trample* (2 Kgs. 7:17; 14:9; Mic. 5:8[7]) *to the ground,* adds a vivid touch to the grisly scene. *And my glory* in poetry seems to be an idiom for self-reference.[69] *In the dust* is an apt metaphor for desiccation and ignominy (Gen. 3:14; 1 Sam. 2:8; 1 Kgs. 16:2; Isa. 47:1; Pss. 22:15[16]; 44:25[26]; 119:25).

2. Petition That Disaster Terminate Wicked (7:6-9[7-10])

a. Plea to convene court (7:6-7[7-8])

6[7]: Plea to Decree Justice On the one hand, God's king must not begin holy war without God's presence, as the prophet Samuel had to teach King Saul (1 Sam. 10:8; 13:1-4). On the other hand, God desires the king to prosecute holy war with unqualified zeal, as the prophet Elisha had to teach King Joash (2 Kgs. 13:14-19). David does not disappoint. With unqualified zeal for righteousness and justice, three times he petitions "I AM" to rise up and engage the enemy.[70] "I AM" waits for David's zeal to rouse him from his apparent slumber and decree justice. "Apparent slumber," for God neither slumbers nor sleeps (Ps. 121:3-4). *Arise, "I AM"*

---

69. After considering different explanations of this use of "my glory," C. John Collins (*NIDOTTE*, 2.573, s.v. *kbd*) draws the conclusion: "Actually none of these explanations for this use is self-evidently superior to *BDB*'s poet. as the seat of honour in the inner man, the noblest part of man." For defense of the traditional interpretation see McKay, "My Glory — A Mantle of Praise," *Scottish Journal of Theology* 31 (1978): 161-72.

70. The force of these imperatives is not that of orders from a superior to an inferior, but that of urgent requests from an inferior to a superior (*IBHS*, P. 34.3b, p. 568).

reprises Moses' old war cry (Num. 10:35f.). The faithful warriors call upon God to arise from his throne of judgment between the cherubim and to commence holy war against their enemies. In holy war the strength of the enemy is discounted, for "the battle is not yours, but God's" (2 Chron. 20:15). An index of what happens when God fights *in . . . anger* — that is to say, "in . . . moral indignation" — can be seen in David's own plight when he was the target of God's anger (Ps. 6:1-8[2-9]). *Rise up* in parallel to the war-cry "arise" probably has the same sense here and in Psalm 94:2, although it could mean "exalt yourself" or "be exalted" (2 Chron. 32:23; 1 Chron. 14:2; Isa. 33:10; 52:13; 57:15). *And awake* means to rouse somebody to activity that requires extra effort, such as war, work, or love.[71] *My God* (*'ēlay*) presumably has the same meaning as other words for God (*'ĕlôah*, and its intensive plural *'ĕlôhîm*), which signify the quintessence of divine transcendence.[72] *Decree* denotes a superior stating something with authority and/or force to a subordinate with the purpose of eliciting a response. The Most High speaks with authority to bring about *justice* (מִשְׁפָּט), which may mean "to act as lawgiver, governor" in a most comprehensive sense, or, as in this context, "to decide cases and/or execute justice by delivering the oppressed and punishing the oppressor." In this sense מִשְׁפָּט implies the interaction of three parties: the oppressor(s), the oppressed, and a "judge" who has the sanction to condemn and punish the former and to clear and reward the latter.

7[8]: Plea for God to Assume Role as Cosmic Judge   The innocent king now asks the Most High to hold an assize of peoples from near and far, and, as God takes his place on high, vindicate his innocent king by punishing his enemy. *The assembled* denotes a company assembled together by appointment. *Peoples* (לְאֻמִּים) refers to *foreign* peoples. *Let gather around you*[73] more literally means "to go in a circle."[74] *Return* (see n. 41) also reprises Moses' war-cry upon the return of the Warrior to his throne. *On high* glosses an idiom, "to the height" (Ps. 75:5[6]; LXX εἰς ὕψος, "on high").

b. Plea for a Verdict (7:8-9[9-10])

8[9]: Plea to Be Vindicated   *Let "I AM" judge* (יָדִין) means "to issue [just] verdicts or edicts." *The peoples* (עַמִּים; *'ammîm*), probably a synonym for "foreign

---

71. Victor P. Hamilton, *NIDOTTE*, 3.337, s.v. *'ăl*.
72. It is not clear how the meaning of *'ĕlôah* is distinct from *'ēl*. The significance of the *h* ending is unknown. Furthermore, *'ĕlôah* and *'ĕlôhîm* can both be either indefinite or definite nouns.
73. *BDB*, p. 686.
74. *HALOT*, 2.739, s.v. *sbb*.

peoples," denotes any community of people, often larger than a clan but less numerous than a race, who are related and unified in some way as by blood, history/ memory, and/or culture. *Judge me* (*šāpaṭ*, v. 7[8]) petitions "I AM" to hand down a verdict that proves David's innocence and his enemy's guilt. By rescuing David, who relies totally on prayer against an enemy who relies totally on human might, God displays his righteousness and justice in the sight of all peoples. Unlike penitential psalms, David asks no favors, no mercy. Rather, he wants all nations to see that Israel's God judges *according to my righteousness* (Ps. 5:8[9]). The issue is guilty or not guilty (i.e., "declared right"), not of moral self-qualification to merit God's favor.[75] *Integrity* signifies "completeness," and "integrity," not in the sense of one who perseveres in his work and completes it, but with reference to a process that has already been accomplished in a person or thing and "through imminent necessity will produce either a good or bad result."[76] Here this comprehensive term denotes that he is wholeheartedly committed to communal loyalty. There is not a treacherous bone in David.

9[10]: Plea That Disaster Terminate the Wicked   *Let a disaster* (1 Sam. 26:10) *bring to an end* (Pss. 12:1[2] and 77:8[9]), *I pray, the wicked* (see n. 44). The wicked, the antonym of the righteous, are the guilty and are always spoken of in terms of a community.[77] *But establish* connotes firmness, stability, and permanence. Only God is able to test a person's true character, and so hand down a just verdict. The verb glossed *the one who tests* is used in Proverbs 17:3 for the process of cupellation in testing the karat of silver and of a fiery furnace in testing the karat of gold. *The heart* denotes the inner forum where a person decides one's religious and moral conduct on the interplay of thoughts, feelings, desires, and religious affections.[78] *And emotions* glosses "kidneys." "Of all human organs," says Kellermann, "the OT associates the kidneys in particular with a variety of emotions," from joy (Prov. 23:15f.) to deepest agony (Ps. 73:21).

---

75. Hans-Joachim Kraus (*Psalms 1-59*, p. 173) notes: "We are here dealing not with *iustificatio impii* but with the *iustificatio iusti*, in other words, with the fact that God brings to light the righteousness of the righteous against all questioning and temptation."

76. Cf. K. Koch, *TLOT*, 3.1425, s.v. *tmm*.

77. K. Richards, "A Form and Traditio-historical Study of *rš'*" (Ph.D. dissertation, Claremont, CA, 1970; cf. *ZAW*, 83:402).

78. B. Waltke, *The Book of Proverbs: Chapters 1-15* (Grand Rapids: Eerdmans, 2005), pp. 90-92.

3. Confidence: Righteous God Will Execute Poetic Justice (7:10-17[11-18])

a. Cosmic Judge Is Righteous and a Mighty Warrior (7:10-13[11-14])

As David describes his enemies in the plural and in the singular, he also applies God's justice to peoples and to himself. "It would be contrary to every principle of just reasoning to suppose," says Calvin, "that he who governs many nations neglects even one man."[79] The strophe is unified by "I AM's" armament: a shield on defense, and a swordsman and archer on offense.

i. God Is a Righteous Judge and Divine Warrior (7:10-11[11-12])
10[11]: God a Shield That Defends Innocent King My shield (מָגִנִּי, *māginnî*) is a round, light shield, made of wood or wicker and covered with thick leather rubbed with oil (Isa. 21:5) to preserve it and to make it glisten; it is carried by the light infantry to ward off the enemy's sword, spear, or arrows (Pss. 18:2[3], 30[31], 35[36]). The larger shield (*ṣinnâ*, cf. 2 Chron. 14:8) was either oblong or rectangular in shape and carried by the heavy infantry or armor bearer (Ps. 5:12[13]; Gen. 15:1). *The one who saves* (see 7:2[3]) . . . *heart* (v. 9B[10B]). *Upright* derives from a word whose literal meaning has the geometric notion of being straight, either flat horizontally ("smooth") or upright vertically. Its predominant figurative use assumes a fixed ethical order by which action can be judged as straight, upright, and level.

11[12]: Filled with Moral Indignation Usually the verbs associated with the Hebrew lexeme for *indignant* have a clear judgment aspect (Ps. 69:24[25]; Ezek. 21:31[36]; 22:31; Zeph. 3:8), and "I AM's" indignation finds expression in human pain and suffering (Pss. 38:3[4]; 69:24[25]; 78:49; 102:10[11]; Jer. 15:17). Kidner comments: "His *indignation every day* . . . is more constant than any human zeal, having no tendency to cool down into either compromise or despair."[80] Without constant moral indignation, his longsuffering would lose meaning (Exod. 34:6-7; 1 Pet. 3:9).

ii. God Is a Mighty Warrior (7:12-13[13-14])
12[13]: His Sword The imagery of "I AM" as divine Warrior is strikingly similar to Moses' song (Deut. 32:36-44). *If a sinner does not repent* (see n. 49), God dispatches his guilty enemies quickly and decisively, as indicated by *he will sharpen his sword* in contrast to a blunt sword. The sword is the most important weapon of

79. John Calvin, *Commentary on the Book of Psalms*, vol. 1 (Grand Rapids: Baker; reprinted 2003), p. 83.
80. D. Kidner, *Psalms 1–72*, p. 64.

warfare in the biblical world. "Ranging from sixteen inches to three feet in length, with one or both sides sharpened, this implement was used for thrust and slashing opponents in armed conflict."[81] *He will tread his bow* on the ground with his foot while he bends it with his hand in order to bend it for maximum power. *And* [with the other hand] *will string* glosses a verb that means "to fix" (Pss. 11:2; 21:12[13]; Isa. 51:13)[82] *his bow.* The archer may shoot his arrows from afar (Gen. 21:16) or from ambush (Jer. 9:8). His arrows strike suddenly (Ps. 64:7[8]) and so swiftly that time stands still (Hab. 3:11). These qualities — long-range, lightning-quick, unseen — made the bow and arrow the prime symbol of divine justice meted out.[83]

13[14]: His Flaming Arrows   Verse 12B[13B] refers to the bow and verse 13[14], to its arrows. *He will prepare* is the same Hebrew lexeme for "and he will string." *His . . . weapons* glosses the genus for anything that is finished/made/or produced, and here functions as metonym for the specie flaming arrows (Ps. 7:13B[14B]). *He will make ready* (lit., "to execute") signifies that the divine warrior puts into action the necessary means to secure the success of his flaming arrows (lit., "he makes his arrows into burning ones"). Incendiary arrows (tipped with tow or pitch) are even more fearful than ordinary arrows. Are they metaphors for lightning bolts (Ps. 18:14[15]; Zech. 9:14)?

b. Praise: God Is Righteous (7:14-17[15-18])

The final strophe strings together three original or well-known proverbs that teach the wages of sin is death (vv. 14-16[15-17]),[84] followed by praise to God

---

81. Leland Ryken, James C. Wilhoit, Tremper Longman III, eds., *Dictionary of Biblical Imagery* (Downers Grove, IL: InterVarsity, 1998), p. 835.

82. "Analogous to cocking a pistol" (Peter Craigie, *Psalms 1–50*, Word Biblical Commentary [Nashville: Thomas Nelson, 2004], p. 102).

83. Literary tragedies, such as *Prometheus* and *Oedipus*, in contrast to comedies, are short, and tragedy strikes quickly and decisively.

84. In an unfortunately influential thesis, K. Koch argued that righteousness and justice refer to a power-charged area *(tatsphären)* created by human deeds and that the notion that Yahweh rewards or punishes is lacking in Hebrew thinking. Yahweh's task in Hebrew thinking, according to Koch, is to ensure that the cosmic system functions properly (see K. Koch, "Gibt es ein Vergeltungsdogma im Alten Testament?" *Zeitschrift für Theologie und Kirche* 52 [1955]: 1-42; *TLOT*, 2.1046-65, s.v. *ṣdq*). One could argue Koch's interpretation on the basis both of verse 9[10] ("let the disaster, I pray, bring the wicked to an end") and these proverbs in isolation from the rest of the psalm. R. L. Hubbard ("Dynamic and Legal Processes in Psalm 7," *ZAW* 94 [1982]: 267-79), however, argues that the whole psalm is appealing to "I AM" to render a verdict. But Hubbard stops short and sees the divine verdict as merely enabling the dynamic process of the created world order to be effected. J. R. John Samuel Raj ("Cosmic Judge or Overseer of the World Order? The Role of Yahweh as Portrayed in Psalm 7," *Bangalore Theological Forum* 34, no. 2 [December 1, 2002]:

for upholding justice (v. 17[18]). *Observe* functions as a macro-syntactic sign to highlight the psalm's conclusion.

i. Proverbs Teaching Poetic Justice (7:14-16[15-17])

14[15]   The first proverb, using the metaphor of gestation, describes the development of the misuse of power from its conception to its parturition. The collocation, *conceives,* always followed by *and brings forth,* describes the act and result of sexual intercourse, more often than not a metaphor referring to the birth of *evil* (Job 15:35),[85] the misuse of power by deception and lying to hurt others (Ps. 5:5[6]; 6:8[9]).[86] *Malice* frequently designates the mendacious, outrageous, violent deeds of the enemy without being specific.[87] *Lies* signifies aggressive deceit intended to harm the other; it is used of Judas Iscariot (Ps. 109:2; Acts 1:20).

15[16]   The next proverb reinforces the last word of verse 14[15], "lies," by the figure of digging a pit (v. 14A[15A]). The figure depicts the enemy's cunning deception and deadly intention (Prov. 26:27A). A *pit* refers to a hole large enough that a person could not escape from it. A dry pit could function as a dungeon, and one with water as a cistern. *And hews it out* signifies the pit was given shape and form with heavy cutting; here to function as a booby-trap to kill the victim (Exod. 21:33). *Then they* [singular] *fall* (Ps. 5:10[11]) *into the trap they* (singular) *make* (v. 13[14]). *Trap* specifies a pit as a place designed to capture an animal or a person (Ps. 9:15[16]; Ezek. 19:8) and/or a place of decay and death (Job 33:24, 28; Jonah 2:6).

16[17]   As the proverb in verse 15[16] reinforces verse 14B[15B], so also the last proverb reinforces the notion of poetic justice in verse 15B[16B]. The third proverb uses the figure of a weight bashing a skull, as by stoning (Lev. 20:2, 27; 24:14, 16) or by dropping a stone on it (Num. 15:35). The proverbial string is brought full circle by the catchword *their* (singular) *malice* (v. 14[15]). The malice they conceived and

---

1-15) regards the psalm as a composite of these two viewpoints. But against all three, "I AM" is presented as a Divine Warrior who dynamically enacts the verdict; he sharpens his sword, bends his bow, and prepares his deadly weapons. Moreover, the binding together of the song of praise in verse 17[18] with the proverbs prevents the misunderstanding that this is a dynamic process within the created order, not a part of God's intervention in salvation history (see Bruce Waltke, *Proverbs 1-15,* pp. 73-76)

85. Victor Hamilton, *NIDOTTE,* 1.1058, s.v. *hrh.*

86. K. H. Bernhardt, *TDOT,* 1.143, s.v. *'awen.*

87. In designating the unspecified evil activity of enemies against the godly, *'āmāl* stands in connection with *'āwen* "iniquity" (Job 15:35; Pss. 10:7; 55:10[11]), *šeqer I* "lies" (Ps. 7:14[15]), *mirmâ* "deceit" (Job 15:35), and *ḥāmās* "violence" (Ps 7:16[17]); cf. Schwertner, *TLOT,* 2.926, s.v. *'āmāl.*

brought to birth in deception *recoils on their head,* the most important part of the other party. The vulnerable head in battle had to be protected by a helmet (1 Sam. 17:5). *And on their* (singular) *skull* refers to that part of the head as the base for hair (Ps. 68:21[22]; Jer. 2:16). H. Haag defines *"violence" (ḥāmās)* as "cold-blooded and unscrupulous infringement of the personal rights of others, motivated by greed and hate and often making use of physical violence and brutality." He also notes: "a favorite instrument of *chāmās* is false accusation and unjust judgment."[88]

ii. Song of Praise to the Most High for His Righteousness (7:17[18])

These gnomic truths are not due to some inexorable fixed order within the creation but due to *"I AM" Most High,* whose nature is righteous (v. 9[10]) and who decrees justice in human affairs (vv. 6[7]; 8[9], 11[12]). So the righteous king concludes the stanza in praise of his righteous God. *I will give thanks* (Ps. 6:5[6]) *to "I AM"* (יְהוָה) *because of his righteousness.* From the root of *and I will sing praise* is derived *mizmōr,* "a psalm" (Psalm 5: Superscript). The verb's core meaning denotes playing a musical instrument in the context of praise and worship, usually a stringed instrument (Pss. 33:2; 98:5; 144:9; 147:7), but sometimes also a percussion instrument (149:3). Usually it has the developed sense of sing to a musical accompaniment (Ps. 71:22-23).[89] *Of the name of* (Ps. 5:11[12]; "Literary Context") *"I AM" Most High* (*'elyôn,* Gen. 14:18-22). *'Elyôn* occurs in parallel with both "God" (*'ēl,* Pss. 73:11; 107:11) and with "I AM" (Pss. 7:16[17]; 21:7[8]; 83:18[19]). *'Elyôn* is the great King over all the gods (Ps. 18:13[14]); over all the earth (Ps. 47:2[3]); dwells in the heights above the clouds (Isa. 14:14); thunders from heaven (Ps. 18:13[14]); and is sovereign over good and ill (Lam. 3:38). This name is most fitting in a psalm that called upon "I AM" to return on high over the assembled people (v. 7[8]) and decree justice (v. 6[7]), and whose flaming arrows may be lightning bolts (v. 13[14]). This verse segues into the postscript that pertains to the psalm's musical performance.

4. Postscript

For the director of music (Psalm 6: superscript) *upon the gittîth* occurs in postscripts of Psalms 80 (Psalm 81: superscript) and 83 (Psalm 84: superscript); it probably refers to music that accompanied the performance of the psalm in Israel's worship. R. H. O'Connell makes a case that *'al haggittît* indicates "According to 'The (female) Winepresser' (melody)."[90] Whatever the meaning, the postscript

---

88. H. Haag, *TDOT,* 4.481f., s.v. *chāmās.*
89. L. C. Allen, NIDOTTE, *zāmar* 1.1116.
90. Robert H. O'Connell, *NIDOTTE,* 1.904, s.v. *gittît.*

and "selah" (end of v. 5[6]) give evidence that the psalm was shaped for use in Israel's worship at the temple. At a still later period it became associated with the Feast of Purim, which celebrated the victory of Esther after Haman had falsely accused the Jews.

Part IV. Conclusion

Psalm 7 spiritually fortifies the church in its struggle against the Devil, who from the beginning was a liar and a murderer. Aristotle once made a perceptive remark on the function of tragic drama: it "purged the emotions of pity and fear."[91] He seems to say that great plays have a cleansing function. The fate of a tragic hero universalizes emotions, and makes people see that in their sufferings and pain they are part of a whole, a sharer in humankind. Something of this sort happens to the saints in praying the psalms. Their emotions of outrage and fear at the apparent triumph of might over right are purged as they become part of Christ's victory over evil. When the weary years seem to bring them no relief, no intervention from on high, they participate in the historic victory of God's King over the diabolical enemy that he won through prayer of faith in crisis.

Psalm 7 portrays David as a type of Jesus Christ. Like David in this psalm, he was falsely accused of blasphemy against God and of treason against Caesar and of being a pretender to God's throne. Like David, he did not take military armor in his own hand to avenge himself but depended on God to deliver him. By rescuing them from the realm of death God displayed their innocence. Christ tasted the worst of human folly without recrimination and so shows himself fit to judge all people (John 1:29; 5:27; 20:31).

91. Aristotle, *Poetics* 1447a13 (1987, 1).

CHAPTER 5

Psalm 32: Forgiveness for the Justified

PART I. VOICE OF THE CHURCH

I. Introduction

Of the seven penitential psalms, 32 and 51 are the most overtly "penitential" although, as Bruce will argue, the form of Psalm 32 is mixed. But as we have already discussed in our historical survey of Psalm 51,[1] the church's history on penance and penitence is long and complex. This we have further outlined in chapter 1. The terms in the semantic range of "penitence" are not always clearly distinguished, for cultural changes produce subtle differences in the usage of distinct terms during different periods. Confession, contrition, repentance, penitence, penance, conversion, as well as baptism, forgiveness, reconciliation, are all intertwined in the cultural changes and teachings of the church. For this psalm we shall simply focus upon Augustine's pastoral theology to recover an incarnational paradigm distinctive of this great Father of the church. We say "incarnational," for he takes up an already-accepted early church tradition of reading the Psalter as the transcript of Christ's early life. He proceeds further, using 1 Timothy 2:5, to understand the mediatorial work of Christ as mediating the interrelation of the old and new covenants.[2]

---

1. See Bruce K. Waltke and James M. Houston with Erika Moore, *The Psalms as Christian Worship (PACW)* (Grand Rapids: Eerdmans, 2010), pp. 446-62.
2. Michael Cameron, "The Christological Substructure of Augustine's Figurative Exegesis," in *Augustine,* trans. and ed. Pamela Black (Notre Dame: University of Notre Dame Press, 1997), pp. 74-103.

II. Augustine's Hermeneutic of Divine Grace

To appreciate **Augustine**'s commentary we also need to recover Augustine's hermeneutic of divine grace. We will trace the development of this hermeneutic chronologically, focusing on his Christological and figurative interpretation, on his confessions, and on grace. With Ambrose bishop of Milan as his mentor, Augustine was baptized in 387. But he tells us that already a year before, in 386, he had read all of Paul's epistles "with the greatest attention and care."[3] A number of episodes described later in the *Confessions* bear out that claim. In 391 Augustine was ordained a priest, and by 396 he was elected a bishop, producing the most dramatic decade of his life. Halfway through it he developed a crucial Christological and figurative approach peculiar to his interpretation of the Psalms. This interpretation became his defense first against the heresy of the Manichees, and then later against the heresy of Pelagius. In his first notes on the Psalms (392), he demonstrates his awareness of the voice of Christ in the psalms.

The *Confessions*, written soon after 397, just after Augustine had been consecrated as a bishop,[4] is one of the most remarkable works of early Christianity, for it has made Augustine personally known as no other writer of antiquity. Currently he is being recognized afresh, as "the Father of Western Consciousness." He explored the inner life of the self as no other had ever expressed before or indeed for many centuries after him. The literary, philosophical, and theological character of his *Confessions* has drawn more attention and intense debate among scholars than most other works.

But many modern scholars profoundly misunderstand him.[5] Augustine's *Confessions* are not, as they suppose, the fruit of "self-understanding" any more than his new identity as a Christian could ever be self-making. Their misunderstanding is the product of "modernity,"[6] not of biblical faith. Even Christians today distort their "Christian identity" when it is conceptualized largely as the product of their self-achieved professional ambitions. Augustine is not Descartes'

---

3. Carol Harrison, *Rethinking Augustine's Early Theology* (Oxford: Oxford University Press, 2006), p. 117.

4. Frederick Van Fleteren, *Confessiones: Augustine through the Ages*, ed. Allan D. Fitzgerald, O.S.A. (Grand Rapids: Eerdmans, 1995), pp. 227-32.

5. For example, Charles Taylor traces the origins of "the self" from Plato, to Augustine, and then on to Descartes. See Charles Taylor, *Sources of the Self* (Cambridge, MA: Harvard University Press, 1992), p. ix. Peter Brown succumbs to the same lack of understanding regarding the radical nature of Augustine's *Confessions* in his magnum opus, *Augustine of Hippo* (Berkeley: University of California Press, 1967), pp. 88-114.

6. See Anthony Giddens, *Modernity and Self-Identity: Self and Society in the Late Modern Age* (Stanford, CA: Stanford University Press, 1991).

forebear, for he is "anti-modern" theologically, as we shall see from his reflections on Psalm 32.[7] Rather, Augustine's task is to demonstrate that human self-knowledge is only possible in the light of knowing God, that is, as a sinner in need of the Redeemer, Jesus Christ. For the "self-made individual" today, both Psalm 32 and the *Confessions* are wholly irrelevant!

Biblically, "confession" has two basic forms: confession of faith (Matt. 3:6; James 5:16) and confession of sin/s (Matt. 10:32; 1 John 1:9). Confession of sin/s has four dimensions: to God alone (Pss. 32:3-6; 51:4-6[6-8]); to one another (James 5:16); to a spiritual adviser (Acts 19:18); and to the entire church, publicly (1 Cor. 5:3ff.; 2 Cor. 2:6ff.). In Augustine's writings we have examples of all four forms of confession. The immediate context for the writing of the *Confessions* has been variously explained. It may have been the accusation of the Donatists, that the new bishop of Hippo was still a crypto-Manichean. If so, this forced Augustine to describe intimately the circumstances of his Christian conversion in his own defense. Or, it has been argued that his *Confessions* is a polemic against Pelagianism.[8] More positively, for Augustine, the act of making "confession" was for "making the truth," indeed of seeking to "live the truth."[9]

His first homily on Psalm 32 dates from the 390s; it is more of a brief "spiritual paraphrase" of only sixty lines in two pages that could have been annotated within his Bible. Yet already it is an innovative kind of mini-Confessions, a preparation for his great work on "living-the-truth-through-grace," the *Confessions*. Possibly in 412/13[10] he expanded his second homily on Psalm 32 to 826 lines (twenty-three pages), which is the text used here. "Grace-reading" now becomes more boldly "grace-provoking" and "grace-living," with all the richness of the *Confessions* behind it. He begins boldly: "This is a psalm about God's grace, and about our being justified by no merits whatever on our own part, but only by the mercy of the Lord our God."[11] He devotes the first ten pages to the apostle Paul's teaching on grace in order to demonstrate that the Christian can only read David's lament through the lens of the apostle Paul. Since it is a Pauline exegesis, we cannot appreciate Augustine's exegesis without understanding his pastoral concerns.

7. Thomas Harmon, "Reconsidering Charles Taylor's Augustine," *Pro Ecclesia* 20, no. 2 (Spring 2011): 189-209; Wayne Hankey, "Between and Beyond Augustine and Descartes: More Than a Source of Self," *Augustinian Studies* 32, no. 1 (2001): 65-74.

8. P. Courcelle, *Les Confessions de saint Augustin dans la tradition littéraire: Antécédents et postérité* (Paris: Études Augustiniennes, 1963).

9. James J. O'Donnell, *Augustine's Confessions*, vol. 1 (Oxford: Clarendon, 1992), p. xxx.

10. Henri Rondet, S.J., "Essai sur la chronologie des 'Enarrations in Psalmos de saint Augustin," *Bulletin de littérature ecclésiastique* 61 (1960): 281-86.

11. Saint Augustine, *Expositions of the Psalms, 1–32*, vol. 1, trans. Maria Boulding, O.S.B. (Hyde Park, NY: New City Press, 2000), p. 362.

Based on the chilly correspondence between Jerome and Augustine,[12] it is evident Jerome did not appreciate this style of commentary! He tells Augustine that there are ". . . certain commentaries on the Psalms, that if [Jerome] so wished to discuss them, I would indicate they were at variance *(discrepare)*, not with my own interpretation — I who am a nobody — but with that of the venerable Greeks."[13] Listing the illustrious commentators by name,[14] Jerome asks Augustine: ". . . in the face of so many and so revered interpreters of the Psalms, why will you come up with different meanings?"[15] However, it was more than Augustine's freshly original style that upset Jerome. It was his bold Pauline interpretation of the text, his call to interpret *totius Christi* in the Psalms, with its threefold levels of the Christological, Ecclesiological, and Eschatological. Gregory of Nyssa could get away with the eschatological, but for the irascible monk in Bethlehem, whose scholarship anticipated the grammatical-historical method of interpretation, this was not acceptable. Augustine was now in radical departure from Jerome's canons of scholarship. That Augustine followed Origen's allegorical approach, and had been mentored by Ambrose — whom Jerome detested — made things worse.

But Jerome had not faced the wholesale rejection of the Old Testament as Augustine had experienced when for over nine years he was "a hearer" of the Manichees,[16] reading Paul very differently. Later, the Pelagian controversy post-dated Jerome's remarks, when there was now a common cause of concern. Apart from the clash of different personalities, there were also numerous educational differences between the two scholars.

III. The Augustinian "Paul" in Psalm 32

Augustine identifies himself with the psalmist and also identifies the psalmist with Paul. At least five times Augustine quotes from Psalm 32 in his *Confessions*.[17] In his first homily on the psalm, he uses the word "confession" six times, placing himself within David's lament. At the same time he identifies

12. For further details, see Stefan Rebenich, *Jerome: The Early Church Fathers* (London and New York: Routledge, 2002), pp. 45-47.

13. Pierre Jay, "Jérôme et la pratique de l'exégèse," in *Le Monde Latine Antique et la Bible, Bible de tous les temps,* vol. 2 (Paris: Beauchesne, 1985), pp. 323-541.

14. These were Origen, Eusebius of Caesarea, Theodore, Asterius, Apollinaris, Didymus of Alexandria, Hilary of Poitiers, as well as some later translators.

15. Thomas F. Martin, "Psalmus Gratiae Dei: Augustine's 'Pauline' Reading of Psalm 31," *Vigiliae Christianae* 55 (2001): 137-55.

16. Brown, *Augustine of Hippo,* p. 46.

17. Martin, "Psalmus Gratiae Dei," p. 143.

Paul's citation of Psalm 32:2 in Romans 4:7-8: "Blessed are those whose transgressions are forgiven, whose sins are covered . . ." (NIV). Pivotal to Augustine's own experience is this confession of the apostle in Romans 7:24-25a: "What a wretched man I am. Who will rescue me from this body of death? Thanks be to God — through Jesus Christ our Lord." In sum, just as Paul expresses Augustine's existential despair, so too David voices Paul's confession. By this threefold identification Augustine legitimizes eight lengthy introductory paragraphs to teach his hearers "Pauline Christianity" before he even begins to comment upon the psalm!

Finally, before turning to Augustine's exposition of Psalm 32, it should be noted that many scholars have observed the strong fascination given to the writings of the apostle Paul at this period of the church. Peter Brown calls it "the generation of Paul,"[18] while others mark 350-450 as "the century of Paul."[19] Both the Manichees and the Pelagians claimed the authority of the apostle. Yet here was Augustine at the height of his secular career as a rhetorician, in deep despair, hearing the voice of Paul in his epistle to the Romans, "Take! Read," which he later narrated in the *Confessions* (viii.12.29). Paul's voice was so compelling for Augustine to once and for all be embraced by the grace and love of God.

IV. Augustine's Exposition of Psalm 32

With a passionate mind, Augustine reads the Greek superscription of Psalm 32 as "For David himself, for understanding." Here then for Augustine was a cry of both the mind and the heart to reach out to the source of the Christian life, seeking for the basic vitality of God's grace in forgiving and justifying the sinner. For the last forty years of his life, in his roles as rhetorician, priest, bishop, preacher, pastor, public leader, and polemicist, Augustine sought to "understand" what David sought. Now he begins his interpretation: "The psalm is so called because it enables us to understand that we are set free not because we earned it, but by God's grace, as we confess our sins"[20] (Ps. 32:1). Perhaps unique in all his voluminous expositions on the Psalms, as another translation puts it more forcibly: "This is a psalm about God's grace, and about our being justified by no merits whatever on our part, but only by the mercy of the Lord our God, which forestalls

---

18. Brown, *Augustine of Hippo*, p. 151.

19. Thomas F. Martin, *Rhetoric and Exegesis in Augustine's Interpretation of Romans 7:24-25A*, Studies in Bible and Early Christianity 47 (Lewiston, NY: Edwin Mellen, 2001), p. 5.

20. Augustine, *Exposition of the Psalms*, p. 362.

anything we may do. It is a psalm to which the apostle's teaching has called our attention in a special way."[21]

With all the heresies around him claiming Paul's authority, Augustine uses Psalm 32 to define the essential balance of truth for the Christian life. It is like the cable of divine grace being stretched over the abyss, which is neither received by human pride *(superbia)* in self-achievement, nor is it morally achievable in passive complacency *(pigritia)*. The example of Abraham's faith *(fides)* in trusting God is set against James's assertion that "faith without works is dead" *(opera)*. The balance is only achievable by Paul's statement in Galatians 5:6b: ". . . the only thing that counts is faith expressing itself through love." Augustine makes this into an aphorism: "as you are about to act, hold on to faith."

After a life given over to many experiences of conversion, Augustine pours out a flood of scriptural citations[22] with cumulative impact on his hearers, to resolve this pride/complacency dilemma, about the acceptance of grace being lived out truthfully. Unlike our own reading, there is no dichotomy for Augustine between textual meaning and living the text.

Using the examples of Nathaniel (John 1:48) and the contrasting prayers of the Pharisee and the Publican (Luke 18:13-14), he describes the conditions of receiving God's grace in Psalm 32:1-2. He warns his hearers about being silent concerning their sins, while shouting about their merits (v. 3). Their "bones" or virtues will begin to get "old," when confession would keep them reinvigorated. Better for the Lord to "cover" our sin than for it to be exposed in humiliation (vv. 4-5). For in our humble intent to confess everything, God has already acted in forgiving us. Moreover, our confession is not only to God, but to ourselves, with the self-conscious awareness, "I will confess" (v. 5).

Augustine understands verse 6 to be "the time of grace," now under the New Covenant (Gal. 4:4-5), when the cry of Romans 7:24, "O wretched man that I am, who can deliver me?" has been already answered. This is when the Lord "may be found" to forgive and to liberate. Being kept safe from "the mighty floods" meant for Augustine being guarded against the flood of heretical teachings, all claiming Paul as their authority, "whether Epicurean, Stoic, Manichean, or Platonist."[23] In "relying wholly upon God," the psalmist can rejoice (vv. 6-7).

Since Augustine understands the psalm is vital for gaining a new understanding, he spends over nine pages in the introduction explaining the paradigm change needed. "I will instruct you" (v. 8) Augustine translates as "I will give

21. Martin, "Psalmos Gratiae Dei," pp. 143-44.

22. Augustine cites the following passages: Rom. 13:10; Gal. 5:14; Rom.13:9-10; 1 Cor. 13:13; 1 Tim. 1:5; Rom. 3:28; Gal. 5:6; 1 Cor. 13:2; Rom. 4:5; 1:2; 3:23; 4:3-4; he also cites the parable of the Good Samaritan, Luke 10:30.

23. Augustine, *Exposition of the Psalms*, pp. 180-81.

you understanding," an echo of the superscription for which Paul's teaching on justification provides instruction. With this reorientation we can be assured we are on the right way, and the eyes of the Lord will be upon our journeying through life. Those who are stubbornly proud, like an undisciplined mule, are devoid of doctrinal understanding, need to be humbled, and their boastful mouths controlled. For unrepentant sinners are like a wild animal that needs to be disciplined.

In conclusion, Augustine interprets "the righteous" (v. 11) as those who are now "just" (in the Pauline understanding, which he outlined at the beginning). This causes them "to rejoice in the Lord," not in themselves, but solely in God's grace. "They are just. And how did that happen to them? Not by their own merits, but by his grace. In what sense are they just? Just because justified."[24] "This leads to rejoicing in the Lord of all those who are upright in heart" (v. 11). Again Augustine points to Paul: "Look at this rightness of heart as evinced by Paul: we even glory in our sufferings, knowing that suffering fosters endurance, and endurance constancy, and constancy hope; but hope does not disappoint us, because the love of God has been poured out into our hearts through the Holy Spirit who has been given to us" (Rom. 5:3-5).[25] Not only have David and Paul become inseparable in this Psalm, but Augustine would have himself and his hearers also living within Psalm 32, in his hermeneutic of *totius Christi*.

PART II. VOICE OF THE PSALMIST: TRANSLATION

Of David. A maskil.

1   Blessed is the one whose transgressions are forgiven,[26]
        whose sins are covered.
2   Blessed is the human whom "I AM" does not hold guilty
        and in whose spirit is no deceit.
3   When I kept silent, my bones wasted away[27]
        through my groaning all day long.
4   For day and night your hand was heavy on me;

24. Augustine, *Exposition of the Psalms*, p. 384.
25. Augustine, *Exposition of the Psalms*, p. 386.
26. Unusual *nᵉśûî* was chosen for its alliteration with *kᵉsûî*, "covered."
27. Several (11-20) Heb. mss. read כָּלוּ ("consumed"), not בָּלוּ ("wear out"). /B/ and /k/ are easily confounded in the Aramaic script; *blh* can be explained away as the much more frequent lexeme.

> my vigor[28] was sapped as in[29] the dryness of summer.[30]   Selah[31]
> 5   [Then] I acknowledged my sin to you
>   and did not cover up my guilt.
>   I said, "I will confess my transgressions[32] to 'I AM.'"
>   And you forgave the guilt of my sin.   Selah
> 6   Therefore, let all the godly pray to you at the time you[33] may be found;
>   Surely,[34] at the time of a torrent of mighty waters, they will not reach
>   them.[35]
> 7   You are a shelter for me; you protect me from trouble
>   and surround me with ringing shouts[36] of deliverance.[37]   Selah

28. Literally, "my moisture." LXX, Sym., Theod., Vg., confronted with the rare lexeme lšd, read lšdy as l^e + šōḏ ("into devastation"). Syriac read b^e šaday ("in my breasts"). Some conjecture lšny "my tongue," because to them lšdy ("my juice"?) makes little sense (Peter Craigie, Psalms 1–50 [Word Biblical Commentary, vol. 19; Waco, TX: Word Books, 1983], p. 264). Almost all the English versions found the figure sensible, although some gloss the figure by "moisture," "strength," and/ or "vitality."

29. Lit., "turned in the dryness." Preposition b^e is pregnant with the thought: "as happens in the dryness" (IBHS, P. 11.4.3d, p. 224). NIV did not emend בְּחַרְבֹנֵי to בְּחַרְבֹנֵי (pace Stephanus D. Snyman, "Psalm 32 — Structure, Genre, Intent and Liturgical Use," Psalms and Liturgy, Journal for the Study of the Old Testament Supplement Series 410 [Sheffield: JSOT Press], p. 159).

30. The difficult but plausible MT text was misunderstood by the ancient versions. See C. A. Briggs, A Critical and Exegetical Commentary on the Book of Psalms, I (ICC; Edinburgh: T. & T. Clark, 1906), p. 283. Against the canon of textual criticism of accepting the reading that best explains another and against almost all English versions, Briggs prefers the facilitating reading of LXX: "I became thoroughly miserable while a thorn was fastened in me."

31. See p. 80, n. 39.

32. LXX, without an oral tradition, and two Heb. mss. pointed 'ly as 'ālay ("upon/against me"), not as the poetic form of 'al (cf. IBHS, P. 1.6.3, pp. 24-28). Also, LXX and Vg. point p^e šā'ay (my transgressions) as piš'î (my transgression) to agree with sing. "my sin" and "my guilt."

33. In the other three instances of this construction (Deut. 4:29; Hos. 5:6; Jer. 29:13), when God is referenced in the preceding clause, he is elided as the object of māṣā'. In Job 23:3 God as the object is expressed because there is no preceding reference to him.

34. BHS emends the difficult מְצֹא רַק into מָקוֹר or מָצוֹק ("time of distress"). This radical surgery — changing /r/ to /w/, dropping the /'/, restructuring and repointing the words — is unnecessary (cf. A. S. van der Woude, "Zwei ale cruces im Psalter," in Studies of the Psalms, ed. B. Gemser et al. [Oudtestamentische Studien 13; Leiden: Brill, 1963], pp. 131-36). Delitzsch (Commentary on the Old Testament: vol. 5, Psalms [Peabody, MA: Hendrickson; reprinted from the English edition originally published by T. & T. Clark, Edinburgh, 1866-91], p. 254) helpfully explains the usual syntax of 32:6B by the figure of hypallage — the reversal of the syntactic relation of two words. Raq modifies "not reach," not "at the time . . . waters" (cf. Prov. 13:10).

35. Singular, with "godly" as its antecedent.

36. Presumably masculine רֹן, a hapax, has the same sense as its feminine doublet רִנָּה (IBHS, P. 6.4.3, p. 106).

37. Hebrew text alliterates /t~ṭ~[t]ṣ and /s~ṣ and /r/ sounds: 'tth str ly mṣr tṣṣrny rnny plṭ

8   I will[38] instruct you[39] and teach you in the way you should walk;
        I will counsel [you] as my eyes are upon you.[40]

9   Do not be[41] like horse or mule, which do not have understanding —
        with[42] bit and bridle, its trappings,[43] to control[44] them,[45]
        or[46] they will not come to you.

10   The wicked have many woes,
        but as for "I AM's" unfailing love, it surrounds those who trust in him.

11   Rejoice in "I AM": and celebrate, you righteous;
        Shout out, all you who are upright in heart!

PART III. COMMENTARY

I. Introduction

A. Literary Context

Several striking marks link Psalms 31 and 32. In both, the king introduces his dire distress with "I said" (31:14[15], 22[23]; 32:5); describes the distress in terms of bodily blows (31:9-13[10-14]; 32:3-4), and instructs the congregation, which instruction "stands in the relation of a general inference to the whole Psalm"

---

tswbbny, and especially *mṣṣr tṣṣrny.* LXX points text differently, prompting a grammatical anomaly, and adds to it: "You are my refuge from the affliction that encompasses me; my joy, to deliver me from them that encompass me." J. Leveen ("Textual Problems in the Psalms," *Vetus Testamentum* 21 [1971]: 55) emends the *hapax ronê* into *'dny* ("Lord") and reads *plṭny,* yielding: "Rescue me, O Lord, and encompass me with loving kindness." Budde (see BHS), supposing *tiṣṣᵉrēny* occasioned *ronnê,* emends *rny* to *mgny* ("shields"). Both emendations are gratuitous and fail to note the brilliant alliteration of MT.

38. Cohortative expresses resolve (*IBHS,* P. 34.5.1a, p. 573).

39. Singular "you."

40. According to Delitzsch (*Book of Psalms,* p. 254), since *y'ṣ 'l* always has a hostile sense ("to counsel against"), it is better to take עָלֶיךָ with עֵינִי, not with אִיעָצָה, although Delitzsch inserts *śam* ("keeping my eye upon you").

41. Plural. Hebrew writers can switch number as is well attested in the Book of Deuteronomy.

42. Terse poetry gaps "do not be like the horse or mule," which the adverbial phrase modifies.

43. Literally, "its ornaments."

44. *Blm* is a hapax legomenon whose meaning is determined by cognates and by cognate languages (F. E. Greenspahn, *Hapax legomena in Biblical Hebrew* [Atlanta: Scholars, 1984], p. 105).

45. Literally, "for controlling."

46. Literally, "not drawing near to you." Terse poetry elides a logical connection between the infinitives "to curb" and "not to draw near," such as "or" (= "otherwise").

(31:23f.[24f.]; 32:8-11).[47] Catchwords also connect these psalms.[48] Also, a case can be made for regarding Psalms 32 and 33 as originally a unified psalm, as happens in some Hebrew manuscripts. Only Psalms 10 and 33 in Book I lack a superscript, and most scholars agree that Psalms 9 and 10 were originally a unified psalm. The same is true of Psalms 42 and 43 in Book II. Moreover, Psalm 32 ends and Psalm 33 begins with a call to the righteous and the upright to give a ringing cry to "I AM." The form and content of the two psalms, however, differ strikingly. Psalm 32 is in part a penitential psalm; Psalm 33 is a typical praise psalm. Moreover, both psalms have their own integrity. Psalm 33 is an alphabet psalm, having twenty-two verses matching the twenty-two letters of the Hebrew alphabet. Finally, the conspicuous similarity of Psalms 32:11 and 33:1 can be explained as a tagline, leading from one psalm to the next.

Wilson questionably suggests a liturgical connection of these two independent psalms because: (1) Psalm 33 could be viewed as a response to the didactic instruction in the way the godly should go (32:8). (2) God's kindness (32:10) is expanded in 33:16-19; and (3) the willingness of the godly to wait for "I AM" (33:20-22) contrasts with the danger of being impatient as a horse (32:9).[49]

Whereas the penitential Psalm 51 was written "when the prophet Nathan came to him after David had committed adultery with Bathsheba," Psalm 32 probably presents his later reflections on his pangs of conscience before that confession (vv. 3-4) and his making good his promissory instruction to the godly (51:13-15[15-17]). Both psalms begin with the removal of King David's sin, followed by restoration to fellowship (51:1-12[3-14]; 32:1-5), and both are drawn to conclusion with instruction to the godly based on King David's experience of godly repentance (51:13-19[15-21]; 32:6-11).

B. Form Criticism

The church traditionally labeled Psalm 32 "penitential," a few as "wisdom,"[50] and the majority as "thanksgiving."[51] All three designations are apt, but not in their

---

47. F. Delitzsch, *Commentary on the Old Testament*, p. 251.

48. "Seek refuge in God," 31:1[2]; 32:7; "escape," 31:1[2]; 32:7; *zû* (a rare relative pronoun, 31:4[5] 32:8); "trust," 31:6[7]; 32:10; "rejoice," 31:7[8]; 32:11; "kindness," 31:7, 16, 21[8, 17, 22]; 32:10; "bone," 31:10[11]; 32:3; "time," 31:15[16]; 32:6; "human," 31:19[20]; 32:2; "shelter," 31:20[21]; 32:7; "godly," 31:23[24]; 32:6; "guard," 31:23[24]; ט.

49. G. H. Wilson, "The Use of Untitled Psalms in the Psalter," *Zeitschrift für die alttestamentliche Wissenschaft* 97 (1985): 407.

50. E.g., R. E. Murphy, "A Consideration of the Classification of 'Wisdom Psalms,'" *VT* Sup 9 (1963): 161.

51. Mitchell Dahood, *Psalms 1–50* (Garden City, NY: Doubleday, 1966), p. 194.

pure forms. As for penitence, the psalm unlike Psalm 51 praises, rather than pe-titioning God for forgiveness. As for wisdom, the superscript labels Psalm 32 a *maskil* (possibly, "to be/make prudent"; v. 8), and it begins and ends with typical sapiential motifs: beatitudes (vv. 1-2), parable (v. 9), and proverb (v. 10).[52] On the other hand, unlike sapiential literature, instruction takes place within a cultic setting, involving prayer, refuge, and praise, and by conditioning wise conduct on confession and forgiveness.[53] As for thanksgiving, Psalm 32, like other psalms of this genre, includes: looking back on a situation of distress and an experienced deliverance, expressing trust, and calling for praise. However, it lacks typical mo-tifs of that genre: an introductory first person resolution to praise; a formal *tōḏâ* (i.e., a thank offering of words and sacrifice); and a conclusion that returns to the theme and wording of the introduction.[54] In sum, the psalm is a unique mixture of penitence, wisdom, and praise. It mixes addresses to God (vv. 3-7 [esp. v. 6]) with addresses to the congregation (vv. 1-2, 8-11).

C. Rhetorical Criticism

Apart from the typical call to praise that draws the psalm to conclusion (v. 11; Ps. 51:18[20]), the psalm falls into two equal stanzas of five verses each. The first fo-cuses on forgiveness of sin as seen in its framing inclusio of terms in the semantic domains of sin and forgiveness (vv. 1-2, 5). The framing inclusion of the second stanza pertains to judgment for the wicked but salvation for those who trust God (vv. 6B and 10). In the first stanza the king recalls his confession of godly sorrow that led to his salvation; in the second, he prays that the godly community will not keep silent regarding their sin (vv. 6-7), and then, addressing the congregation directly, instructs them not to be like a mule that resists coming to its master for its own good. The logical particle "on account of this" (i.e., my experience or removal of guilt and restoration of fellowship) connects them: the grounds and conclusion, experience and exhortation. Also, Craigie observes a concentric pattern linking the stanzas:

52. J. Kenneth Kunz ("The Retribution Motif in Psalmic Wisdom," *Zeitschrift für die alttes-tamentliche Wissenschaft* 89, no. 2 [1977]: 223-33) on both rhetorical and thematic grounds finds nine compositions in the Psalter merit designation as wisdom psalms (1, 32, 34, 37, 49, 112, 127, 128, 133).

53. William P. Brown, "'Come, O Children . . . I will teach you the fear of the Lord' (Psalm 34:12): Comparing Psalms and Proverbs," in *Seeking Out the Wisdom of the Ancients: Essays in Honor of Michael V. Fox* (Winona Lake, IN: Eisenbrauns, 2005), p. 93.

54. Cf. James D. W. Watts, "Psalms of Trust and Praise," *Review & Expositor* 81, no. 3 (1984): 395-406, esp. 399.

A. Wisdom: blessed person (of the congregation in third person)   1-2
   B. Confession of sin and forgiveness (first person addressed
       to God)   3-5
   B'. Confidence of salvation in distress (first person addressed
       to God)   6-7
A'. Wisdom: instruction with proverb (of the congregation in
    second person)   8-10[55]

Verses 6-7 function as a janus, for in them David continues in the posture of prayer, but conceptually looks ahead to the salvation of the godly community. Also water imagery links verses 5 and 6.

Each stanza consists of strophes of two and three verses (vv. 1-2, 3-5; and 6-7, 8-10), and the three-verse strophes consist of a couplet (vv. 3-4, 8-9) and a single verse (vv. 5 and 10). Other rhetorical features also unify the psalm:[56] (1) a subtle inclusio of the first and last terms: *'šry* ("blessed") and *yšr* ("upright"); (2) twofold repetition of terms: "blessed" (vv. 1, 2), "forgive" (vv. 1, 5), "day" (vv. 3, 4), "cover" (vv. 1, 5), "confess (twice, v. 5), "many" *rbbym* ("mighty" [v. 6] and "many" [v. 10]), *'th* ("you," vv. 5, 7), "shout" (vv. 7, 11), "surround" (vv. 7, 10), "instruct" (twice, v. 8), *ḥsd* ("godly" [v. 6], "unfailing love" [v. 10]); (3) the role played by the number three, including words for: (a) sin (*ḥṭ'h, 'wn, pš'*, vv. 1, 5); (b) forgiveness (*ksh, nšh, ḥšb*, vv. 1, 2); (c) confession (*'wdh, 'dy'k, l' ksyty*, v. 5); (d) protection (*str, nṣr, sbb*, v. 7), (e) "teach" (*'śkylk, 'wrk, 'y'ṣh*, v. 8); *selâ* (vv. 4, 5, 7); and (f) three lessons from the mule (v. 9).[57]

D. Message

The psalm is by a godly sinner and for those like him (superscript, vv. 3-6). From his own experience King David offers other "godly sinners" two choices — there is no third: silence and stubborn resistance against God's blows of conscience and death, or confessing sin and finding forgiveness and life. God's grace to offer the "godly sinner" forgiveness and salvation calls for songs of loudest praise to "I AM."

---

55. Adapted from Craigie, *Psalms 1–50*, p. 265.

56. Snyman, "Psalm 32," p. 158.

57. Amazingly, though noting the inclusio, the twofold and threefold repetitions, and Craigie's chiastic structure, S. D. Snyman (*Psalms and Liturgy*, p. 164) questions that the psalm comes from one hand and suggests it developed in three stages (3-7; 1-2, 8-10; 11)!

II. Exegesis

A. Superscript

By David: see Psalm 5: superscript. *Maskîl,* from a root "to be prudent," outside of psalm-superscripts (Psalms 42, 44, 45, 52, 53, 54, 55, 74, 78, 88, 89, 142) refers to a prudent/insightful person, or, as object of "sing/play" (Ps. 47:7[8]), to a specific type of psalm. Most agree this technical expression has something to do with wisdom/skill.[58] Some think it refers to the content of the psalm, but apart from Psalms 32 (v. 8), 45 (v. 10), and 78 (v. 2), that notion does not uniquely fit the content of the other *maskîl* psalms. Others think it refers to an "artfully molded song,"[59] but all the psalms are artfully crafted; also the other *maskîl* psalms differ in their artistic forms. Craigie suggests it may refer to "musical accompaniment,"[60] but superscripts pertain to composition and postscripts pertain to performance.[61]

B. First Stanza: Forgiveness (32:1-5)

The first stanza develops the theme of forgiveness in two strophes: the blessedness of forgiveness (vv. 1-2) and the conditions for it (vv. 3-5). The opening strophe in the form of a third person beatitude strikes the stanza's tone and message: "the blessedness of the forgiven" (vv. 1-2). The autobiographical second strophe recounts the spiritual pangs of godly sorrow that led King David to godly repentance and finding forgiveness. The two strophes are linked by: (1) "when" (lit., "I say this because") (v. 3); (2) catchwords for sin (vv. 1-2, 5); and (3) a pun on "cover" (vv. 1 and 5) — that is to say, by not covering his sin (5Aa), his sin was covered (5B; 1B). In sum, David coins his experience of forgiveness (3-5) as universal beatitudes (1-2).[62]

1. Forgiven Pronounced Blessed (32:1-2)

The repetition of initial "blessed" unites, underscores, and illuminates the beatitudes. Verse 1 presents forgiveness by divine passives ("lifted up," and "covered

---

58. Ancient versions render *maskîl* by "knowledge, intelligence, [good]-understanding."

59. Hans-Joachim Kraus, *Psalms 1–59: A Continental Commentary,* trans. Hilton C. Oswald (Minneapolis: Fortress Press, 1993), 1.25f.

60. Craigie, *Psalms 1–50,* p. 264.

61. Bruce Waltke, "Superscripts, Postscripts, or Both," *Journal of Biblical Literature* 110 (1991): 583-96.

62. Robert Davidson, *Wisdom and Worship* (London: SCM Press; Philadelphia: Trinity Press International, 1990), p. 32.

over"); verse 2 by the active voice with "I AM" as the agent. Verse 1 uses two metaphors to depict forgiveness; verse 2 explains them.

1 Sages reserve the laudatory exclamation "blessed" for people who experience life optimally, as the Creator intended. W. Janzen notes that the largest number of these twenty-six pronouncements has the near or distant future in view, but that future depends on a present relationship with God.[63] For that reason Eliphaz calls even those whom "I AM" disciplines "blessed" (Job 5:17; cf. Matt. 5:3-12). In Psalm 1 the Torah lover and keeper is pronounced blessed; in Psalm 32 the forgiven Torah-breaker is pronounced blessed, for they have experienced God's mercy and forgiveness.

The two beatitudes use three words for sin. (1) *Transgression* refers to the human's open and brazen defiance of God's person and a willful, knowledgeable violation of his ethical norms (Ps. 5:10[11]). Picture it as a raised fist against God. (2) *Sin* refers to the wrong of superior against an inferior (1 Sam. 19:4; 26:21).[64] Etymologically, "sin" means "miss (mark)," "fall short,"[65] "a disqualifying error,"[66] or "a disqualifying offense." The mortal's sin against an inferior and their rebellion against God are inseparable, since God made the inferior in his image and counts all humans as equal (Job 34:19; Prov. 14:31; 17:5; 22:2; 29:13). Picture it as falling short of the jumper's bar. (3) *Guilt* is the most holistic term, for it encompasses both religious and ethical crime and their consequent judicial guilt. Picture its etymology as twisting or bending something straight.[67] All the Hebrew words for sin involve a standard; namely, God's *torah*.

The two beatitudes match these three terms that "specify the full dimensions of human evil" with three terms that "indicate the completeness of the divine deliverance from evil which makes happiness possible."[68] Two of the three metaphors are: (1) *forgiven* (lit., "lifted up," "borne away," like the scapegoat that carried on itself all Israel's sin and carried them into the wilderness, Lev. 16:21-22); and (2) *covered,* and so removed out of the sight of the Holy One whose fierce anger blazes against sin.

2 The metaphors are explained in verse 2 and universalized to humanity. *Human ('āḏām),* the broadest term for humankind, differentiates the mortal on earth

---

63. W. Janzen, "'AŠRÊ in the Old Testament," *Harvard Theological Review* 58 (1965): 223.

64. Alex Luc, *NIDOTTE,* 3.706, s.v. *pš'.*

65. For its nontheological sense of missing a standard or way see Judg. 20:16; Job 5:24; Prov. 19:2.

66. M. Saebo, *TLOT,* 1.406-8, s.v. *ḥṭ'.*

67. R. Knierim, *TLOT,* 2.862, s.v. *'āwōn.*

68. Craigie, *Psalms 1-50,* p. 266.

from God in heaven, who determines the earthling's potentialities and limitations (Prov. 11:7; 12:3; 27:20; 30:2-4). Only God can forgive their sin absolutely because: (1) he searches out the human heart (Prov. 15:11; 20:27) and so justly blesses or punishes them according to their piety toward God and their ethics to others. (2) By definition terms for sin (rebelling against, falling short of, twisting/bending his standard) are against "I AM" (YHWH; Ps. 5:1[2]), for he set the standard by which human conduct is judged. Therefore only he can forgive (Mark 2:7). *Does not hold* (lit., "does not reckon") always expresses an intellectual act of evaluation that occurs in the heart. It may be used of reckoning a person justly (i.e., according to what properly belongs to them, as when Judah thought/reckoned Tamar a prostitute because she appeared as such [Gen. 38:15]). On the other hand, it can be used to reckon something to someone that did not properly belong to them before the reckoning (Num. 18:27). Shimei's appeal to David to not reckon him guilty for cursing the king illustrates this use: "May my lord not reckon me/ hold me guilty. Do not remember how your slave did wrong" (2 Sam. 19:19-20). Likewise, in Psalm 32:2 the human being is reckoned according to grace for what one properly is not (2 Tim. 4:16; Philem. 18).

The fundamental condition that God requires for his grace to pervade and cleanse the guilty conscience is: *and in their spirit is no deceit.* "Spirit" here functions as a synecdoche for a person's entire disposition (Eccles. 7:8, 9; Ezek. 11:19; 18:31; 36:26); whole inner life (Job 7:11; Ps. 78:8), including opinions or desires (cf. Ezek. 13:3); mind (Ps. 77:6[7]); will (Prov. 16:32); and motives (2 Chron. 36:22).[69] *Deceit* usually refers to speech and is parallel to "lies" (Ps. 120:2, 3) or to "injustice" (Job 13:7; 27:4). This lynchpin condition connects the beatitudes to his autobiographical confession, as Weiser explains:

> The fact that he feels constrained to let God once more gain an insight into the uttermost depths of his conscience's strivings, of which he himself is deeply ashamed when he recalls them (notice the form of prayer in vv. 4-7 in which God himself is addressed!), proves more clearly than anything else that to display the utmost candour in the presence of God, no matter what the cost will be, still remains for the psalmist the foundation of his relationship with God after he has obtained the forgiveness of sins.[70]

---

69. Cf. R. Albertz and C. Westermann, *TLOT*, 3.203, s.v. *rûaḥ*; R. G. Bratcher, "Biblical Words Describing Man: Breath, Life, Spirit," *Biblical Translator* 34 (1982): 204.

70. Artur Weiser, *The Psalms: A Commentary* (Philadelphia: Westminster, 1962), p. 284.

2. Silence and Agony versus Confession and Forgiveness (32:3-5)

The second strophe consists of both a couplet (vv. 3-4) that presents the problem and a single verse that presents its solution (v. 5). Barentsen notes: "verses 3-4 mention concepts like . . . silence, judgment, and misery, while v. 5 . . . contain[s] the opposite concepts, those of confession and forgiveness."[71]

a. Silence and Agony (32:3-4)

Verses 3-4 are linked in several ways: (1) the semantic notion of the pangs of a guilty conscience; (2) a chiasm pertaining to the duration of guilt: "all day long" (3B) and "day and night" (4A); and (3) the cause ("your hand was heavy upon me" [v. 4]) and consequence ("my groaning" [v. 3]), and (4) the motif of body parts: "bones" (v. 3A), "hand" (v. 4A), and body "moisture" (v. 4B).[72]

3 His distress was extreme both in quality ("groaning") and quantity ("all day long"). *I kept silent* signifies active, intentional silence. *My bones* refers to the hardest part of his body, his skeletal frame, and is a metonymy for his psychical and whole self (Ps. 6:2[3]). *Wasted away* means "something that is ordinarily used daily that has become worn out and can hardly continue to be used even if it is repaired." Here the lexeme is "used to describe the most severe distress of the worshiper."[73] *Through my groaning* refers to loud cries of pain and anguish. Four of its seven uses denote the roar of a lion (Isa. 5:29; Ezek. 19:7; Zech. 11:3; Job 4:10). Ironically, because he did not cry out to God, he cried out loud in misery. *All day long* lasted over many days, since he is withered away (v. 4).

4 The merismus *day and night* presents more poignantly the extreme all-day-long duration of anguish as "all day long." The verse halves consist of two metaphors to describe his distress. The first, using the anthropomorphism of God's heavy hand, denotes God as the agent of his extreme distress; the second, using the metaphor of moisture turned to drought, refers to a sudden burning spiritual fever, a symptom of his fatal spiritual sickness. *Your hand* stands for God's "power and strength," and/or "authority, control, or possession" (1 Sam. 5:6, 11).[74] "*Was heavy* may be applied to anything that weighs down human life. Guilt and sin,

---

71. Jack Barentsen, "Restoration and Its Blessings: A Theological Analysis of Psalms 51 and 32," *Grace Theological Journal* 5, no. 2 (1984): 247-69, esp. 263.

72. Cf. Snyman, *Psalms and Liturgy*, p. 161.

73. Gamberoni, *TDOT*, 2.128, s.v. *bālāh*.

74. Leland Ryken, James C. Wilhoit, and Tremper Longman III, eds., *Dictionary of Biblical Imagery* (Downers Grove, IL: IVP Academic, 1998), p. 361.

misfortune and disaster, can burden people and oppress them (Ps. 38:4[5]; Job 6:3; Gen. 18:20; Isa. 24:20; Prov. 27:3)."[75] The anthropomorphism denotes the extreme punishment "I AM," in his authority and power, inflicts on the guilty (1 Sam. 5:6, 11). *Upon me* further connotes that he feels the Sovereign's extreme punishment as a heavy burden. *My vigor* is used elsewhere only in Numbers 11:8 for the taste of manna as dainty cakes baked in oil, suggesting it means "juice" or "sap," a metaphor for "life-moisture." *Was sapped* (lit., turned) refers to "an action that brings about a sudden change or to a process that suddenly and abruptly upsets a chain of events or a condition, often changing into its opposite."[76] David's withering from moisture to drought was due to the sudden and abrupt intervention of God, not to the natural process of aging. The metaphor of *as in the dry heat*, a *hapax legomenon* from the root "to become dry," must be understood from the aridity of the land of the Bible, a dry and thirsty land (Ps. 63:1[2]; Ezek. 19:13), particularly in the heat and drought of summer (Job 24:19).

b. Confession and Forgiveness (32:5)

Sin, transgression, and guilt expressed in abstract beatitudes now become personal: "my sin," "my iniquity," "my transgression." The inclusios of *my sin* (v. 1), the first and last words of the verse, and of *guilt* in the second and penultimate positions, frame the verse and demarcate it from verses 3 and 4.[77] *I acknowledge* means "to make known." John Goldingay comments: "This openness needs to operate toward other people and God."[78] In his openness David even confesses his own cover-up. Solomon counsels the sinning nation to confess: "We have sinned, we have done wrong, we have acted wickedly." On that condition, he assures them of salvation (see 1 Kgs. 8:46-53). *I confessed to you* (1 Kgs. 8:33, 35 [= 2 Chron. 6:24, 26]; Prov. 28:13) means "to respond to another's action or behavior with public praise" — the opposite of "deliberately to keep silence."[79] By acknowledging his need of forgiveness and deliverance from sin he gives God public praise and glory. This entails praising his greatness (i.e., one cannot hide sin from him), his justice (i.e., he has the right to punish the transgressor), and his grace (i.e., he forgives and delivers; cf. Josh. 1:9). *I said* is unnecessary and so emphatic. The manifold resolve to confess suggests that a half confession is no confession. *And you*, in emphatic contrast to "I confessed," *forgave* (v. 1). The

75. Stenmans, *TDOT*, 7.17-18, *kābēd*.
76. Seybold, *TDOT*, p. 423, *haphak*.
77. Snyman, *Psalms and Liturgy*, p. 161.
78. John Goldingay, *Psalms*, vol. 1, *Psalms 1–41*, Baker Commentary on the Old Testament Wisdom and Psalms, ed. Tremper Longman III (Grand Rapids: Baker Academic, 2006), p. 454.
79. C. Westermann, *TLOT*, 2.507, s.v. *ydh (hiphil)*.

collocation, *the guilt of my sin,* shows that the wronging of an inferior incurs guilt before God.

C. Second Stanza: Prayer and Instruction to the Godly (32:6-10)

The second stanza consists of two strophes pertaining to the godly: a prayer for them to be saved from inevitable judgment (vv. 6-7) and instruction to them not to stubbornly resist drawing near to God (vv. 8-10). "He who thus seeks Jehovah when He may be found shall not be swept away when His judgments are let loose like a flood of waters upon the earth."[80]

1. Prayer for Godly to Pray and Escape Judgment (32:6-7)

David combines his prayer that "I AM" extend his grace to the godly so that they escape certain judgment (v. 6) with his personal confidence that God will protect and deliver him from the coming distress (v. 7). Without that promise, apprehended by faith, the godly would despair and continue in sin. As David modeled confession in verses 3-5, he now models faith in God's saving grace (v. 7).

6 The king universalizes his experience of forgiveness to *all the godly.*[81] The godly accept God's covenant, namely, to love, trust, and be loyal to him and to his people. To such a person God shows "unfailing kindness to help the helpless" (Ps. 18:26[27]); he will not be angry forever with them (85:5[6]). "Godly men are the only ones who in the nature of the case will heed the admonition."[82]

The hortatory wish, *let . . . pray to you,* on the vertical axis asks God to grant the godly grace to pray, and on the horizontal axis caroms his prayer as a hortatory appeal to them to pray to escape sin's inevitable judgment. In his truly penitential psalm, Psalm 51, David promised God that if God removed from him the guilt of his transgression and sins, he would teach transgressors God's ways — that is to say, his grace, mercy, patience, and unfailing kindness (51:13A[15A]; Exod. 34:6; cf. Ps. 145:17). Now he asks God to give them the grace to confess sin,

---

80. J. J. Stewart Perowne, *The Book of Psalms* (Grand Rapids: Zondervan, 1976), p. 292.

81. Parallel terms to "the godly" are "those who made a covenant with [God]" (Ps. 50:5); "who love 'I AM' " (Ps. 97:10); "his people" (85:9[10]); "a slave who trusts in you" (86:2); "blameless" [i.e., "having integrity"] (2 Sam. 22:26); "faithful" (Pss. 12:1[2]; 31:23[24]); "upright" (Mic. 7:2). By contrast the "ungodly" are parallel to "deceitful and vile" (Ps. 43:1); "those who return to folly" (Ps. 85:8[9]); the "proud" (Ps. 31:23[24]); and the "wicked" (1 Sam. 2:9).

82. H. C. Leupold, *The Psalms* (Grand Rapids: Baker, 1977), p. 268.

as he had, and experience God's salvation from the disaster that threatens those who live outside of his holy presence, as verse 6B clarifies.

At the time refers to a determined time; namely, the time *you may be found* (Deut. 4:29; Jer. 29:13; Isa. 55:6). In the other three instances of this construction, finding God occurs after seeking him with all the heart. The notion of timely prayer implies God's patience has limits (cf. Hos. 5:6; Prov. 1:27-29). Verse 6B instructs the godly why they should pray. *At the time of a torrent of mighty waters* utilizes the mythic imagery of the sea as an unruly, destructive force that, unlike land, threatens life. The sudden overwhelming and totally destructive tsunami depicts God's judgment (Isa. 8:8; 10:22; 28:2, 15, 17, 18; 30:28).[83] In the presence of "I AM" the godly, who earnestly pray to him for salvation beforehand, cannot be touched by the unruly, deadly chaos that is persistent within the creation and is unleashed when God removes his restraint (Joel 2:32).

7   In the horrendous destruction that God's righteousness demands, the king is confident that God, who is his *shelter*, will protect him (v. 7A) and deliver him amidst shouts of praises to "I AM" from the godly surrounding/encircling him. Elsewhere in the Psalter God's tent (Pss. 27:5; 61:4[5]) or God's presence (Ps. 31:20[21]) provides protection; here *you* (i.e., God himself) protects the psalmist from the coming torrential floods of judgment. *From trouble* denotes a situation from which he cannot extricate himself.

As a consequence of God's protecting his king from the overwhelming flood, he confesses, *you surround me* (Ps. 7:7[8]) *with songs* (lit., "ringing cries") *of deliverance* (from danger), presumably sung by the godly, whose own salvation is bound with that of their king. Instead of being encompassed by the mighty waters, he is encompassed by shouts of praise.

2. Do Not Be Obstinate and So Escape Pain (32:8-10)

David devotes a whole verse with three synonyms to underscore the importance of what he is about to say to his flock at the temple: "I will make you prudent," "I will teach you," "I will counsel/admonish [you]" (v. 8). His instruction derives from three lessons to be learned from the simile of a stubborn horse or mule (v. 9). Singular pronouns "you" in verses 8 and 9b surround the plural pronoun in verse 9A. The combination compels individuals to see themselves as part of a

---

83. An account of the rise to power of Nabonidus (555-539 BCE) recounts: "He (the king of the Manda-hordes) swept on like a flood storm, above and below, right and left . . . laying waste their (sacred) towns worse than a flood storm" (James B. Pritchard, ed., *Ancient Near Eastern Texts* [Princeton: Princeton University Press, 1969], p. 309).

group but not as a group they can hide behind.[84] A proverb in the third person supplies the basis for the instruction, drawing the strophe to its conclusion (v. 10).

a. Turn to God Now and Escape the Coming Judgment (32:8-9)

8 Some think "I AM" is the antecedent of *I*, but King David is the only antecedent in verses 3-5, 7.[85] Exegetes who think God is the speaker err, I suggest, because they do not realize that the psalmist speaks as a king and/or that a king speaks as an oracle of God (Prov. 16:10). The root of *I will instruct you* designates to give attention to a threatening situation, have insight into its solution, act decisively, and thereby effect success and life and prevent failure and death. David's success against Goliath (1 Samuel 17) is a textbook example of the prudent person (1 Sam. 18:4, 14, 15).[86] *And teach you* denotes a catechetical context.[87] The metaphor *in the way* evokes three notions: (1) "course of life" (i.e., the character and context of life); (2) "conduct of life" (i.e., specific choices and behavior); and (3) "consequences of that conduct" (i.e., the inevitable destiny of such a lifestyle). *I shall counsel you* has a range of meanings from "advise," to "counsel," to "admonish," to "prophesy," to "purpose with an immutable will," depending on the social relationship between the speaker and his audience and the situation in which he speaks. Since the king is addressing his subjects, they do not have the choice to accept or reject counsel as merely good advice but a responsibility to accept it. As a shepherd king keeping watch over his flock, the king adds *as my eyes are upon you*. One may fix one's eyes "upon" another to inflict appropriate judgment (Jer. 32:19) or, as here, to watch over and protect (Zech. 12:4). He gives his counsel with passionate concern for them, not with a "take it or leave it" indifference.

9 His instruction comes in the form of a parable: don't be like a stubborn mule. The three clauses that modify this command explain the parable: (1) to be without the understanding of disastrous judgment that will sweep away all sinners; (2) to

---

84. Cf. Goldingay, *Psalms 1–41*, p. 459.

85. A. F. Kirkpatrick (*The Book of Psalms* [Grand Rapids: Baker, 1982; from the 1902 edition of the University Press, Cambridge], p. 165) gives several reasons why God, not the psalmist, is the speaker. I will add a rebuttal to each: (1) "Would any human teacher venture to say 'I will counsel thee with mine eye upon thee'?" But a good king would to his flock. (2) For the ever-wakeful "eye of God's loving Providence" see Pss. 33:18; 34:15[16]; Jer. 24:6. But the king represents God to the people. (3) The view that God is the speaker is confirmed by the parallels in 25:8, 12; 16:7; 73:24. But the king also instructs his people, as the Book of Proverbs shows. (4) It avoids the abruptness of the transition from verse 7 to verse 8. But the change of speaker would be even more abrupt. (5) [It avoids] the change to the plural in verse 9. But see Psalms 5:9[10] and 32:7.

86. So William McKane, *Prophets and Wise Men* (London: SCM, 1965), p. 67.

87. S. Wagner, *TDOT*, 6.339, s.v. III *yārâ*.

not need prolonged pain to do the right thing; and (3) to not resist drawing near to God in faith.

The plural, *do not be,* shifts the focus from the individual to the group. The mood is urgency, demanding immediate, specific action.[88] He explicitly compares a wrong response to that of a stubborn war *horse* (Prov. 26:3; Jer. 8:6) *or a mule,* a "hybrid offspring of the stallion and she-ass," a proverbial intractable animal. The nature of both horse and mule *is without understanding* — that is to say, they are incapable of giving heed and considering their situation with the senses in such a way that insight about the situation takes place. *With bit* is located in the animal's sensitive lips (2 Kgs. 19:28) and is used with *and bridle,* perhaps including the lead line attached to the bit. Archaeology verifies that bits were placed in the horse's mouth, for at their side are plates with eyes for the bridle. A bridle includes both the headstall that holds the bit and the reins that are attached to the bit. *Its trappings* glosses a word that elsewhere refers to ornaments such as of silver and/ or gold to decorate the body (Exod. 33:4-6; 2 Sam. 1:24; Jer. 2:32; 4:30). Perhaps David is using sarcasm: what makes the stubborn animal attractive is the bit and bridle to curb it. Tremendous energy is required to tame the wild spirit of horses and mules, and even when tamed, they demand great energy *to control* or "curb" *them* for useful activity.

b. Proverb (32:10)

A proverb grounds the parable (vv. 8-9) in antithetical universal truths, involving a double contrast: (1) between two people: the wicked versus the one who trusts "I AM"; and (2) between their two portions: sorrows versus mercies. What the two portions have in common is abundance, of either many sorrows or of being surrounded with kindness. *The wicked has* (Ps. 7:9[10]) *many* (v. 6) *pains.* The abstract term, *pains,* sums up the sufferings of Israel in Egypt (Exod. 3:7) and of the suffering servant (Isa. 53:3). In both cases the pains bring the afflicted close to death. Both physical pain (Gen. 34:25) and/ or psychic pain (Prov. 14:13) are entailed.[89] *Trust in "I AM"* means "to rely on 'I AM' out of a sense of security in the face of danger." The biblical confession that "I AM" alone is worthy of faith gives these confessional statements their peculiar strength and inner dynamic.

---

88. *IBHS,* P. 34.4a, p. 571.
89. See Terrence E. Fretheim, *NIDOTTE,* 2.576f., s.v. *k'b.*

D. Praise (32:11)

"I AM's" loving kindness calls for praise from the *righteous* and the *upright in heart* (v. 10). Their praise escalates from *rejoice* and make merry with their whole disposition, to *celebrate* with outward shouts of joy, to *shout out* (vv. 7-8) and make the temple ring. Praise is their right and duty.

PART IV. CONCLUSION

Psalm 32 is like a cargo ship carrying a heavy and precious load of theology: the doctrine of sin; the doctrine of God's forgiveness; and the doctrine of double agency.

I. Doctrine of Sin

The doctrine of sin in Psalm 32 includes its nature (see the three words for sin in vv. 1-2, 5), its universality, and its punishment. As for its universality, all humans, including those whom Scripture calls "the godly," sin (1 Kgs. 8:46). The oxymoron "godly sinners" expresses a profound truth. The psalm's beatitudes are proclaimed upon law-breakers. Augustine said: *intelligentia prima est ut te nôris peccatorem* ("the beginning of knowledge is to know oneself to be a sinner").[90] Luther loved the psalms because they show "the heart of all the saints,"[91] and that includes their sinful nature.

As for sin's punishment, let us not take comfort that we are fashioned as sinners by nature.[92] Rather, Paul warns the church: "Do not be deceived: God cannot be mocked. People reap what they sow" (Gal. 6:7). In Psalm 32 David threatens the godly with punishment if they do not confess their sin before God loses patience. Like the farmer who must reckon with the seasons of the year, the godly must reckon with the time of favor and the time of judgment (Isa. 49:8; 2 Cor. 6:2).

II. Doctrine of Punishment

The psalm assumes that if the faithful do not humble themselves under God's mighty hand of guilt, they will suffer under his rod. "If the righteous person is repaid in the earth/land, how much more the wicked and the sinner!" (Prov. 11:31).

90. Cited by Delitzsch, *Commentary on the Old Testament*, p. 474.
91. Peter Jensen, "Psalm 32," *Interpretation* 33, no. 2 (1979): 172-76.
92. Waltke and Houston, *Psalms as Christian Worship*.

Regarding sin's punishment, one needs to distinguish between historical guilt, sin's built-in consequences, and, as in Psalm 32, God's intervening judgment. Historical guilt pertains to the irreversible consequences of sin; e.g., David could not restore purity to Bathsheba or life to Uriah. God's intervening judgments are judgments beyond and/or apart from sin's built-in consequences. The wicked do not necessarily experience their just deserts on the earth (i.e., within their own lifetimes), but certainly will be punished eternally when they are finally torn from the land (Prov. 2:21-22; 10:30). On the other hand, godly sinners may be punished temporally within history, as the apostle Peter taught (1 Pet. 4:17-18) and as the psalm infers. Even Moses and Aaron, though undoubtedly they will be rewarded in the glory of an eschatological future for their lifetimes of faithful service, for their incidental disobedience were denied the honor of leading Israel into the Promised Land (Num. 20:12). The disobedient prophet from Tekoa was killed by a lion (1 Kgs. 13:2-24); Hezekiah's pride cost him his treasury (Isa. 39:1-8); and Solomon's loss of wholehearted commitment to "I AM" cost him more than half of his kingdom (1 Kgs. 11:9-11). Paul commanded the church at Corinth: "Hand this [sexually immoral man] man over to Satan for the destruction of the sinful nature so that his spirit may be saved (σωθῇ) on the day of the Lord" (1 Cor. 5:4-5; cf. 1 Cor. 11:29f.). All of these were godly/saints but suffered pain. Nevertheless, it is also true: "if we are faithless, he remains faithful, for he cannot disown himself" (2 Tim 2:13; cf. v. 19).

III. Doctrine of Forgiveness

The doctrine of forgiveness as taught in Psalm 32 includes the nature of forgiveness (see the terms for forgiveness in vv. 1, 5), the basis for forgiveness, and the conditions for God's forgiveness. As for the nature of forgiveness in general, it includes the removal of sin and the restoration to fellowship.[93] The two movements are like the light and heat of the sun; they are distinct notions, yet inseparable. As for the basis of forgiveness, God's forgiveness is not based on human effort or on human merit. God does not reckon to the forgiven the guilt that they properly own. Paul uses the psalm to teach that God grants forgiveness as a gift to those who trust God, not as a wage they earn for their circumcision or their keeping the Law (Rom. 4:4-9).[94] Calvin comments on Psalm 32: "They only are blessed who rely upon God for mercy."[95] Psalm 32 teaches that four spiritual conditions

---

93. Ryken, Wilhoit, Longman, *Dictionary of Biblical Imagery*, p. 302.

94. Craigie, *Psalms 1–50*, p. 268.

95. John Calvin, *Commentary on the Book of Psalms* (Grand Rapids: Reprinted by Baker, 2003), p. 524.

must be met for that mercy to flow freely into the human spirit: (1) no deception (v. 2B);[96] (2) godly sorrow for sin (vv. 3-4; 2 Cor. 7:10); (3) open confession of sin (v. 5; cf. 1 Kgs. 8:46-53; Jer. 17:9; Ps. 139:23f.; Prov. 16:2-3);[97] and (4) faith in God's salvation from the punishment of sin (6-10). "Self-righteous Pharisees have no portion in this blessedness," says Spurgeon. "It is over the returning prodigal that the word of welcome is pronounced and the music and dancing begin."[98] Psalm 32, however, is silent about God's justice in not reckoning the guilty as not guilty. That concept is handled in the priestly liturgy of sacrifice that points to the vicarious sacrifice of Christ to satisfy God's justice.

IV. Doctrine of Double Agency

God's will and the human will dance in step. Theologians differ on who takes the lead in this dance, but in this psalm God takes the lead. His heavy hand upon David, a severe mercy, in cooperation with David's conscience, opened up David's clammed-shut mouth (Job 33:16-30). Moreover, David does not tell the people to pray. Instead he prays that God, the Author of virtue, will make them willing to pray (James 1:17-18; 1 Pet. 1:7).

---

96. Both Shimei and Saul confessed to David their wrongdoing, but David did not commit himself to either one, for their behavior deconstructed their words (1 Sam. 15:24, 30; 26:21; 1 Kgs. 2:36-46; cf. John 2:23-25). Humans ought to love their neighbor (Lev. 19:18), not judge their motives (Matt. 7:1), and to forgive seventy-times seven (Matt. 18:21f.), but they should evaluate whether to commit themselves to their neighbor (cf. Matt. 7:16-20) or to hold them guilty after due process of law by what they do, not by what they say (Titus 1:16). If they are not proved guilty, humans should judge the person innocent on the basis of their confession of innocence (Ps. 7:3-5[4-6]). Since only God truly knows the spiritual disposition of a person (John 2:25), only he is able to hold or not hold a person guilty according to absolute justice (1 Cor. 4:1f.). God does not reckon guilt to the honest penitent; not so for hypocrites.

97. In the case of sin, silence is not golden; it is killing.

98. Charles Haddon Spurgeon, *The Treasury of David: Spurgeon's Great Commentary on Psalms.* An updated edition in today's language, updated by Roy H. Clarke (Nashville: Thomas Nelson, 1997), p. 237.

CHAPTER 6

Psalm 38: The Dance between Deserved and Undeserved Suffering

PART I. VOICE OF THE CHURCH

I. Introduction

As will be seen in the exegetical study, this third penitential psalm is the prayer-lament of an individual who is seriously sick. It is a textually intricate psalm. Its complexity has led commentators to differ widely in their interpretations. Is God a judge or a surgeon in this psalm? Are Satanic attacks behind the sufferings of the psalmist, as Ambrose suggested? Is the suffering expressly the result of the physical sickness of the psalmist, as understood by Antiochene interpreters? Or is it anticipatory of the sufferings of Christ within his body the church, as Augustine preaches? Is it analogous to the sufferings of Job, physical and spiritual, as Cassiodorus interprets it? Or is it even the sufferings of self-inflicted penance, as Richard Rolle contends? How was the psalm related to the vice of gluttony, as late medieval commentators interpreted? In other words, Psalm 38 has been understood as a testing lament with many possible contexts.

Psalm 38's textual complexity is compounded by the psychological complexity of mourning.[1] In cultures prior to the modern discoveries of medical science, mortal sickness was experienced as a mixed confusion of diverse agencies: personal sin(s), the devil and his demons, recognized physical illness, and the emotional afflictions experienced by the commentators themselves. Add to this the Stoic mindset of the classical world, its renewal in post-Reformation cultures, and the penitential culture of the Middle Ages, and the history of commentary on such a psalm as this is understandably complex.[2]

---

1. Biblical mourning itself is a recent topic of study. See Saul M. Olyan, *Biblical Mourning: Ritual and Social Dimensions* (Oxford and New York: Oxford University Press, 2004).

2. Two contemporary efforts to explore the ethics of suffering are: Frank E. Young, *Good*

The psalm's textual and psychological complexity is illustrated by the titles given to it by modern commentators: Peter Craigie, "A Sick Person's Prayer";[3] Hans-Joachim Kraus, "Prayer from Sickness, Guilt, and Hostility";[4] John Goldingay, "Suffering and Sin."[5] "Prayer and Sickness"[6] seem to be the overall themes. It is one thing to lament over one's intense and confused feelings and thoughts about the cause(s) of one's sufferings, and another to develop moral resilience in the process. A central coping strategy for intense suffering is to find meaning in the stress. David Bosworth, in his study on David's mourning or lack of mourning over the losses of his children, observes: "it is easier . . . to find yourself guilty of some sin than to admit how helpless you really are."[7] When there is no meaning, then helplessness is intensified. This seems the case in Psalm 38.

We now give a broad historical perspective of interpretation of Psalm 38, extending from Ambrose (339-397) to Richard Rolle (1300-1349).

II. Ambrose as a Mystagogical Interpreter

As heir of the Constantinian church, challenged by a wide range of Christian communicants, **Ambrose** (339-397) governed the church in Milan for twenty-three years. The Roman emperor held his court in Milan, which afforded Ambrose extensive political experience as a lawyer and provincial governor. He held what was considered the most important see of the West. His religious policy was therefore to protect the church from the violence of the civil powers; to nourish respect for the moral law; and to foster a close union between church and state. Ironically, lacking political ambitions, Ambrose gained greater power than the emperors themselves. Dealing with "principalities and powers," Ambrose was highly sensitive to satanic attacks, which he sees well evidenced in Psalm 38. As in the book of Job, Satan may afflict the psalmist, but the power of hurting the psalmist is given by God. He comments: "[while] the Devil wounds him, the ar-

Grief: Love's Final Gift (Washington, DC: Eleuthera Publications, 2011); and Hans C. Boersma, "Hope-Bridled Grief," *First Things* (Jan. 2012): 45-49.

3. Peter C. Craigie, *Psalms 1–50*, Word Biblical Commentary (Nashville: Thomas Nelson, 2004), p. 300.

4. Hans-Joachim Kraus, *Psalms 1–59*, trans. Hilton C. Oswald (Minneapolis: Fortress Press, 1993), p. 409.

5 John Goldingay, *Wisdom and Psalms. Psalms 1–41*, vol. 1, Baker Commentary on the Old Testament (Grand Rapids: Baker Academic, 2006), p. 536.

6. R. Martin-Achard, "La prière d'un malade: Quelques remarques sur le Psaume 38," *Verbum Caro* 45 (1958): 77-82.

7. David A. Bosworth, "Faith and Resilience: King David's Reaction to the Death of Bathsheba's Firstborn," *Catholic Biblical Quarterly* 73, no. 4 (Oct. 2011): 691-707.

rows are the Lord's. . . . There is too, that . . . reason why the Lord gives power to the tempter; it is so that one's love might be tested by temptations"[8] (v. 21[22; cf. Deut. 13:3]). Ambrose's great contribution was in mystagogy, the rite of Christian initiation of adults. As a preacher of the rites of initiation into church membership by penitence and baptism, he led catechumens in their spiritual formation of having a new, Christian identity.[9] He wrote on the critical significance of penitence in an age when great numbers of pagans were becoming Christians.[10] As new converts often experience Satanic attacks on their new life, Ambrose interpreted the third penitential psalm as an expression of such attacks.

III. Augustine (354-430) as Interpreter of the "Whole Christ"

The idea expounded by the apostle Paul in 1 Corinthians 12:12-27 ("For as the body is one, and has many members, and all the members are of that one body, being many, are one body, so also is Christ . . .") had a major influence on **Augustine**'s Christology. Augustine relied extensively on this in his interpretation of the Psalms. The Psalms became no longer simply the voice of David, but the *vox totius Christi,* the "voice of the whole Christ." After his death and resurrection, Christ continues to live in all Christians by communication and relationship; "it is no longer I but Christ lives in me" (Gal. 2:20). Frequently Augustine quotes Matthew 25:31-46: "Lord, when did we see you hungry or thirsty or a stranger or naked or sick or in prison . . . ? Truly I say unto you, as you did not do it to one of the least of these, you did not do it to me" (v. 45).[11] Augustine depicts graphically the various aspects of suffering described by the psalmist in 38:1-11[2-12] as typical of all human suffering. But already in the context of verse 2[3] he has introduced Matthew 25:42, first as an echo of the psalmist's affliction; then ever more clearly there is the voice of Christ the sufferer, as Augustine asks: "Who is speaking here?"[12] Just as Christ identified himself with the petitioner of Psalm 22, he who is without sin now identifies with sinners who are his body. Augustine interprets "the Body" describing the consequences of sin until the end of verse 11[12], and from verse 12[13] to the end of the psalm, "the Head speaks of his sufferings, which are also ours."[13] Christ's enemies are seeking to destroy his life (v. 12[13]),

---

8. Ambrose, *Commentary on Twelve Psalms,* ACTP, p. 119.

9. Craig Alan Satterlee, *Ambrose of Milan's Method of Mystagogical Preaching* (Collegeville, MN: Liturgical Press, 2001).

10. *Ambroise de Milan: La Penitence,* trans. Roger Gryson (Paris: Cerf, 1971).

11. So also in Acts 9:4: "Saul, Saul, why do you persecute me?"

12. Saint Augustine, *Expositions of the Psalms,* vol. 2, p. 150.

13. Saint Augustine, *Expositions of the Psalms,* p. 158.

yet the Lord is silent under attack (vv. 13-14[14-15]). His enemies gloat over him (v. 16[17]), scourge him (v. 17[18]), and yet they live well themselves (v. 19[20]). Nevertheless, Christ pursues justice (v. 19[20]), for his intent is that we should be transfigured by his death, so that he does not remain alone, but part of the *totius Christi.* "Contemplating God's glory and seeing him face to face we shall be enabled to praise him for ever. ..."[14]

IV. Theodore of Mopsuestia (350-429)

The Antiochene commentator **Theodore of Mopsuestia** interprets the psalm as didactic, teaching how the righteous should live through calamity, even when it appears undeserved.[15] He identifies this as one of the penitential psalms and declares that it has more moral worth than the novel rite of public confession or penance. He identifies the historical context of the psalm as David's sin with Bathsheba, "when he fell foul of the calamities brought on by Absalom; and God allowed him to be caught up for the same reason, to teach him about his sin and make him stronger in future."[16] What follows is a portrait of the truly penitent one, centered on the prayer, "Lord, all my desire is before you" (v. 9[10]). Theodore argues that the psalmist's declaration in verse 15[16], "Because it is in you, Lord, that I hoped: you will hearken to me, Lord my God," is more than confession of sin(s), "for it is trusting in the foreknowledge and grace of God as what I suffered, you know that I hoped in you, you know that I confessed my sin, you know that I never stopped suffering troubles, you know what was inflicted on me by my friends."[17]

V. Theodoret of Cyrus (393-460)

Living a generation later, **Theodoret of Cyrus** is a "desk theologian," who wrote over thirty works. Like Chrysostom he trusts the inspired authority of the Septuagint text. Theodoret is able to read Syriac and Greek, but he is not a Hebrew scholar like Jerome. Contrasted with the earlier commentators we have selected, he does not seem to have a deep pastoral intent. Rather, as a bishop, he wants to present a reliable commentary for his clergy to consult, studying the Psalms

---

14. Saint Augustine, *Expositions of the Psalms,* p. 167.
15. Theodore of Mopsuestia, *Commentary on Psalms 1-81,* trans. Robert C. Hill (Atlanta: Society of Biblical Literature, 2006), p. 413.
16. Theodore of Mopsuestia, *Commentary on Psalms,* pp. 441-43.
17. Theodore of Mopsuestia, *Commentary on Psalms,* pp. 459, 463.

objectively and critically, to let the text speak for itself. He is aware of the church's use of seven penitential psalms, as well as others that prefigure the sufferings of Christ.[18] Theodoret loosely connects the background of Psalm 38 to the stories of David's reign preserved in 2 Samuel. He links the psalm with Psalm 6, as both ask the Surgeon not to apply the knife to one's wound but to pour in ointment. "He begs for the remedy, not the knife" (v. 19[20]).[19] He focuses on the symptoms of the penitent's sinful condition as "the extraordinary degree of depression, by which the light does not appear to be light, and the deprivation of divine care . . . while those of my friends . . . took the actions of my enemies."[20] Theodoret's matter-of-fact approach is not very inspiring for the sufferer!

VI. Cassiodorus's Use of Job in Psalm 38

Cassiodorus (485-580), who served as a Roman senator before becoming a monk, often follows Augustine in his commentaries on the Psalms. But in Psalm 38, Cassiodorus hears in the voice of David the voice of Job[21] rather than Augustine's *vox totius Christ*. He divides the psalm into four parts. "First there is an exordium in which the penitential life moves the pity of the kindly Judge. Next comes the narration in two parts, in which he relates the affliction to his body by different punishments, and the harsh wounding of his spirit by the accusations of friends. Since no consolation remains in either respect, he prays to the Lord with all his strength. Appended as the third part is the consolation of the saving remedy: this he says is the hope that he has placed in the Lord in the midst of manifold disasters. . . . After this emerges the joyful conclusion always granted to penitents, in which he is now delivered from all disasters and proclaims God as the Author of his salvation."[22] Using the Psalms to illustrate rhetorical devices, Cassiodorus cites this psalm as illustrative of *ethopoeia* (i.e., what is "expressive of character"), specifically of moral resilience, "as Christ's unconquered soldier. . . . He is pierced by the pain of wounds, he oozes with worms, and in addition he is wounded with reproaches. Besieged by these numerous disasters, he retains total health solely by rigor of faith. I believe with reason that this persona is to be

18. Theodoret of Cyrus, *Commentary on the Psalms, Psalms 1–72*, trans. Robert C. Hill (Washington, DC: Catholic University of America Press, 2000), p. 17.

19. Theodoret of Cyr[us], WGRW 9:121.

20. Theodoret of Cyr[us], WGRW, p. 230.

21. Ancient Christian Writers, *Cassiodorus, Explanations of the Psalms*, vol. 1, trans. P. G. Walsh (Mahwah, NJ: Paulist, 1990), p. 377.

22. *Cassiodorus, Explanations of the Psalms*, p. 70.

attributed to blessed Job, for he endured similar hardships, and the very words seem virtually to represent him."[23]

Cassiodorus links the words of Psalm 38:3[4] ("Because of your wrath there is no health in my body; my bones have no soundness because of my sin") with Job's cry, "the arrows of the Lord are in me . . . the terrors of the Lord war against me" (Job 6:4). The suffering of the psalmist in verse 4[5] is echoed in Job 30:17. He comments: "It is the man who punishes his soul with griefs and weeping who is *afflicted with miseries.*[24] So Job with reference to his sufferings says: *I have done with hope. I shall now live no longer. Spare me, O Lord, for my days are nothing* (Job 7:16). . . . Sad weeping possessed him, and this — a common experience of the faithful — without in any sense his despairing of the Lord's love."[25] Coming to his friends for consolation (Ps. 38:12, 13[13, 14]), the psalmist is again like Job, who cries out: "He has put my brethren far from me, and my acquaintances like strangers have departed from me" (Job 19:13). Both Job and the psalmist cry out in physical pain, although in receiving the mental pains of their false friends, both remain silent (Job 4:5). Cassiodorus concludes: "Having finished the account of his sufferings [physical and mental], he now passes to the aid brought by saving healing, for in the course of his harsh disasters his trust never failed. . . . as Job himself says: 'though he should kill me, I will trust in him' (Job 13:15)."[26] Illustrative of verses 18, 19[19, 20] of the psalm is now the patience of Job, which Cassiodorus notes is expressed in two ways: "First we proclaim ourselves to the Lord as sinners [as Job did in 7:20]: 'I have sinned against the Lord.' Yet at the same time we rebuke the false accusations against us, saying with Job, 'you will not find iniquity on my tongue' (Job 6:30)."[27]

Cassiodorus concludes by holding up Job as a model of *ethopoeia* (i.e., exemplary resilience): "How courageous, how triumphant over himself this Job, described by David, became! Among the many agonies of his wounds he did not cease to moderate his cries. His body lay in ordure but his spirit dwelt in heaven. He was gnawed by worms, but he overcame unclean spirits. . . . Let us understand the dignity of those who repent; even Job was not excluded from it, for he was praised by the words of so great a Judge."[28]

Cassiodorus maintains that biblical lament is not expressive of emotional defeat. There are times when exemplars like Job are struggling to affirm their innocence before the righteousness of God, since they inhabit a moral universe

---

23. Cassiodorus, *Explanations of the Psalms*, p. 377.

24. *Cassiodorus, Explanations of the Psalms*, p. 379.

25. *Cassiodorus, Explanations of the Psalms*, p. 381.

26. *Cassiodorus, Explanations of the Psalms*, p. 384.

27. *Cassiodorus, Explanations of the Psalms*, p. 383.

28. *Cassiodorus, Explanations of the Psalms*, p. 387.

expressive of "the Judge who does right." But self-reliance in the depth of one's sufferings is the worst form of divine defiance. Despair and bitterness in the abandonment of all hope are other tragic expressions of suffering. Rather, a co-operative relatedness between God and the sufferer, as Psalm 38 communicates, is "the way of the righteous." It is the biblical understanding of "moral resilience." It is not gained as a trait of an achieved character, but is an ongoing process, gained by prayer alone.[29] There is always a balance to maintain, as Cassiodorus argues, between being aware we remain sinners, and yet at times experiencing afflictions that appear unjust and unaccountable.[30]

VII. Medieval Penitential Commentaries

Using the Bible as both literature and revelation, as Cassiodorus in the "Dark Ages," educated monks compiled the *libri Carolini* as a basis for the Carolingian "renaissance" of universal Christendom. For its theological contributors, such as Theodulf of Orléans and Alcuin of York (734-804), were trying to steer a middle course between the break of the Latin West and the Greek East.[31] Moreover, the emperor Charlemagne was creating a new Christendom out of diverse pagan tribal morals. This gave new impetus to penitence for cardinal vices, to replace the morals of tribal common laws.[32] A further contribution was the Irish monastic codification of penalties, for penalties to match the seriousness of the crimes needing penitence.

Further, there was the development of the notion of purgatory, introduced by Tertullian, substantiated by Augustine and Gregory the Great, and now (c. 1170-80) given a location.[33] Purgatory linked the confession of venial sins (lesser sins that do not result in damnation) with the penitent who had not had time in this life to be able to complete the process. Purgatory allowed an extension of the process before the final Day of Judgment.[34] For some, it meant that the final

---

29. Recent literature on the psychology of "resilience" deals primarily with childhood hardships, or the disabled, both in secular categories: *Resilience Across Contexts: Family, Work, Culture, and Community,* ed. Ronald D. Taylor and Margaret C. Wong (Mahwah, NJ: Lawrence Erlbaum, 2000).

30. *Cassiodorus, Explanations of the Psalms,* p. 377.

31. Irena Backus, ed., *The Reception of the Church Fathers: From the Carolingians to the Maurists,* vol. 1 (Leiden: E. J. Brill, 1997).

32. Alasdair MacIntyre, *Beyond Virtue* (Notre Dame: University of Notre Dame Press, 1984), pp. 166-68.

33. Jacques Le Goff, *The Medieval Imagination,* trans. Arthur Goldhammer (Chicago: University of Chicago Press, 1988), pp. 66-67.

34. For the contemporary revival of "purgatory" see Gary Anderson, "Is Purgatory Biblical?" *First Things* 217 (Oct. 2011): 39-44.

moments before death might lead to the beginning of contrition, which purgatory would then mercifully complete.[35]

The penitential system relied upon the monasteries for its execution until priestly confession was introduced by the Lateran Council of 1125. However, as Sir Richard Southern notes, "after 1300 there began a process of over-elaboration and confusion, not indeed caused by any special moral or intellectual failure on the part of the popes, but by the relentless pressure on every side to drive the system to its limit."[36] The role of the penitential psalms received special emphasis within this religious-social fabric of medieval culture.

Alcuin of York at the request of bishop Arno of Salzburg wrote a handbook, or *enchiridion,* on the seven penitential psalms for the private devotions of monks. He followed the list already selected by Augustine and Cassiodorus. His motive (quoting 1 Cor. 14:15) was that "they [i.e., the monks] might know and understand in the heart what the mouth and tongue sounded out [in chants]," a much deeper form of devotion.[37]

Moreover, unlike Cassiodorus, Alcuin reverts to Augustine's lens of reading Psalm 38 as expressing the *totius Christi,* of both Christ and his church. He claims: "The entire psalm is in the person of the penitent [ex persona poenitentis]."[38] The "arrows" and "lashings" of verse 2[3] are now those of chastisement, "so that I might do penance," while the wounds and sickness described are the consequence of penitence. "The rotted wounds" of Psalm 38:5[6] express a lack of repentance, while being purified comes only from confession. "All his desire" in verse 9[10] refers to the desire to be pardoned. Alcuin makes an interpretive shift as he understands verses 1-10[2-11] to refer to the penitent believer, but applies verses 11-22[12-23] to the sufferings of Christ.[39]

Between 1050 and 1215, the Gregorian reform modernized the church to become independent of the secular society. The Cistercian reform began to emphasize the conversion and penitence of the individual as an act of personal confession; this was legalized by the fourth Lateran Council of 1215. Now the communicant had to practice private confession to the priest, at least once a year. Sexual tolerance was abolished, as punishable in hell. Further, with the rise of commerce, payment as a substitute for physical punishment now became more

---

35. Jacques Le Goff, *The Birth of Purgatory,* trans. Arthur Goldhammer (Chicago: University of Chicago Press, 1986), p. 136.

36. R. W. Southern, *Western Society and the Church in the Middle Ages* (Harmondsworth, UK: Penguin, 1973), pp. 142-43.

37. Alcuin, *Enchiridio seu exposita pia brevis in psalmos penitentiales,* PL 100:57A.

38. Alcuin, *Enchiridio,* 579A.

39. Alcuin, *Enchiridio,* 579C.

the norm, certainly for the wealthy, by prayers officiated by the church.[40] **Richard Rolle** (c. 1300-1349), a lay graduate of Oxford, wrote a commentary on the Psalms in Middle English. Due to its status as a lay commentary, it was uncensored by the church, which afforded a unique freedom for it to be used by the reforming Lollards, although still set within the penitential culture.[41] Rolle hears the strong voice of the penitent in Psalm 38, and even attributes the penitent's sickness (v. 3[4]) to the severity of the penance inflicted upon his body. "There is no health in my body . . . as I have been weakened and exhausted by fastings, prayers, disciplines, and stresses and vigils . . . so justly, I have harshly afflicted myself."[42] Rolle suggests the psalmist cannot distinguish between his own penitential self-inflicted sufferings and the judgment of God upon him, confessing: "I am afflicted (v. 8) for my sins by divine chastisement and salutary repentance (poenitentia salutari), and being humbled exceedingly."[43]

Rolle describes "true repentance" as "compunction in the most heartfelt manner, and that we might wholly groan, be scourged and be humbled." Unlike Job's friends, Rolle's former friends are those now who "proposed inane and useless persuasions to me so that they might call me away from the taken paths of penance and entangle me in the former vanities [i.e., of worldliness]." The penitential logic of Rolle's conclusion is that the latter part of the Psalm describes both the sufferings of the penitent sinner as well as the sufferings of Christ. He admits that the psalm is "somewhat obscure," "but since this psalm is one of the penitential psalms, we ought especially to labor that we may understand . . . how clearly it instructs what sort of thing a truly penitent person should do."[44] A century later, Denys the Carthusian sums up aptly what a model of penitence Psalm 38 had become: "Behold how affectionate this psalm is, and how clearly it instructs what sort of thing a truly penitent person should do, namely that he should vehemently exaggerate his sins, he should humbly reveal them, and be ready to bear every punishment. But since this is one of the penitential psalms, we ought especially to labor that we might clearly understand (for it is somewhat obscure) and devoutly read it."[45]

---

40. Margaret Deanesly, *A Short History of the Medieval Church, 590-1500* (London: Routledge, 1972), pp. 184-85.

41. See B. Waltke and James M. Houston with Erika Moore, *The Psalms as Christian Worship (PACW)* (Grand Rapids: Eerdmans, 2010), pp. 283-85.

42. Richard Rolle, *The Psalms of David, with a Translation and Exposition in English by Richard Rolle of Hampole*, ed. Henry Bramley (Oxford: Clarendon, 1884), Psalm 38, verse 3.

43. Rolle, *The Psalms of David*, verse 8.

44. Rolle, *The Psalms of David*, verse 11.

45. Denys the Carthusian, *D. Dionysii Cartusiani insigne opus commentariorum, in psalmos omnes Davidicos*, vols. 5-6 (Monstrolii: Typis Cartusiae S. M. De Pratis, 1898), p. 643.

As we shall see with later medieval commentators of the other penitential psalms, this culturally rigid mindset of medieval penance could not be changed until the shattering events of the Reformation.

PART II. VOICE OF THE PSALMIST: TRANSLATION

A psalm of David. For remembrance.

1 "I AM," stop rebuking me in your anger;
    stop[46] disciplining me in your wrath;
2 for your arrows have pierced into me,
    and[47] your hand comes down[48] upon me.
3 Surely, there is no soundness[49] in my body because of your indignation;
    there is no well-being in my bones because of my sin;
4 for[50] my iniquities overwhelm my head;
    like a heavy burden, they are too heavy for me.
5 My wounds have become a stench and fester[51]
    because of my folly.
6 I am bent over and exceedingly bowed down;
    all day long I go about[52] mourning.[53]
7 For my back is filled with searing pain;
    there is no soundness[54] in my body.
8 I am benumbed and utterly crushed;
    I growl from the groaning of my heart.
9 Lord, all my desires lie open[55] before you,
    my sighing is not hidden from you.
10 My heart palpitates, my strength fails me;

46. *'al* ("stop") is gapped (so also a few Hebrew mss. and the ancient versions; cf. 1:5; 9:19[20]; 75:5[6]; see Ps. 6:1[2]).
47. Narrative *waw* ("and then").
48. *Have pierced into me* (נִחֲתוּ בִי) and *have come down* (וַתִּנְחַת) play upon the diverse meaning of *nht* (to move from a higher to a lower place [cf. Job 21:13; Jer. 21:13]) in *Piel* and *Qal* stems respectively.
49. Since no other noun has the nominal pattern of מְתֹם, the form may be תֹם + enclitic מ (*IBHS*, P. 9.8, pp. 218-60).
50. I.e., "[I say 'my sin'] because 'my iniquities . . .'"
51. LXX and Syriac; MT omits "and," probably due to haplography.
52. Frequentative *piel* (*IBHS*, P. 24.5a,b, pp. 414f.).
53. Literally, "being dark."
54. See n. 49.
55. Literally, "are before you."

even the light has gone from my eyes.[56]

11 My friends and companions stand aloof from my wounds;
my close neighbors keep their distance.[57]

12 And those who seek my life set their traps,
those who would harm me[58] talk to ruin me;[59]
all day long they scheme and lie.

13 I am like the deaf, who cannot hear,
like the mute, who cannot speak;

14 and so I have become like one who does not hear,
whose mouth can offer no reply.

15 Surely, "I AM," I wait for you;
you will answer, Lord my God.

16 For I thought: otherwise[60] they will rejoice over me;
when my foot slips they will exalt themselves over me.

17 For I am poised to stumble,
and my pains are ever in front of me.

18 I declare my iniquity;
I am in dread of my sin.

19 And the enemies of my life[61] are numerous;
and those who hate me wrongfully are many.

20 Indeed, those who repay my good with evil
lodge accusations against me for my pursuing good.

21 Do not forsake me, "I AM";
do not be far from me, my God.

---

56. *Hēm* is the unmarked form, unlike *hēn*, and may have a feminine antecedent (*IBHS*, P. 6.5.3a, p. 108).

57. Note the assonances of *neged nigʿî* ("aloof from my wounds") and *qᵉrôbay mērāḥōq* ("close neighbors [stand] from afar").

58. Lit., "the searchers of my evil" may be a double entendre: "those who search for the evil I have done" (genitive of agent) and ". . . for the evil to me" (an objective genitive).

59. Lit., "ruin." The pronominal suffix "of me" is gapped.

60. After *'mr*, the purpose clause introduced by *pen* may be regarded as dependent on an elided clause (GKC 152w).

61. MT reads וְאֹיְבַי חַיִּים, literally "my enemies of life." Many emend *'oyᵉbay* to *'oyᵉbê* (enemies of life). H. D. Hummel ("Enclitic *Mem* in Early Northwest Semitic," *JBL* 76 [1957]: 99) thinks the original text was וְאֹיְבַי חַי- ם עָצְמוּ, an enclitic *mem* construction. MT is better construed as a broken construct chain. Amos Ḥakkam (*The Bible: Psalms with the Jerusalem Commentary*, vol. 1, *Psalms 1–57* [Jerusalem: Mosad Harav Kook, 2003], p. 303) notes Ps. 17:9 אֹיְבַי בְּנֶפֶשׁ, "my mortal enemies." Others, plausibly in light of the parallel *šeqer*, emend חַיִּים to ם חִנָּ ("without reason"; cf. Pss. 35:19; 69:4[5]). Yet the emendation does not explain the second *yodh*. LXX also reads MT: "But my enemies live, and are mightier than I."

²²   Come quickly to help me,
        my Lord and my salvation.⁶²

For the director of music. For Yedutun.⁶³

PART III. COMMENTARY

I. Introduction

A. Literary Context

The obvious acrostic of Psalm 37 alerts the audience that Psalm 38 consists of twenty-two verses, labeled "an alphabetical psalm," because there are twenty-two letters in the Hebrew alphabet. Also, the final *taw* strophe of Psalm 37 matches the final verse of Psalm 38. Finally, Psalm 37 is a wisdom psalm, and Psalm 38:5[6] uniquely characterizes sin by the sapiential term "folly." Also, Psalm 38 is connected with Psalms 39–41 by the theme of confession of sin.⁶⁴

B. Form Criticism

The psalm's superscript identifies its form as a remembrance/petition psalm,⁶⁵ and its motifs support this identification: direct address to God with introductory petition (v. 1[2]); lament (vv. 2-20[3-21]), mingled with confidence (vv. 9, 15[10, 16]) and a final petition proper with a hint of praise (vv. 21-22[22-23]).⁶⁶ More specifically, it is a penitential psalm (Psalms 6 and 32). Although the psalmist attributes his awful sufferings as due to his sins, he does not repent *sensu stricto,* asking for forgiveness.

---

62. Possibly, the *lamed* is gapped, yielding "O Lord, to save me."

63. Many medieval Hebrew mss. and Targum read as Q, *yedutun;* LXX reads as K, *yeditun.*

64. *Zondervan TNIV Study Bible,* ed. Kenneth L. Barker, John H. Stek, and Ronald Youngblood (Grand Rapids: Zondervan, 2006), p. 889.

65. Jewish tradition has it that לְהַזְכִּיר means that this prayer liturgically accompanied the offering of the *Azkara* (cf. Lev. 24:7; cited by H. C. Leupold, *Exposition of the Psalms* [London: Evangelical Press, 1969], p. 308). However, terms pertaining to a psalm's performance, not its composition, belong in the subscript, not superscript (p. 308).

66. Bruce Waltke and James M. Houston, *PACW,* p. 95.

C. Rhetorical Criticism

Psalm 38 is truly a great piece of literature. The psalmist enables his reader to feel his eventual numbness from his unremitting pain by his unrelenting verbal depictions of them. No psalm depicts sickness in such an extended, numbing way. As the psalmist can endure no further suffering, neither can his audience endure further reading about them.

Several rhetorical features unify the psalm and give it a sense of harmony within the cacophony of unrelenting maladies: (1) An alphabetic psalm is more than a cute technique. The structure enables the poet to express fully what cannot be expressed fully. The alphabetic limits function as an emotional catharsis; he has purged himself from his unending pain by a restraining, yet complete, structure. (2) A persistent complaint of ceaseless sufferings permeates the psalm, even in the motifs of confidence (vv. 9-10[10-11]) and petition (vv. 1-2[2-3]). (3) The psalm consists of eleven strophes of quatrains (i.e., two parallel versets × two verses). (4) The eleven strophes are grouped together into five stanzas; the first four consists of two strophes (vv. 1-4[2-5], 5-8[6-9], 9-12[10-13], 13-16[14-17], 17-20[18-21]) and are followed by a concluding stanza of two verses (21-22[22-23]). (5) At exactly the halfway point (v. 12[13]), the focus shifts from the psalmist's physical afflictions to his concern that his enemies, who plot to take away his life judicially through treachery, will triumph over him. This semantically crucial verse is formally marked out by a unique tricolon. (6) The central stanza functions as a janus to assist the transition from physical affliction in the first two stanzas to his social rejection in the next two stanzas. Moreover, ostracism by his friends (v. 11[12]) segues easily into hostility from his adversaries (v. 12[13]). (7) The placement of God's name and titles are carefully chosen. "I AM" introduces the first two closely connected stanzas; "Lord" introduces the third transitional stanza; "I AM" and "Lord my God" occur in the middle of the fourth strophe to contrast his deserved sufferings from God with his undeserved sufferings from his opponents; and "I AM," "God," and "Lord" are used as inclusios in framing the psalm (vv. 21-22[22-23]). (8) The psalm is framed with two unique petitions, escalating from "stop rebuking/disciplining me" to "do not abandon me/be far off from me" but "come quickly to help me" (vv. 1, 21-22[2, 22-23]).

These rhetorical features profile the outline followed in the exegesis.

Superscript	
Plea for Relief from "I AM's" Rebuke through Bodily Affliction	1-4[2-5]
Introductory Petition to Cease Discipline	1-2[2-3]
Not a Healthy Spot in His Body	3-4[4-5]
Devastating Physical Afflictions	5-8[6-9]

Wounds Fester; Posture Bent	5-6[6-7]
Not a Healthy Spot in His Body Elaborated	7-8[8-9]
"I AM" Knows His Desires as Enemies Conspire to Kill Him	9-12[10-13]
Confident "I AM" Knows His Desires	9-10[10-11]
No Friends to Defend Him against Treachery of Enemies	11-12[12-13]
"I AM" Must Defend Him	13-16[14-17]
Cannot Defend Himself in Court	13-14[14-15]
Waits for God to Defend Him	15-16[16-17]
"I AM's" Discipline Deserved; Enemy's Accusations Undeserved	17-20[18-21]
"I AM's" Discipline Deserved	17-18[18-19]
Enemies' Accusations Undeserved	19-20[20-21]
Invocation for Help with Praise	21-22[22-23]
Subscript	Psalm 39: superscript A

D. Message

These rhetorical features also point to the psalm's message. Its logic is dense, not apparent upon first reading. On the one hand, his deserved sufferings from God (i.e., sickness) provoke his undeserved sufferings from his opponents (i.e., treachery). On the other hand, his undeserved sufferings from his opponents provoke God to relieve him of his deserved sufferings.

The psalmist finds himself conflicted between his just sufferings from God and the unjust false accusations of his enemies. The first two stanzas feature the former; the next two stanzas feature the latter. The fifth stanza juxtaposes the two kinds of sufferings. They are related. "Those who seek his life" see his physical maladies from God as an opportunity to discredit the chosen king by their vicious speech: "they talk of my ruin." They set traps, plot treachery, lodge false accusations, and spread slander against him. Richard J. Clifford explains: "It [sickness] is a sign of divine rejection, and people should withdraw from such an accursed wretch."[67] Since he can be maligned as accursed, the opponents of all that this covenant-keeping king represents can ruin his dynasty by falsely making him out to be a pretender to the throne.

The complaints of the first two stanzas implicitly aim to move God to pity and so to cease punishing him; the complaints of the third and fourth stanzas aim to move God to do what is right. He neither makes a direct claim upon

---

67. Richard J. Clifford, *Psalms 1–72* (Abingdon Old Testament Commentaries; Nashville: Abingdon, 2002), p. 193.

135

God's benevolent attributes to save him (Exod. 34:6; Psalm 51) nor petitions God for forgiveness. He accepts his just deserts. Rather, he asks God for reprieve for himself and for reproof of his opponents.

The psalm represents his two kinds of sufferings as having come to a crisis point. If God does not relent from afflicting him for his sins — he does not minimize them as "sins of ignorance or inadvertence"[68] — his physical death is imminent and certain (v. 17[18]); and, because of his afflictions, he cannot defend himself against the treacherous false accusations of his enemies. Yet, though his enemies did not intend it, his undeserved sufferings from their hands give him hope for deliverance from his deserved sufferings from God's hands. "I AM," his God and Sovereign, will do what is right; he will answer their false accusations by raising him from the realm of death.

Embedded in the psalm are other reasons why he hopes for God's salvation. First, he has already paid a heavy — he does not claim sufficient — price for his sin. Second, he never loses his sense of intimacy with God and faith in him (vv. 9a; 15a, b; 22b[10a; 16a, b; 23b]).

While the psalm ends with a faith that still supplicates for salvation, not with the triumphant faith that celebrates salvation, the subscript shows that in the history of the psalm's use it was understood that ultimately God saved his chosen king. If God had not answered him, the church would not hail as its King the heir to David's throne.

II. Exegesis

A. Superscript

A *psalm of David* (Psalm 5: superscript). Martial terms, such as "your arrows that pierce me" and "your hand that comes down on me," do not necessarily support Davidic authorship, for Job uses similar language (Job 6:4). Nevertheless, the author's psychology is that of a leader under attack. Moreover, the psalm was handed over to Jeduthun, a contemporary of David. David's biographers in our historical sources pass over the sin and the sickness described in this psalm (Pss. 25:7, 18; 40:12[13]; 130:3). A *remembrance/petition* (לְהַזְכִּיר, "to make oneself remembered"), presumably its genre, occurs uniquely in the superscripts of Psalms 38 and 70. Both end with the petition, "come quickly to help me." God's chosen saints actively vitalize the truth that God knows the desires of their heart and do

---

68. Monsignor Edward J. Kissane, *The Book of Psalms Translated from a Critically Revised Hebrew Text with a Commentary*, vol. 1: *Psalms 1–72* (Dublin: Browne & Nolan, 1952), p. 170.

not passively fall back upon that verity. When Israel went to war she sounded a blast on the ram's horn to remind God they were going to battle! Sound theology entails a personal and relational encounter between God and humans based on truth propositions. When God remembers, he acts upon a previous commitment he has made with his covenant partner (Gen. 8:1).[69] God elected David to be his king, and now David calls upon God to remember and to act according to that covenant commitment.

B. Plea for Relief from "I AM's" Rebuke of Bodily Affliction (38:1-4[2-5])

1. Introductory Plea to Cease Discipline (38:1-2[2-3])

David's introductory plea is blunt and terse, not grandiloquent (Ps. 5:1). The strophe features God punishing David with severe physical affliction.

1[2] "I AM," *stop rebuking me in your anger, and in your wrath stop disciplining me* (see 6:1[2]). When God disciplines a person in his anger, they are reduced to nothing. This is the terminal fate of the ungodly, not of the godly (Jer. 10:24).

2[3] King David now pictures himself as a badly wounded warrior, and "I AM" as a mighty warrior — first, as an archer, who from a distance pierces his opponent's body with deadly arrows, and then, in close-up battle, smashes it as with a war club. The term for "arrow" *(ḥṣṣ)* may derive onomatopoetically from the arrow's swift hissing sound. The arrow consisted of a shaft and head. Its light and balanced shaft, usually made of wood or reed, had a tail designed with eagle, vulture, or kite feathers to stabilize its flight. In David's day the arrow's head was usually made of sharpened copper or iron and to make it even more lethal was dipped in poison (Job 6:4). The metaphor of arrows piercing him refers to his searing pains (v. 5[6]). Commentators commonly allege that the psalmist here reflects the conventional thinking of his world that all suffering is due to sin and that he employs the standard motifs of a tortured body, mental anguish, rejection by friends, and wrath of God against sin.[70] Both notions misrepresent the true situation. Elsewhere the psalmist endures suffering while protesting his innocence (Psalms 7, 26, 44). To reduce the psalmist's depictions of his sufferings as simply conventional language is cynical. The anthropomorphism, *your hand* (Ps. 32:3[4]),

---

69. Bruce K. Waltke with Cathi Fredricks, *Genesis: A Commentary* (Grand Rapids: Zondervan, 2001), p. 140.

70. C. Broyles, *Psalms* (New International Biblical Commentary; Peabody, MA: Hendrickson, 1999), p. 185.

signifies God's punishing power and strength. The same mighty hand that struck Pharaoh such a blow that he was compelled to liberate the Israelites (Exod. 3:19-20; 6:1; 7:4-5; 13:9, 14, 16; Deut. 9:26) now *has come down upon me*.

2. Not a Healthy Spot in His Body (38:3-4[4-5])

The second strophe states explicitly that David was under God's wrath for his *sin* (Ps. 32:4[5]). His are deserved sufferings.

3[4] "I AM's" blows afflict his whole being, from his fleshly substance without (3A[4A]) to his bones within (3B[4B]). The two other occurrences of the phrase, *there is no soundness*, illustrate the severity of David's affliction (Judg. 20:48; Isa. 1:6). *Body* denotes its fleshly substance (Mic. 3:3). *Indignation* glosses a lexeme that originally meant "to snap at in anger, to scold strongly,"[71] and, as its parallels show, denotes "I AM's" experiencing or expressing intense anger (Isa. 10:5, 25; 13:9); 66:15; Jer. 10:10). Matching the entire wounding of the body without, *"there is no well-being in my bones"* (Pss. 6:2[3]; 32:2[3]) within. The bones usually combine the physical with the psychological and so does "well-being" *(šālōm)*, for the transition from concrete well-being occurs almost effortlessly into psychological satisfaction.

4[5] God's judgments are as vast in quantity as waves or a waterfall overwhelming the head of a drowning person (Jonah 2:3[4]) and as great as a heavy load upon the head. "My sin" is escalated to the plural and more comprehensive term, *my iniquities* (32:1, 5[2×]). His peril of drowning in the depths of the sea, as it were, connotes chaos and death outside of God's benevolent presence, threatening his very being. His guilt on his head is *like a burden* or load (2 Kgs. 5:17; 8:9) *too heavy* for him; he is like a donkey lying helpless under its load (Exod. 23:5).

C. Devastating Physical Afflictions (38:5-8[6-9])

The first two stanzas, 1-4[2-5] and 5-8[6-9], are linked by the phrase "because of my sin" and "because of my folly" at the end of 3[4] and 5[6] and by the repetition of "there is no soundness in my flesh," the first and last terms chiastically arranged in verses 3A[4A] and 7B[8B].

---

71. C. A. Keller, *TLOT*, 2.1143, s.v. *qll*.

1. Wounds Fester; Posture Bent (38:5-6[6-7])

5[6] "I AM's" constant blows left the battered warrior with putrefying, rotting wounds. His moral corruption corrupted his body. *My wounds* refers to the welts on the body left by a whip or a rod (Isa. 1:6) that *have become a stench.* The meaning of *fester* (i.e., "to putrefy and rot") is well illustrated in reference to the plague coming upon those invading Jerusalem (Zech. 14:12). His stinking and festering wounds are due to his *folly.* Fox says this sapiential term denotes "*moral corruption* [italics mine] from the standpoint of its impact on judgment and reason."[72] "A man does not commit a transgression until a spirit of folly has entered into him" (*Soṭah,* 3a).

6[7] His battered body is so doubled-over that he looks like a darkened mourner. The extreme quantity of affliction is matched by its extreme duration, "all day long." *Bowed down* refers here "to bow down" in defeat (Pss. 35:14; 107:39; Prov. 14:9). "Bent over," expanded to "bowed down [to the ground]," is further emphasized by *exceedingly.* The quality of his affliction now gives way to quantity: *all day long. Mourning* occurs thirteen times, only in poetry, with the concrete sense of "grow dark," and is used in contexts of judgment (Jer. 4:28; Joel 2:10; 3:15[4:15]). Coppes observes: "Darkness denotes the whole range of what is harmful or evil. Our root connects darkness and sorrow — a connection not limited to the ancient Near East." Mourning entails that "he was dirty, unattended and in mourning attire (2 Sam. 19:24)."[73] In later times, at least, the accused appeared before the court in mourning. "Whosoever comes before this court of the Sanhedrin to take his trial, presents himself in the guise of humility and fear, appealing to your compassion, with hair neglected, and clad in black garments."[74]

2. No Healthy Spot Elaborated (38:7-8[8-9])

7[8] He is bent over to the ground *because* of the searing pain in his lower *back,* more specifically his "loins," the sides between the lower ribs and pelvis and the lower part of the back (Isa. 21:3; Nah. 2:10[11]). *Is filled* suggests his loins contain as much pain as is possible. The Hebrew lexeme for *searing pain* means "to roast, burn, or parch"; literally, "my back is full of burning flesh."

8[9] *I am benumbed* occurs only three other times in the Old Testament; Jacob "was stunned" (lit., "his heart became numb," deprived of sense and feeling) when

72. Michael V. Fox, *Proverbs 1–9* (Anchor Bible; New York: Doubleday, 2000), p. 40.

73. L. C. Coppes, *TWOT,* 2.786, s.v. *qādar.*

74. Josephus, *Antiquities,* xiv.9.3, cited by A. F. Kirkpatrick, *The Book of Psalms* (Grand Rapids: Baker, 1982; from the 1902 edition of the University Press, Cambridge), p. 200.

he heard Joseph was still alive in Egypt (Gen. 45:26; cf. Hab. 1:4; Ps. 77:2[3]). After God's hand has beaten his king into a bloody pulp, the king is deprived of sense and feeling, a notion confirmed by its compound: *and I am utterly crushed* (10:10; 44:19[20]; 51:8[10]). Psychologically, *crushed* signifies "a high degree of dehumanization and depersonalization."[75] Totally pulverized, no physical resistance is left; only a growling-groan. *Growl* in its other twenty uses always refers to the growl/ roar of a lion. His growl comes *from the groaning of my heart* (Ps. 7:9[10]). The nominal derivatives of *to groan* are used of a lion's roar (Prov. 19:12; cf. 28:15; Isa. 5:29) and of the groaning of a human sufferer (Prov. 5:11 and Ezek. 24:23). This groaning is worse and less vital than that of mourning and weeping (Ezek. 24:23). The ancients attributed all the body's functions to the *heart*: its facial expressions (Prov. 15:13), its tongue (Prov. 12:23; 15:28), and its other members (Prov. 6:18).

D. The Lord Knows His Desires as Enemies Conspire to Kill Him (38:9-12[10-13])

The third, the janus stanza, segues into his greater concern: the triumph of his enemies.

1. Confident "I AM" Knows His Desires (38:9-10[10-11])

Its initial strophe (vv. 9-10[10-11]) looks back to verses 1-8[2-9], bringing closure to his physical sufferings with two assertions. First, by noting that "I AM" knows them all, he implies there is no need further to remind God of them (v. 9[10]). Second, he is at the end of his rope: the vital energies for life, as expressed by his heart, his strength, and his eyes, are gone (v. 10[11]).

9[10]   Since the heart lies open before God, he segues into his confident confession of faith: "Lord, all *my sobbing* (see 6:6[7]) lies open before you." *Lord* or Sovereign relates "I AM's" transcendence specifically to the social order wherein he is "supreme lord and master," "the Lord par excellence," "Lord of all."[76] The slave hands over all his desires to his Master. *All* encompasses more desires than he can list (2 Sam. 7:20). *Desire* denotes his aspiration rooted deep in his personality that draws him along to a desired state (Pss. 78:30; 106:14). In other words, the king still hopes God will answer his appeals. *Lie open before you* (*negd ka*, lit., "are in front of you") is a stronger preposition than the usual preposition *liphnê*

75. J. Swart/C. Van Dam, *NIDOTTE*, 1.946, s.v. *dkh*.
76. See *IBHS*, p. 124, P. 7.4.3e, f.

("before"); in connection with Lord, *neged* has the collateral idea of being "open" or "known to." Repetition of his confession and implicit appeal by its negative counterpart emphasize it: *My desire is not hidden from you.*

10[11]   The lamenter combines his implicit appeal with a final description of his physical condition — he is about to die: his *heart* (v. 8[9]) palpitates, his *strength* (i.e., his power to produce) fails (lit., abandons me), and *light* (the sign of life) fades from his *eyes*. *Palpitates* glosses a rare Hebrew form, a $p^{e\epsilon}al$, that repeats the last two radicals and represents movements repeated in quick succession.[77] *Even* (lit., "even they [the eyes]") emphasizes that the last sign of his physical and emotional well-being (1 Sam. 14:28f.) is gone (Ps. 13:3[4]).

2. No Friends to Defend Him against Treachery of Enemies (38:11-12[12-13])

As vital physical energies fade away, his concern shifts to his social situation. Verse 11[12], a reference to his friends forsaking him, functions as a janus to his real concern; namely, that his enemies — God's enemies — will triumph over God's chosen king. Friend and foe function as a merismus for the entire spectrum of humanity. His concern, however, is not so much his ostracism by friends but that God's covenant king will be stripped of his glory and so will the God he represents. He, the glory of God, is about to depart earth, leaving the world in profound spiritual darkness.

11[12]   As his physical energies dissipate, no friend or neighbor comes to his aid. *My friends* glosses a term that denotes those who used to have a strong desire for an attachment to him. *And my neighbors* refers to "those persons with whom one is brought into contact and with whom one must live on account of the circumstances of life."[78] By Jesus' definition of a neighbor, David has none (Luke 10:29-36). *They keep their distance* or "stand aloof" is a metonym of cause, implying the effect "to offer no help" (2 Sam. 18:11; Obad. 11). *Wounds* refers to a violent assault that inflicts pain on the recipient. *Close neighbors* refers to neighbors who are "close" to him in space and/or metaphorically in sympathy and spirit (Lev. 21:2-3; Ruth 2:20; cf. Ps. 148:14). Juxtaposing "close one" with *stand aloof* (lit., "stand from afar") creates a striking oxymoron.

12[13]   *And so* signifies that *those who seek* (i.e., strive to fulfill a wish) his *life* (*nepeš*, his "passionate vitality," Ps. 6:3[4]) take advantage of God's discipline to take

---

77. GKC, P. 55e, p. 152.
78. *HALOT,* 3.1,254, s.v. *rēaʿ.*

away whatever life the battered king has left.[79] *They set traps (naqšû),* a rare word that occurs with textual certainty only two other times (Deut. 12:30; 1 Sam. 28:9), meaning "to knock, strike, only in the specific sense of to strike or bring down (a bird)." The poet chose the rare word for its assonance with the next three words, yielding *naqšû mᵉḇaqšê napšî wᵉḏōrᵉšê.* And those who search *(wᵉḏōrᵉšê)* denotes persons who carefully[80] and energetically[81] strive to fulfill a passion. *To harm me (rāʿātî)* refers to the morally wrong effort to diminish his life even to death; he has done his enemies no evil. *Speak (dibbᵉrû)* assumes the dynamic spiritual powers of speech for good and evil. (The poet chooses his words to alliterate /r/: *wᵉḏōrᵉšê rāʿātî dibbᵉrû.*) *To ruin me* denotes destructive forces that bring ruin.[82] The destructive force, always plural in this use, is usually evil speech, which in many instances is associated with lies and treachery (Pss. 5:9[10]; 52:2[4]; passim). *And they utter (yehgû)* etymologically means "to utter inarticulate sounds" (Ps. 1:2). *Treacheries* denotes their evil designs to deceive their victim in order to harm him. Evidently, they hope to trap him into saying something that will justify their killing him (Matt. 22:15-18). Ironically, his friends stand aloof and his enemies never leave him alone.

E. God Must Defend Him (38:13-16[14-17])

The fourth stanza contrasts the suffering king's inability to defend himself, apparently because he appears under a curse (vv. 13-14[14-15]), with his certainty that "I AM" will defend him by healing and restoring his chosen king (vv. 15-16[16-17]).

1. Psalmist Cannot Defend Himself in Court (38:13-14[14-15])

The psalmist first likens himself to a deaf and mute person (v. 13[14]) and then explains his similes (v. 14[15]); an unreliable witness is unable to defend himself; his silence stands in marked contrast to his enemies' plotting. The strophe's semantic connection is strongly underscored by three grammatical connections: (1) *waw* consecutive ("and so," v. 14[15]); (2) verbal repetitions in their A versets; (3) and repetition of "his mouth" in their B versets.

---

79. "To seek the life" is a common Hebrew idiom meaning "to take away life" (*BDB*, 2.a, p. 134).

80. L. C. Coppes, *TWOT*, 1.198, s.v. *dāraš.*

81. S. Wagner, *TDOT*, 3.294f., s.v. *dāraš.*

82. *HALOT*, 1.242 s.v. *hawwâ.*

13[14]   *But I* strikes the contrast. *Like the deaf,* unlike its verbal root that means "to keep silence intentionally," in its nine usages refers to a person who is indeed "deaf." Since that is the case, *cannot hear* is probably the appropriate gloss of a Hebrew form that could have other senses, such as "must not hear." *Like the mute* means literally "to have the lips tightly closed."[83] The nonrestrictive clause similarly signifies *who cannot open his mouth.* The two similes, "deaf" and "dumb," signify that he cannot defend himself against the adversaries' calumny.

14[15]   *And so I have become like an unreliable witness* (lit., "like a person who does not hear"). The meaning of this simile is apparent in Proverbs 21:28: "Those who give false witness will perish, but a careful listener/reliable witness [lit., 'a person who hears'] will testify successfully" — that is to say, a false witness is not a reliable listener whereas the true witness listens attentively and critically. Thus, *whose mouth can offer no correction,* a judicial term (Job 23:4), meaning essentially "to determine what is right," and when referred to someone in the wrong, means "to reprimand," "to call to account."[84]

2. Waits for God to Defend Him (38:15-16[16-17])

Verses 15-16[16-17] contrast his inability to defend himself (vv. 13-14[14-15]) with his confidence that God will defend him. "Surely" introduces the reason why he turned his defense over to God; namely, so that his adversaries may not celebrate the fall of God's chosen king.

15[16]   The Hebrew lexeme *wait (yāḥal)* is used of "hope" in confident expectation; it is "a close synonym of *bāṭaḥ* 'trust' and *qāwâ* 'wait for, /hope for'" (Mic. 5:7[6]; 7:7). This hope "is not a pacifying wish of the imagination which drowns out troubles, nor is it uncertain (as in the Greek concept), but rather . . . is the solid ground of expectation for the righteous."[85] This is so because it is directed toward *you* and so is based on the character of God himself. The B verset clause explains. Tautological *you (ʾattâ)* — and so emphatic — stands in marked contrast to "I," which began the stanza. *Will answer* means a good and effective answer to his enemies' false testimonies against him. God does not author an evil and/or ineffective answer (Prov. 15:23; 16:1). Presumably God's answer will take the form of healing his chosen king, not that of words.

83. J. N. Oswalt, *NIDOTTE,* 1.412, s.v. *'lm.*
84. G. Liedke, *TLOT,* 2.541f.
85. P. R. Gilchrist, *TWOT,* 1.373f., s.v. *yāḥal.*

16[17] *For I said* allows his audience to overhear his self-talk behind his confidence. *Otherwise they* (i.e., those who seek his life, see v. 12[13]) *will rejoice,* which denotes being glad and merry with one's whole disposition; it may have a cultic nuance, because they probably would have celebrated their military and political triumph in the temple. Their glee *over me* exhibits their animus against God's chosen king and so against God himself. When a warrior's *foot* (i.e., from the knee to the toe) *slips,* he is defenseless and so in extreme danger of being killed. "To slip" is both a metaphor, signifying falling headlong into calamity, and a metonym of cause for the effect: death (Deut. 32:35; Ps. 94:17f.). Since death, not life, has the last word in his experience, he must be reckoned as a pretender to Israel's throne. If God's chosen king dies, the enemies of all that is right will *exalt themselves over me* (lit., "cause themselves to be great") and negate God's promise to David: "I will make your name great" (2 Sam. 7:9). This cannot happen; and so God must defend his king.

F. "I AM's" Discipline Deserved; Enemies' Accusations Undeserved (38:17-20[18-21])

The fifth stanza climactically juxtaposes his deserved affliction for sin (vv. 17-18[18-19]) with his undeserved affliction through human machinations (vv. 18-19[19-20]). The contrast is the key to the psalm's message.

1. "I AM's" Discipline Deserved (38:17-18[18-19])

The stanza's opening strophe (vv. 17-18[18-19]) repeats the theme of the first two stanzas and of the first strophe of the third — the janus — stanza (vv. 1-8, 9-10[2-9, 10-11]). Verse 17[18] picks up where verse 10[11] left off. He drew his reflections on his deserved afflictions to conclusion with a sigh; his vital energies are gone. Now he begins: "I am poised to stumble"[86] to my death.

17[18] *I* shifts the focus away from "I AM" (vv. 15-16[16-17]) back to self and his desperate situation. *Am ready* (or "prepared," cf. Exod. 19:11) *to stumble* (Job 12:5) glosses an idiomatic oxymoron: "established for stumbling." All four instances of *stumble/stumbling* occur in a context of personal calamity for which others have no concern (Job 18:12) or over which they rejoice (Pss. 35:14[15]; 38:17[18]; Jer.

---

86. John Goldingay, *Psalms,* vol. 1: *Psalms 1–41* (Baker Commentary on the Old Testament Wisdom and Psalms; Grand Rapids: Baker Academic, 2006), p. 548.

20:10). That he is "established to stumble" is validated by *my pains* (cf. Ps. 32:10) *are ever* (i.e., repeatedly, constantly) *before me* (*negdî,* see v. 9[10]).

18[19] *Because* explains the previous statement. *I declare ('aggîd)* — from the same Hebrew root as *ngd* ("with/before," v. 17[18]) — signifies the process whereby someone communicates to another a vitally important message; namely, *my iniquity/guilt* (v. 4[5]). Verse 18B[19B] emphatically repeats 18A[19A]. The seven instances of *to be in dread of* refer to the inward emotional response to threat (1 Sam. 9:5; 10:2; Isa. 57:11; Jer. 17:8; 38:19; 42:16); here, namely, to death as a consequence of *sin.*

2. Enemies' Accusations Undeserved (38:19-20[20-21])

As the first strophe of the stanza (vv. 17-18[18-19]) looked back to verses 1-10[2-11]), so the second strophe (vv. 19-20[20-21]) looks back to the second strophe of the janus stanza (vv. 11-12[12-13]) and the fourth stanza (vv. 13-16[14-17]). The king's enemies are numerous, and they have no right or just reason to hate him (v. 19[20]). This is true, because they return evil for good (v. 20[21]).

19[20] *And the enemies of my life* picks up where the shift to his enemies began: "and those who seek my life" (v. 12[13]). Though the verb glossed *have become numerous* in contexts that speak of threats may mean "to be strong," the parallel, *and those who hate me* (Ps. 5:5[6]) *wrongfully* (Ps. 7:15[16]) *are many,* shows it signifies quantity. That they hate him "wrongfully" signifies their misconceptions and/or misrepresentations of him. The conspirators greatly outnumber God's anointed king.

20[21] *Indeed, those who repay* is a legal term "to pay," "to settle," "to make good," "to compensate." God rewards a person according to what one has done: good with good (1 Sam. 24:19[20]; Ruth 2:12) and evil with evil (2 Sam. 3:39; Ps. 31:23[24]). But David's enemies pervert justice: they repay *evil (rāʿâ)* in exchange for[87] *good. Rāʿâ* conveys the factual judgment that something is bad, whether it be a concrete physical state (e.g., "ugly" cows, Gen. 41:3), an abstraction ("calamity/disaster"), or moral behavior that injures others (Ps. 15:3). By contrast, "good" refers to what is beautiful and enhances life. *They lodge accusations* — the Hebrew root is *śāṭan* — *against me* occurs six times with the consistent sense "to oppose" (Ps. 71:13); here the hostility takes the form of accusation (Zech. 3:1; Ps. 109:4, 20,

---

87. Bruce Kenneth Waltke, "The Theological Significations of *'anti* and *'uper* in the New Testament" (Th.D. dissertation, Dallas Theological Seminary, 1958).

29). They do so *[in exchange] for my pursuing* (Ps. 7:1[2], 5[6]) *good,* as in a chase or hunt so as not to allow his beneficiaries to escape.

G. Invocation for Help with Praise (38:21-22[22-23])

The broken warrior draws his petition psalm to conclusion with negative and positive petitions (vv. 21[22] and 22[23] respectively). The petitions subtly paint a tone of pathos, but the three titles for God — "I AM" (v. 1[2]), "my God" (v. 15[16]), and "Sovereign/Lord" (v. 9[10]) — frame them in tender intimacy.

21[22]   His strength has left him; his friends stand aloof from him. His only, and yet his best, hope is his covenant-keeping God. His pleas, *do not forsake me* and *be not far off from me,* retain the mood of covenant intimacy. God's personal name, "I AM," reminds him that his God is eternal and that he has marked him out as his chosen king, his personal property, by the fine oils Samuel poured on him in the midst of his brothers (1 Sam. 16:13).

22[23]   His final petition is terse (four Hebrew words, with two in each parallel) and to the point. *Come quickly* assumes "I AM" is tarrying in an emergency situation (Isa. 60:22). *To help me,* like the English term "to help," assumes a subject who has sufficient strength to come to the aid of/to support an object with insufficient strength. Although the etymology of *salvation* is uncertain,[88] it signifies a military/political/judicial intervention and deliverance because it is a person's legal right. Sawyer says that in the Old Testament salvation and deliverance seldom, if ever, express a spiritual state exclusively: their common theological sense is that of a material deliverance attended by spiritual blessings.[89] The responsibility to deliver for the cause of justice fell particularly upon the king (2 Kgs. 6:26) and,

---

88. The customary etymology, which sees the basic meaning in Arabic *wasiʾa* "to be wide, spacious," is now called into question because it meets with difficulties in the discrepancies in expected consonantal correspondences in South Arabic. Nevertheless, the etymology is enticing because its antonym is *ṣrr,* "to be narrow" (Isa. 63:8f.; Jer. 14:8; cf. F. Stolz, *TLOT,* 2.584). The nominal form *ṣar* is glossed "foe" in Ps. 3:1[2].

89. J. Sawyer, "What Was a *Môšiaʿ*?" *VT* 15 (1965): 479. He summarizes his argument that *môšiaʿ,* the *nomen opificum* of the root *yšʿ,* has forensic sense: Negatively, (1) there are no cases in the Old Testament where a forensic meaning is impossible, and (2) there is no other word used so consistently in similar contexts; and positively, (1) three quarters of its occurrences suggest . . . the language of the law court, (2) the most probably [sic!] etymology . . . suggests a forensic origin for the root *yšʿ,* (3) there are other examples of forensic words appearing in wider and more general contexts, but still retaining forensic overtones, (4) the *môšiaʿ* was always on the side of justice, (5) his activity seems to have been verbal rather than physical in many contexts, unlike

above all, upon "I AM." If God fails to help the innocent sufferer, the afflicted is put to shame (Ps. 44:8[9]). The wronged party, however, has the responsibility to cry out (Deut. 22:23-27). This is why the psalmists frequently emphasize that they have raised their voice, presumably in public (Ps. 3:4[5]). God's help belongs especially to the king (Ps. 20:6[7], 9[10]), who in turn delivers the poor and needy (Pss. 72:4; 109:31). Because salvation is one's legal right, a lament psalm is structured like a legal brief.[90] The human role is to trust God *alone,* as well as to ask (Pss. 33:1; 60:11, 12[12, 13]; 146:3).

The psalm draws to a conclusion with a supplicating faith, not of triumphant faith. "The light has not yet dawned upon the darkness of God's wrath," says Delitzsch. "*Fides supplex* is not yet transformed into *fides triumphans.* But the difference between Cain's repentance and David's repentance is shown in the concluding words. True repentance has faith within itself, it despairs of itself, but not of God."[91]

H. Postscript (38:39: superscript)

For the director of music (see Psalm 5: postscript). *For (l^e)* Jeduthun, aka Ethan (1 Chron. 6:44), whom David appointed along with Asaph and Heman as temple prophets with musical instruments (1 Chron. 25:1). In the postscripts of Psalms 61 and 76 Jeduthun occurs with *'al* ("according to" or "over" [the family or guild of singers called after him]).

PART IV. CONCLUSION

The psalm has the signature of the Author of salvation history. The chosen king's situation and petitions in Psalm 38 typify the passions of our Lord Jesus Christ in many ways.

(1) Both suffer God's holy wrath against sin: David for his own sin, Christ to atone for the sins of his people (Isa. 53:6; 2 Cor. 5:15). (2) David's relentless depictions of his sufferings match the unremitting afflictions of Christ, as memorably depicted in Mel Gibson's *The Passion of the Christ.* (3) Their closest friends

---

its synonyms, and (6) there was a place in ancient Israel for an "advocate" or a "witness for the defense," as also for a "witness for the prosecution."

90. F. Stolz, *TLOT,* 2.585.

91. F. Delitzsch, *Psalms,* trans. Francis Bolton, Commentary on the Old Testament by C. F. Keil and F. Delitzsch (Peabody, MA: Hendrickson, reprinted from the English edition originally published by T. & T. Clark, Edinburgh, 1866-91; 1996), p. 292.

respond to the chosen kings' tortured pain of body (vv. 5, 7[6, 8]) and anguish of mind (vv. 6, 8[7, 9]) by deserting them (v. 11[12]), leaving them without human aid to defend them against those who aim to take their lives away (v. 12[13]; Matt. 26:31, 56). (4) Their enemies try to trap them verbally (v. 12[13]; Matt. 22; 26:49). (5) They do not speak to defend themselves in a kangaroo court (vv. 13-14[14-15]; Isa. 53:7; Matt. 27:11-25; 1 Pet. 2:23). (6) Their enemies lodge false accusations against them in their endeavor to topple them and to discredit them as pretenders (vv. 12, 17[13, 18]; Matt. 26:60). (7) Both have their pursuit of good to all repaid by evil from their opponents (v. 20[21]; Acts 2:22-24). (8) Both enter the realm of death — David partially; Christ fully. (9) Both ask God not to abandon them as they confront imminent death (v. 21[22]; Matt. 27:46). (10) God uses the machinations of his enemies to bring salvation. God's justice demanded that he vindicate his chosen k/King (vv. 15-16[16-17]; 1 Tim. 3:16). The enemies' false accusations against David prompted his assurance that his God would answer his accusers in a righteous deed. By crucifying Jesus Christ, the rulers of this world condemned themselves and brought salvation to others (1 Cor. 2:7-13). Had the accusers of God's chosen known the craftiness of God to use them for salvation before destroying them, they would never have opposed his chosen kings. (11) In the midst of their pathos, both retain faith's intimacy with God (vv. 21-22[22-23]; Luke 23:46).

CHAPTER 7

Psalm 39: The Lament of Silence in the Pastoral Theology of Erasmus

Part I. Voice of the Church

I. The Hermeneutic of Lay Nourishment

Richard Rolle (c. 1300-1349), an English hermit and writer, pioneered in the effort to emancipate the Psalter from the tyranny of monastic litany for the benefit of lay piety. So too, Erasmus' pastoral concern was how the laity could grow in spiritual maturity through the use of the Psalms. Political concerns led reformers such as Martin Luther to condemn Erasmus for staying in the Catholic Church, but Erasmus focused his own criticism on judging the church for its pastoral failure in not correcting false and superstitious practices. He deemed most Christians of his age to be more superstitious than pious, teaching that piety would result in a life characterized by thoughtful prayer. Toward the end of his life, Erasmus composed his own prayer book. This book demonstrates that he understood prayer had to be personal, not merely liturgical, and that he appreciated the need for prayer to be Christ-centered and biblically based.[1] For Erasmus, prayer was intended to promote much more than virtue and morality; it nurtures the participant's entire spiritual life. Erasmus' focus on the "spiritual malnutrition" of the Christian laity can be contrasted with the early Fathers' emphasis on "soul-sickness" in their appropriation of the psalm. Erasmus' concern with "spiritual malnutrition" directed his biblical scholarship toward the hermeneutic of lay nourishment, reliably and faithfully, in the use of the Scriptures. How does the Good Shepherd feed his flock in "green pastures"?

---

1. Era Hilmar M. Pabel, *Conversing with God: Prayer in Erasmus' Pastoral Writings* (Toronto: University of Toronto Press, 1997).

II. Erasmus as a Pastoral Theologian

Desiderius Erasmus Roterdamus (c. 1469-1536) has been the icon of secular scholars for the furtherance of classical scholarship in the Northern Renaissance.[2] This perspective of him has eclipsed his truer contribution as a major pastoral theologian of his tumultuous times. "An Erasmus nobody knows"[3] — he has remained probably the most distorted public figure in the history of the church! Early in his career Erasmus had intended to write a commentary on the Psalms, which he never did. "Who has not written on the Psalms?" he writes wearily to Sadoleto in 1530.[4] He has been likened to Jerome, but he had no knowledge of Hebrew. Yet he sought the appropriate mode of psalm studies. He selected eleven psalms that he wrote about extensively over a period of twenty years in his later life (1515-35). His pastoral concerns regarding "spiritual nourishment" are clearly demonstrated in his work on these psalms. Ironically, in a divided Christendom he appreciated that the Psalms had common interest, both for the Catholic conservatives in their cultic practice of devotion as well as for the Protestant reformers.

He experiments with five hermeneutical modes over this twenty-year span: *enarratio* (homiletic exposition; Psalms 1, 3, 22, 33, 38); *commentarios* (a discontinuous narrative, textually based commentary; Psalm 2); *paraphrases* (a paraphrase of the psalm; Psalm 3); *cocio* (the deliberative oratory of a sermon for a particular public audience; Psalms 4, 85); and *concordia* (an appeal for concord and unity among diverse groups; Psalm 83).[5]

In his personal life, as he left his position as a Canon Regular in the community of Steyn (1487-93), Erasmus also retired from being the public officer in conducting the liturgical use of the Psalter in order to concentrate on his own personal use of the psalms.[6] He critiques the monastic practice of his day, remarking: "Those who, day after day, mumble their way through psalms they don't understand are not 'meditating on the law of the Lord,' but beating thin air, like St.

---

2. The eighteenth-century view of him was as "a rationalist and precursor of enlightened agnosticism." See M. M. Phillips, *Erasmus and the Northern Renaissance* (New York: Collier, 1965), pp. 199-203.

3. *Collected Works of Erasmus* [CWE], 69, *Spiritualia and Pastoralia*, ed. John W. O'Malley and Louis A. Perraud (Toronto: University of Toronto Press, 1999), p. xi.

4. *CWE, Expositions on the Psalms*, ed. Dominic Baker-Smith (Toronto: University of Toronto Press, 1997), vol. 1, p. xv.

5. Susan Gillingham, *Psalms Through the Centuries*, vol. 1 (Oxford: Basil Blackwell, 2008), pp. 133-34.

6. This personal use of the psalms was what the new orders of the Theatines in 1524 and the Jesuits in 1534 were also doing.

Paul's shadow boxer (1 Cor. 9:26)."[7] He exemplified, as the *Devotio Moderna* had already demonstrated, that religious life need not be confined to monasteries.[8] More than ever, Erasmus and the Reformers further appropriated the psalms to express their own inner spiritual struggles. As Erasmus notes in his comments on Psalm 39, "the word meditation does not mean 'deliberation,' but . . . a passionate desire to do something."[9]

Of the fourfold levels of medieval exegesis, Erasmus embraced "the tropological" (etymologically, "speech that has changed direction"), or moral application. For Erasmus that meant from being spoken by the psalmist to being embraced within the soul of the one who meditates upon it.[10]

III. Erasmus' Use of Psalm 39 as a Pastoral Theology

His tropological interpretation is well illustrated in his exposition of the lament of Psalm 39 (Vulgate Psalm 38). Erasmus selected it in 1532 and dedicated his exposition to Stanislaus Thurzo, Bishop of Olomuc in Moravia. For over a decade Erasmus had been pilloried by slander and malice, so his choice of Psalm 39 is in part autobiographical. He faced much misunderstanding both from Catholics and Reformers. The Reformers appreciated his work on the Greek text of the New Testament (1515), as he aimed to establish an accurate text for the restoration of sound doctrine. Yet, to the Reformers' consternation, he had not left the ecclesial institution. The conservative Catholics, on their part, viewed him as treacherous and unfaithful to the status quo. In 1532, in a plea to his friend Ursinus, Erasmus expresses his exhaustion as a broken old man, declaring his inability ever to write again. Nevertheless, he was eventually persuaded to do further psalm study on Psalm 39, which idealizes a spiritual leader who laments in the context of slander. In his dedicatory letter he describes how "among so many plagues, there is none more pestilential, than tongues dipped in deadly poison — they reign supreme in this age more than any other."[11]

Like the early Fathers (i.e., Gregory of Nyssa, see Psalm 6),[12] Erasmus comments at length on the superscription of Psalm 39. He suggests the biblical context

---

7. Dominic Baker-Smith, "Erasmus as Reader of the Psalms," *Erasmus of Rotterdam Society Yearbook* 20 (2000): 2.

8. Richard L. Demolen, *The Spirituality of Erasmus of Rotterdam* (Nieuwkoop: De Graaf, 1987), p. xviii.

9. Baker-Smith, "Erasmus as Reader of the Psalms," p. 15.

10. Baker-Smith, "Erasmus as Reader of the Psalms," pp. 14-16.

11. *CWE, Expositions of the Psalms,* ed. Dominic Baker-Smith, p. 10.

12. See above on Psalm 6, pp. 43-70.

is when Shimei insulted David (2 Samuel 16), although he finds it more apposite to apply it to the way Jesus was treated by his enemies. Following Jerome, he spells Jeduthun as Idythun, which he translates as "leaping over."[13] He idealizes "the leaper" as playing the cithara or lyre. His idealized musical "leaper" figurally "leaps over his own desires" to present the truth of the text of Scripture, or "leaps over pleasing his audience" to serve Christ. Fully a third of his exposition[14] dwells on this theme of "leaping over" all of our own subjective needs, desires, concerns, ambitions, rather than directing ourselves to what honors God and emulating the psalmist who "listens to the God who speaks."[15]

Erasmus often associates the emotions communicated within the psalms with its accompanying music, saying that when "a song" is referred to, it is "not uttered in a loud voice but with strong inner emotion. One might say a song occurs in suffering, while music is produced in grief."[16] Erasmus reflects on Christ in his sufferings as transcending the afflictions of David,[17] so that the voice of Christ is more important in reflecting on this psalm. Christ is the unique "Leaper over," "playing most melodiously . . . when his body was stretched out on the cross."[18] "Singing" and "leaping over" reflect for the aging Erasmus the suffering involved in transcending one's own self-interest for the glory of God.[19]

The pastoral theology of Erasmus was essentially, then, the promotion of "Idythun," of "leaping over" all the inner dispositions that would hinder us from becoming Christ-like, even the wounds of slander — or indeed — our own sins. Whereas Gregory of Nyssa uses the principle of anagogy to pursue virtue as an "ascent," the focus of Erasmus is upon the inner dispositions of the soul. While he also uses the language of "ascent," it is, he says, "through the emotions and not by the feet; with the heart and not with steps."[20] In contrast to the late-medieval public enactment of the penitential system, Erasmus directs us toward *affectus* (i.e., to internalize rather than to externalize the reform and growth of the spiritual life). Erasmus also argues against an exaggerated *sola fideism*, which

13. Jeduthan the choirmaster is mentioned in 1 Chron. 25:1-2.

14. The first 30 of 112 pages of his exposition.

15. Such was the theme and life of our dear colleague, Klaus Bockmuehl, *Listening to the God Who Speaks* (Vancouver: Regent Publishing, 1991).

16. *CWE, Expositions of the Psalms*, ed. Dominic Baker-Smith, pp. 11-12.

17. Erasmus understands David to be a cithara player based on 1 Sam. 16:23.

18. Erasmus, *Psalm 38*, pp. 26-27.

19. Abraham Heschel observed: "May I suggest that our [old people's] potential for change and growth is much greater than we are willing to admit and that old age be regarded not as the age of stagnation but as the age for inner growth? The old person must not be treated as a patient, or regard his retirement as a prolonged state of stagnation." Abraham J. Heschel, *The Wisdom of Heschel*, introduced by Ruth M. Gordhill (New York: Farrar, Straus & Giroux, 1986), p. 89.

20. *CWE, Expositions of the Psalms*, vol. 65, p. xvi.

he ascribes to Luther. Erasmus argues that as a penitential culture had driven the sinner to despair, now the Reformers' reaction leads to moral complacency in a doctrinaire justification; it is like lurching from Scylla to Charybdis, argues Erasmus.[21]

IV. Erasmus' Commentary on Psalm 39[22]

In 1531, in his homily on Psalm 34 (Vulgate, 33) Erasmus commented on the fluidity and fallibility of the early Fathers, which resulted in "intellectual errors." As he observed: "those whose error is a merely intellectual one, and whose emotions have not been seduced are easily brought back to the path."[23] Similarly, in the preface to his edition of the *de Trinitate* by Hilary of Poitiers, Erasmus noted, "God has willed that the happy state of freedom from error be reserved for the salvation books alone [i.e., the Bible]. Scripture apart, all human authors have their blind spots so that we read them with scholarly discrimination and judgment, and yet also with indulgence."[24] Thus, the theme of charitable accommodation to human authorities, even the Fathers, forms an extensive introduction of some sixteen pages to his commentary on Psalm 39. Herein he shows how Origen, Cyprian, Augustine, Jerome, Chrysostom, as well as eminent medieval fathers, all made errors — "a vast ocean" of mistakes that can be outlined. Yet we do not judge them all as "heretics"!

With this historical context in mind, he shows how slander has always afflicted God's people. Since Psalm 39 laments slander, so it is applicable to us all. Luther could attack Erasmus with the epistle to the Galatians; instead Erasmus sought church unity through the personal piety of the Psalms. Psalm 39, writes Erasmus, "presents us with a devout and right-thinking man who, in accordance with God's will, has been persecuted by ungrateful and wicked people"[25] — indeed viciously with slander. Wisely he refrains from further use of the tongue, quoting Isaiah 30:1-2 and 40:5: "I have said, I shall guard my ways that I may not sin with my tongue."[26]

Erasmus relates the story of Shimei's "furious insolence" against David.[27]

21. *CWE, Expositions of the Psalms*, vol. 76, p. 86.

22. Erasmus used the Vulgate enumeration, as Psalm 38; to avoid confusion we refer to it with the MT and Septuagint as Psalm 39.

23. *CWE, Expositions of the Psalms*, vol. 64, p. 368.

24. Erasmus, *Psalm 38*, p. 50.

25. *CWE, Expositions of the Psalms*, vol. 65, p. 60.

26. *CWE, Expositions of the Psalms*, vol. 65, p. 66.

27. 2 Sam. 16:5-14; 1 Kgs. 2:8-9.

Turning back to Psalm 39:3[4] he notes, "the just man in this psalm is unable to bear so much human malice: his soul seethes and his heart grows hot . . . and having carefully considered all human remedies, but seeing no escape from his misfortunes and no effective relief; realizing that he is hemmed in on all sides, he inevitably turns to the Lord" (v. 4[5]).[28] "Let me know my end," prays the psalmist, as the end of his misery, and yet also as the measurable nature of his mortality. "What in man appears as great substance is as nothing in God's eyes,"[29] not even his intellect that he values most. But this perspective is not seen by us introspectively; it is seen only in the presence of God (v. 5[6]). So at this point Idythun, "this great leaper of ours, has made an exceptional leap . . . over all earthly things . . . all things affected by time and change" to view all things in the light of eternity. "Here the pause or 'diapsalma' [Hebrew *selâ*], inserted at this point [end of v. 6]," gives him time to turn from earthly things with increasing desire "that he might be inflamed for that life in which there is no change," knowing with the writer of Ecclesiastes "that there is nothing under the sun which is not deceptive . . . all things being prey to a terrible insecurity."[30]

Continuing his reflections on verse 6[7] of the psalm, Erasmus notes we should not use "this passing world" capriciously, nor store its wealth selfishly, nor bustle about aimlessly. Rather, with the psalmist we should acknowledge that our hope is from God alone (v. 7[8]). "Human hope frequently fails, but hope that is placed firmly in the Lord never causes despair or shame because it never fails. . . . Blessed is the man who is dead to the world and lives for the Lord."[31] Referencing the Satanic attack (permitted by God) that Job endured, Erasmus adds: "anyone who reveals his offenses to God . . . in this life will have his sins hidden from the wicked slanderer."[32]

The psalmist remains silent in verse 9[10], for it is God who has allowed his afflictions; it is God who judges us righteously. As Job's friend Eliphaz states: "Happy is the man whom the Lord rebukes" (Job 5:17). "This just man is aware that, although misfortunes are inflicted by men, they do originate from God, and he abandons confidence in his own capabilities and worthiness; instead he entrusts himself wholly to God."[33]

Throughout his treatment of Psalm 39, Erasmus uses the analogy of the patient and his doctor, so that "even if he [i.e., God] drives the knife in quite deeply,

---

28. *CWE, Expositions of the Psalms*, vol. 65, pp. 74-75.

29. *CWE, Expositions of the Psalms*, vol. 65, p. 83.

30. *CWE, Expositions of the Psalms*, vol. 65, pp. 86-87. One of his greatest commentaries was *Ecclesiastes: On the Art of Preaching*, begun about 1523 but not published until 1535.

31. *CWE, Expositions of the Psalms*, vol. 65, p. 95.

32. *CWE, Expositions of the Psalms*, vol. 65, p. 101.

33. *CWE, Expositions of the Psalms*, vol. 65, p. 107.

he does not do so with the intention of killing but to cure the patient."[34] This is the condition then of Everyman, a mere "breath." To further reflect on all this, another "Selah" or pause is needed at the end of verse 11[12] to let the inevitable truth sink in. That is why "lament" expresses our condition.

In the conclusion, Erasmus sums up the three petitions: "Desire impels us to pray, need urges us to cry out, while tears cause us to get what we want by force. Where there is desire there is no pretense; where there is a cry there is no respite; where there are tears, there violence is in some sense brought to bear on God's mercy."[35] "For you will prevail upon the Lord more quickly if you tell him all your problems rather than your merits."[36] This is the language, then, of exile; of our body dwelling here, but our soul belonging to another country. Pleading to be released from the hand of God, as a wrestler pinned by a stronger opponent, the psalmist's request seems still unanswered. But Erasmus notes that while this may remain "an old song" of repentance, the next psalm can begin to sing with "a new song": "I waited patiently for the Lord and he heard me," redemptively so.

Erasmus concludes by indicating his awareness of the diversity among the early Fathers regarding Psalm 39. His life's mission was to be a conciliator between contestants, between those free with allegory and those who seek to be only textual literalists. The two poles are illustrated by the tensions between Augustine and Jerome who are always before Erasmus' lens. "I have preferred to follow the interpretation which seemed to me to be the least complicated and most suited to the tone and the logic of the psalm as a whole. . . . I consider it to be the mark of a good teacher to at no point consciously depart from the true sense of Scripture; and if this is not absolutely clear, it is better to refrain from making dogmatic assertions."[37]

True to form, Erasmus treads the via media, a course that caused him to lament like the psalmist for all the blows he received from both Reformers and from the conservative Catholic leaders.[38] His conclusion would be that given by Augustine: "God can permit evil only in so far as he is capable of transforming it into a good." Or as the apostle Paul affirms: "all things work together for good, to those who love him" (Rom. 8:28).

---

34. *CWE, Expositions of the Psalms*, vol. 65, p. 111.

35. *CWE, Expositions of the Psalms*, vol. 65, p. 113.

36. Marcia L. Colish, *Medieval Foundations of the Western Intellectual Tradition, 400-1400* (New Haven: Yale University Press, 1997), p. 40.

37. *CWE, Expositions of the Psalms*, vol. 65, p. 123.

38. A century later, the Puritan Henry Scougal wrote his classic *The Dumb Christian under the Rod of Affliction*, on how and why to keep true from false silence, in meditating upon this psalm.

PART II. THE VOICE OF THE PSALMIST: TRANSLATION

A psalm[39] by David[40]

1   I said, "I will guard my ways[41] so that I do not sin[42] with my tongue.
    I will guard[43] my mouth with a muzzle,[44] as long as[45]

---

39. מִזְמוֹר "refers to a song that is sung to the pizzicato of a stringed instrument." Bruce K. Waltke and James M. Houston with Erika Moore, *The Psalms as Christian Worship (PACW)* (Grand Rapids: Eerdmans, 2010), p. 195.

40. לַמְנַצֵּחַ לִידִיתוּן ("for the director of music, for Jeduthun"), reading the *Qere* [לִידוּתוּן], is understood as the subscript pertaining to the liturgical performance for Psalm 38. Jeduthun (Pss. 62:1; 77:1) is mentioned along with Asaph and Heman as temple musicians during David's reign (1 Chron. 16:37-42; Neh. 11:17). See Waltke and Houston, *PACW*, pp. 86-90; 207-8; Randall Xerxes Gauthier, *Psalms 38 and 145 of the Septuagint Version (Old Greek): An Inception Oriented Exegetical Study*, Ph.D. dissertation, University of Stellenbosch, December 2010, pp. 136-37.

41. Reading "my words" (דְּבָרַי) with Dahood, and contra Hermann Gunkel and H.-J. Kraus, who emend to "my ways" (דְּרָכַי). See Hermann Gunkel, *Die Psalmen* (Göttingen: Vandenhoeck & Ruprecht, 1929), p. 166, and H.-J. Kraus, *Psalmen I, Biblischer Kommentar Altes Testament* (Neukirchen-Vluyn: Neukirchener Verlag, 1961), p. 299. But reading חֲטוֹא ("sin" *qal* inf. con.) contra Dahood's reading "lest I stumble over my tongue," which he bases in part on his strained translation of Ps. 15:3, "He who does not trip over his tongue," reasoning that חֲטָא "is seen to carry a physical rather than a moral connotation. Better to understand the psalmist's concern that voicing his complaint might be maliciously misunderstood by the wicked and seized as an opportunity to malign "I AM." See Mitchell Dahood, *Psalms 1–50,* The Anchor Bible, vol. 16 (New York: Doubleday, 1986), pp. 83, 238-39.

42. Separative (ablative) *min* with infinitive construct introducing negative clause; see *IBHS,* P. 36.2.2b #16, p. 604.

43. Bardtke's *(BHS)* suggested emendation of אֶשְׁמְרָה to אָשִׂימָה (referencing the LXX's ἐθέμην τῷ στόματί μου φυλακήν, "I appointed a guard over my mouth"), and Gunkel's pronouncement that this second אֶשְׁמְרָה is "unzulässig" (excessive) are misguided. (See Gunkel, *Die Psalmen,* p. 166.) The repetition of אֶשְׁמְרָה serves to bind together the first bicolon of the stanza.

44. BDB derives מַחְסוֹם, a *hapax,* from root חסם, "stop up, muzzle" (Deut. 25:4; Ezek. 39:11); so too Aquila interpreted with φιμός ("muzzle"). Syriac reads "from iniquity" (*mn'wl; מֵחָמָס) transposing the ס and מ of מחסם. LXX reads "watch" or "sentinel" [φυλακὴν]. Gauthier, citing Donner and Röllig, mentions a Phoenician inscription attesting מחסם as a golden "lip plate," referencing the ancient Near Eastern practice of sealing a dead person's mouth to obstruct the entrance of demons. Gauthier cautions, "However, it is unlikely that such a notion, even by figurative extension, underlies the Hebrew Psalm insofar as a wicked or impious person (רשע) is present before the psalmist" (Gauthier, *Psalms 38 and 145,* pp. 144-46).

45. Bardtke's *(BHS)* suggested emendation of בְּעֹד to בַּעֲמֹד (qal inf. con. + בְּ) based on the temporal infinitive construction of the LXX (ἐν τῷ συστῆναι) "when stood" is unnecessary. The shortened form of עוֹד also occurs in Jer. 15:9 (Gen. 8:22; 19:12; *IBHS* P. 11.2.12b, p. 215). Dahood's translation, "while the wicked man is full of glee before me," based on rendering בְּעֹד as an infinitive construct and relating it to Ugaritic *ǵdd,* "be gleeful," and seeing this as sharpening the contrast between the afflicted believer and the smirking skeptic, is unwarranted. The MT is clear enough.

> the wicked[46] are in front of me."

2 I was completely silent.[47] I kept myself silent[48] for a good reason.[49]
But my anguish proved ruinous.[50]

3 My heart grew hot within me. In my meditation, a fire began to burn.[51]
I spoke with my tongue.

4 "I AM," make me to know my end,
and the extent of my days,[52] what it is.

---

46. Read as a collective singular.

47. The Hebrew verb אלם "to be dumb, silent" always occurs in the *niphal* (Isa. 53:7; Ezek. 3:26; 24:27; 33:22; Pss. 31:18[19]; 39:9[10]; Dan. 10:15) except in Gen. 37:7, where the *piel* participle מְאַלְּמִים is used for the binding of sheaves. The apparent redundancy of the Hebrew word that follows (דוּמִיָּה) has incited many unnecessary emendations (Gauthier, *Psalms 38 and 145,* pp. 152-53). NET's "I was stone silent" captures well the accusative of manner (*IBHS*, P. 10.22e, p. 172).

48. The asyndetic clause begins with an internal *hifil, IBHS* P. 27.2f., pp. 439-40.

49. The prepositional phrase מִטּוֹב is difficult. Many English versions translate emphatically, "even from good" (GNV, NIV, NAS, KJV, so too Aq, Chald); others variously understand "good" as "the law" or "the praise of God" or any "good words" of response to the psalmist's detractors. Perowne, citing Hupfeld, argues against such an interpretation, contending that *min* after a verb of silence is either privative ("far from good," i.e., without relief, Job 28:4), or denotes "the negative consequence of the silence," reading טוֹב as an infinitive for מִטּוֹב לִי (i.e., "I held my peace to no avail"; see RSV), reading in parallel with the final colon of the verse, "My distress grew worse." See J. J. Stewart Perowne, *Commentary on the Psalms,* 2 volumes in 1 (Grand Rapids: Kregel, 1989), pp. 330-31. Another way to construe the *min* is causally, "because of, for, on account of," what *BDB* (p. 380) refers to as "of the remoter cause, the ultimate ground *on account of* which something happens or is done" (italics original); Exod. 2:2; Ps. 38:18[19]. Here in verse 2[3] "for a good reason" fits the psalmist's psychological self-awareness, demonstrates his concern for "I AM's" reputation, and fits with the narrative flow of the psalm. The psalmist here is ultimately basing his commitment to silence (his envious struggle; see below in commentary) on his resolve to withhold from his enemies any fodder for discrediting "I AM." In his general comments about the psalm, Perowne observes, "It is the sorrowful complaint of a heart, not yet subdued to a perfect resignation, but jealous with a godly jealousy, lest it should bring dishonour upon its God . . ." Perowne, *Psalms,* p. 326.

50. The *nifal* of עָבַר occurs elsewhere only in Prov. 15:6; all other occurrences are in the *qal,* treating the *nifal* participle as a gerundive here as in Prov. 15:6 (*IBHS* P. 23.3d, p. 387).

51. Incipient past imperfect (*IBHS* P.31.2c, P. 503.31.2.b) parallels the ingressive stative, "my heart grew hot."

52. The collocation יְמַי מַה־הִיא is unique. Clifford's efforts to ease the tension between the psalmist's request here for a deeper appreciation of the transitoriness of life, and his eloquent demonstration of such knowledge (vv. 6-7, 12c[7-8, 13c]), is misguided. Why shouldn't the end of the psalmist's affliction coincide with the end of his life (v. 13[14]; Job 6:11; Jer. 51:13; Amos 8:2)? Richard J. Clifford, "What Does the Psalmist Ask For in Psalms 30:5 and 90:12?" *JBL* 119, no. 1 (2000): 60.

Let me know[53] how transient[54] I am.

5   Behold as handbreadths[55] you have allotted my days.

My lifespan[56] is as nothing before you.

Surely all people,[57] even those who are solidly established,[58] are nothing but a breath.[59]   Selah.[60]

6   Surely a person walks about as fleeting shadows.[61]

Surely they heap up fleeting wealth without knowing who will gather it.[62]

---

53. A number of Hebrew mss. read וָאֵדְעָה, perhaps prompting the LXX translation with a purpose clause, "that I may know."

54. *BDB* (p. 293) suggests emending חָדֵל to חֶלֶד (Ps. 89:48 חָלֶד "fleeting"). This is not necessary and has no textual warrant. The meaning of the verbal root חָדֵל includes "to forbear," "to cease," "to stop" (*TWOT*, 1.606), hence, translating the adjective with "transience" in this verse.

55. The *hapax* טְפָחוֹת ("handbreadths") occurs elsewhere only in 1 Kgs. 7:9 (with the article), where it is usually translated with the architectural term "coping" (the covering of a wall). LXX translates with παλαιστής, here in Ps. 39:5[6]; Syriac translates as "measure." Commenting on the LXX translation, Gauthier notes, "Literally παλαιστής signifies the 'length equivalent to 4 fingers' or '77-78 mm.' . . . [It] was one of the smallest measures in the Hebrew system of measuring, so that the metaphor reduces the span of human life to something tiny from the perspective of God. The imagery in G* [LXX] is the same as it is in M [MT]" (*Psalms 38 and 145*, p. 170).

56. Epexegetical *waw*. See *IBHS* P. 39.2.4, pp. 652-53.

57. The final clause of this tricolon is syntactically difficult. The absence of the first כָּל ("all") in a number of Hebrew mss. plus the Syriac leads BHS to suggest deleting it due to dittography.

58. Gauthier argues cogently for translating כָּל-הֶבֶל as the predicate in a nominal sentence, while כָּל-אָדָם is the subject. *BDB* treats the *niphal* participle נצב ("to stand") adverbially, presumably based on the disjunctive accent (כָּל-אָדָם). With this interpretation, following NET, נצב introduces a concessive clause: "Surely all people, *even* those who seem secure, are nothing but vapor." נצב in this instance then has a broader social viewpoint: "even those who are firmly established in this life are but a disappearing vapor." According to Gauthier, most English translations, however, disregard the disjunctive accent, rendering נצב "as a simple adjectival participle" (e.g., NRSV, "Surely everyone stands"). Gauthier, *Psalms 38 and 145*, p. 176.

59. Buttenweiser's conjectural emendation for 5C[6C], "a mere breath is every man," based on the refrain-like recurrence of the phrase in 11C[12C], and the deletion of both the כָּל (due to dittography) and נָצָב based on the LXX rendering, is unwarranted. See Moses Buttenweiser, *The Psalms Chronologically Treated with a New Translation* (Chicago: University of Chicago Press, 1938), p. 551.

60. See p. 80 (note 39 in chapter 4).

61. Construing *beth* on בְּצֶלֶם as *beth essentiae* ("like a fleeting shadow"). See Harry M. Orlinsky, *Library Biblical Studies: The Psalms* (New York: Ktav, 1969), p. 151.

62. The transitive verb יִצְבֹּר ("heap/pile up") lacks an object, and the pronoun "them" on אֹסְפָם ("gathers them") lacks an antecedent. These anomalies can be resolved by reading הֶבְלֵי הָמוֹן ("vain/fleeting things of wealth"), instead of הֶבֶל יֶהֱמָיוּן ("in vain they strive"), assuming the *yodh* of הבלי is a *hireq compaginis* (IBHS, P. 8.2e, p. 127), a misdivision of words, and a dittography of final *yodh*. See NET Bible.

7   And now,[63] what am I eagerly waiting for, Lord?[64]
      My hope[65] is in you.
8   From all my transgressions[66] save me;
      Do not make me[67] the reproach of the fool.
9   I am silent; I do not open[68] my mouth;
      because you[69] did it.
10   Remove your scourge[70] from me;
      I am consumed by the blow[71] of your hand.
11   With rebukes you discipline a person for sin;
      you consume like a moth what is dear to them.
      Surely all humankind is a breath.   Selah.[72]

12   Hear my prayer, "I AM," and listen to my cry for help.
      Do not[73] be deaf to my tears,
      for I am a resident alien with you, a sojourner[74] like all my ancestors.
13   Look away[75] from me so that I may be comforted;
      Before I go and am no more.

For the director of music. (Psalm 40:1a)

---

63. וְעַתָּה can be understood in a temporal sense, in opposition to the psalmist's previous mindset (so J. A. Alexander, *The Psalms: Translated and Explained* [New York: Charles Scribner, 1853], p. 175) or as a logical particle, "based on what was just said."

64. Many Hebrew mss. read יהוה instead of אֲדֹנָי.

65. Literally, "as for my hope, it."

66. Bardtke's *(BHS)* emendation, פֹּשְׁעַי ("those who rebel against me"), is unwarranted.

67. Bardtke's *(BHS)* suggestion to omit אַל due to haplography is spuriously based on the LXX ὄνειδος ἄφρονι ἔδωκάς με ("you made me an object of criticism for a fool"). For Gauthier's argument against this, see *Psalms 38 and 145*, p. 198.

68. LXX and two late Hebrew mss. read "and I cannot open."

69. Independent personal pronoun אַתָּה is emphatic.

70. "Scourge" renders נֶגַע, translated as "wounds" in 38:11[12].

71. The meaning of מִתִּגְרַת is disputed. Based on the LXX ("from the strength"), Bardtke *(BHS)* suggests emending to מִגְּבוּרַת. *HALOT* (p. 1684, s.v. מִתְגָּרֶה) thinks a meaning such as "blow" is better because it is the more difficult reading.

72. See n. 60.

73. A number of Hebrew mss. read "and do not."

74. תּוֹשָׁב signifies a landless individual, dependent on another as a vassal (Gen. 23:4 of Abraham; Lev. 25:23 of all Israel; 1 Chron. 29:15 David of his contemporaries).

75. Bardtke's *(BHS)* suggested emending of the *hifil* imptv. הָשַׁע to *qal* imptv. שְׁעֵה based on LXX ἄνες ("leave [me] alone") is unwarranted because the LXX, unlike MT, lacks an oral tradition (see *IBHS*, P. 1.6.3, pp. 24-28).

PART III. COMMENTARY

I. Introduction

A. *Literary Context*

This psalm of individual lament comes near the end of Book 1, the so-called Davidic Psalter (Psalms 1–41). It has been identified as an elegy for some serious affliction (Dahood), be it illness (Briggs) or an overwhelming sense of the psalmist's own mortality (Craigie). The psalmist understands his suffering as punishment for his sins and cries out to the Lord to cease from afflicting him (vv. 8-9[9-10]). The psalm shares the theme of confession of sin with Psalms 38, 40–41, which in Book 1 is found elsewhere only in Psalms 25 and 32.

Zimmerli identifies Psalms 38 and 39 as "twin psalms" *(Zwillingspsalmen)*[76] noting themes that connect the two: resolution to silence before enemies (38:13-14[14-15]; 39:1-2[2-3]); urgent appeal for reprieve from severe illness (38:21-22[22-23]; 39:8, 10, 12[9, 11, 13]); acknowledgment that the illness is a divine rebuke for sin (38:1, 3[2, 4]; 39:9[10]); confession of sin (38:13-14, 18[14-15, 19]; 39:8[9]); and declaration of trust in the LORD (38:15, 22[16, 23]; 39: 7[8]). Unlike Psalm 38 (*lᵉhazkîr*, "to bring to remembrance"; Psalm 70), in Psalm 39 David replaces an extended lament of his physical (and psychological) sufferings with a brief lament and sapiential reflection on the transitoriness of human life before petitioning "I AM" in repentance (compare 38:2-15[3-16] with 39:4-6, 11[5-7, 12]). Instructively, both Psalms 38 and 39 fall short of a full confession of praise that typically ends the psalms of lament.[77] The emphasis on perverse personal enemies so dominant in Psalm 38 is abandoned in Psalm 39, as the psalmist focuses on the transitory nature of life and his suffering at "I AM's" hand due to his sin. However, thanksgiving and praise for deliverance from illness follow in 40:1-10[2-11], before the theme of lament for suffering is resumed in 40:12-17[13-18]. Praise for deliverance from illness follows in Psalm 41, closing Book I on a note of praise.[78]

---

76. For other pairs of Psalms that Zimmerli identifies as *Zwillingspsalmen*, see Walther Zimmerli, "Zwillingspsalmen," in *Wort, Lied, and Gottesspruch: Beiträge zu Psalmen und Propheten*, ed. J. Schreiner (Würzburg/Stuttgart: Echter, 1972), pp. 105-13.

77. Westermann identifies as "constituent parts of the LI (individual lament): address, lament, confession of trust, or assurance of being heard, petition, vow of praise." See Claus Westermann, *Praise and Lament in the Psalms* (Atlanta: John Knox, 1981), p. 64.

78. In DSS 11QPsd. Psalm 39 (only extant for vv. 12-13[13-14]) is preceded by Ps. 37:1-4 and followed by Psalm 40; in 4QPsa, Psalm 39 is omitted, with Psalm 71 following Psalm 38. See Gauthier, *Psalms 38 and 145*, p. 121.

B. Form Criticism

The psalm's superscript identifies the psalm as a *mitkam*[79] of David. From a form-critical perspective, this prayer does not follow the order and the motifs of a typical lament psalm:[80] the expected opening address to "I AM" is replaced with a statement of the psalmist's resolution to silence in the midst of his intense suffering and pain (compare 38:1[2] with 39:1-4[2-5]). The description of the psalmist's intense suffering (39:2B-3[3B-4]), his confidence (39:7[8]), and his petition for relief (39:8[9], 10[11], 12[13]) are typical; but the wisdom-style reflection on the ephemerality of human life is somewhat unexpected (39:4-6[5-7], 11[12]). Instead of the expected praise to "I AM" for deliverance, David petitions "I AM" for relief from his gaze: "Frown on me no more" (NEB), so that the psalmist may once again rejoice (v. 13[14]).

C. Rhetorical Criticism

A dizzying array of suggestions have been offered regarding the psalm's structure. Alexander divides the psalm into two parts:[81] verses 1-6[2-7] and 7-13[8-14], in which the first part describes the psalmist's conduct at a former period in relation to God's providential dealings; the second expresses what he now feels and believes in reference to the same subject, closing with an earnest appeal for divine compassion.[82] Spurgeon observes a tripartite structure: verses 1-2[2-3], the stifling of unbelief; verses 3-6[4-7], a complaint regarding the "desponding picture of human life"; and verses 7-13[8-14], submission to God's sovereignty, as "the cloud has evidently passed, and the mourner's heart is relieved."[83] Kirkpatrick divides the psalm into four stanzas: (a) resolution to silence in the face of temptation (vv. 1-3[2-4]); (b) impossibility of silence (vv. 4-6[5-7]); (c) humanity's ephemerality (vv. 7-9[8-10]); and (d) petition for help (vv. 10-13[11-14]).[84]

Though there is no unanimity regarding proposed structures, from a rhetorical viewpoint, there is good reason to divide the psalm into a four-stanza

---

79. Waltke and Houston, *PACW*, p. 327.

80. Waltke and Houston, *PACW*, p. 95.

81. So too Limburg and Perowne, but both divide: verses 1-3(2-4) and 4-13(5-14). See James Limburg, *Psalms* (Louisville: Westminster John Knox, 2000), p. 130; Perowne, *Psalms*, p. 326.

82. Alexander, *The Psalms*, p. 172.

83. C. H. Spurgeon, *The Treasury of David*, vol. 1 (McLean, VA: Macdonald Publishing Company, n.d.), p. 214.

84. A. F. Kirkpatrick, ed., *The Book of Psalms* (Cambridge: Cambridge University Press, 1910), pp. 202-3.

lament,[85] with verse 6[7], a sapiential meditation, serving as the hinge verse. NIV Study Bible notes: "The first two stanzas of five and three Hebrew poetic lines are balanced by the last two stanzas of five and three lines." The first stanza (vv. 1-3[2-4]) depicts "the inner turmoil of a silent sufferer,"[86] followed by the second stanza in which the psalmist laments the fleeting nature of his own life (vv. 4-5[5-6]). Verse 6[7] stands alone as a wisdom-like reflection on the transitoriness of human life in general. The third stanza (vv. 7-11[8-12]) contains a plea to "I AM" for forgiveness of sin and deliverance from suffering. Its initial strophe (vv. 7-8[8-9]) shifts the psalmist's focus from his problems to the source of resolution: "I AM." After acknowledging that his hope is in "I AM" (v. 7[8]), the psalmist's tone in the third stanza alternates between pleas to "I AM" for forgiveness (v. 8[9]) and deliverance (v. 10[11]), with indicative statements providing a rationale for the psalmist's requests: acknowledgment of divine sovereignty in suffering (v. 9[10]), and the nexus between sin and suffering (v. 11A[12A]). In the final stanza (vv. 12-13[13-14]) the psalmist petitions "I AM" to hear his prayer, because he shares the status of resident alien and sojourner with Israel's ancestors under the protective care of "I AM" (v. 12B[13B]). The concluding verse (v. 13[14]) falls short of the expected note of resounding praise, but the supplication to "I AM" is given in faith and contains an implicit nod in that direction.

In verses 1-6[2-7] the tricolon pattern dominates. In each case the second colon expands on the first (Kugel's "A < B"), with the third colon functioning to demonstrate the significance of the first two.[87] The tricolon pattern is broken in verse 7[8], which also marks a break in the thought flow of verses 1-6[2-7], as the psalmist shifts from a horizontal to a vertical perspective. A bicolon pattern dominates verses 7-10[8-11], before returning to the tricolon pattern in verses 11-12[12-13]. The psalm ends with an abrupt bicolon (v. 13[14]). The two Selahs (after vv. 6[7] and 11[12]) follow the statement that "humankind is but a breath."[88]

The asymmetrical structure of the psalm mirrors the psalmist's vacillations between lament, petition, and reflection. This give-and-take rings true to the life

85. Clifford observes that a fourfold structure can be supported by the Hebrew word count: "verses 1-3 (24 words); verses 4-6 (36 words); verses 7-11 (37 words); verses 12-13 (22 words). Parts 1 and 4 have approximately the same number of words, as do parts 2 and 3. The parts are tied together thematically: the themes of silence and suffering that dominate part 1 are repeated in part 3 (v. 9); and the theme of transience of human life in part 2 is repeated in part 4 (v. 12cd)." See Richard J. Clifford, *Scripture: Psalms 73–150* (Nashville: Abingdon, 2002), pp. 197-98.

86. Mark D. Futato, *The Book of Psalms*, Cornerstone Biblical Commentary Series (Carol Stream, IL: Tyndale, 2009), p. 151.

87. Robert G. Bratcher and William D. Reyburn, *A Handbook on the Psalms*, UBS Handbook Series (New York: United Bible Societies, 1991), p. 373.

88. Bratcher and Reyburn, *A Handbook*, p. 377.

of faith: "There is no steady march toward resolution of the silence, transience, or sin-suffering themes. On the contrary, these themes reappear and disappear, and in the end there is a build-up focusing upon the unbearable lightness of existence, in which the poet asks God to 'look away' from him so that he can enjoy his short moment before he becomes a nothing."[89]

I. Retrospective resolution to silence	1-3[2-4]
A. Statement of intent to be silent	1[2]
1. Mental resolve	1a[2a]
2. Metaphorical statement	1b[2b]
B. Impact of silence on the psalmist	2-3[3-4]
1. Increased anguish	2[3]
2. Intense internal burning	3[4]
II. Wisdom-type reflection on the transitoriness of life	4-6[5-7]
A. Petition for knowledge about the length of the psalmist's life	4[5]
B. Acknowledgment of the transitoriness of life	5[6]
1. Fleetingness of psalmist's individual life	5a[6a]
2. Fleetingness of humankind in general	5b[6b]
C. Acknowledgment of the futility of humankind's activities	6[7]
III. Address to "I AM"	7-12[8-13]
Declaration of the psalmist's trust in "I AM"	7[8]
A. Petition for forgiveness	8[9]
B. Acknowledgment of "I AM's" hand in his suffering	9[10]
C. Petition for deliverance from present sufferings	10[11]
B'. Acknowledgment of "I AM's" hand in humanity's sufferings	11[12]
A'. Petition for deliverance	12[13]
IV. Implicit confidence in the psalmist's final petition for deliverance	13[14]

Another way to understand the rhetoric of the psalm is to divide it into two equal halves with verse 7[8] at the center:

A. Psalmist's silence leads to anguish	(vv. 1-2[2-3])
B. Fleetingness of human life	(vv. 3-4[4-5])
C. Brevity and vanity of human life	(vv. 5-6[6-7])
D. Psalmist's declared hope is in the Lord	(v. 7[8])
C'. Petition for spiritual salvation	(vv. 8-9[9-10])
B'. God's power and sovereignty in human affairs	(vv. 10-11[11-12])
A'. Prayer anticipating relief	(vv. 12-13[13-14])

---

89. Bratcher and Reyburn, *A Handbook*, p. 373.

II. Exegesis

A. *David's Retrospective Resolve of Silence (39:1-3[2-4])*

1[2]   The word translated "muzzle" *(maḥsôm)* is a *hapax;* the verbal root occurs in Deuteronomy 25:4 and Ezekiel 39:11 where it means to incapacitate the mouth of an ox and block the way of passers-by, suggesting the noun is best translated as muzzle rather than a curb or bridle, which functions to control but not silence the mouth.[90] *In front of me* glosses *lᵉnegeddî*, with preposition *lᵉ* denoting a hostile sense.[91] The nature of the opposition that David is facing is not expressed, although this latter reflection on the futility of amassing great wealth (vv. 5-6[6-7]) suggests a struggle with envy over the prosperity of the wicked in light of the psalmist's own personal strife (hence Terrien translates, "But my pain became intolerable in view of [his] prosperity").[92]

This is not the coercive silence of Habakkuk 2:20b; rather, the psalmist feared lest his complaint should be misinterpreted as murmuring.[93] Calvin: "it is generally understood . . . lest he should give occasion of blasphemy to the wicked, who, as soon as they see the children of God fail under the weight of their afflictions, insolently break forth into derision against them, which amounts to a contempt of God himself."[94] David is aware of his enemies' relentless efforts to trap him.

2[3]   *I kept myself silent for a good reason* translates the obscure second colon *(heḥᵉšêtî)*. If the preposition *min* is read as a privative *min,* the sense is that the psalmist's silence proved harmful. In his desire to avoid the language of complaint he was altogether silent "and suppressed even what might have been said without sin or what he was in duty bound to say. The natural effect was that his inward grief, instead of being soothed, was roused, excited and exasperated."[95] It is better read, however, as a causal *min,* "for a good reason," that is, David understood the damaging effects of openly complaining about the prosperity of the wicked, and he did not want to give the wicked any opportunity to denounce "I AM" (Psalm 37; Prov. 13:3; 21:23). The psalmist elaborates on the results of his resolution to

90. Alexander, *The Psalms*, p. 173.

91. BDB p. 617.

92. Samuel Terrien, *The Psalms: Strophic Structure and Theological Commentary* (Grand Rapids: Eerdmans, 2003), p. 39.

93. Perowne, *Psalms*, p. 326.

94. John Calvin, *Commentary on the Book of Psalms,* vol. 1 (Grand Rapids: Baker; reprinted 2003), p. 73.

95. Alexander, *The Psalms*, p. 173.

silence, rehearsing the misery he experienced during his time of vowed silence. Determined not to give his calumniators any ammunition with which to mock "I AM," he resolves not to complain about "I AM's" perplexing providences. Anguish consumes him.

3[4] *My heart grew hot within me* vividly describes the inner turmoil experienced by David as he refuses to vent his frustrations. *Ham* (grew hot) is used to describe the burning with perverse lust by those practicing pagan cultic fertility rituals in Isaiah 57:5. The only other occurrence of the root *ham* (grew hot) with *lēḇ* (heart) is Deuteronomy 19:6, where it is used to describe the rage felt by the avenger of blood. Here in Psalm 39 it describes the anxiety-stoked fire raging in the psalmist's bosom, building up to a boiling point as he refuses to vent his feelings.

I *spoke with my tongue* is not the psalmist's admission that he is breaking his vow of silence (v. 2[3]). Rather, the repetition of *ne'elamtî* (with *dûmiyyāh*, 2[3] "was completely silent") coupled with "I do not open my mouth" (v. 9[10]) indicates that his vow was not unqualified and that he had in fact maintained his vow. His speaking is not a violation, but a breakthrough. Instead of concealing, his silence exasperated his despair. "[T]he less he said, the more he thought and felt until at last it burst forth with more violence than if expressed at first. . . . Without, all seemed calm and cool; within, his heart was in a glow on fire."[96] According to Spurgeon, "As he thought upon the case of the wicked and his own daily affliction, he could not unravel the mystery of providence, and therefore he became greatly agitated. While his heart was musing it was fusing, for the subject was confusing."[97]

B. Sapiential Reflection on the Transitoriness of Life (39:4-5[5-6])

4[5] David had resolved to keep quiet in the presence of the wicked, but before "I AM" he is able to open his mouth and acknowledge his transience (v. 4[5]). Exasperated and overcome by despair under growing emotional pressure, he finally burst forth in speech like a volcanic eruption. Clifford contends that the psalmist's imploring, *"I AM," make me know my end and the extent of my days, what it is,* is a petition to know when his personal affliction will end rather than seeking more information on life's ephemerality.[98] According to Clifford, the psalmist is not asking for enlightenment regarding the transitoriness of life — he

96. Alexander, *The Psalms*, pp. 173-74.
97. C. H. Spurgeon, *Treasury of David*, p. 310.
98. Clifford, "What Does the Psalmist Ask For?" p. 165.

clearly demonstrates that he knows this already in vv. 5, 6, 11(6, 7, 13). Instead Clifford argues that the psalmist is expressing his desire to know the duration of his own sufferings.[99] Clifford derives lexical support by translating *qēṣ* as "term/end/limit" and *ḥāḏēl* as "cease/stop" rather than "fleeting." Discussing a similar interpretive issue in Psalm 90, Clifford notes, "As in Psalm 39, two themes appear to have been confused in the interpretive tradition, the theme of human transience and fragility designed to win God's mercy and the theme of requesting the time that only God knows. Psalm 39 combines the two to make a single argument: let me know how long this affliction will last (v. 5), for you know that human life is too short to be entirely spent in suffering (vv. 6-7)."[100] Contra Clifford, David poses a rhetorical question; the psalmist is not seeking more information about life's brevity.[101] Nor does the passage accord with Hengstenberge, Qimchi, and Calvin, who all interpret the question negatively as expressing impatience in the psalmist's tone ("Just tell me when my life will end"). Such an interpretation, according to Alexander, is "at variance with the tone of sad resignation which breathes through the Psalm."[102]

It is better to translate *qiṣṣî* ("my end") as the end of life (so also Gen. 6:13 [the end of humanity]; Job 6:11 [the end of Job's life]; the destruction of Jerusalem [Lam. 4:18]; and the final adversary [Dan. 11:45]).[103] The appositional clause *what it is (mâ hî')* emphasizes the psalmist's concern with his own mortality.

5[6]   The psalmist's appeal to "I AM" continues with the deictic particle "behold" *(hinnēh)*, which draws attention to what immediately follows, the wisdom reflection on the vanity of amassing wealth. Continuing with the theme of life's transience, the psalmist opines that "I AM" has dealt out life to him in the scantiest measure, *a handbreadth;* that is, he only appears in "I AM's" presence long enough to disappear; his life is inconsequential (*ke'ayin*, "as nothing"). Calvin, commenting on the significance of handbreadth, notes, "as if it had been said, the life of man flies swiftly away, and the end of it, as it were, touches the beginning."[104] *Transient* translates the lexeme *ḥebel* as denoting anything impalpable and evanescent — an inconsequential puff (vapor or breath) that vanishes into thin air. *Selah.*[105]

99. Clifford, "What Does the Psalmist Ask For?" pp. 161-62.
100. Clifford, "What Does the Psalmist Ask For?" p. 166.
101. Contra the LXX (ἵνα γνῶ τί ὑστερῶ ἐγώ) and contra Limburg who comments on this verse, "The writer of this psalm asks the Lord to give it to him straight" (*Psalms,* p. 130).
102. Alexander, *The Psalms,* p. 328.
103. *BDB,* p. 893.
104. Calvin, *Psalms,* p. 77.
105. On *selâ* see p. 80, n. 39.

6[7]   This verse beginning with the asseverative *'ak* ("Surely") is differentiated from the foregoing verses by its reflective style and reference to sapiential observation. The psalmist recognizes that he is being punished for his sin (vv. 8, 10[9, 11]), and so, in light of this existential reality, he exclaims how utterly foolish is the feverish activity and prosperity of the wicked. The reflection functions as a janus verse: summarizing his observations formulated in verses 4-5(5-6), and segueing into his plea for "I AM's" help in light of these sobering realities (vv. 7, 8, 10[8, 9, 11]). The psalmist imports sapiential reflections into his lament, likening humankind to a phantom, here one minute and gone the next, echoing similar passages in Job and Ecclesiastes (Job 7:7, 16; 8:9; 10:20; Eccles. 2:26; 5:16; 6:12).[106] It is instructive to note that David proceeds to contrast himself with the wicked in a following verse (8[9]). "Since the psalmist draws this distinction while he determines to restrain his speech, . . . it appears that the matter about which he was so anxious to talk concerns the dilemma of the wicked prospering and the godly envying that prosperity."[107]

According to Calvin, this is where David begins truly to pray; by the word *shadow,* the psalmist means that there is nothing substantial in humanity, "but that he is only, as we say, a vain show, and has I know not how much of display and ostentation." People disquiet themselves in vain, indicating "the very height of their vanity . . . born for the purpose of rendering themselves more and more contemptible: for only shadows, they involve themselves needlessly in harassing cares, and vexing themselves to no purpose . . . for by their insatiable desire of gain, they eagerly grasp at all the riches of the world, as if they had a hundred times the life of man."[108] Commenting on this verse in his *Treasury of David,* Spurgeon quotes from Shakespeare's *Macbeth*:

> To-morrow, and to-morrow, and to-morrow, / Creeps in this petty pace from day to day, / To the last syllable of recorded time; / And all our yesterdays have lighted fools / The way to dusty death. Out, out, brief candle! / Life's but a walking shadow; a poor player, / That struts and frets his hour upon the stage, / And then is heard no more; it is a tale / Told by an idiot, full of sound and fury, / Signifying nothing.[109]

---

106. Bratcher and Reyburn, *A Handbook,* p. 376.

107. Craig C. Broyles, *The Conflict of Faith and Experience in the Psalms: A Form-Critical and Theological Study,* Journal for the Study of the Old Testament (JSOT) Supplement Series 52 (Sheffield: Sheffield Academic Press, 1989), p. 197.

108. Calvin, *Psalms,* pp. 79-80.

109. C. H. Spurgeon, *Treasury of David,* p. 227.

C. Address to "I AM" (39:7-11[8-12])

Instead of leading to despair, these sobering reflections lead the psalmist to cry out to "I AM" as the only one in whom the burden of life's ephemerality can be ameliorated. In this section the psalmist addresses "I AM" with escalating petitions, two positive and one negative. The two positive requests are: 1. *save me* (*haṣṣîlēnî*, v. 8[9]) *from all my transgressions*, acknowledging his need for full forgiveness; and 2. *remove your scourge* (v. 10[11]), acknowledging that his affliction is the result of "I AM's" punishment of his sins. Negatively, he petitions "I AM" not to make him the scorn of fools (v. 8[9]). Throughout this stanza, David's imperatives alternate with indicatives that provide the basis for his urgent pleas. He can ask to be saved from his transgressions and the scorn of fools (v. 8[9]) because he acknowledges that the source of both his hoped-for salvation and sufferings is "I AM" (v. 9[10]). As Spurgeon puts it, "He misses often the result of his ventures, for there are many slips between the cup and the lip."[110]

7[8] The initial *but now, wᵉʿattâ* (both a temporal marker indicating discontinuity with the preceding verses[111] and a logical marker indicating a turn in the psalmist's mindset — "but now, as opposed to the past" [based on what has been said]) of this pivotal verse expresses the psalmist's confidence and hopeful expectation (Ps. 38:15[16]). Here, at the halfway point of the psalm, focus shifts from the psalmist's afflictions and wisdom reflections to his hope in "I AM" as he prays to be delivered from the consequences of his sin. The threefold repetition of *'ak* ("surely") in verses 6(7) and 7(8) unifies the two stanzas, as the anguished psalmist's march toward resolution is interspersed with further sapiential reflection on transience and silence. This imbalance functions to underscore the spiritual turbulence that accompanies the psalmist's suffering. The stylistic asymmetry matches the psalmist's spiritual state of disorientation (Job 16:19-20). Commenting on what is so remarkable about Old Testament faith, Perowne observes, "In the midst of the riddles of the present and in view of a future, losing itself in a night of gloom, it casts itself absolutely and without hesitation into the arms of God."[112]

8[9] Here David's prayer for deliverance includes an implicit recognition of God's governance. His declaration of trust in "I AM" is immediately followed

---

110. C. H. Spurgeon, *Treasury of David*, p. 312.

111. B. L. Bandstra, "Making Turns in Poetic Text: Waw in the Psalms," in *Narrative and Comment: Contributions Presented to Wolfgang Schneider*, ed. E. Talstra (Amsterdam: Societas Hebraica Amstelodamensis, 1995), p. 51.

112. Perowne, *Psalms*, pp. 328-29.

by two imperatives, one positive *(from all my transgressions save me)* and one negative *(do not make me the scorn of fools)*, denoting a sense of urgency as the psalmist acknowledges his sin and vulnerability. His sins go undescribed, though the consequence, *scorn of fools*, with Calvin, perhaps is intentionally polyvalent, "either that God would not abandon him to the mockery of the wicked,[113] or that he would not involve him in the same disgrace to which the ungodly are given over."[114]

9[10] The stanza's second strophe (vv. 9-11[10-12]) repeats the theme of the opening stanza (the psalmist's resolve to silence, vv. 1-2[2-3]), though the focus on the psalmist's enemies is muted in comparison with other psalms of individual lament.[115] David combines his appeal for deliverance with a return to "silence" (v. 2[3] and 38:13[14]). Medial logical particle *kî* introduces the second colon. He is not simply repeating his resolution to silence from verses 1-2[2-3], but advances his petition, acknowledging the sin-suffering nexus as he attributes his suffering to divine punishment. His earlier silence stemmed from his attempt to quell his envious questioning, but here "he is kept silent by a filial submission to his father's chastisements."[116] The significance of this silence is that it stems from his acknowledgment of "I AM" as the agent of his afflictions. "Nature failed to muzzle the mouth, but grace achieved the work in the worthiest manner."[117]

10[11] The pressure is more than he can bear, and so he prays for reprieve. *Remove your scourge from me* asks "I AM" to relieve him because he has been overcome by the blow of "I AM's" hand.[118]

11[12] With this verse, the psalm returns to a tricolon pattern. In the second colon, the psalmist draws a comparison between "I AM's" actions in judgment and the activity of a moth, a biblical image for destruction, decay, and consumption. Some versions (JPS, KJV) translate "and like a moth Thou makest his beauty to consume away," understanding the comparison to be between the fading and fleeting nature of what humanity treasures (i.e., "his beauty") and the frail, perishing character of the moth. This comparison requires a textual emendation that is not supported in any of the Hebrew manuscripts.[119] Better to understand

---

113. So Erasmus, see above, pp. 150-55.
114. Calvin, *Commentary*, p. 82.
115. C. Westermann, *Praise and Lament*, pp. 180, 190.
116. Alexander, *The Psalms*, p. 176.
117. C. H. Spurgeon, *Treasury of David*, p. 218.
118. See pp. 137-38 above (on Ps. 38:2[3]).
119. See n. 71.

the simile as comparing God's visitations in judgment to the silent, secret, yet destructive and decaying activity of the moth on a garment. In the context of pronouncing judgment on Ephraim, God likens himself to a moth (Hos. 5:12; cf. Job 4:19; 13:28; Isa. 50:9; 51:8; Matt. 6:19-20). Calvin notes, "although God does not openly thunder from heaven against the reprobate, yet, his secret curse ceases not to consume them away, just as the moth, though unperceived, wastes by its secret gnawing a piece of cloth or wood."[120]

Still haunted by humanity's ephemerality, the tricolon ends with the brief observation, *Surely all humankind is a breath* (v. 11C[12C]; cf. v. 5[6]). The two metaphors of *moth* and *breath* together emphasize humanity's tenuous existence as the psalmist has come full circle back to the point where he started but with an extraordinary change in perspective as he acknowledges "I AM's" hand in his afflictions before moving on to verse 12(13), in which the psalmist resists the impulse to turn inward in light of his reflections and instead turns to "I AM" as his only source of help.

D. Only Hope in "I AM" (39:12-13[13-14])

The fourth stanza climactically contrasts the psalmist's desire for an audience with "I AM" (v. 12[13]) with his wish for "I AM" to look away (v. 13[14]). At the heart of these paradoxical requests lies the psalmist's relationship to "I AM." He can appeal to "I AM" to listen to his urgent pleas because, like his fathers, he recognizes that life on this earth is a pilgrimage. In the first two cola of this stanza (v. 11a, b[12a, b]) the psalmist appeals to "I AM's" hearing, petitioning him both positively ("Hear my prayer"; 11a[12a]) and negatively ("Do not be deaf"; 11b[12b]). Medial logical particle *ki* (v. 12C[13C]) offers the basis for imploring "I AM" to respond; namely, because he is a member of the sojourning covenant community. In the concluding bicolon the psalmist implores "I AM" to *Look away* (13a[14a]), so that he may enjoy comfort before his death.

1. Pleas for "I AM" to Listen (39:12[13])

12[13] The stanza's opening strophe (v. 12[13]) is a tricolon that begins with the psalmist petitioning a sympathetic "I AM" to listen. Having recognized that his resolute silence kept him from the divine help, he now repeats his plea for divine deliverance. Brueggemann notes, "At the beginning of the psalm, the speaker noticed what has happened to him because he has kept silent too long. Now, at the

---

120. Calvin, *Commentary*, p. 86.

end, he is noticing that what happens to him is because God kept silent too long.”[121] *Deaf to my tears* (v. 12b[13b]) glosses *’el-dim‘āṭî ’al-teḥᵉraš*, a metonym for cry for help. Kirkpatrick notes a rabbinic saying: “there are 3 kinds of supplication, each superior to the other: prayer, crying, and tears. Prayer is made in silence, crying with a loud voice, but tears surpass all. ‘There is no door, through which tears do not pass,’ and ‘The gates of tears are never locked.’”[122] Medial logical particle *kî* links the psalmist’s pleas with the grounds for his bold appeal: *for I am a resident alien with you; a sojourner like all my ancestors* (v. 12c[13c]). *Resident alien* translates the Hebrew lexeme *gēr* (one who is but a passing guest); *sojourner* glosses the lexeme *tôšāḇ* (“one who settles for a time in a country but is not a native of it”). The two words together connote someone who has left their homeland in order to dwell as a “newcomer and resident alien without the original rights of the host community . . . in order to find protection, a resting place and home in another community.” The *gēr* is one who “possesses no land and so is usually poor and depends on the good will of the host.”[123] *Like all my ancestors:* David invokes “I AM’s” covenant promises, especially recalling the wilderness wanderings, as he summons “I AM” to action: the term *gēr* is applied to Abraham (Gen. 23:4); by Moses to the entire congregation of Israel (Lev. 25:23); and by David to himself and his contemporaries (1 Chron. 29:15). An image from the ancient Near East depicts starving nomads applying to an Egyptian official for status as protected aliens.[124] Here, the psalmist “now begs for the compassion that was legally granted to pilgrims and sojourners when Israel settled in the land (Exod 20:10; Deut 1:16).”[125] The sojourning metaphor is also used to describe the status of the New Testament covenant community as we await the return of Christ to establish his kingdom (Heb. 11:13; 1 Pet. 2:11).

As king, the psalmist appeals to God’s past dealings with the covenant community, the patriarchs in particular. What connects David with the past covenant community is his status as *before thee* (12c[13c]). Conversely, he closes his petition (v. 13[14]) by pleading with “I AM” to leave him alone.

2. Implicit Praise in the Psalmist’s Petition for Deliverance (39:13[14])

13[14]   The ambiguous note on which the psalm ends is a departure from the typical lament paradigm, which usually offers an actual praise to God for deliv-

121. Walter Brueggemann, “Voice as Counter to Violence,” *CTJ* 36 (2001): 29.

122. Kirkpatrick, *The Book of Psalms*, pp. 206-7.

123. Waltke and Houston, *PACW*, p. 296.

124. Othmar Keel, *The Symbolism of the Biblical World: Ancient Near Eastern Iconography and the Book of Psalms* (Winona Lake, IN: Eisenbrauns, 1997), p. 320.

125. Terrien, *The Psalms*, p. 333.

erance, or anticipates an outburst of confident expectation at the end.[126] "The last words of Psalm 39 are perhaps the most provocative and disturbing in all the Psalter, asking not for God's presence, but imploring God's absence: 'Turn your gaze from me, that I may smile again, before I depart and am no more' (v. 13)."[127]

The tension that arises as the psalmist moves from imploring God to deliver him (v. 12[13]) to a plea for relief from the divine gaze upon him (v. 13[14]) bears truthful testimony to the vagaries of the life of faith as both petitions cohere in God himself: it is to "I AM" that David prays for help and relief from the only one able to provide that help. This dissonance, which appears in several of the lament psalms (Psalms 38, 88, 143), is heightened here by the psalmist's compressed thought: he finishes his petition with six Hebrew words. Firth rightly observes, "The inclusion of these few unrelieved psalms in the Psalter is vivid testimony to ancient Israel's willingness to retain a record of unresolved anguish. And it has enabled many a believer in subsequent eras to express similar anguish, using them as both a model and a resource."[128]

Calvin, noting parallels between David and Job, concludes that the psalmist errs in his request to die in calmness and peace: "It is obvious, therefore, that although David endeavoured carefully to restrain the desires of the flesh, yet these occasioned him so much disquietude and trouble, that they forced him to exceed the proper limits in his grief."[129] But it is Calvin who errs, not reading the psalmist's words in the context of his profession of faith and hope in "I AM" (vv. 7-8[8-9]). It is in this context of covenant faith that David's pleas for reprieve from "I AM's" heavy hand of judgment must be read.

Before I go and am no more, a euphemism for death (1 Kgs. 2:2; 1 Chron. 17:11; Job 7:9b; Ps. 88:8), conveys the psalmist's desire for brief respite as he contemplates his own death. As Book 1, which is primarily about the life of David, draws to a close, we see a focusing on the end of David's life: Psalm 37:25 ("I was young and now am old"); Psalm 38 laments failing health, which may be connected with old age (vv. 3, 7[4, 8]); Psalm 39, as we have demonstrated, reflects on the transience of life in general and David's imminent death (vv. 4-6, 11, 13[5-7, 12, 14]). "Book I concludes with Psalm 41, which also makes references to death. It seems that David is finally on his deathbed."[130]

---

126. Westermann's "constituent parts" of individual laments. See *Praise and Lament*, p. 64.

127. Gary W. Charles, "Preaching the Psalms: Psalm 39," *Journal for Preachers* 31, no. 4 (Pentecost 2008): 17.

128. Philip S. Johnston and David G. Firth, eds., *Interpreting the Psalms: Issues and Approaches* (Downers Grove, IL: InterVarsity, 2006), p. 80.

129. Calvin, *Psalms*, p. 88.

130. Michael Barber, *Singing in the Reign: The Psalms and the Liturgy of God's Kingdom* (Steubenville, OH: Emmaus Road, 2001), p. 91.

PART IV. CONCLUSION

In this psalm, "I AM" afflicts his chosen king in response to sin to stir him to reflect upon the transience of life in a general and personal sense and to stir him to pray. David has the moral acumen to discern the sin-suffering nexus and responds by declaring the source of his hope is to be found in "I AM" alone. "I AM's" chosen king is able to distinguish between deserved and undeserved suffering. Unlike his protestation of innocence in Psalm 26, David here by faith acknowledges his sin, and it is this moral discernment that leads him to seek forgiveness from "I AM."

David's suffering and alienation (but not the sinful cause) typify the passions of our Lord in many ways. As Childs notes, "However one explains it, the final form of the Psalter is highly eschatological in nature. . . . The perspective of Israel's worship in the Psalter is eschatologically oriented."[131] We see this eschatological (messianic in particular) impulse in the following typological connections: (a) Both David and Jesus suffer God's wrath against sin, David for his own sin, Jesus vicariously for the sins of the world (vv. 7-8[8-9]; 2 Cor. 5:21; 1 Pet. 2:24); (b) David's resolve to silence before his enemy builds up internally until he can no longer contain it and he bursts forth in petition to God, confessing his sin and acknowledging his only hope is to be found in "I AM" (vv. 3-8[4-9]). Jesus remains silent and does not defend himself when falsely accused (Matt. 27:14; Mark 15:5; 1 Pet. 2:23): "He was oppressed and afflicted, yet he did not open his mouth; he was led like a lamb to the slaughter, and as a sheep before its shearers is silent, so he did not open his mouth" (Isa. 53:7, *NIV*). When our Savior did break his silence, it was not to confess his sins or to reflect on the transience of life in light of the inevitable death that awaits us all but to announce the defeat of death (John 19:30) and offer life eternal to those who believe in him (John 3:16-17; John 10:10); (c) After seeking forgiveness from "I AM," David petitions "I AM" to turn his holy gaze away from him, unable to stand under the scrutiny of his holy gaze; David wants it both ways and the tension is unsustainable (v. 13[14]); this tension between seeking divine presence and distance is shattered on the cross where Jesus suffers complete abandonment (Matt. 27:46; Mark 15:34) when "God made him who had no sin to be sin for us, so that in him we might become the righteousness of God" (2 Cor. 5:21) and members of the covenant community could stand in "I AM's" presence without fear, clothed in Christ's righteousness (Gal. 3:26).

In his reflections on Augustine and the Psalms, former Archbishop of Can-

---

131. Brevard Childs, *Introduction to the Old Testament as Scripture* (Philadelphia: Fortress Press, 1982), p. 518.

terbury Rowan Williams asks and answers, "But how can we understand words that imply alienation from God when they occur on the lips of Jesus? Only by reading them as spoken by the whole Christ, that is, Christ with all the members of his Body.[132] He speaks for us, makes his own the protesting or troubled cry of the human being, so that his own proper and perfect prayer to the father may become ours."[133] The believing community today can appropriate this psalm because of the finished work of Christ.

132. Perhaps reflecting on Augustine's *corpus Christi,* see above, pp. 18, 25.
133. Rowan Williams, "Augustine and the Psalms," *Interpretation* 58 (2004): 19.

CHAPTER 8

Psalm 44: Lament in National Catastrophe

PART I. VOICE OF THE CHURCH

I. Introduction

Lament over the loss of a battle is one thing. Lament for the captivity and exile of a nation, not once, but several times, reaches another depth. But who can plumb the unfathomable terrors of the genocide of a whole people! Uniquely Psalm 44 has been used for all these catastrophes. As the Jewish scholar Herbert J. Levine has attested: "Few verses in the Psalms have been as important as this one [Ps. 44:22] in the history of Jewish response to catastrophe."[1] For of all the verses of the Psalter quoted by its victims, none was more frequent and more prominent than this verse: "It is for Your sake that we are slain all day long, / that we are regarded as sheep to the slaughter." Throughout the Holocaust literature — memoirs, poems, rabbinic responses, in public arguments over Jewish resistance or passivity — this one verse has echoed its distinctive death knell.[2]

The Jerusalem temple was destroyed twice (587 BCE and 70 CE) and desecrated under Antiochus IV (168 BCE). In 1492, half a million Jews were expelled from Spain, preceded by earlier expulsions from England, France, and German towns. In our generation there has been the greatest tremendum of all: the Holocaust of 1933-45.

Affliction and lament may often fit together, but occasions like that expressed in Psalm 44 are too devastating to be fully understood. Various voices and diverse cultural contexts are needed to explore the depths of lament in such a psalm. We shall give voice to four great theologians of the church: Origen, Thomas Aquinas, Martin Luther, and John Calvin.

---

1. Herbert J. Levine, *Sing Unto God a New Song* (Bloomington and Indianapolis: Indiana University Press, 1995), p. 183.
2. Levine, *Sing Unto God*, p. 205.

175

II. Origen (c. 185-254)

Origen was born in the turbulent years that witnessed the beginning of the demise of the Roman Empire. Fierce persecution of the church in the midst of a growing confidence that highly educated Christians could outmatch the pagan philosophers (as Origen did with Celsus) was the context for Origen's writings. He argued, as a Platonist, that faith and reason were not incompatible, but both were essential for two differing levels of knowledge, rational and revelatory. Correlatively, he argued that prayer was as vital as thought; indeed, prayer should be the thought-life of the Christian, and that thought-life entails sharing in Christ's sufferings. Origen's two treatises, *On Martyrdom* and *On Prayer,* complement each other, for having the mind of Christ in communion with him is to enter into the fellowship of his sufferings. Von Balthasar has noted: "Origen's view of martyrdom, prayer, and Scripture merge into one vision of the Christian's life as a movement, towards perfect knowledge of God and perfect fellowship with Him through Christ."[3] Origen interprets the Christian life as a double journey: morally in this life, and spiritually in the life to come. This is why for Origen there is no lament about the prospect of martyrdom, which he encouraged his father to embrace, and which as a youth he would have volunteered to share with him.

In his treatise *On Martyrdom* he meditates on Psalm 44. Reflecting on verses 13-16[14-17] he notes: "It is likely that we shall both be reproached by our neighbors and scorned by those who surround us and shake their heads at us as fools. But in these circumstances let us say to God, "You have made us a reproach to our neighbors, the scorn and derision of those around us. You have made us a byword among the nations; the peoples shake their heads at us. I live in disgrace all day long, and my face is covered with shame at the taunts of those who reproach and revile me, because of the enemy, who is bent on revenge." But when all this happens, it is blessed to speak to God the next words (vv. 17-18[18-19]) boldly uttered by the prophet: "All this has come upon us, and we have not forgotten you, and we have not been false to your covenant, and our heart has not turned back."[4] Commenting on verses 21 and 22[22 and 23], Origen suggests that this picture of accepting external martyrdom is also an inward matter of the submissive heart before God: "Then we shall say to God what can only be said by martyrs, 'For your sake we are slain all the day long; we are accounted as sheep for the slaughter.'"[5] Quoting from the martyrdom of the seven brothers noted in

---

3. *Origen,* trans. Rowan A. Greer, and introduction by Hans Urs von Balthasar, The Classics of Western Spirituality (Ramsey, NJ, and New York: Paulist, 1979), p. 17.

4. *Origen,* pp. 54-55.

5. *Origen,* p. 55.

2 Maccabees, and then from the Gospel narratives in which Jesus tells his disciples to endure in their sufferings for his sake, Origen uses this psalm as the model prayer of the martyrs.

III. Thomas Aquinas (1226-1274)

Toward the end of his life, **Thomas Aquinas** wrote a commentary, *Super Psalmos,* on at least Psalms 1–54. Though the commentary was little studied by scholars, Thomas himself considered his reflections on the Psalms to be important. In many ways Origen is Aquinas's exemplar, for the latter takes Aristotle as seriously as Origen had taken Plato. He, too, integrated scholarship, prayer, and suffering as a continuum in the journey of the faithful Christian.

Aquinas also suffered. Born into an aristocratic Neapolitan family, his family imprisoned him as a youth to prevent him from joining the Dominican order. Later in his life he was subjected to adversity from his theological colleagues at the university of Paris.

Thomas reads Psalm 44 through the lens of Luke 6:22: as Christ suffered for us, we too should share in his sufferings. Basing his exegesis of Psalm 44 on Peter Lombard's *Glossalia,* he elaborates upon each verse. He identifies "the sons of Korah" (in the superscription) as "the sons of the passion of Christ which in these last days are appropriately called martyrs, because they imitate Christ. Christ has suffered for us, leaving us an example that we should follow in his steps."[6]

Thomas divides the psalm into three sections: the past prosperity of Israel (vv. 1-8[2-9]); the present adversity (vv. 9-22[10-23]); and the cry for divine help (vv. 23-26[24-27]). "Awake, why are you sleeping, O Lord?"[7] He interprets the psalm as a prayer "which elevates the intelligence towards God," whether in adversity or in blessing. In adversity the mind is raised toward God in need of help; in blessing the mind is also elevated in joy; both states promote transcendence.[8]

For Thomas, listening to God "through the use of the mind" is essential,[9] and this implies for him, listening to the Fathers as the source of wisdom. Far more serious, however, is the neglect and denial of God as the source of our salvation in idle boasting that is not true, as, according to his interpretation, occurs in verse 8[9]: "In God we make our boast all day long, and we will praise your name for-

6. Thomas Aquinas, *Commentaire sur les Psaumes,* trans. Jean-Éric Stroobant de Saint-Éloy, O.S.B. (Paris: Cerf, 2004), p. 551.

7. Thomas Aquinas, *Commentaire,* p. 551.

8. Thomas Aquinas, *Commentaire,* p. 552.

9. Thomas Aquinas, *Commentaire,* p. 552.

ever."[10] Whenever this boasting happened in Israel's past, Thomas continues, then disaster followed as the psalmist recites in verses 9-16[10-17]. When the afflicted protest that they have done no wrong against God (vv. 17-18[18-19]), then their sin of self-deception prevents them from seeing the reality. "But God knows the secrets of the heart" (v. 21[22]). It is this blindness to sin that makes martyrs of God's people "who are killed all day long" (v. 22[23]). At times, even the persecuted, claiming that they are being afflicted "for God's sake," may be in self-deception.

In the conclusion, the perplexed psalmist demands that God "Wake Up!" (v. 23[24]). Yet in Exodus 3:7 God states to Moses: "I have surely seen the affliction of my people who are in Egypt and have heard their cry because of their taskmasters. I know their sufferings. . . ." For Thomas, as we have noted, prayer is on a continuum between faith and reason, and thus it has to be communicated appropriately. When we think God has forgotten us, we cry out "Help us!" When we think God is asleep, we cry out, "Wake up!" And when we think God has forgotten us, we cry, "Rise up!" As an educated patient may call for the appropriate medical attention, so the pray-er utters the appropriate form of lament.

Yet Thomas was too early before the Reformation to appreciate the much greater complexity concerning the whole realm of human suffering, affliction, penitence, and salvation that would all have to be reassessed three centuries later.

IV. Martin Luther (1483-1546)

In **Martin Luther**'s first commentary on Psalm 44, the Reformer cheerfully assures us, "everything in this psalm is easy"![11] Between 1513 and 1515, Luther's first lectures as a university professor were on the biblical exposition of the Psalms. Based on notes *(glossia)* on the text that he handed out to his students, he would then give his impromptu notes *(scholia),* based on the four medieval levels of exegesis: the literal/historical, the allegorical/figural, the moral/tropological, and the anagogical/future glory.[12]

For nearly twenty years Luther was an Augustinian friar, and only gradually was he to discover that the Christian expression of devotion in the liturgical recitation of the Psalms had not two, but three levels: those wholly ignorant of its words and context, as expressed by "nuns" and indeed the common people; those who followed special "counsels" as monks or clergy, submitting to the threefold vows of poverty, chastity, and obedience; and now he was discovering a third level,

---

10. Thomas Aquinas, *Commentaire*, p. 555.
11. *Luther's Works*, ed. Hilton C. Oswald, vol. 10 (St. Louis: Concordia, 1974), p. 205.
12. *Luther's Works*, pp. 3-5.

where the whole people of God, by the indwelling Spirit of God, could sing the psalms, live by them, and have all their devotional life transformed by "being in Christ," *sola gratia* indeed! This was happening to Luther, probably still early in 1514, some seven years before he wrote *De votis monasticis iudicium* (*Judgment on the Monastic Vows,* 1521). An entirely new paradigmatic shift (the redefinition of the Christian's life — *sola Scriptura, sola gratia*) was now unfolding to Luther, for "Christ has opened the mind of those who are His so that they might understand the Scriptures."[13] This is why Luther could exclaim, "everything in this psalm is easy." Unfortunately, we have no record of any later homily by Luther on this psalm. What he writes in these *Dictata super Psalterium* is a fumbling reaching out to exercise "new ears" "to hear openly" "the spiritual meaning" of the text, as the operation of divine grace.[14] Luther is already interpreting this psalm as God's judgment against the self-righteous, quoting 1 Peter 4:17, "The time has come for judgment to begin at the household of God."

Although he had been an exemplary monk from 1505 until 1524, Luther began to see that the distinction between those seeking "perfection" in the monastic tradition of poverty, chastity, and obedience, according to "the Church counsels," and the lax religious life of the laity was not scriptural. Nor were theologies of human glory, or religious devotion exhibiting human performances, or "works" that God rewards. Instead his pastoral theology had become the "theology of the cross." Essentially, this expresses four realities: 1) who God is, in his holiness and as judge of sin, as well as lover and redeemer; 2) the human response to God must be in repentance and trust; 3) what the human, sinful condition is apart from God, and how God has acted to alter that; and 4) what kind of life trust in Christ brings to his disciples, as a cruciform way of being.[15] A lament psalm like Psalm 44 only deepened Luther's anguished conscience: before God he was not "perfect." Outward human deeds were no substitute for the inward gift of divine grace. Radical and comprehensive repentance is the beginning of a reunderstanding of what it is to be "human." Without God, we have no human identity; "our soul is humbled down to the dust" (v. 25[26]).

While Luther's pastoral theology is radical and clear, he shared the late-medieval ignorance and confusion about diseases and physical afflictions.[16] As

13. See the excellent essay by Dorothea Wendebourg, "Luther on Monasticism," in *The Pastoral Luther: Essays on Martin Luther's Practical Theology,* ed. Timothy J. Wengert (Grand Rapids: Eerdmans, 2009), pp. 32/*54.

14. *Luther's Works,* vol. 10, pp. 205-7.

15. This is well summarized in Robert Kolb, "Luther on the Theology of the Cross," in *The Pastoral Luther,* ed. Timothy J. Wengert, pp. 33-56.

16. Ronald L. Numbers and Darrel W. Amundsen, eds., *Health and Medicine in the Western Religious Tradition* (New York: Macmillan, 1986), pp. 65-107.

God's instruments, these adversities humble saint and sinner alike, generating terrifying images of the afterlife and making pestilence a purification of the life to come. Thus Luther shared in interpreting suffering in a positive role, driving the sinner from self-complacency to patient endurance, although he also tended to relativize the sinner's ills with almost Stoic indifference.

In 1520, when the Elector Frederick the Wise was taken gravely ill, Luther composed his Fourteen Consolations. He eliminates medieval advocacy of the help of the "canonized saints" in our illnesses, but still sees evils and blessings so intertwined that finally death is expressive of God's mercy, seeing in the sufferings of the risen Christ the ultimate resolution between good and evil. As June Strohl concludes in her study of Luther's thought: "The powerful theological and pastoral insight Luther offers in the Fourteen Consolations is the realization that what is perceived as evil can be transformed into a blessing, that sufferings of all kinds, and most especially death, become for believers signs of God's love and means of Christ's grace. This true consolation, like the righteousness of faith, is wholly God's gift."[17]

V. John Calvin (1509-1564)

Late in his life (1557), **John Calvin** completed his *Commentary on the Psalms*. He had been preaching every Sunday afternoon on the Psalms since 1547; later he developed more formal lectures as well. Writing later than Luther, his approach is less personally existential, and with growing apprehension of more persecution of the Protestants, he writes with a wider apprehension of the church's suffering. As strongly as Luther, his is "a theology of the cross," namely, that in deeper suffering the Christian knows God better.[18] But Calvin also sees the church militant as in a continual warfare with Satan and the world as his domain.

Commenting on Psalm 44:1[2], he argues that just as the return from captivity did not bring an end to the sufferings and struggles of Israel, so also will the church continue to experience hardship even after the death, resurrection, and ascension of Christ. Until the time of Christ's Second Coming, "we should war under the banner of the cross, until we are received into the rest of the heavenly kingdom."[19] Christians are the soldiers of Christ.

17. Jane E. Strohl, "Luther's Fourteen Consolations," in *The Pastoral Luther*, ed. Timothy J. Wengert, p. 324.

18. Herman J. Selderhuis, *Calvin's Theology of the Psalms* (Grand Rapids: Baker Academic, 2007), p. 286.

19. John Calvin, *Commentary on the Book of Psalms,* trans. Rev. James Anderson, vol. 2 (Grand Rapids: Baker, 2005), p. 149.

Calvin interprets the first eight verses of Psalm 44 not just as a historical recitation of God's past benefits to Israel. The church, too, benefits from that recitation by being reminded of God's unchanging character, so that "we should assuredly believe that we shall also in due time experience some relief, since God continues unchangeably the same."[20] Comparing our misery with the blessings others previously seemed to enjoy does not give us this perspective. It is the presence of the Holy Spirit that removes the language of complaint. "He communicates . . . the doctrine of salvation. . . . from age to age." As verse 3[4] emphasizes, this is only achieved by God. "The best means, therefore, of cherishing in us habitually a spirit of gratitude towards God, is to expel from our minds this foolish opinion of our own ability."[21] The psalmist "does not suppose any worthiness in Abraham," nor does the Lord. Calvin cites Moses: "The LORD did not set his affection on you and choose you because you were more numerous than other peoples. . . . But it was because the LORD loved you (Deut. 7:7, 8)."[22] In verse 4[5] Calvin suggests that the psalmist is praying for God to continue to send new deliverances to his people, for the church today as he did for Israel in the past. The conclusion is in verse 8[9], namely, that joy continues to go on flowing from all God's people, at all times.

From verse 9[10] onwards, there is a dramatic shift into lament about the present circumstances. The people's complaints multiply: God has rejected them; God no longer accompanies them into battle; they have been enslaved cheaply and contemptibly; they have been exposed openly to derision and scorn; and there is no end to their miseries (v. 15[16]). Verse 17[18] is pivotal, Calvin argues, for while the people "already attributed to God all the afflictions which they endured, if they should now say they were undeservedly afflicted, it would be the same thing as to accuse God of injustice; and thus what is here spoken would no longer be a holy prayer, but rather an impious blasphemy. . . . God has some good reasons for treating them so severely."[23] Nevertheless, God knows the hearts of the faithful — that they have kept covenant; they have not forgotten God; that their footsteps have not abandoned the ways of God; nor have they sought the help of false gods. Yet their destitution has been such that like Jonah, they have been abandoned to the sea monsters in the depths, despairing of life in the shadows of death. The third stanza of the psalm, according to Calvin, opens with verse 22[23], which the apostle quotes in Romans 8:36. It is the unmerited persecution of the church, in not denying Christ, which is cause for such affliction. "No," affirms

---

20. Calvin, *Commentary on the Book of Psalms*, p. 151.
21. Calvin, *Commentary on the Book of Psalms*, p. 153.
22. Calvin, *Commentary on the Book of Psalms*, pp. 153-54.
23. Calvin, *Commentary on the Book of Psalms*, p. 163.

the apostle, "we are more than conquerors through him who loved us . . . so that nothing can separate us from the love of God in Christ" (Rom. 8:37, 39). But the psalmist without this "Christian" interpretation has to pray: "Are you sleeping, O God? . . . Why do you hide your face? . . . Come to our help . . . redeem us for the sake of your steadfast love!" They are crushed in their affliction, and only God's redemption can save them. Calvin concludes: "They are contented to ascribe their salvation to the unmerited goodness of God as the sole cause of it."[24] No other commentator can probe this despairing issue of theodicy any deeper. God's ways of governance are a mystery to us, such that "human suffering emanates from God but he is not to be blamed."[25]

PART II. VOICE OF THE PSALMIST: TRANSLATION

By[26] the Sons of Korah. A *maskil.*

1   God, we have heard it with our ears,
          Our fathers have told us
          What[27] you did in their days,
              In days long ago.
2   You — your hand — drove out the nations and planted our fathers; [28]
          You broke[29] the peoples but made them flourish.
3   Surely, they did not possess the land by their sword
          Nor did their own arm bring them victories;
          Surely [it was] your right hand, your arm, and the light of your face,
              For you favored them.
4   You alone are[30] my King and my God,

---

24. Calvin, *Commentary on the Book of Psalms,* p. 172.

25. Selderhuis, *Calvin's Theology of the Psalms,* p. 103.

26. Construing, with LXX and Talmud, *lamedh* with personal name to signify authorship. See Bruce K. Waltke and James M. Houston with Erika Moore, *The Psalms as Christian Worship (PACW)* (Grand Rapids: Eerdmans, 2010), pp. 89f.

27. Lit., "the deed," a collective singular (*IBHS,* P. 7.2.1b) and a cognate effected accusative (P. 10.2.1f).

28. Lit., "them."

29. רָעַע *rāʿaʿ* means: "treat badly, cause difficulties and injury" (*PACW,* p. 301). In a figure involving trees and branches, רָעַע probably means "to break" (cf. Jer. 11:16; Amos 2:9). The prefix conjugation is construed as a customary imperfect (i.e., "you broke time and again," *IBHS,* 31.2b).

30. Grammar signifies "you" has a "selective-exclusive" force (*IBHS,* P. 16.3.3c).

Who[31] decrees victories[32] for Jacob.

5   Through you we gore[33] our adversaries;
     Through your name we trample our assailants.

6   Surely, I put no trust in my bow,
     My sword does not save me;

7   Surely, you save us[34] from our enemies,
     You put our adversaries to shame.

8   In God we make our boast all day long,
     And to your name we will give credit forever.[35]

9   But no, you rejected[36] and humiliated us;
     You no longer go forth[37] with our militias.

10   You routed us[38] before the adversary,
     And those who hate us have plundered us.[39]

11   You gave us up[40] as a flock to be devoured as food[41]
     And have scattered[42] us among the nations.

12   You sold your people for a pittance,
     You did not set a high price on them.

---

31. Reading retroversion of LXX *(ho theos mou)* and Syriac מַצֻוֶּה אֱלֹהָי *ʾelōhay mᵉṣawweh* in place of MT's אֱלֹהִים צַוֵּה *ʾelōhîm ṣawēh*, because incorrect word division is a common scribal error, and MT's petition in a stanza on confidence is atypical.

32. The relatively rare plural יְשׁוּעוֹת *yᵉšûʿôt* is construed as a countable plural, for vv. 5, 7[6, 8] of the strophe (vv. 4-7[5-8]) have many past historic enemies in view in contrast to the singular enemy of the lament stanza (vv. 9-16[10-17], esp. 10[11] and 16[17]).

33. Construed as a habitual imperfect *(IBHS, P. 31.3e)*.

34. Construed as gnomic perfective *(IBHS, P. 30.5.1c)*.

35. For meaning of סֶלָה *selâ* see p. 80, n. 39, above.

36. Construed as a preterite *(IBHS, P.30.5.1b)*.

37. Construed as present progressive imperfect *(IBHS, P. 31.3b)*.

38. Lit., "you caused us to turn (see Ps. 6:4[5]) back[ward]," a picture of a retreat in flight.

39. A gloss for "for themselves" (לָמוֹ, *lāmô*, "benefactive dative" [*IBHS*, P. 11.2.10d]): "Their enemies destroyed them at their pleasure and without any resistance" (Calvin, *Commentary on the Book of Psalms*, p. 158).

40. Yigal Bloch ("The Prefixed Perfective and the Dating of Early Hebrew Poetry — A Re-Evaluation," *Vetus Testamentum* 59 [2009]: 34-70, esp. 64-66) construes the prefixed conjugation in vv. 9-16[10-17] as the old prefixed conjugation that signified a preterite situation *(IBHS, P. 31.1.1)*. But this form can also be construed as an incipient past imperfective *IBHS, P. 31.2c)*. A conclusive decision between these two interpretations cannot be reached, because aspect represents the author's subjective view of a situation. More certainly, Bloch's thesis that the short prefix conjugation does not point to early Hebrew poetry does not hold, because he arbitrarily late dates Ps. 44 to the sixth century BCE (see "superscript," below).

41. Lit., "flock of food" (genitive of mediated object, *IBHS*, 9.5.2d).

42. Construed as present perfect *(IBHS, P. 30.5.2b)*.

13   You have made us a reproach among the nations,
         The laughter and derision of those around us.
14   You have made us a byword among the nations;
         Foreign peoples wag their heads.[43]
15   All day long my ignominy is before me,
         And the shame of my face covers me[44]
16   at[45] the voice of the one who reproaches and blasphemes,[46]
         Because of[47] the enemy and the avenger.

17   All this came[48] upon us, though[49] we had not forgotten you;
         We had not been false to your covenant.
18   Our hearts had not turned back;
         Our steps[50] had not[51] strayed from your path.[52]
19   But no![53] You crushed us in a haunt for jackals;[54]
         You covered us over with a shadow of death.[55]

43. The Leningrad Codex has the improbable reading מְנוֹד רֹאשׁ בַּל-אֻמִּים *mᵉnôḏ rōʾs bal-ʾūmmîm*, "a wagging of head, not peoples." But more than twenty medieval mss. plus editions of the Hebrew text according to Kennicott, de Rossi, and Ginsburg have the more probable reading מְנוֹד-רֹאשׁ בַּל-אֻמִּים *mᵉnôḏ rōʾš bil ʾūmmîm*, "a wagging of heads among the peoples."

44. Facilitating emendation changes MT's כִּסָּתֵנִי *kissāṭᵉ nî*, "[shame of my face] covers me" into כִּסְּתָה *kissᵉtâ*, "[shame] covers my face." See e.g., W. O. E. Oesterley, *The Psalms: Translated with Text-Critical and Exegetical Notes* (London: SPCK, 1962), p. 246. But MT cannot readily be explained away; the emendation obviously involves more than "a change of a single consonant" (pace Robert Alter, *The Book of Psalms: A Translation with Commentary* [New York and London: W. W. Norton, 2007], p. 156).

45. Lit., "from."

46. מְחָרֵף וּמְגַדֵּף *mᵉḥārēp ûmᵉgaddēp* and מִפְּנֵי אֹיֵב וּמִתְנַקֵּם *mippᵉnē ʾôyēḇ ûmiṯnaqqēm* are a word pair similar in sound. Note the consonance of /m/ and the assonance of /ē/ of this verse.

47. Construing the literal "from the presence of" as having causal significance (*HALOT*, p. 943, s.v. פָּנֶה, entry 5d); note the parallel to "at the voice of" (see n. 45).

48. BDB, p. 98, s.v. *bôʾ*, entry 2b.

49. Lit., "and" (see *IBHS*, P. 649. 39.2.1c).

50. Reading אֲשֻׁרֵנוּ *ʾᵃšūrēnû* with many Mss., a collective singular agreeing with the third fem. sing. verb.

51. לֹא *lōʾ* is gapped in the B verset. The Greek Lucianic recension adds it.

52. אֹרַח *(ʾōraḥ)*, a poetic synonym for דֶּרֶךְ *derek̲*, may have been chosen for its assonance with אָחוֹר *(ʾāḥôr)*.

53. See *HALOT*, 2.470, s.v. *kî*, entry 3.

54. In the older versions תַּנִּים *tannîm* was mistakenly thought to mean "dragon" through a confusion with *tannîn* ("sea-monsters").

55. Reading צַלְמָוֶת *ṣalmāwet* with MT and LXX rather than the popular emendation צַלְמוּת *ṣalmût*. See Walter A. Michel, "Ṣlmwt, 'Deep Darkness' or 'Shadow of Death'?" *Biblical Research* 29 (1984): 5-20.

20   If we had forgotten the name of our God
         Or spread out our palms to a foreign god,
21   Would not God have searched this out,[56]
         Since he knows the secrets of the heart?
22   Yet for your sake[57] we are killed all day long;
         We are considered as sheep to be slaughtered.

23   Wake up, Lord! Why do you sleep?
         Rouse yourself! Do not reject us forever.
24   Why do you hide your face?
         Forget our misery and oppression?
25   Our lives[58] sink down to the dust;
         Our bodies cling to the ground.
26   Rise up as our helper[59];
         And redeem us on account of your unfailing love.

45:1   For the director of music. To the tune of "Upon Lilies."[60]

PART III. COMMENTARY

I. Introduction

A. *Literary Context*

The ten psalms[61] by the sons of Korah (42, 44, 45, 46, 47, 48, 49, 84, 85, 87) roughly frame the second and third books of the Book of Psalms (42–89), which consist largely of the so-called Elohistic Psalter (Psalms 42–83).[62]

---

56. The question expecting an affirmative answer is an emphatic assertion (i.e., "Most certainly God would have").

57. עַל *'al* (lit., "upon"), signifying advantage (*IBHS*, P. 11.2.13c).

58. The polyvalent נֶפֶשׁ *nepeš* could be glossed by "neck."

59. Lit., "as help (accusative of state modifying the subject [*IBHS*, P. 10.2.1c]) to us."

60. The gloss is an intelligent guess.

61. The superscription of Psalm 88, "A psalm of the sons of Korah," is part of an original subscript for Psalm 87. See *PACW*, pp. 80–88; 207–8.

62. The Elohistic Psalter is so named because it strikingly differs from the rest of the Psalter in the use of the divine names YHWH ("He Is") and *'lhym* (Elohim, "God"). In Psalms 1–41 and 84–150 YHWH occurs 584 times and *'lhym* 94 times. In Psalms 42–84, however, *'lhym* occurs 210 times and YHWH 45 times. In the rest of the Psalter YHWH mostly occurs in the A verset and Elohim in the B verset, but in Psalms 42–83 the reverse happens. Otherwise unknown combinations occur in

The Psalter's editors paired Psalm 44 with Psalms 42–43 — originally a unified psalm. Both psalms are included in the Korahitic collection, are a *maskil*, and complain in conclusions that their "life *(nepeš)* is bowed down" (*šûaḥ*, 42:5[6], 11[12], 43:5). Elsewhere they complain that God "rejects" (*zānaḥ*, 43:2; 44:10[11]) and "forgets (*šākaḥ*, 42:9, 10[10, 11]; 44:24[25]) them," while they are a "reproach" (*ḥārap*, 42:10[11]; 44:13[14]), and have to endure their affliction "all day long" (*kol-hayyôm*, 42:3; 44:22[23]). Yet both count on God to "command" (*ṣāwâ*, 42:8[9]; 44:4[5]) salvation and are confident of his "unfailing love" (*ḥesed*, 42:8[9]; 44:26[27]). Thus the second book of the Psalter deliberately begins with the lament of the individual (Psalms 42–43) and of the nation. Psalm 45 presents a striking contrast; the king's suffering under the feet of Gentiles (Psalm 44) is followed by his glory, including his marrying a Gentile bride who forsakes her family. Perhaps Jesus opened to his disciples this amazing contrast when he rebuked them from the Scriptures for not understanding that Messiah must first suffer before entering into his glory (Luke 24:25-27).

B. Form

The superscript labels Psalm 44 a *maskil* ("making prudent"). As such, it aims to instruct the covenant people in the theology of prayer for martyrs. According to contemporary form criticism the Psalm is a national lament.[63] "National," for

---

42–83: *Elohim Elohai* (43:4) and *Elohim Elohekha* (45:7[8]; 50:7). In synoptic Psalms the names are reversed (cf. Pss. 14:2, 4, 7 with 53:2[3], 4[5], 6[7]; 40:13[14a], 17[18] with 70:1a[2a], 5[6]; cf. also Ps. 50:7 with Exod. 20:2; Ps. 68:1[2], 7-8[8-9] with Num. 10:35 and Judg. 5:3-5). Interestingly, the Elohistic anthology features the number forty-two: it begins with Psalm 42 and contains forty-two Psalms. Forty-two in Scripture symbolizes premature death through divine punishment (Num. 35:6; Judg. 12:6; 2 Kgs. 2:24; 10:14; Rev. 13:5). Perhaps this number features prominently in the Elohistic Psalter because Korah, the eponymous ancestor of the Korah family, died an unnatural death for rebelling against "I AM" (Numbers 16). The plague that ensued from that rebellion killed 14,700, a multiple of 42 (Num. 16:49); see Joel S. Burnett, "Forty-Two Songs for Elohim: An Organizing Principle in the Shaping of the Elohistic Psalter," *JSOT* 36 (2006). Possibly, then, the Korahites avoided using God's personal name in order to revere it by not taking it to vanity. It is well known that during the second temple period Israel ceased using God's personal name for this very reason. This explanation finds confirmation in that the Elohistic Psalter includes Psalms such as Psalm 44, which on a superficial reading border on what could be interpreted as blasphemy (Psalms 88 and 89). According to Amos Hakan (*The Bible: Psalms with the Jerusalem Commentary*, vol. 1: *Psalms 1-57* [Jerusalem: Mosad Harav Kook, 2003], p. 349, n. 13) the Tosefta (*Soṭah* 9:10) explains why Yoḥanan the High Priest removed this psalm from the temple liturgy. He was concerned that ignorant people might err and "think that the Jewish people believe that its God goes to sleep and must be woken."

63. Craig C. Broyles, "The Conflict of Faith and Experience: A Form Critical and Theological Study of Selected Lament Psalms," *Journal for the Study of the Old Testament* (Supplement

the speakers oscillate between "I," a warrior king (v. 6[7]), and "we," the people of Israel (2 Chron. 20:13), who refer to "our armies" (*ṣib'ôṯēnû*, v. 9[10]), more precisely, "our militias." "Protest," not penitence, because beyond a national lamenting (vv. 9-16[10-17]), they protest God's handing his army over to a humiliating defeat although they had been God's faithful covenant partners.[64] In his covenant with Israel God promised his people blessings for fidelity and threatened curses for infidelity (Deuteronomy 28). The law-keeping king and people who survived the rout assemble at the temple and pour out their protest. Contrary to Thomas Aquinas and John Calvin, suffering in this psalm is not punishment for sin, but as Derek Kidner puts it, "a battle-scar" for righteousness, "the price of loyalty in a world which is at war with God."[65]

The Psalm has the typical motifs of the hymnal lament genre: direct address (first word), confidence and praise (vv. 1-8[2-9]), lament (vv. 9-16[10-17]), and petition (vv. 21-24[22-25]). However, Psalm 44 atypically includes the motif of protest (vv. 17-22[18-23]) and is structured so that praise issues into petition.

Perhaps the original setting and later use of the Psalm resemble Jehoshaphat (870-840 BCE) assembling at the temple all God's chosen people to plead with God to spare Israel from the attack of neighboring nations (2 Chron. 20:3-12).[66]

C. Rhetoric[67]

These typical motifs nicely match both Thomas's analysis of the psalm as having three stanzas: the past prosperity of Israel (vv. 1-8[2-9]), the present adversity (vv.

Series 52; Sheffield: JSOT Press, 1989). By protest he means they protest against what the psalmists experience as unjust or unintelligible treatment by God. Thus he uses the term differently than Erhard S. Gerstenberger (*Psalms, part 1, with an Introduction to Cultic Poetry,* The Forms of Old Testament Literature, XIV [Grand Rapids: Eerdmans, 1988]), who applies the term to the whole group of what is more often called "lament psalms." See also Claus Westermann, "The Role of Lament in the Theology of the Old Testament," *Interpretation* 18 (1974): 20-38; Robert Davidson, *The Courage to Doubt: Exploring an Old Testament Theme* (London: SCM Press, 1983), pp. 6-177. By doubt he also means protest.

64. Dalit Rom-Shiloni ("Ps. 44: The Powers of Protest," *Catholic Biblical Quarterly* 70, no. 4 [2008]: 683-97, esp. 685) distinguishes between complaint and protest: "complaint" recognizes punishment for sin (Psalm 79) while one "protests" unmerited distress. Without distinguishing lament from complaint or protest, Psalm 44 is the first of eleven community laments (Psalms 60, 74, 79, 80, 83, 85, 90, 94, 123, and 127).

65. Derek Kidner, *Psalms 1–72: An Introduction & Commentary* (TOTC; Leicester, UK: InterVarsity, 1973), p. 170.

66. See Carl J. Bosma, "Discerning the Voices in the Psalms: A Discussion of Two Problems in the Psalmic Interpretation," *Calvin Theological Journal* 45 (2008): 183-212.

67. The term "rhetoric" is meant to question the arrangement of material and the choice of

9-22[10-23]), and the cry for divine help (vv. 23-26[24-27]); and Calvin's division of the second part into two stanzas, labeled here as lament and protest.[68] In the first stanza the martyrs recite their king's awesome history to bolster their faith after the bewildering defeat.

Loren D. Crow notes the Psalm's chiastic structure:

A.   Hymnic description of God's past aid   (1-3[2-4])
   B.   The present community's faithful trust in God   (4-8[5-9])
      C.   God's violence against the community   (9-16[10-17])
   B₁. Community's innocent contrast with God's action   (17-22[18-23])
A₁. Petition that God aid in the present   (23-26[24-27])[69]

Ridderbos ingeniously argued that the psalm was intentionally structured to resemble a Babylonian temple ziggurat. The ziggurat was a pyramidal structure, built in receding tiers, ranging from two to seven, with an ascending stairway and possibly a shrine at the summit, where petitions may have been offered. The tiers were covered with glazed bricks often in varying colors. The Psalm's fourfold tiered structure becomes apparent when one realizes that verses 1[2] and 3[4] are quatrains (i.e., consisting of two lines). Accordingly, the psalm's motifs and stanzas consist structurally of a receding number of ten, eight, six, and four poetic lines. "This," says Ridderbos, "could hardly have occurred by chance. The psalm rises up like a ziggurat; and only when the poet has come to the topmost flight does he raise up his prayer to God."[70]

In addition to this harmonious structure, each stanza consists of two balanced strophes. In the first strophe of the confidence stanza the people recite their salvation history (vv. 1-3[2-4], five lines), and in the second strophe they confess their unequivocal faith in God, acknowledging their victories as his (vv. 4-8[5-9], five lines). The first strophe of the second stanza laments their withering defeat (vv. 9-12[10-13], four lines), and its second strophe laments their humiliation (vv. 13-16[14-17], four lines). In the protest stanza, the first strophe asserts their innocence (vv. 17-19[18-20], three lines), and the second proves it (vv. 20-22[21-23],

the discourse to persuade. See Susan E. Gillingham, *One Bible, Many Voices: Different Approaches to Biblical Studies* (Grand Rapids: Eerdmans, 1988), p. 182).

68. John Calvin, *Commentary on the Book of Psalms*, translated from the original Latin, and collated with the author's French version by James Anderson, vol. 2 (Grand Rapids: Baker, 2003, originally printed for the Calvin Translation Society, Edinburgh, n.d.), p. 148.

69. Loren D. Crow, "The Rhetoric of Psalm 44," *Zeitschrift für die Alttestamentliche Wissenschaft* 104, no. 3 (1992): 394-401, esp. 394.

70. Nic. H. Ridderbos, "The Psalms: Style, Figure and Structure," in *Oudtestamentische Studien*, vol. 13 (Leiden: Brill, 1963), p. 50.

three lines). The petition consists of two appeals: that God wake up from his apparent indifferent slumber (vv. 23-24[24-25], two lines) and an urgent plea that he go forth in holy war on account of his unfailing love (vv. 25-26[26-27], two lines).[71]

These moieties produce a sense of serenity and pleasure, and reveal the psalmist's composed psyche. He confronts his peril with fervency balanced with equanimity. The combination resembles a Beethoven symphony: fervent harmony.

Here is a sketch of the psalm's structure:

Superscript
  I. Confidence   1-8[2-9]
    A. Recital of Israel's salvation history   1-3[2-4]
      1. Introduction to recitation   1[2] [two lines]
      2. God, not technology, dispossessed the land   2-3[3-4]
    B. Affirmation of Israel's continuing faith and victory   4-8[5-9]
      1. God gives Israel victories   4-5[5-6]
      2. Israel does not credit technology for victories   6-7[7-8]
      3. Concluding praise   8[9]
  II. Lament   9-16[10-17]
    A. Lament of being handed over to defeat   9-12[10-13]
      1. Literal account   9-10[10-11]
      2. Metaphorical account   11-12[12-13]
    B. Lament of being handed over to humiliation   13-16[14-17]
      1. National humiliation   13-14[14-15]
      2. Individual humiliation   15-16[16-17]
  III. Protest   17-22[18-23]
    A. Assertion of innocence   17-19[18-20]
      1. Nation faithful to covenant   17-18[18-19]
      2. God crushed nation   19[20]
    B. Proof of innocence   20-22[21-23]
      1. God does not condemn nation   20-21[21-22]
      2. Nation killed daily   22[23]
  IV. Petition   23-26[24-27]
    A. Wake up   23-24[24-25]
    B. Redeem us on account of your unfailing love   25-26[26-27]
Postscript

71. Amazingly, C. A. Briggs and E. G. Briggs (*A Critical and Exegetical Commentary on the Book of Psalms* [ICC 15; Edinburgh: T. & T. Clark, 1906], pp. 374ff.) find the psalm so disorganized that they posit two different strains!

The poet's skillful rhetoric can also be seen in the inclusios that frame the stanzas and strophes. The first three stanzas end with "all day long" (vv. 8[9], 15[16], 22[23]),[72] yielding the amazing paradox that Israel praises God all day long, while they are reviled and being put to death. Contrary to Brueggemann, orientation and disorientation are not opposed voices in the psalm but one voice of disorientation within orientation. Moberly comments that Psalms 44 and 89 "pose a theological dilemma . . . the disparity that may arise between what faith trustingly affirms about God (Ps. 44), or what believers expect of a faithful and powerful God who has made promises (Ps. 89), and circumstances in life that are entirely otherwise." But "faith in YHWH and His steadfast love remains the premise. The problem is not the conflict of opposites in itself, but rather a probing of surprising and difficult dimensions of what is entailed by trust in God."[73]

Chiasms, catchwords, and other rhetorical features link the stanzas and strophes to one another so as to form a prayer of fervent power and arresting art.

D. Message

This *maskil* ("making prudent") teaches martyrs, among other things, that the calculus of covenant blessings and curses is not a simplistic *quid pro quo;* before enjoying covenant blessings the faithful may expect to suffer undeservedly. Moberly notes that "the predominance of laments at the very heart of Israel's prayers means that the problems that give rise to lament are not something marginal or unusual but rather are central to the life of faith. . . . Moreover they show that the experience of anguish and puzzlement in the life of faith is not a sign of deficient faith, something to be outgrown or put behind one, but rather is intrinsic to the very nature of faith."[74]

II. Exegesis

A. Superscript (44:1[2])

The sons of Korah who authored the psalm (see n. 26) are the descendants of those sons of Korah of the clan of Kohath of the tribe of Levi who did not follow

---

72. So also Martin Kessler ("Ps. 44," in *Unless Some One Guide Me . . . Festschrift for Kaarel A. Deurloo,* ed. Janet W. Dyk et al. [Maastricht: Shaker, 2001], pp. 193-204, esp. 198).

73. R. W. L. Moberly, *Old Testament Theology: Reading the Hebrew Bible as Christian Scripture* (Grand Rapids: Baker Academic, 2013), pp. 231, 240.

74. R. W. L. Moberly, "Lament," *NIDOTTE,* 4.879.

their eponymous ancestor in his rebellion against Moses and Aaron. By Korah's unnatural death his survivors learned their lesson well: to fear "I AM" and not to treat God's name or his elect with contempt (Num. 16:1-50; 26:10f.). Indeed the Korahites were among the few Israelites who suffered with God's chosen king in his exile during Saul's harsh reign (1 Chron. 12:6). God elected this priestly family to play a prominent role in the temple liturgy. They guarded the entrances to the temple (1 Chron. 26:19) and served as musicians in the sanctuary (2 Chron. 20:19). In war and in music they were like David; they would rather be doorkeepers in the house of the Lord than dwell in the tents of the wicked (Ps. 84:10[11]). Unlike David, however, these noble Levites fought, sang, and composed psalms as a family, not as famous individuals.

The superscript does not situate the psalm within Israel's sacred history as known in her national treasury,[75] but Psalm 44 can best be imagined, as Delitzsch argues,[76] as a counterpart to Psalm 60, whose superscript reads: "A *miktam* of David, for teaching, when he fought Aram Naharaim and Aram Zobah, and when Joab returned and struck down twelve thousand Edomites in the Valley of Salt." Like Psalm 44, Psalm 60 laments a national defeat under David's kingship, a defeat that is not mentioned elsewhere in Scripture. Also, like Psalm 44, Psalm 60 complains "You have rejected us" and continues "you no longer go out with our armies" (Pss. 44:9[10]; 60:1[3], 10[12]). The two psalms belong to a unique moment in salvation history when covenant faithfulness is wedded to military defeat. In short, an anonymous Korahite put this inspired plea into the mouth of the suffering king and his people, who are in corporate solidarity, to pour out an antiphonal, liturgical lament and protest.

B. Confidence and Praise (44:1-8[2-9])

The foundational tier of the literary ziggurat shines brightly with confidence and praise. It consists of two strophes: a recital of past salvation history, with a focus

75. For a helpful bibliography of recent discussion of dating Psalm 44, see Dalit Rom-Shiloni, "Ps. 44: The Powers of Protest," *CBQ* (2008): 683-97. Suffice it to note here that the Antiochene school (Chrysostom) and later exegetes, including Calvin, proposed a Maccabean setting, but recent commentators reject this setting. Cf. A. A. Anderson, *Psalms (1-72)*, in *The New Century Bible Commentary*, vol. 3 (Grand Rapids: Eerdmans, 1972)], p. 337.

76. C. F. Keil and F. Delitzsch, *Psalms*, in *Commentary on the Old Testament*, trans. Francis Bolton, vol. 5 (Peabody, MA: Hendrickson, 1996, reprinted from English edition, originally published by T. & T. Clark, Edinburgh, 1866-91), pp. 318-20. Scholars marginalize this brilliant commentary because it accepts with erudition the Bible's claim to its authorship; tragically, contemporary evangelical publishers and scholars tend to follow suit!

on the Conquest, and a confession of present trust in God and praise of him. A chiastic structure unites the two strophes, the past and the present, as discerned by Willem VanGemeren.[77] Here is an adaptation of his analysis:

A. Forefathers' praise of God	1[2]
B. Victory of forefathers	2[3]
C. Victory of forefathers not by human strength	3a[4a]
D. Victory of forefathers by God	3b[4b]
E. Confession of king's confidence in God alone	4[5]
D'. Victory of present generation by God	5[6]
C'. Victory of present generation not by human strength	6[7]
B'. Victory of present generation	7[8]
A'. Present generation's praise of God	8[9]

The stanza moves from past (vv. 1-3[2-4]), to present (vv. 4-7[5-8]), to future (v. 8[9]); its horizon extends from the remote past (v. 1[2]) to the remote future (v. 8[9]). The epithet "God" frames the stanza (vv. 1, 8[2, 9]). By God's saving acts from the beginning of Israel's history to its consummation, his name becomes ever-more glorious and gains significance from salvation history. The chiastic repetitions emphasize this teaching: God, not human strength and technology, saves Israel.

1. Recital of Salvation History (44:1-3[2-4])

The recital of *Heilsgeschichte* consists of an introduction (v. 1[2]) and of a recounting of God's hand — emphatically, not their own — in dispossessing the nations (vv. 2-4[3-5]).

a. Introduction to Recitation (44:1[2])

Though the stanza gives voice to confidence and praise, it begins with the typical introduction of laments: a direct address to *God,* his generic title, which exalts him higher above human beings than the heavens are above the earth. The parallels of the A verset mention the hearing children (44:1Aa[2Aa]) and the B verset, the telling ancestors (44:1Ab[2Aa]), emphasizing an oral communication linking the generations. Israel preserved her traditions in writing for accuracy and in oral

---

77. Willem A. VanGemeren, *Psalms,* The Expositor's Bible Commentary, revised edition (Grand Rapids: Zondervan, 2008), vol. 5, p. 391.

form for dissemination.[78] *With . . . ears* infers the oral preservation of Israel's biography; oral traditions in the ancient Near East were transmitted with accuracy and fervency. In written communication readers tend to control the process of communication, for they can refuse to open the document; in oral communication speakers tend to control the situation, for those who are addressed can scarcely walk away from a speaker who speaks with soul-stirring passion. *Our* refers to the people in corporate solidarity with their king. *We have heard* implies the children by faith accepted the inherited tradition. *Our fathers,* which does not exclude mothers,[79] presumes that they themselves were true children and that they fulfilled their obligation to teach their children the ways of God constantly and diligently (Exod. 10:2; Deut. 6:6-9; 32:7; Prov. 4:1-9). The plural refers to successive generations. *Have told us* assumes a successful transmission of the gospel proclamation in spite of the common parental ailment of being tongue-tied (Judg. 2:10; 2 Kgs. 22:10f.). *What you did* (see n. 27) *in their days, in days long ago* (קֶדֶם, *qedem*), will become focused in verse 2[3]. קֶדֶם can denote the divine sphere (i.e., "the eternal," Deut. 33:27; Hab. 1:12), but here it refers to historical acts in Israel's remotest past (Deut. 33:15; Pss. 68:33[34]; 74:2) — namely, at the time of Israel's founding fathers under the leadership of Moses and Joshua.

How long ago is unimportant, but the fact of transmission of founding events over generations is very important, both how events happened and what events mean. *Heilsgeschichte* is not merely a story about the past but functions like pagan myths, albeit based on factual history. Both myths and *Heilsgeschichte* feature the events of a people's founding and both shape their cultures; they determine the worldview of its individual members.[80] Moreover, the *magnalia Dei* are unique to the founding generation; otherwise history would be like a yo-yo, not advancing. God builds his catholic covenant community by the mouths of faithful parents (Deut. 30:11-13; Rom. 10:6-10) and disciples (Matt. 28:19f.).

b. The Tradition (44:2-3[3-4])

The psalmist singles out of Israel's salvation history her conquest of the land (Joshua 1–12) and distribution and settlement of it (Joshua 13–19) because at issue in this national protest is the possession of the land.

78. For example, the *Torah* was passed down in both written and oral forms (Deut. 6:6; 17:18), and so was Israel's wisdom literature (Prov. 1:8; 22:20).

79. Bruce K. Waltke, *The Book of Proverbs: Chapters 1–15* (Grand Rapids: Eerdmans, 2004), pp. 116-19.

80. Bruce K. Waltke, "Myth, History and the Bible: With a Focus on the Old Testament," in *"But My Words Will Never Pass Away": The Enduring Authority of the Christian Scriptures,* ed. D. A. Carson (Grand Rapids: Eerdmans, forthcoming).

i. Prosperity of Israel through Canaanite Misfortune (44:2[3])

The poet depicts the founding generation as the Gardener's choicest slip of a vine that later spreads out its branches over the entire land.[81] This successful planting is due to the Gardener, not the plant. The physical nation is a shadow of the true Vine and its branches, the church (John 15:1-6), which today covers every continent. The poet's grammar emphasizes "you": it is followed by *paseq*,[82] a Masoretic accent that signals a slight disjunction; it is followed exceptionally by the apposition "your hand";[83] and stands in antithesis to the fathers in verse 3(4).[84] Anthropomorphic *your hand*, the appendage from elbow to fingertip, symbolizes "power" and coincides — as is often the case — with *arm* (Deut. 4:34; 5:15; 7:8; 26:8; Josh. 24:1-13), the appendage from shoulder to elbow. In light of that coincidence, A. S. van der Woude asserts: "Thus [hand] stands for a person's power or capacity to rule over others (1 Chron. 18:3), to exercise force (1 Sam. 23:7), to punish (Ps. 21:9), to save oneself from a dangerous situation (Josh. 8:20), to grant gifts in abundance (only of the kings: 1 Kgs. 10:13) . . . and to act zealously (Prov. 10:4). This power is made concrete in property (Lev. 25:28; Ps. 44:3, 4[4, 5]) and wealth (Lev. 5:7)."[85] The Hebrew lexeme glossed *you dispossessed* (cf. Exod. 34:24) in *qal* in Deuteronomistic literature, which is presumed here, denotes "by right of conquest one people or action succeeds another in ruling over a territory. This right of conquest is undergirded by divine providence and action." In *Hiphil*, as here, it denotes "to destroy someone so that his property can be taken."[86] Seven of the many dispossessed *nations* are named in Deuteronomy 7:1. *You planted them* (Exod. 15:17) glosses a more literal "to insert a slip into the soil" — here probably on a large scale — and metaphorically signifies "to establish" the founding generation securely so that they could eventually succeed in ruling over the conquered peoples. The United States drove out Saddam Hussein and his regime from Iraq, but presently it cannot be said that it has planted democracy to overcome demagoguery. *Ad sensum* the antecedent of "them" must be the founding fathers. *You broke* [the branches of, see n. 29] *the peoples*, a stock-in-trade parallel to "nations"

---

81. The vine is a well-known symbol of Israel (Exod. 15:17; Isa. 5:1-7; Jer. 2:21; 12:10; Ezek. 17:22ff.; Joel 1:7; and esp. Ps. 80:8-11[9-12]). In Assyrian bas-reliefs Israel is symbolized by a vine, and the Herodian Temple had a symbolic golden vine for Israel placed over the porch before the sanctuary.

82. A. J. Maas, "The Use of Paseq in the Psalms. II," *Hebraica* 8, no. 1/2 (Oct. 1891–Jan. 1892): 89-97.

83. *IBHS*, 16.3.4a. The exceptional construction prompts Bardtke (BHS) to delete אַתָּה *'attâ* and to join יָדְךָ *yād^ekâ* with קֶדֶם *qedem*, and prompts the LXX and Syriac to omit it.

84. *IBHS*, 16.3.2a,d.

85. *TLOT*, 2.500, s.v. *yād*.

86. N. Lohfink, *TDOT*, 6.371, 375, s.v. 396, *yrš*.

(Ps. 2:1). The Hebrew lexeme in *piel* glossed *and you spread them out* (lit., in *Qal,* "set in motion away from the actor") in this horticultural metaphor means "to hold (roots, twigs, tendrils) outstretched, expanded" (Ps. 80:8-11[9-12]).[87]

ii. Prosperity of Israel Solely through God's Power (44:3[4])

No! establishes the emphatic "you" that introduces verse 2[3]. The antithetic parallels of the A and B versets, by juxtaposing the negative, signaled by *not* in Aa, and the positive, signaled by another negative, an emphatic *No!* in Ba, heighten the tradition that God, not Israel's own strength, gave Israel the rule over Canaan. Human effort could no more explain Israel's impossible dispossessing of nations greater and stronger than she, with their large cities walled up to the heavens (Deut. 9:1), than human power could explain the victory of Christian lambs over mighty Rome. *By their sword* (Josh. 24:12) functions as a synecdoche for the offensive weapons of the founding fathers. To be sure Joshua fought with a sword (cf. Josh. 6:21), but Israel's arm did not dry up the swollen Jordan (Joshua 3–4), or fell the walls of Jericho (ch. 6), or hurl giant hailstones (10:11), or make the sun stand still (10:11-13), or send a plague of hornets (24:12) that dispossessed (v. 2[3]) *the land* that God had sworn by himself to give Israel's patriarchs (Gen. 15:10-21; cf. 22:15-18). "Their sword" is intensified by *their arm,* which makes the sword effective. But in itself it *did not bring them victories.*[88] Spurgeon comments: "Canaan was not conquered without the armies of Israel, but it is equally true that it was not conquered by them."[89] The Owner of earth has the legal right to give the Land to whomever he will. God gave Israel the Land as a usufruct out of sheer grace (Deuteronomy 9), saving his chosen people from the attacks first by five Amorite kings at Gibeon (Josh. 10:1-43) and then from the five kings of the Canaanites, Amorites, Hittites, Perizzites, and Jebusites at the Waters of Merom (Josh. 11:1-23).

The anthropomorphisms, *right hand and . . . arm,* speak of power (Exod. 15:6-12; Lam. 2:3), but the emphasis is on *your.* The repetition in verses 2[3] and 3[4] underscores God's grace. *And the light of your face* is a frequent metaphor for the king in the Babylonian, El Amarna, and Ugaritic texts to signify the ruler's beneficent favor toward someone. The symbol probably has a solar background; the king is called "sun," because of his beaming face that dispels the darkness. The meaning of the metaphor is certified and underscored by the explanatory clause introduced by "for." *You favored them* signifies "to delight in" and "to accept fa-

---

87. M. Delcorcor/E. Jenni, *TLOT,* 3.3,334, s.v. *šlḥ.*

88. See p. 60, nn. 47 and 48.

89. Charles Haddon Spurgeon, *The Treasury of David,* updated by Roy H. Clarke (Nashville: Thomas Nelson, 1997), p. 359.

vorably." "I AM" dispossessed the nations because he elected and loved his chosen people (Deut. 7:7f.; 10:15), although the poet could have added, but chose not to, *because of the sin of the Canaanites* (Gen. 15:16; Deut. 9:4). Israel's salvation, as Calvin insisted, is solely the gift of God's merciful, sovereign grace that is rooted in his person and defies rational explanation; the timing of the predetermined salvation, however, is contingent upon human merit and demerit.

2. Affirmation of Confidence with Petition and Praise (44:4-8[5-9])

Faith in God's unchangeable nature assures the faithful that his fidelity to his covenant promises pertains as much to the present and future as to the past. Maclaren comments: "The Psalmist did not think that God was nearer in some majestic past than now. His unchangeableness had for consequence . . . continuous manifestation of Himself in the same character and relation to His people. Today is as full of God as any yesterday."[90] The nation confesses this in three strophes (vv. 4-5[5-6], 6-7[7-8], 8[9]). The first two strophes alternate between the king's (vv. 4, 6[5, 7]) and people's confession of faith (vv. 5, 7[6, 8]).[91] A concluding verse of eternal praise draws the strophe and stanza to its conclusion. The second strophe proves their confessions of faith in strophe 1 by their rejecting the secular alternative of faith in themselves and in technology.

a. Confession of Faith in God (44:4-5[5-6])

i. By King (44:4[5])

Another emphatic *you* (see v. 2[3]) intensified further by *alone* (see n. 30) introduces the second strophe. The anthropomorphic identification of "I AM" as *my King* speaks of the chosen nation's acceptance of the God of Jacob as the One who is invested with final and absolute authority (Deut. 33:2-5).[92] Its combination with *my God* unites God's transcendence with the personal intimacy of the covenant relationship. Israel's king derives his authority from God

---

90. Alexander Maclaren, *The Psalms*, vol. 2, The Expositor's Bible (London: Hodder & Stoughton, 1900), p. 57.

91. VanGemeren explains the alternation "as a literary convention rather than a liturgical alternation between people and king (see Craigie, 331-32)." But Peter Craigie (*Ps. 1-50*, in Word Biblical Commentary, vol. 19 [Waco, TX: Word, 1983]) says: "though the alternation may be merely a literary convention, it is more likely to reflect the alternation of the speakers."

92. Cf. Sumerian King List (James B. Pritchard, *Ancient Near Eastern Texts* [Princeton: Princeton University Press, 1953; hereafter *ANET*], 265b; S. N. Kramer, *Sumerians* [1963], pp. 43-53, 328-31; H. Frankfort, *Kingship and the Gods* [1948], pp. 148ff.; E. Hornung, *Einführung in die Ägyptologie* [1967], pp. 76-81).

who (uniquely) *commands* (Ps. 7:6[7]) *victories* (i.e., acts of salvation; see n. 32). "Commands" refers to a ruler's ordering a subordinate; here God orders the beneficent and lasting destiny of Jacob, a poetic gentilic of the nation derived from her eponymous ancestor.

ii. By People/Army (44:5[6])

Through you, the source of Israel's strength (Ps. 18:2[3]), *we gore* (Deut. 33:17; 1 Kgs. 22:11; Ezek. 34:21),[93] a metaphor of David's many victories (Ps. 18:37-45[38-46]). The incomplete zoomorphic metaphor pictures Israel as having horns, an ancient Near East symbol of an effective defensive weapon. Horns "give the animal a regal look and provide such an impressive defense mechanism that their imagery was widely employed to represent power. . . . In Mesopotamian art, horns indicate deity and deified kings from Naram-Sin on."[94] The trajectory of this imagery finds its fulfillment in the Messiah (Ps. 148:14; Ezek. 29:21). In Revelation 5:6 the Lamb paradoxically has seven horns — that is to say, the most submissive One's kingly power is absolute!

God's army validates their faith in God by going to war *in your name* (1 Sam. 17:45; Ps. 20:7[8]). To act in God's name is to recognize his authority, directions, and empowerment, and to act in union and communion with him.[95] The goring imagery is escalated to *we trample,* connoting their humiliation of their enemies (see Mic. 4:13; Dan. 7:7).[96] *Those who rise up against us,* or "who attack us," refers to nations who seek to wipe God's kingdom off the map.[97]

b. Rejection of Faith in Weapons (44:6-7[7-8])

i. By King (44:6[7])

Employing the same logic to validate that it was God who gave the founding fathers' victory (v. 3[4]) by rejecting the secular alternative that technology gave them victory, the poet warrior again validates that God gives victory by again rejecting the secular alternative. Verses 3[4] and 6[7] both begin with emphatic

---

93. In the Ugaritic texts, Baal and Mot gore each other like wild bulls (*ANET* p. 141, entry I AB [vi], line 18).

94. Leland Ryken, James C. Wilhoit, and Tremper Longman III, eds., *Dictionary of Biblical Imagery* (Downers Grove, IL: IVP Academic, 1998), p. 400.

95. Joseph Addison Alexander, *The Psalms: Translated and Explained* (Grand Rapids: Zondervan, n.d., reprinted from the edition of 1864), p. 196.

96. "Similarly, Shalmanezer III refers to his military exploits, saying, 'his land I trod down like a wild ox'" (Anderson, *Psalms,* p. 340, citing S. R. Driver, *Deuteronomy* [ICC; Edinburgh: T. & T. Clark, 1896], p. 407).

97. Cf. Ps. 3:1 (*PACW,* p. 198).

substantiation, *surely,* followed by *not* in both versets. In place of "by their sword" he substitutes *with my bow,* a common parallel to "sword" (Ps. 7:12[13]). I *trust* (Ps. 4:5[6])[98] denotes reliance in face of crisis. Likewise, *my sword does not save me* replaces "their arm does not save them" (v. 3[4]B).

ii. By People/Army (44:7[8])

As verse 6[7] matches verse 3[4]A, so verse 8[9] matches verse 3[4]B. Both begin with an emphatic *surely.* These repetitions between the two strophes, pertaining first to the past situation, then to gnomic present, implicitly affirm that God does not change. This notion is reinforced by the gnomic *you save us* (vv. 3, 4, 7[4, 5, 8], n. 30), a catchword binding together the second strophe. With this verb the significance of figural goring (v. 5[6]) is clearly explicated. The catchword, *from our foes,* links strophes 1 (v. 5[6]) and 2. The B verset exposes the foe's inner psyche: *those who hate us* (Ps. 5:5[6]). *You put to shame* (Ps. 6:10[11]) validates that "trample" connotes humiliation.

iii. Conclusion: Israel's Everlasting Praise of God (44:8[9])

Verse 8[9] stands apart as the conclusion by functioning as an inclusio with verse 1[2] (see above), by referring to God in the third person, by moving from the present to the eternal future, and by shifting from the motif of confidence to praise. *In God* (v. 1[2]) *we praise* denotes an interpersonal exchange in which Israel makes a favorable judgment of God's virtue and expresses their admiration by extolling his person and his sublime attributes to others. Though this is an obligation of the living (Deut. 26:19; Isa. 43:21; Jer. 13:11), the successive generations of Israel do so because it is the right and proper thing to do. If we do not admire what is praiseworthy, says C. S. Lewis, "we shall be stupid, insensible, and great losers."[99] The hyperbole *all day long* (Deut. 28:32; 33:12; Judg. 9:45) could be glossed "always, ever" (Gen. 6:5; Exod. 10:13). The B verset returns to direct address: *and to your name* (Ps. 22:22[23]).[100] *We will give credit* (Ps. 6:5[6]) *forever* (Ps. 5:11[12]).

C. Lament of Being Handed Over to Defeat (44:9-16[10-17])

The inspired poet now ascends to the second tier of his literary ziggurat, a desolate waste, covered with black clouds that conceal the heavens. "No longer are

---

98. Waltke and Houston, *PACW,* p. 237.

99. C. S. Lewis, *Reflections on the Psalms* (New York: Harcourt, Brace & World, 1958), p. 92.

100. Waltke and Houston, *PACW,* p. 409.

we to hear Miriam's timbrel (Exod. 15:20). We are to hear Rachel's weeping (Gen. 35:16)."[101] Timbrel and tears, however, complement each other. Lament and protest are possible only because the holy nation assumes the covenant doctrine of blessings and curses as reward for virtue and punishment for vice respectively. D. Rom-Shiloni comments: "Protest reaches its height *because* of the unresolved dissonance between the circumstances of crisis and accepted doctrinal conventions."[102]

With a sustained rhythm, and a sevenfold "you" introducing the first six verses, the psalmist blames God for Israel's defeat (strophe 1, vv. 9-12[10-13]) and humiliation (strophe 2, vv. 13-16[14-17]). It is not merely that God has allowed other nations to desolate Israel, but rather that God has actively sought to defeat them.[103] Catchwords link the confidence and lament tiers; "adversaries" and "those who hate us" occur in verses 7[8], 10[11]. There is a mysterious sovereignty that directs Israel's undeserved sufferings: the undeserved sufferings of martyrs, not merely those of the innocent.

The first quatrain of the first strophe describes the military debacle literally (vv. 9-10[10-11]), and the second quatrain, metaphorically (vv. 11-12[12-13]).

1. Lament for Devastating Defeat (44:9-12)

a. Literal Account (44:9-10[10-11])

The quatrain first attributes the defeat to the Commander-in-Chief having gone AWOL[104] (v. 9[10]); he then describes it as a plundering rout (v. 10[11]). The stanza is framed by the lexeme כָּלַם (*kālam*, "humiliation"; vv. 9, 15[10, 16]).

9[10] The coordinator *but you for your part* (-אַף, *'aph*)[105] correlates and semantically contrasts God's being an apparent loose cannon against Israel's eternal praise for his victories. *Rejected* stands opposed to the previous favor God had toward the forefathers (Ps. 77:7[8]; Zech. 10:6).[106] *And* as a consequence *you humiliated us* (2 Sam. 19:4): to be in a state of being in public dishonor. *And*, in

---

101. Spurgeon, *Treasury of David*, p. 361.

102. Rom-Shiloni, "The Powers of Protest," p. 698; emphasis in original.

103. Crow, "The Rhetoric of Psalm 44," p. 39.

104. Military acronym for "absent without leave."

105. *IBHS*, P. 39.3.4d.

106. Reuven Yaron ("The Meaning of *Zanah*," *Vetus Testamentum* 13 [1963]: 237-39) contends זָנַח *zānaḥ* entails God's anger, but this psalm supports only the notion of rejection, not of anger. For the semantic field of divine desertion and neglect, and its consequences in military defeat, see Monica J. Melanchthon, *Rejection by God: The History and Significance of the Rejection Motif in the Hebrew Bible* (Studies in Biblical Literature 22; New York: Peter Lang, 2001), pp. 75-80.

that connection, *you no longer go forth* (see n. 37) as our leader, *with our militias* (1 Sam. 28:1; Deut. 20:4; 23:14[15]). The lexeme glossed "armies" (צָבָא, *ṣābā'*) means the service "that one does not do of one's own volition but that is required of one by a superior. As a rule it was service in war, but it could be labor. Thus *ṣābā'* means (esp. in conjunction with . . . *yṣ'*) 'to go out to serve in the military. . . .'"[107] The plural may refer to tribal militias.

10[11] By God's not going with the militias he himself drafted, in effect, as they protest, *you routed us* (see n. 38) *before the foe* (v. 5[6]). *And those who hate us* (v. 7[8]) *have plundered us* (see n. 39). The reference is probably to the property, including precious articles and food supplies, and the fleeing troops left behind on the battlefield (Num. 31:32-54; Judg. 8:23-26; 1 Sam. 23:1; 30:16; Hos. 13:15).

b. Metaphorical Account (44:11-12[12-13])

The next quatrain pictures the dead soldiers as defenseless sheep being butchered (v. 11[12]) and the survivors as being sent into exile. These figures are then expanded by another figure: God sold them for a pittance — that is to say, it cost the enemy almost nothing in loss of their own lives. The image of butchery draws the stanza to its conclusion (v. 22[23]).

11[12] *You gave us up* (with the object "food"; see Gen. 28:20; Exod. 16:15; Neh. 9:15; 9:20) implies that its indirect object is the enemy, not wild animals and birds of prey as is common with מַאֲכָל (*ma'ᵃkal*, "food"). The simile *as a flock* (usually of sheep and/or goats) *to be devoured as food* (see n. 41) depicts the battlefield as a slaughtering house (v. 22[23]). *You scattered us* (זֵרִיתָנוּ, *zērîtānû*, Lev. 26:33) signifies that God separated them from one another and sent them off as slaves in various directions. "With peoples *zārâ* pictures a defeat so devastating that no one survives to resist the victor to take root again."[108] The image of scattering is intensified by adding *among the nations*, an equivalent to the normal expansion, "to the winds" (Jer. 49:32, 36; Ezek. 5:10, 12).

12[13] The mercantile figure *you sold* (Deut. 32:30) is a frequent metaphor "to describe people as completely at the disposal of their enemies, as if they were slaves, the property of their foes."[109] *Your people* identifies "us" as a community

---

107. A. S. van der Woude, *TLOT*, 2.1041, s.v. *ṣābā'*.

108. Bruce K. Waltke, *Book of Proverbs: Chapters 15-31* (Grand Rapids: Eerdmans, 2005), p. 134.

109. Anderson, *Psalms*, p. 341.

larger than a clan related and unified with God by history and covenant[110] as his inalienable relationship.[111] "For a pittance" glosses "without wealth," elliptical for "without getting anything substantial." The Hebrew lexeme glossed "wealth" denotes "what stands ready" (i.e., "property, possessions, wealth").[112] *You did not set a high price on them* glosses a Hebrew text that could mean "you did not make great[113] with[114] their price," or "you did not increase [wealth] with the price you set on them," with little difference in significance.

2. Lament for Being Handed Over to Humiliation (44:13-16[14-17])

By granting success to the enemy, "I AM" abased his people (vv. 13-14[14-15]) and his king (vv. 15-16[16-17]). The catchword "reproach" frames the strophe (vv. 13, 16[14, 17]), and "among the nations" unites its two bicola.

a. Nation's Humiliation (44:13-14[14-15])

13[14] *You made us* implies that God has authority and exercises power over Israel to transform her identity from being an object of respect to that of being repulsive.[115] Thus they become *a reproach:* an object of verbal abuse, of scoffing. *By our neighbors* refers to those who reside in some geographically proximate relationship to them and so may designate a next-door neighbor, the closest neighbor in proximity in space and metaphorically expected to be such in sympathy and spirit.[116] Their reproach escalates to *laughter,* which expresses the inward joy and disdain a conqueror feels toward the defeat of his enemies (Pss. 37:13; 59:8[9]). The victory is so lopsided that there is a comic side to the reversal of the fortunes. Their laughter escalates to mockery and jeering *derision* (2 Kgs. 2:23).[117] The "church militant" cannot escape the "scoffing rudeness" from *those round about us* on all sides (Ps. 79:4).[118]

14[15] The repetition of initial *you made us* sews the second bicolon of the quatrain to the first (vv. 13-14[14-15]). The reproach, laughter, and derision of the first

---

110. G. Van Groningen, "ʿ*m*," *TWOT* 2.676; E. A. Speiser, "ʾPeoplesʾ and ʾNationsʾ of Israel," *JBL* 79 (1960): 156-63.

111. A genitive of relationship (*IBHS*, P. 9.5.1h,i).

112. E. Kutsch, *TDOT*, 3.366, s.v. *hôn.*

113. Factitive *Piel* of רָבָה "to be many" (*IBHS*, P. 24.2b).

114. בְּ of specification (*IBHS*, P.11.2.5e).

115. Sam Meir, *NIDOTTE*, 3.1238f, s.v. שִׂים.

116. R. H. O'Connell, *NIDOTTE*, 4.112, s.v. *šākēn.*

117. *HALOT*, 3.1105, s.v. *qls.*

118. *HALOT*, 2.740, s.v. *sb.*

is now packaged together into one word: a *byword* (מָשָׁל *māsal*, Deut. 28:37). Landes, following McKane, defines מָשָׁל as "a comparison or analogy [constructed] for the purpose of conveying a model, exemplar, or analogy."[119] "Israel" *among the nations* represents a type, class, or quality of army that is absurdly impotent and repulsive. *Foreign peoples* (Ps. 7:8[9]) accompanies the byword with a gesture of "malicious astonishment,"[120] *wagging their heads* (Ps. 22:7[8]; Isa. 37:22), thereby unwittingly typifying the sufferings of Christ on the cross (Matt. 27:27-44).

b. King's Humiliation (44:15-16[16-17])

15[16]   As in the first stanza, "we" (i.e., the people) oscillates with "I" (i.e., the king). "All" is a common closure technique in Hebrew poetry,[121] and *all day long* points to the closure to the second stanza (see "Rhetoric" above). It also signals a shift from the past to the present. *My ignominy* refers to the disintegration and degradation of the king's person both subjectively ("disdain") and objectively ("insult"). His feeling of being isolated, cut off from communication, and his sense of worth being impugned[122] attend his public humiliation. The inapposite juxtaposition of *before me* with "ignominy" suggest his disgrace is a metonymy of effect from the derision of those conspicuously in front of him. The king ventured to win glory on the battlefield and returned home in *shame* (Isa. 49:1-4).[123] The inapposite juxtaposition of an abstract noun, "shame," with a concrete phrase, *of my face*, suggests "shame" is a metonymy of cause for his crimson blushing. The blushing embarrassment *covers me* (see n. 44) as a mantle enveloping his whole person; the hyperbole is similar to "the iniquity of my heels shall compass me about" (Ps. 49:5[6], KJV).[124] His ignominy accompanied by his blushing face occurs *at the voice*, which is implied with "laughter" and "byword," *of the one who reproaches* (v. 13[14]) *and blasphemes* (see n. 46). The latter Hebrew lexeme in its other four occurrences is used of heaping reproach upon God — that is to say, "blasphemes" (Num. 15:30; 2 Kgs. 19:6 [= Isa. 37:6], 19:22 [= Isa. 37:23]; Ezek. 20:27). Blaspheme means to speak irreverence toward God or a person uniquely related to him, such as his holy people and sacral king. *Because* (see n. 47) links

---

119. G. M. Landes, "Jonah a Māsal?" in *Israelite Wisdom*, ed. J. G. Gammie et al. (Missoula, MT: Scholars, 1978), p. 140.

120. Delitzsch, *Psalms*, p. 322.

121. B. Smith, *Poetic Closure* (Chicago: University of Chicago Press, 1968), pp. 182 ff.

122. S. Wagner, *TDOT*, 7.186, s.v. *klm*.

123. Cf. H. Seebass, *TDOT*, 2.52, s.v. *bsh*.

124. J. J. Stewart Perowne, *Commentary on the Psalms*, 2 volumes in 1 (Grand Rapids: Kregel, 1989); originally published as *The Book of Psalms*, 4th rev. ed. (London: George Bell & Sons, 1878-79), p. 363.

the voice as that of the *enemy and the avenger* (Ps. 8:2[3]),[125] perhaps a reference
to the blaspheming kings.

D. Protest (44:17-22[18-23])

The inspired psalmist now ascends to the third tier of his literary ziggurat; it is
covered with fog so thick he cannot see. Though hotly protesting, the martyr
remains completely rational, for the stanza exhibits alternating moieties, each
beginning with a quatrain testifying in first person to the people's covenant fidelity (vv. 17-18, 20-21[18-19, 21-22]) and ending in a single bicolon introduced
by an emphatic כִּי (*kî*, "surely"), glossed *but no!* and yet, followed by the protest
that "you," God, are killing us (vv. 19, 22[20, 23]).[126]

1. Assertion of Innocence (44:17-19[18-20])

17[18]   *All this,* linking the protest stanza to the lament, *came upon us* (see n. 48),
though we had not forgotten you (see n. 49; Pss. 42:9[10]; 43:2). The Hebrew lexeme for "to forget" in relationship to people means "to dismember oneself from
a former allegiance, a synonym for 'to abandon.'" "Significantly, the vb. ʿzb ("forsake") occurs in close proximity in seven cases."[127] In human relationship to
God, "'forgetting' refers . . . less to the human act of remembering [i.e., a mental
process] than to practical behavior: active turning away and opposition."[128] *We
had not been false to* could also be translated "we have not dealt treacherously
against"[129] *your covenant,* a reference to the Ten Commandments given by God
at Sinai, expanded in Moses' Book of the Covenant (Exodus 21–23) and in its full
elaboration in the Book of the Law that Israel accepted in a covenant renewal
ceremony at Moab.

18[19]   The covenant had two aspects: the heart's commitment to love "I AM"
(Deuteronomy 6–11; Ps. 44:18[19]A) and the behavior that follows (Deuteronomy
12–26; Ps. 44:18[19]B). *Our hearts* (Ps. 7:9[10]) *had not turned back,* and consequently *our steps had not strayed from your path,* an incomplete metaphor for the

---

125. See Waltke and Houston, *PACW*, pp. 263f.

126. Crow, "Rhetoric of Ps. 44," pp. 397-99, also noted the A A B//A' A' B' structure of the
strophe.

127. Leslie C. Allen, *NIDOTTE*, 4.104, s.v. *škḥ*.

128. W. Schottroff, *TLOT*, p. 1325, s.v. *škḥ*.

129. The equivalent idiom, *šqr bᵉ*, occurs in the Aramaic Sefire treaty (J. Fitzmyer, "The
Aramaic Suzerainty Treaty from Sefire in the Museum of Beirut," *CBQ* 20 [1958]: 455-56).

commandment of the Mosaic covenant with its particular stipulations and judgments. To the common metaphor of "way," signifying lifestyle, "steps" adds the notion of a precise conformity to the piety and ethics that the covenant demanded.

19[20] *But no*, on the contrary (see n. 53) *you crushed us*, an incomplete metaphor for the intense physical and psychological affliction described in the lament. Ironically, their steps in precise conformity to God's covenant ended *in a haunt for jackals*, which cry mournfully in waste places (Job 30:29), deserts (Isa. 43:20), and deserted sites (Jer. 9:10[9]; 10:22; 49:33). *And*[130] in that desolate and dreadful place *you covered us over with the shadow of death* (see n. 55).

2. Proof of Innocence (44:20-22[21-23])

20[21] Semantic pertinence dictates that *if we had forgotten* (v. 17[18]) be interpreted as a contrary-to-fact conditional clause. *The name of our God* identifies his essential eternal being and destiny.[131] *Spread out our palms*, one of several gestures for praying in the Old Testament,[132] *to a foreigner* (i.e., one who distances and removes himself)[133] colors forsaking the living God as petitioning and praising a senseless god. Prayer is an exchange of confidence (Ps. 99:6-7), and so there is a commitment of a person to a deity, and when prayer is offered from the heart, as assumed here, there is a deep and necessary connection between praying and living (Prov. 15:24).[134]

21[22] *Would he not search it out* (Ps. 139:1),[135] a metonymy of cause, infers the effect that he would have rebuked Israel before punishing her. The rhetorical question presumes that God is not derelict in caring for his own people (Prov. 3:11-12). Although a question, in the Hebrew idiom it is a highly emphatic assertion (see n. 56). If Israel's suffering was condign punishment, God would have rebuked the nation, as when Joshua complained of Israel's catastrophic defeat at Ai (Josh. 7:10-12), perhaps through a prophet (Judg. 2:1-5).

The apodosis of verset A presumes God is good, and the protasis asserts he is omniscient: *since he knows the secrets*, a rare word for "what is hidden," *of the heart* (v. 18[19]; cf. Job 31:4). Only God can issue the verdict that the human heart

---

130. *Waw-consecutive* for a co-relative situation.

131. If this were the oath formula ("if we . . . , [then may God kill me]" [i.e., "I swear we have not . . ."]), the apodosis would be lacking; but verse 21[22] is the apodosis.

132. *HALOT*, 3.976, s.v. פָּרַשׂ.

133. L. A. Snidjers, *TDOT*, 4.53, s.v. *zr, zûr.*

134. Ryken, Wilhoit, and Longman, *Dictionary of Biblical Imagery*, pp. 659-60.

135. Waltke and Houston, *PACW*, p. 546.

keeps faith with him. In sum, since God is omniscient and too good not to censor his sinful people, we can be sure the nation's testimony is true.

22[23]   *But no!* (v. 19[20]). *For your sake:* see n. 57. The Hebrew lexeme *we were killed* originated in the terminology of warfare. *All day long:* see verses 8, 15[9, 16]. Israel's plight is worse than that of Job, for although Job suffered undeservingly, he suffered as an innocent person, not as a martyr. *We are considered* expresses an intellectual act of evaluation that occurs in the heart (Ps. 32:2). His evaluation of Israel *appears* sadistic: they are *as sheep to be slaughtered* [and cooked] (1 Sam. 8:13; 25:11; v. 11[12]). Yet, the sardonic poet speaks as a prophet, for who knows the mind of God, but the Spirit of God (1 Cor. 2:11)?

E. Petition (44:23-26[24-27])

The psalmist now ascends above the thick fog to the fourth and uppermost tier of his literary ziggurat, where his petitions give voice to hope. The catchword "reject" links the petition to the lament (vv. 9, 23[10, 24]); the catchword "forget" links the petition to the protest (vv. 17, 24[18, 25]). An initial petition, "Wake up," introduces the first strophe (v. 23[24]) and a concluding petition, "Rise up," a parallel elsewhere with "wake up" (Ps. 7:6[7]), draws the second strophe to its conclusion (v. 26[27]). In sum, petitions that God awake from his indifference frame the stanza.

1. Wake Up (44:23-24[24-25])

23[24]   A repeated accusatory *why* links the strophe's two bicola, forming a quatrain. The fervent imperative, *wake up* (Pss. 7:6[7]; cf. 35:23; 59:4f.[5f.]; 78:65; Joel 3[4]:9; Matt. 8:25), aims to rouse the Warrior from his slumber and have him exert extra effort to save Israel. In theological doctrine Israel knows that God neither slumbers nor sleeps (Ps. 121:4), but in religious experience God requires his people to energize their relationship. Similarly, the disciples had to arouse Jesus from sleep during the storm when waves threatened to swamp the boat and drown them (Matt. 8:23-27). The rhetorical, accusatory question *why* (see Ps. 2:1)[136] vents Israel's feeling of anger and indignation. The metaphor *do you sleep* signifies, as the parallel shows, that God appears to be socially unaware of his surroundings and so uninvolved, unconcerned, and indifferent to his people's plight and their urgent need for his help (Ps. 3:7[8]). The epithet *Lord* (Ps. 2:4)[137] represents God as Sovereign over all

---

136. Waltke and Houston, *PACW*, p. 163.
137. Waltke and Houston, *PACW*, p. 167.

social relationships. The parallel, *rouse yourself* (see Ps. 139:18),[138] is used of waking from sleep; here in connection with social indifference. *Do not reject* (v. 9[10]) *us* (gapped) *forever* (לָנֶצַח), *lāneṣaḥ*, a synonym of לְעוֹלָם *le'ôlām* (v. 8[9]), refers to perpetuity without limits.

24[25] In the second bicolon of the strophe, the anthropomorphism of hiding one's face replaces the metaphor of sleeping, both connoting indifference.[139] *Why* (v. 23[24]) *do you hide your face* (Pss. 19:6;[140] 22:24[25]) signifies to prevent yourself from perceiving Israel in its need and so to exert yourself to protect her when human sin does not enter the picture.[141] Emphatically, they ask, [Why do you] *forget* (see v. 17[18]) *our afflictions* (עָנְיֵנוּ, *'onyēnû*)? According to Birkeland עָנָה (*'ānâ*) means "to find oneself in a stunted, humble, lowly position."[142] The abstraction finds concrete expression in the lament. The concrete meaning of *our oppressions* (לַחֲצֵנוּ, *laḥ°ṣēnî*) is graphically pictured in the situation when Balaam's donkey "squeezed up" (לָחַץ, *lāḥaṣ*) against the wall and thereby "crushed" (לָחַץ, *lāḥaṣ*) Balaam's foot (Num. 22:25).

2. Redeem Us for the Sake of Your Unfailing Love (44:25-26[26-27])

25[26] The logical, medial coordinator כִּי (*kî*, "for") probably has the elliptical sense "we pray thus because," linking the second strophe to the first. *Our life* (נַפְשֵׁנוּ: *napsēnû*, see Ps. 3:1[2])[143] *sinks down to the dust* (Ps. 7:5[6]) here is only a symbol of humiliation, not entailing punishment (Ps. 102:14; cf. Gen. 3:14). The Hebrew lexeme glossed *our belly* denotes the lower abdomen of a man or a woman; probably the outward portion of the anatomy is meant; here it functions as a synecdoche for the whole person. Their bodies *cling*, as bone to flesh of a starving person (Ps. 102:5[6]), and as the tongue to the roof of the mouth in thirst (Ps. 137:6), *to the ground* (i.e., to the surface of the earth),[144] a symbol of abject humiliation, even more so than that of Jehu's bowing on hands and knees before the Assyrian king, Shalmaneser III.[145]

---

138. Waltke and Houston, *PACW*, p. 563.

139. On the significance of God's hiding his face, see Samuel E. Balentine, *The Hidden God: The Hiding of the Fact of God in the Old Testament* (Oxford: Oxford University Press, 1983).

140. Waltke and Houston, *PACW*, p. 364.

141. Waltke and Houston, *PACW*, p. 411.

142. Cited by L. J. Coppes, *TWOT*, 2.682.

143. Waltke and Houston, *PACW*, p. 192, n. 35.

144. *BDB*, s.v. אֶרֶץ, p. 76, entry 3a.

145. See James B. Pritchard, *The Ancient Near East in Pictures Relating to the Old Testament* (Princeton: Princeton University Press, 1969), Numbers 351, 355.

26[27] *Rise up* reprises Moses' old war cry (Ps. 7:6[7]). *As our help* (see n. 59) assumes God has sufficient strength to come to their aid. The help needed is metaphorical, *and redeem us* (וּפְדֵנוּ, *ûpᵉdēnû*). In profane legal literature and in cultic literature פָּדָה *(pādâ)* means "to ransom," that is, to transfer or free someone from another's ownership through the payment of a price. According to J. Stamm, however, a "religious linguistic use" of *pdh* (as here) distinguishes itself from the profane legal and cultic literature in that it knows only the Lord as the subject of the freeing/liberating action and correspondingly never the paying of a compensating price: "In this use the specifically legal notion steps to the background and the liberating/freeing notion steps to the foreground."[146]

The psalm is drawn to conclusion with the sole reason for God to act: *on account of*[147] *your unfailing love* (Ps. 5:7[8]). The living, unchanging, everlasting God helps his helpless people as a responsible keeping of faith with them.[148]

F. Postscript[149]

Handing the psalm over *for the director of music* (Ps. 45:1) transforms the psalm from a particular historical situation to all God's covenant people. The psalm ends with the plea to God, not with God's response. But that the plea was set to the tune of *"Upon Lilies"* (see n. 60) implies that the Warrior awoke and vindicated his people. That the covenant community passed down this *Maskil* for three millennia in uninterrupted regular use also implies that God's people found in this psalm the spiritual strength to accept unmerited suffering for God's sake. Anderson notes: "A war has been fought and lost, but the fight for the meaning of history goes on."[150] By contrast, "many other prayers, from many ancient cults and religions, are known to us, some of them even older than the Psalms. But those texts are museum-pieces, relics of a dead past, addressed to divinities long since deserted by men and almost forgotten."[151]

---

146. J. Stamm, *THAT*, 2.389.

147. H. A. Brongers, "*Die Partikel Lᵉma'an* in der biblisch-hebräischen Sprache," *OTS* 18 (1973): 87.

148. K. D. Sakenfeld, *The Meaning of Ḥesed in the Hebrew Bible* (Harvard Semitic Museum 17; Missoula, MT: Scholars, 1978), p. 233.

149. Bruce K. Waltke, "Superscripts, Postscripts, or Both," *JBL* 110 (1991A): 583-96.

150. Anderson, *Psalms*, p. 341.

151. Leopold Sabourin, S.J., *The Psalms: Their Origin and Meaning*, vol. 2 (Staten Island, NY: Alba House, 1969), p. 143.

PART IV. CONCLUSION

This *maskil* was written to give martyrs the theology they need to survive suffering for righteousness' sake. As a pilot who loses visual contact in a cloud turns to his instrument panel to fly his airplane safely, so the inspired psalmist, when having lost rational contact in the fog of undeserved sufferings, finds his bearings by locating himself within the metanarrative of salvation history and by reflecting on God's attributes.[152] The reason why martyrs suffer may be unknown, but the reasons for sustaining their faith can be learned from each stanza of this psalm. On the shining first tier of this inspired literary ziggurat, martyrs find their bearing within *Heilsgeschichte*, even as the Founder of the church, while dying on the rude cross, situated himself within that history (Psalm 22).[153] Today the martyr remembers a much greater founding event than the Conquest; namely, the resurrection of the Lord Jesus Christ from the dead. In the shadow of death on the second tier, the martyrs reflect on God's sovereignty: they accept that undeserved suffering is a part of mysterious Providence. Their lament, delivered in staccato hammer blows, drives home the truth, "You did it," without ever deflecting the blows with doubt that perchance their circumstance is due to blind chance (Deut. 32:30).[154] So also the Pioneer of the martyr's faith understood his sufferings as part of a sovereignly designed timetable. Repeatedly he asserted "my hour [to die] is not yet come" (John 2:4; 7:6-8, 30) until the Greeks came, asking to see him. Then he discerned: "my hour is come" (John 12:20-23), for he must first die to become, as John the Baptist prophesied without full comprehension, "the Lamb of God who takes away the sin of the world" (John 1:29).

On the foggy third tier the martyrs grope to understand unmerited suffering. But, unlike Psalm 73, theirs is not a crisis of faith; they never doubt that God is Lord of All.[155] The Lord of the church, however, removes the tone of protest from the psalm, recognizing the necessity, not just the ambiguity, of unmerited suffering (John 15:15-21; 16:33). Likewise Barnabas and Paul incorporate suffering as constitutive of the life of faith (Acts 14:22; Rom. 8:36).[156] Commenting

152. It is important to keep in mind that the Psalm represents the intimate corporate relationship between the king and the community, a type of Christ and his church militant.

153. Waltke and Houston, *PACW*, pp. 376-415.

154. Ingvar Floysvik, "When God Behaves Strangely: A Study in the Protest Psalms," *Concordia Journal* 21 (1995): 298-304, esp. 299.

155. Artur Weiser, *The Psalms: A Commentary* (OTL; Philadelphia: Westminster, 1962) p. 358.

156. Calvin (*Commentary on the Book of Psalms*, p. 172) makes a rare *faux pas* when he describes the inspired cries "Wake up!" "Arise!" "Why do you sleep?" as "morbid affections which belong to the corruption of our nature." But that plea is quite similar to our Lord's existential

on Romans 8:36, R. A. Harrisville notes: "The sufferer's fate is now altered to a descriptive statement of the shape of the Christian life, with (not despair) which the believer is 'more than conqueror,' and which cannot separate from God's love because it is precisely in the shape that Christ makes his appearance in those who are his."[157] Paul argued in Romans 5:3 that we glory in suffering because it produces Christian character. If God immediately applied his covenant promises and curses, his people would be spiritually worse off, for they would use God, confounding morality with pleasure, and/or they would credit their well-being to their own power and/or righteousness (Deuteronomy 8–9). Their Lord graciously for a time turns the Law's blessings and curses on their head to save them from such perils. In truth, God warned his covenant people from the beginning that while the Holy Seed crushes the serpent's head, the serpent will crush its heel (Gen. 3:15). Having only the moral primer of the Mosaic covenant, however, those who lived under the Law and who did not have the benefit of church doctrine protested the "crushed heel."

On the final tier the martyrs reflect on God's sublime attribute of unfailing love, of covenant fidelity. Though not experiencing the covenant blessings in spite of covenant fidelity (Deut. 28:1-14), even the martyrs of the Old Covenant knew their God's character decreed that he upholds justice. For martyrs the present topsy-turvy world, though long and painful, is temporary. Their Lord decisively triumphed over injustice and death by his resurrection. On the fourth tier and through the postscript they learn to persuade God. Patrick Miller notes: "God may not be coerced, but God can be persuaded."[158] Moreover, they reflect on his unfailing love. To be sure, "God's thoughts are not our thoughts, neither are his ways our ways" (Isa. 55:8), but his thought is always for the martyr's good and his way is always directed by unfailing love. And so in the midst of unmerited suffering they pray for victory, confident that God responds to fervent, honest prayer.

---

exclamation in experiencing the human situation: "My God, why have you abandoned me?" His nature was not corrupt, nor did he have morbid affections. Rather, these cries are discharged from the saints' existential situation. Their pleas and questions, like their prayers that God punish their enemy, are orthodox but no longer appropriate in the full light of the gospel of the Lord Jesus Christ (Waltke and Houston, *PACW*, pp. 95-98).

157. Roy A. Harrisville, "Paul and the Psalms: A Formal Study," *Word and World* 5, no. 2 (1985): 168-79, esp. 176.

158. Patrick D. Miller, "Prayer as Persuasion: The Rhetorical Intention of Prayer," *Word and World* 13 (1993): 356-62.

CHAPTER 9

Psalm 102: *The Prayer of an Afflicted Person*

PART I. THE VOICE OF THE CHURCH

I. Introduction

Here, with a focus on the fifth penitential psalm, we shall reflect on diverse commentators of the sixteenth century, whose motives and renderings of the penitential psalms both complement and differ significantly from prior periods. We have categorized this diversity into "Catholic or Traditional Repentance," "Reformed or Evangelical Repentance," and "Courtly Repentance."

II. Catholic or Traditional Repentance

For brevity we shall consider only one commentator to represent the Catholic tradition in interpreting penitential psalms for the sixteenth century.

John Fisher (1469-1535), Bishop of Rochester and a Catholic martyr, like Thomas More was beheaded by Henry VIII, although both martyrs had been his boyhood mentors and friends. In declaring himself head of the church in place of the pope, Henry turned against his mentors, just as Henry II more than three centuries earlier had destroyed Thomas à Becket over the latter's embracing of the Gregorian reforms that asserted the church universal's independence from and supremacy over secular powers. Fisher, who was pastorally responsible for Queen Catherine, condemned Henry VIII's divorce proceedings against her and was destroyed as a result. He drew parallels between the events leading to John the Baptist's beheading, likening himself to John the Baptist, and equating Henry VIII's illicit relationship with Anne Boleyn with the eroticism of Herod's Salome (Mark 6:17-29).[1] Fisher's

---

1. Fisher actually kept in his private chapel an image of the head of John the Baptist. In

great pastoral calling had been to reform both the moral and the scholarly standards of the clergy, which he exemplified as a saintly preacher.

For this clerical reform Fisher recommended the private, daily use of the Psalms. He described the seven penitential psalms as medicine for healing souls, echoing the teaching of Evagrius Ponticus and the Desert Fathers. All prayers of contrite hearts are efficacious, but Fisher taught that the prayers most acceptable were those chosen by the holy church and hence the "seven penitential psalms" were unique and had sacramental efficacy. Another martyr, Savonarola (+1498), had selected Psalm 51, the fourth penitential psalm, for consolation while awaiting execution. Now six years later, in his own rendering of Psalm 102, Fisher read Savonarola's meditations.[2] He reinterpreted metaphorically the Canaanite woman (Matt. 15:22) as a mother of "strong mind," so "mighty" that she can bear any humiliation for her child's sake. Fisher saw her as the archetype of the church in the ecclesial crisis of his day. For Fisher's metaphorical interpretation of Psalm 102, reading the psalm through the lens of the supplication of the Canaanite woman — that is to say, the church, the psalm was food to strengthen the church militant, to execute the severity of God's judgment, while offering mercy for the cleansed penitent.[3] Unlike the later scholars of reform, Fisher did not yet see the need to change the medieval atmosphere of devotion in the veneration of Mary, as conceived without sin, as the advocate of sinners, and as the "means" or mediatrix of divine grace.

He preached two lengthy sermons on Psalm 102, more as prayers than as commentaries.[4] In his first sermon, he reflected from this psalm that we need to pray passionately. Fisher understood the psalmist as meekly making his petition to be heard by almighty God, praying "Lord, hear my prayer effectually."[5] Yes, he argued, the angels can pray on our behalf, but the most effective way to pray is to personally present our prayers, with our own tears, wretchedness, and personal suffering. Secondly, he reflected that we should feed on God's Word. With the ax of judgment descending upon him, now he could only live on the heavenly food of the Word of God. Thirdly, he remembered three things he

---

the late Middle Ages, John the Baptist is often portrayed as the figure of both judgment and of consolation. See Berndt Hamm, *The Reformation of Faith in the Context of Late Medieval Theology and Piety* (Leiden: Brill, 2004), pp. 26-27.

2. Bruce Waltke and James M. Houston with Erika Moore, *The Psalms as Christian Worship* (Grand Rapids: Eerdmans, 2010), pp. 460-61 [PACW].

3. Hamm, *The Reformation of Faith*, pp. 55-65.

4. John Fisher's *Exposition of the Seven Penitential Psalms,* the first of his many works published in 1504, was a very early book in the vernacular.

5. Saint John Fisher, *Exposition of the Seven Penitential Psalms,* in modern English, with introduction by Anne Barbeau Gardiner (San Francisco: Ignatius, 1998), p. 146.

could do as deeds of penance to obtain divine mercy: contrition, confession, and satisfaction.[6]

In Fisher's second homily on Psalm 102 (vv. 12-28[13-29]), he suggested that the more difficult Scriptures are to interpret, the more figurally they are to be understood. Based on Scripture, he understood there to be "three noble places that signify three diverse kinds of covenants in reference to God's people." First there was the covenant with the Jewish people, under the law of Moses. The second is at Mount Sion (Zion), which signified the Christian people under the law of grace. The third is the high celestial calling of the gospel, in anticipation of heaven.[7]

Now the church militant suffers much anguish, but it is heir of the promised heavenly kingdom, which it seeks in meekness and humility. In light of the tension of personal affliction in the first part of the psalm, and the calling forth of God's people from Sinai to Zion in the latter part, he concludes his second homily by contrasting our present mortality of transience to the eternal state. Facing the prospect of personal martyrdom and continuing his stance against the scandalous state of the clergy, "Saint Fisher," as he became venerated, adopted this fifth penitential psalm. In his message we see the transition taking place from the stern mindset of late-medieval penance to the new voice of the Reformers.

III. Reformed or Evangelical Repentance

The Reformers, following Faber and Luther, did not react against penitence (and the centrality of the penitential psalms in the primers and other books of late medieval penitence) per se,[8] but reinforced its importance, albeit with a new evangelical voice. With that voice, the Psalms were reinterpreted from the monastic tradition into the more personal usage of reformed "gracious or evangelical repentance" (i.e., the grace of the gospel leading to repentance). Later they were communicated in a new musical liturgy. The lament psalms, read with the new eyes of the gospel, became a powerful instrument of the Reformation.[9] Luther, Bucer, Calvin, and other reformers all began with emphasis upon the penitential psalms, to vocalize evangelical penitence, repentance, forgiveness, and justification as the great doctrinal issues of the Protestant Reformation.

Jacques Lefèvre d'Étaples (Faber Stapulensis, c. 1450-1536) was the leading

---

6. Saint John Fisher, *Exposition of the Seven Penitential Psalms*, p. 147.

7. Saint John Fisher, *Exposition of the Seven Penitential Psalms*, pp. 175, 181, 183.

8. What was removed from these primers were both the Sacrament of Penance and the Office of the Dead (prayers for the dead).

9. Following Luther's Penitential Psalms, issued in 1517 and 1525, George Joye retained the seven psalms in a primer he edited in 1529, without prayers to the saints or to the dead.

French reformer, who unlike his contemporary, John Calvin, remained in France and within the Roman Church. Faber's pastoral life is summed up in the term "Christiformity."[10] This for him meant more than copying Christ, as in Thomas à Kempis's *Imitation of Christ*. Rather, based on his interpretation of Galatians 4:19 and Colossians 3:1-4, "Christiformity" described for Faber the formation of Christ in the believer.[11] In his pastoral ministry of visiting monasteries, Faber constantly saw the unhappiness of the monks, merely reciting liturgically the Psalms, with no accompanying evidence of living biblically with transformed lives. "Such persons [i.e., in the cloistered life] have dead spirits. And whenever these pious studies cease, monasteries decay, devotion dies out, worship is extinguished, spiritual blessings are exchanged for earthly things, heaven is abandoned and earth welcomed — truly the most disastrous of transactions."[12] This, as we have seen in Erasmus' use of the Psalms, was the same concern to reform monasticism.[13] Faber distinguished two literal interpretations. First, scholars or monks might base the psalms on the literal/historical context of David or some other composer, writing as a historian about a dead past. Second, argued Faber, David is a prophet, inspired by the same Holy Spirit as the apostolic authors of the New Testament, and so passages from the Psalms are to be taken to proclaim their literal fulfillment in the person and work of Christ. For Faber there was a great contrast between "a rabbinical literal text" and "a Christian literal message." Many senses had been applied to the Psalms, such as the medieval fourfold senses, but for Faber the only valid sense was that given by the Holy Spirit,[14] not that of the detached, faithless reading of Holy Scripture, such as that of the rabbis.

Faber, one of the best reforming scholars of his times, was influenced by Origen's Hexapla[15] to compose his Fivefold Psalter (1509).[16] Faber's Commentary on the Psalms consists of: 1) a brief introduction to the title and a short sum-

10. The term "Christiformity," first used in the ninth century, and later used occasionally by Albert the Great, Aquinas, and Nicholas of Cusa, inspired Thomas à Kempis and the Brethren of the Common Life, in which tradition Faber was early nurtured.

11. Philip Edgcumbe Hughes, *Lefèvre: Pioneer of Ecclesiastical Renewal in France* (Grand Rapids: Eerdmans, 1984), pp. 192-97.

12. Jacobus Faber Stapulensis, *Introduction to Commentary on the Psalms*, trans. Heiko Augustinus Oberman, *Forerunners of the Reformation: The Shape of Late Medieval Thought* (New York: Holt, Rinehart and Winston, 1966), p. 297.

13. *Collected Works of Erasmus*, vol. 65, pp. 164, 166-67, 181.

14. Nicholas of Lyra (+1349) and later Paul of Burgos (+1435) had affirmed two literal senses, the historical and the prophetic, which Faber adopted.

15. See Waltke and Houston, *PACW*, pp. 42, 46.

16. "Fivefold" because Faber gives four Latin versions of the Psalms: the Old Latin version revised by Jerome (the Roman version) as Jerome's first version; the Gallic version as Jerome's second revision, which uniquely became the text of the Vulgate; the Hebraic or Jerome's third

mary of the psalm; 2) a continuous verse-by-verse exposition; 3) a concordance of words and themes of the psalm; and 4) a "take note" section.

He begins his commentary on Psalm 102 by describing it as "the prayer of a poor man when he is anxious and pours out his supplication in the sight of the Lord."[17] For Faber this meant: "a prayer to Christ the Lord by the Church, that is, by a faithful people praying ... 'Son of God, Word of the Eternal Father, admit my prayer; and let the outcry of my heart enter before you. . . . Son of God, do not withdraw your grace and favour from me. In whatever time of my trouble, extend your propitiation over me. . . . Son of God, do not defer hearing me, for my times have become empty, without use, like smoke; and whatever was solid and firm in me, is like a thing burnt up, used up, and desiccated ... my soul wasted away because there was not one who would pledge the food of your doctrine being heard.'"[18]

Turning from the personal laments of verses 2-12[3-13], he comments on the psalmist's promise for Zion (i.e., the church [vv. 13-22(14-23)]): "The time has come that you should have mercy on Zion itself, for the saints whom you have raised up were made an acceptable people who are inferred in the building up of Zion. . . . Having heard your name, the nations will revere you, O Son of God, eternal Ruler, and all the rulers of the earth your majesty. . . . They will revere the name of the Son of God, for Christ the Lord will restore his Church. And he will appear in his beauty."[19]

In the psalmist's return to personal laments (vv. 23-28[24-29]), Faber emphasizes that it is Christ himself who "moves his eyes in the prayers of the afflicted and humbled; and he has not spurned their petition" (v. 19[20]). "For the Lord has looked down upon the dwellers of earth so that he might attend the cry of the conquered, that he might snatch away, freed, those contrite ones who had failed in adverse misfortune" (v. 20[21]). He concludes: "The heavens are mutable and pass away, but you will endure. . . . You, O Son of God, will change the heavens, so that like apparel they will be changed; but you are always immutable, and the eternity and duration of your years will in no way fail."[20]

"Take note," he concludes. "You should understand that this psalm should not be interpreted from the literal material *(ab re)* but concerning the Son of God, for Paul also in the first chapter of his Epistle to the Hebrews brings in the

---

version, which became the text of the Vulgate in other books; and fourthly a harmonized version, *Psalterium Conciliatum,* which is Faber's own revision of the Vulgate.

17. Jacques Lefèvre d'Étaples, *Quincuplex Psalterium,* Geneva 1513 (Geneva: Librairie Druz, 1979), folio 146v.

18. Jacques Lefèvre d'Étaples, *Quincuplex Psalterium,* folio 146v.

19. Jacques Lefèvre d'Étaples, *Quincuplex Psalterium,* folio 147r.

20. Peter Martyr Vermigli, *Sacred Prayers: Drawn from the Psalms of David,* trans. and ed. John Patrick Donnelly, S.J., The Peter Martyr Library, vol. 3 (Kirksville, MO: Sixteenth-Century Essays & Studies, 1996), p. 97.

twenty-sixth verse — and incidentally, the two subsequent verses — of this Psalm as directed to the Son of God."[21]

Peter Martyr Vermigli (1499-1562). A generation later, and living in worse times than Faber due to the intensification of the Reformation conflicts, the Italian reformer Peter Martyr fled from Italy (1547), stayed briefly in Strasbourg where he began a warm friendship with Bucer, and then accepted the Regius Chair of Theology at Oxford in 1548.[22] Martin Bucer had been introducing paraphrases of selected psalms into metrical verse since 1524. Clément Marot, a French court poet, helped John Calvin to produce his first collection of metrical psalms in 1539.[23] As a scholar preacher, Peter Martyr added paraphrase as another expression of psalmody, using it at the commencement of his lectures and sermons in order to promote godly scholarship. These were published posthumously as *Preces Sacrae ex Psalmis Davidis desumptae* in Zurich, 1566. Ornate in style, reminiscent of the Roman Missal yet devotional in spirit, these paraphrases aimed to blend biblical scholarship with godliness. Moreover, he concluded his lectures and sermons with an appropriate psalm for the subject being taught.[24]

Martyr rejected the doctrine of transubstantiation, arguing that it was in the Incarnation — not in the Eucharist — that Christ shared in our flesh and blood for the benefits of our redemption, and it is only by the Holy Spirit that we share in all his benefits. These psalmic prayers express his personal trust in the substitutionary atonement of the cross of Christ. As Mariano di Gangi commenting on these prayers notes: "They reflect frequently a spirit of desperation, which is yet completely confident of ultimate victory."[25]

We hear in Martyr's paraphrased prayer of Psalm 102 all the key issues affecting his suffering friends to whom he was writing in Lucca, Italy, in England and Poland, as well as more locally in Switzerland, where he died. He prays, "O almighty God, in ourselves we are unworthy of having our prayers gain access to you, for we have transgressed your commandments and law . . . and we have lived totally unworthy of the Gospel and of our calling. But because of your kindness hide not your face from our prayers and petitions. We are bitterly assailed and oppressed by extreme dangers, so incline your ear to us, and give those who call upon you a

21. Heb. 1:10-12 quoting Ps. 102:25-27(26-28).

22. It was John Fisher who had promoted these lectureships first at Cambridge and then at Oxford, to encourage the training of preachers for the church. He also founded St. John's at Cambridge, which should more truly be named St. John Fisher's College.

23. John Calvin promoted musical psalmody on his return to Geneva in 1541, aided by Clément Marot (a refugee there from 1543). The Genevan Psalter was completed in 1562.

24. Peter Martyr Vermigli, *Sacred Prayers*, p. 2.

25. Mariano di Gangi, *Peter Martyr Vermigli, 1499-1562: Renaissance Man, Reformation Master* (Lanham, MD: University Press of America, 1993), p. 141.

prompt and favourable hearing. We beg you first to deliver us from our sins and vices, then to strengthen our weak heart in your path, and by your Holy Spirit refresh our exhausted strength of soul so that we may live for you. After having been restored and renewed may we cause your name and Gospel to be spoken of favourably. Secondly, turn your power and might against those who heap countless insults and slanders upon the name of your Son and his teaching. We beseech you, take pity now on Zion, that is your church, for it seems time now for you to favour it. We ask you to look down from your heavenly dwelling place, look into our troubles, and listen to the groans of those who are locked up, tortured, and slaughtered in horrible ways because of your name. Rescue . . . your sheep that the Antichrist has condemned not only to death but to vile curses; may your children then be able to live a peaceful . . . life before you. Through Jesus Christ our Lord. Amen."[26]

IV. Courtly Repentance

During the turbulence of the Tudor court, when first Catholic, then Protestant, and then more Catholic diplomats were all imprisoned in the Tower of London, several commentaries on the penitential psalms were composed by its inmates. Their subtleties were a complex of paraphrase, musical rendering, and the inner emotions of their composers. By savage irony the same year (1535) William Tyndale (1494?-1535) was burnt at the stake for his translation of the Bible into English, Miles Coverdale (1488-1568) published his loose translation or paraphrase with the court approval of Henry VIII. The most successful part was the Psalter, set in prose rhythm based on the plain chant tradition, which is traceable back to Ambrose in the fourth century.[27] After the Act of Uniformity this Psalter was incorporated into Cranmer's *Book of Common Prayer*. This is only one of four versions that Coverdale produced. Unlike Faber, he did not seek to establish one critical text from four sources. Coverdale preferred to use paraphrase to overlook, as he confesses, "his ignorance of the three original languages," as well as to cover his ambivalence about its original character as text, or as translation, or as a loose commentary.

In contrast, Tyndale had argued for the reduction of the medieval "four senses" (literal, allegorical, tropological, anagogical) as a church tradition that was invalid, even "damnable."[28] He saw this as undermining the Reformers' rehabilitation of *sola Scriptura*.

---

26. Peter Martyr Vermigli, *Sacred Prayers*, pp. 97-98.
27. Susan Gillingham, *Psalms through the Centuries* (Oxford: Blackwell, 2008), p. 136.
28. James H. Ferguson, "Miles Coverdale and the Claims of Paraphrase," in *Psalms in the*

In addition to paraphrasing the Psalms, another subjective element was the introduction of lyrical and poetic renderings into the popular usage of the Psalms. Consequently, more than seventy new versions of the Psalter were issued between 1535 and 1601; at least six different musical renderings were given to the seven penitential psalms, with many more to individual psalms.[29]

To the biblical dignity of the *imago Dei*, as celebrated in Psalm 8:4 ("what is man, that Thou art mindful of him?"), the Renaissance added the further dignity of the individual's self-determination and powers of judgment. The promotion of science, the revival of Stoicism, the explorations of overseas trade, all gave new secular confidence in humanity itself. For the sake of brevity, we can only select one Tudor example of this self-understanding without the need of divine knowledge.

During his arrest and trial (for his alleged adulterous affair with Anne Boleyn), court poet **Sir Thomas Wyatt** (1503-1542) compiled a poetic version of the seven penitential psalms. He writes a commentary on each penitential psalm using a paraphrase narrative in *terza rima* composed by the Italian Aretino in 1534. According to some scholars, Wyatt, having been chided by Henry VIII for having a mistress, interprets David as persisting in a state of moral confusion, the unfortunate victim of love, until he sorts himself out towards the end of the seven psalms. By the fifth psalm he has taken up his lyre again to eventually win the appropriate plea to God. A humanistic doctrine of comfort is thus achieved through the poetic.[30]

Other scholars, however, interpret Wyatt to be a concealed reformer, who caricatures Catholic penitence in his first three penitential psalms, only then with Psalm 51, to contrast this with what Wyatt now calls "Ryghtfull Penitence."[31] This pivotal change begins with the *Miserere* of Psalm 51, where the kind of practical offering God requires is "a contrite heart." According to this interpretation, only with the fifth penitential psalm does Wyatt introduce the Reformed doctrine of "evangelical repentance." Its posthumous publication in December 1549 came just as the young King Edward was being enthroned to restore the Protestant state. The great medieval popularity of viewing David as the model of penance[32] became in the sixteenth century focused more particularly upon

---

Early Modern World, ed. Linda Phyllis Austern, Kari Boyd McBride, and David L. Orvis (Farnham, UK: Ashgate, 2011), pp. 137-54.

19. Rivkah Zim, *English Metrical Psalms: Poetry as Praise and Prayer, 1535-1601* (Cambridge: Cambridge University Press, 1987), p. 2.

30. Zim, *English Metrical Psalms*, pp. 43-74.

31. Clare Costley King'oo, "Rightful Penitence and the Publication of Wyatt's Certayne Psalmes," in *Psalms in the Early Modern World*, pp. 155-74.

32. Charles A. Huttar, "Frail Grass and Firm Tree: David as the Model of Repentance in the

his adultery with Bathsheba, as a sly polemic against the amorous adventures of Henry VIII.

The Psalms reached new heights of devotion, provided by the musical and lyrical psalmody of the Huguenots, the Calvinists, and indeed of English poets like Sternhold and the Countess of Pembroke. Yet the threshold of modernity also generated more confusion about humanity's position before God. As Wyatt prays lyrically from Psalm 102: "Lord, hear my prayer, and let my cry pass unto the Lord without impediment. Do not from me turn thy merciful face, Unto myself leaving my government."[33]

PART II. VOICE OF THE PSALMIST: TRANSLATION

A prayer by[34] an afflicted person when he grows weak and pours out his complaint before "I AM."

1   "I AM," hear my prayer;
        let my cry for help come to you.
2   Do not hide your face from me when I am in distress.
        Turn your ear to me; when I call, answer me quickly.
3   For my days vanish in smoke;
        my bones burn like[35] glowing embers.[36]
4   My heart is blighted like vegetation and so withers;
        I forget[37] and depart[38] without eating my food.
5   From the sound of my sobbing,

Middle Ages and Early Renaissance," in *The David Myth in Western Literature*, ed. Raymond-Jean Frontain and Jan Wojcik (West Lafayette, IN: Purdue University Press, 1980), pp. 38-55.

33. Costley Kingóo, "Rightful Penitence and the Publication of Wyatt's Certayne Psalmes," p. 174.

34. Or "for" (cf. Psalm 92: superscript).

35. Possibly both *beth* "in" (3A[4A]) and *kaph* "like" (3B[4B]) are doing double duty, yielding "vanish as in smoke" and "burn as in glowing embers."

36. L and many Masoretic mss. read *kāmôqēḏ*. *Qēḏ*, however, is an unknown word. Many medieval manuscripts and editions read more plausibly *kmqd* ("like a burning mass"; Isa. 33:14).

37. In the light of Ugaritic *ṭkḥ* scholars debate the existence of II שָׁכַח ("to be hot, burn, be burned" > "to wither," best attested in Ps. 137:5). (I *škḥ* means "to forget.") Assuming this homonym, 102:4[5] could be glossed: "I am too wilted/limp to eat." According to J. J. M. Roberts ("*NISKAḤTÎ ... MILLĒB*, Ps. XXXI.13," *VT* 25 [1975]: 797-801, n. 13), however, II *škḥ* means "to bow down," and Psalm 102:4[5] could mean "I am too depressed to eat." *HALOT* (IV, 1491, s.v. II *škḥ*) rejects II *škḥ* and emends 137:5.

38. "From" demands a verb of motion, such as "leave" or "depart" (*IBHS*, P. 11.4/3d. p. 224).

      my bones cling to my flesh.

6   I am like a desert owl,
      I have become like a screech owl among ruins.

7   I keep vigil; I have become like a bird
      alone on a roof.

8   All day long my enemies taunt me;
      those who are senseless and against me[39] swear by me.

9   For I eat ashes as my food
      and mix my drink with tears.

10   Because of your indignation and anger,
      surely, you lifted me up and then threw me down.

11   My days are like the evening shadow;
      I wither away like the vegetation.

12   But you, "I AM," sit enthroned forever;
      your renown endures from generation to generation.

13   You arise and have compassion on Zion,
      for time to show her favor —
      for the appointed time is at hand.[40]

14   For your slaves delight in her stones;
      And they show favor to her dust.

15   The nations will fear the name of "I AM,"
      and all the kings of the earth [will revere] your glory.

16   For "I AM" will rebuild Zion;
      He[41] will appear in his glory.

17   He responds to the prayer of the destitute;
      he does not despise their plea.

18   Let this be written for a future generation,
      that[42] a people to be created[43] may praise "I AM":

19   [44]"I AM" looked down from his holy place on high;
      from heaven he viewed the earth,

20   to hear the groans of the prisoners

---

39. Genitive of a mediated object (*IBHS*, pp. 146f., P. 9.5.2d).

40. *Bā'* may be *Qul* ptcp. (= "is about to come") or *Qal* pf. (= "has come" [*IBHS*, P. 37.6f, p. 627; P. 30.5.2b, pp. 490f.]).

41. LXX and Syriac add "and."

42. A conjunctive *waw* that links the prefix cj. with an impv. signifies purpose/result.

43. A gerundive *niphal* ptcp. (*IBHS*, P. 23.3d, p. 387).

44. The *recitative kî* (cf. ὅτι *recitativum*) is represented by quotation marks.

21   and release those⁴⁵ condemned to death⁴⁶
    to proclaim the name of "I AM" in Zion
       and his praise in Jerusalem,
22   when the peoples assemble themselves together,
       and the kingdoms, to worship "I AM."
23   In the course of my life⁴⁷ he broke my strength;⁴⁸
       he cut short my days.
24   I say: "Do not take me away,⁴⁹ my God, in the midst of my days;
       your years go on through all generations.⁵⁰
25   Prior to that you laid the foundations of the earth,
       and the heavens are the work of your hands.
26   They will perish, but you remain;
       they will all wear out like a garment.
       Like clothing you will change them and they will vanish.
27   But you are He Who Is,
       and your years will never end.
28   The sons of your slaves will live in your presence;
       their seed will be established before you."

PART III. COMMENTARY

I. Introduction

A. Literary Context

1. Book IV of Psalter

Book IV is oriented toward the time of Israel's exile in Babylon. Book III ended with the failure of kingship (Psalm 89); Book IV begins with a prayer of Moses and his reflection that "I AM's" kingship endures from ages past. By this juxta-

---

45. The idiom "sons of" presents the nature of the dying (*IBHS*, p. 149, P. 9.5.3b).

46. Lit., "of the dying" (i.e., given a life-sentence without hope of being pardoned). LXX renders the phrase: τοὺς υἱοὺς τεθανατωμένων ("sons of the slain").

47. B^eḏerek may mean "in strength" (Hos. 10:13; Prov. 31:3), yielding "in strength he broke my strength."

48. *Qere. Kethiv* reads "his strength," yielding "his strength afflicted [me] in the way."

49. Normally *'lh hiphil* means "bring up/ascend" with various prepositions. Here it occurs absolutely and seems to be used idiomatically with the sense "to take away [life]," as also in Job 36:20.

50. B^eḏôr dôrîm is an idiomatic absolute superlative (Ps. 72:5; Isa. 51:8; *IBHS*, P. 14.5b, p. 267).

position the Psalter's editor(s) teach that Israel existed before monarchy and that her existence depends upon God's eternal enthronement, not on David's throne. Psalms 90–100 are framed by "you have been our dwelling place throughout all generations" (Ps. 90:1) and "his faithfulness continues through all generations" (Ps. 100:5). Psalm 102:12 reprises that theme. Psalm 102 fits the context of the Babylonian exile. Zion is in rubble (v. 13[14]), the appointed time has come for it to be rebuilt (v. 16[17], Isa. 44:26-28), and prisoners (i.e., the exiles [Isa. 51:14; 61:1]) to be released (v. 20[21]). An anonymous, afflicted psalmist mirrors the humiliation of Zion and finds hope for himself in its restoration.

2. Psalms 101–110

TNIV Study Bible regards Psalms 101–110, though spanning Books IV and V of the Psalter, as an intentionally collected, concentric arrangement. The collection is framed by two psalms that pertain to kingship: the king vows a righteous rule (101) and God commits to his king a universal rule (110). Psalms 102 and 109 are personal laments in intense distress, and 103 and 108 praise God for his love that reaches to the heavens. Psalm 104 celebrates God's wise and benevolent acts in creation, and 107 praises his wonderful deeds in history. Psalm 105 recites Israel's history as a story of redemption, and 106 recites the same history as a history of Israel's rebellion.[51]

3. Psalms 101–103

Psalm 101:7 asserts that "no one who practices deceit will dwell in my house; no one who speaks falsely will be established before my eyes," and 102:28[29] ends with the hope that the descendants of true Israel will be established before "I AM." Psalm 103 knows God will not harbor his anger forever because "I AM" is compassionate and gracious, and 102 looks forward to the appointed time when God will arise and have compassion on Zion and show her favor.

B. Form Criticism

The psalm's superscript labels it "a prayer"; more specifically, "a complaint/ lament."[52] Its motifs also so identify: direct address to God with introductory

---

51. *Zondervan TNIV Study Bible*, ed. Kenneth L. Barker, John H. Stek, and Ronald Young-blood (Grand Rapids: Zondervan, 2006), p. 943.

52. For a compendium of a "bewildering multiplicity of interpretations" regarding the

petition (vv. 1-2[2-3]), lament (vv. 3-11[4-12]), confession of trust and praise (vv. 12-22[13-23]), and a final petition proper (vv. 23-24[24-25]) with confidence (vv. 25-28[26-29]). It is the fifth so-called penitential psalm (Psalms 6, 32, 38, 51) because the psalmist acknowledges he is suffering for his sin.

C. Rhetorical Criticism

Changes of subjects and of mood delineate the psalm's three stanzas: (1) "I AM" and the psalmist in a mood of lament (vv. 1-11[2-12]); (2) "I AM" and Zion in a mood of trust and praise (vv. 12-22[13-23]); and (3) "I AM" and the psalmist in a mood of prayer, trust, and praise (vv. 23-28[24-29]). The first two stanzas are of equal length.

The first stanza consists of an introductory petition strophe of two verses (vv. 1-2[2-3]), followed by a lament of three strophes, each of three verses (3-5[4-6], 6-8[7-9], 9-11[10-12]). The stanza is framed by reference to God's wrath against the psalmist. The lament (vv. 3-11[4-12]) is framed by a chiasm. Its outer frame refers to the brevity of "my days" (vv. 3, 11[4A, 12]); its middle frame, to withering vegetation (vv. 4B, 11[5, 12]); and its inner frame, to eating ashes as his food (vv. 4, 9[5, 10]).

The second stanza, which presents a vision of Zion's future, reverses the pattern. Now three strophes, each consisting of three verses (vv. 12-14[13-15], 15-17[16-18], 18-20[19-21]), are followed by a two-verse strophe (vv. 21-22[22-23]). The stanza is framed semantically by the notion of God being praised eternally in time (v. 12[13]) and universally in space (v. 22[23]). God's covenant name, "I AM" (*YHWH*, six times, vv. 12, 15, 16, 19, 21, 22[13, 16, 17, 20, 22, 23]; *Yah*, v. 18[19]) occurs seven times, the number of divinity, and frames the stanza as its first (after "you") and last words.

The last stanza consists of three quatrains (vv. 23-24[24-25] [linked by "my days"], 25-26[26-27] [linked by "they"], and vv. 27-28[28-29] [linked by the notion of endurance]). "Your years" roughly frames the stanza (vv. 24, 27[25, 28]). Several catchwords link the third stanza to the preceding stanzas: brevity of "my days" (vv. 3, 11, 23[4, 12, 24]); God's existence through all generations (vv. 12, 24[13, 25]); and "your slaves" (vv. 14, 28[15, 29]).

Here is the outline that will be followed in the exegesis below:

---

form of 102 see Leslie C. Allen, *Psalms 101–150*, Word Biblical Commentary, vol. 21 (Waco, TX: Word, 1983), pp. 11-13.

D. Message

An anonymous, desperately sick exile in his midlife is on the edge of the grave at the end of the Babylonian exile (c. 550 BCE). He probably heard the preaching of Isaiah, for his psalm echoes the themes and motifs of Second (40–55) and Third Isaiah (56–66). The afflicted prays that God may share a tiny portion of his unending years with the psalmist's few days so that he might witness the restoration of Zion with his own eyes.

In the first stanza the afflicted invokes an immediate hearing (vv. 1-2[2-3]), for his case is urgent. His bones burn and his heart withers. He is gaunt — nothing but skin and bones — like the prisoners at Auschwitz — for sorrow and sickness have taken away his appetite. His enemies seize his desiccation and emaciation as an opportunity to taunt him. Exposed to their ribald mockery, he is like an owl among ruins; his food is the ashes of a mourner, and his bitter drink is made more potent with tears. Worst of all, he is under divine wrath. Now his life quickly fades away like a shadow about to be engulfed by the darkness of night; he is about to die, unfulfilled.

But the transient mortal is not without hope. In the second stanza, with the eagle eye of faith, he sees "I AM" enthroned on high forever (v. 12[13]). His fleeting, meaningless life must be seen in the metanarrative of the Sovereign's kingship in heaven and its historical realization on Mount Zion. God's everlasting rule guarantees Zion's future, for they are in corporate solidarity with one another. More than that, he knows — from the prophecies of Isaiah (40:1-9) and especially Jeremiah (25:12; 2 Chron. 36:22f.; Dan. 9:2) — that the appointed time for Zion's rejuvenation has come (v. 13[14]). Moreover, the covenant made their return from exile conditional upon their repentance (Deut. 4:29-31; 30:1-5; 1 Kgs. 8:46-53). God's faithful slaves express their regeneration by their taking pity on Zion's rubble (v. 14[15]). When "I AM" rebuilds Zion, the nations will join the slaves in praising the name of "I AM" at the temple in Zion (vv. 15-16[16-17). This new initiative of "I AM" shows that he responds to the prayers of the destitute (v. 17[18]). "I AM's" intentional looking down from heaven to hear the groans of prisoners and to release them from their death sentence must be written down — oral transmission evidently does not suffice — so that future generations may praise "I AM" (vv. 18-20[19-21]). One thing is certain: the peoples, nations, and kingdoms of the earth will gather and praise God in Zion (vv. 21-22[22-23]). The afflicted psalmist longs to see that new age. In sum, within the metanarrative of salvation history, which culminates in eternal life and praise of "I AM," not in death and shame, he is lifted up from his self-immersion to heavenly contemplation and finds hope and meaning to his otherwise unfulfilled, uncertain existence.

In the third stanza he returns to his broken reality, to his fragile and uncertain hold on life. But now armed with faith's vision of God spanning the generations, he prays that he not die prematurely, presumably so that he might glimpse the reality of the appointed time. He lives in hope, confident that the descendants of God's slaves will be established forever under God's protection. Salvation history must end in triumph, not in defeat. His ultimate concern is not for himself but for the kingdom of God. He can accept his own death with equanimity, with the assurance that the future generations of God's slaves will be established and protected. He is in corporate solidarity with the community that sacred history will justify.

II. Exegesis

A. Superscript

The superscript is uniquely in the form of parallelism: "prayer [Ps. 6:9(10)] of an afflicted person"// "pour out his grievance before 'I AM.'" The psalm is by and/ or for this afflicted person (see n. 34). Its content favors the gloss "by," and its function in the canon favors "for." Perhaps the ambiguity is intentional. *Afflicted person ('ānî)* refers to one "in a circumstance of diminished capacity, power and worth."[53] God is their special protector (Prov. 22:22-23; cf. Exod. 22:25[24]). The

---

53. R. Martin-Archard, *TLOT*, 2.342, s.v. ʿnh.

antonyms of *'ānî* include the wicked (Ps. 10:2), the violent (Ezek. 18:10-12), and the oppressor (Amos 4:10). *Grows faint* signifies a feeble hold on life and/or an ebbing away/fading of life (Pss. 61:2[3]; 77:3[4]). Although the lexeme glossed *complaint* can mean "meditation" or "grievance," the former is inappropriate and, unlike Job, the psalmist does not accuse God of acting unjustly. *Pours out his lament/ complaint* metaphorically refers to an abundant prayer, "usually amid tears and deep discouragement."[54] Like Hannah, the afflicted makes his complaint fluid and empties his hurt before "I AM" and so finds healing.

B. Lament for Present Distress (102:1-11[2-12])

1. Introductory Petitions (102:1-2[2-3])

The five urgent introductory petitions are arranged in a chiasm: four positive, escalating petitions around a negative:

A. Hear my prayer,
    B. Let my cry for help come to you.
        X. Do not hide your face from me when I am in distress.
    B'. Turn your ear to me;
A'. When I call, answer me quickly.

1[2] The force of the command, "I AM" (Ps. 6:1[2]) *hear* (Ps. 5:3[4]), is weakened by *my prayer* (Ps. 6:9[10]). *My cry for help* qualifies the prayer as an urgent outcry of one in dire distress (Exod. 2:23; 1 Sam. 5:12) and in need of salvation (Ps. 145:19; Lam. 3:56). *Let come to you* personifies his cry as entering into the heavenly temple where God sits enthroned (vv. 12[13]; Ps. 18:6[7]).

2[3] The litotes *do not hide* (Ps. 38:9[10]) *your face from me when I am in distress* (Ps. 32:2) asks for God's grace. "God conceals his countenance from a person as an expression of wrath," and that entails "concrete acts of divine punishment."[55] *Incline* with *your ear* means to listen attentively and consent to what someone has to say (Prov. 4:20; 5:1, 13; 22:17). With reference to God, the action occurs in the context of prayer (Pss. 17:6; 31:2[3]). *I cry out* signifies audibly to call another's attention to oneself, *answer me* designates the reaction or response.[56] Elsewhere

54. Herbert Wolf/Robert Holmstedt, *NIDOTTE*, 4.222, s.v. *špk*.
55. G. Wehmeier, *TLOT*, 2.817, s.v. *str*.
56. C. J. Labuschagne, *THAT*, 2.668, *'nh*.

the psalmist need only raise his voice and his Father sends him help (Pss. 57:2[3]; 20:1-4[2-5]). But cry he must, for failure to turn to God, the only source of hope, would be tantamount to surrendering to the enemy and to becoming an accomplice with the evildoers (Deut. 22:24).

2. Physical Anguish by Figures of Burning Heat (102:3-5[4-6])

For explains the urgency of the introductory petitions. The quatrains (vv. 1-2 and 3-4) are linked by a play on *yôm* "day" *(bᵉyôm),* "when" (2A, B[3A, B]), and "my days" (3A[4A]).

3[4] The quantity of his life is vanishing in smoke, and the quality of life is a burning fever. *My days* is a rather general and somewhat vague word for the "time" of one's life. The metaphor "vanish"[57] connotes his life is about to end and has come to the point of failure. *In smoke* — perhaps chosen by its association with a burning fever — connotes being insubstantial, short-lived (Hos. 13:3; Isa. 51:6; Ps. 37:20), and unpleasant (Prov. 10:26). *And my bones* (Ps. 38:3[4]) *burn* or "are hot/scorched" (Ezek. 24:11; Job 30:30). *Like glowing embers* intensifies the fever that racks his body.

4[5] He is gaunt, for he is too distracted to eat. His *heart* (Ps. 7:9[10]) is *blighted* (lit., "is struck") because bread sustains a person's heart (Ps. 104:15). *Withers* signifies shortness of life (Pss. 90:6; 102:11[12]; 129:6). This is so *because I forget* due to the overpowering consciousness of distress (Gen. 41:30).[58] That he forgets *and departs from eating* (Deut. 24:19) is an index of his distraction.

5[6] *From the sound* (Ps. 6:8[9]) *of my sobbing* (Ps. 6:6[7]) is a metonym of effect; the unstated cause is his extreme suffering. *My bones* (Ps. 6:2[3]) *cling* (Lam. 4:4; Job 31:7) *to my flesh.* When bones cling tightly to flesh (Ps. 38:3, 7[4, 8]), the bones protrude through it (Job 19:20). He does not sob because he is nothing but skin and bones. Rather, as Delitzsch explains: "Continuous straining of the voice, especially in connection with persevering prayer arising from inward conflict, does really make the body waste away."[59]

---

57. *HALOT,* 2.476-77, s.v. *klh.*

58. W. Schottroff, *TLOT,* 3.1322, s.v. *škḥ.*

59. F. Delitzsch, *Psalms,* trans. Francis Bolton, in C. F. Keil and F. Delitzsch, *Commentary on the Old Testament* (Peabody, MA: Hendrickson, 1996; reprinted from the English edition originally published by T. & T. Clark, Edinburgh, 1866-91; 1996), p. 642.

3. Social Ostracism by Figures of Solitary Birds (102:6-8[7-9])

6[7]   The figure of withered vegetation gives way to that of wretched creatures inhabiting desolate places. The unclean *desert owl (qᵉʾaṭ miḏbār)* is such a bird (Lev. 11:18; Deut. 14:17; Isa. 34:11; Zeph. 2:14). G. R. Driver identifies it with the small scope owl (Latin *strix scops* or *scops giu*) or *jackdaw,* because it cries "kiu-kiu." The simile connotes feelings of isolation, desolation, and loneliness. G. R. Driver identifies the unclean *kôs* (Lev. 11:17; Deut. 14:16) as the small screech owl because it cries "cho-cho-cho."⁶⁰ Owls are notorious for being solitary creatures: "Save that from yonder ivy-mantled tow'r / The moping owl does to the moon complain / Of such as, wand'ring near her secret bow'r, / Molest her ancient solitary reign" (Thomas Gray). *Ruins* refers to cities that are left in ruins — often combined with "desolation" — without inhabitant (Lev. 26:31, 33; Isa. 44:26; 49:19). The Arabs call the owl "mother of ruins."⁶¹ The similes connote feelings of social isolation and desolation.

7[8]   Because owls are scavengers — not the intended connotation — the image shifts to the general word for a nonscavenging *bird* that must keep vigil (Jer. 5:6; Prov. 8:34) to protect its life in an unprotected environment. Birds usually find protection in a group, but the afflicted is *alone* (Hos. 8:9), like a solitary bird without even a mate. Birds seek shelter in a nest, but he finds himself exposed like a bird *on a* [flat] *roof* (Deut. 22:8; Judg. 16:27; 2 Sam. 11:2). Ironically, the psalmist dwells in a place of chaos and ruin and at the same time must keep vigil to protect his solitary, exposed existence.

8[9]   *All day long* (Ps. 38:6[7]) *my enemies* (Ps. 6:10[11]) *taunt* [me] (i.e., denigrate his significance, worth, and/or ability). He labels his enemies as being "mad, senseless" and allows the parallel "taunt me" to interpret *against me. Swear* means to serve as the witness and guarantor of the oath. Elsewhere with *bᵉ* ("by"), "swear" is used with reference to the name of a god as the witness and guarantor of the oath. In other words, his senseless enemies satirically taunt and mock him by treating him as a god to be sworn by!⁶² Their satire is

---

60. Some biblical birds are difficult to identify. Naturalists have identified about 350 bird species in Israel, but the Bible mentions only fifty; it probably classified more than one species by the same name. Also, many birds are mentioned only several times with little clue as to their identity; see Bruce K. Waltke, *The Dance between God and Humanity: Reading the Bible Today as the People of God* (Grand Rapids: Eerdmans, 2013), pp. 476-84.

61. A. F. Kirkpatrick, *The Book of Psalms* (Grand Rapids: Baker, 1982; from the 1902 edition of the University Press, Cambridge), p. 594.

62. Scholars commonly invest *nišbāʿ bᵉ* in Psalm 102:9[10] with the unique meaning "to curse," for they fail to take into account that the context is that of mockery.

similar to that of the Roman soldiers who mocked Jesus as King of the Jews (Matt. 27:28-29).

4. Destruction Due to God's Wrath by Figures of Eating Ashes (102:9-11[10-12])

9[10] His enemies mock him, *for* his banquet is ashes and tears. Food (v. 9A[10A]) and drink (v. 9B[10B]) are a merismus for a full meal. *I eat* (v. 4[5]) *ashes as my food* (v. 4[5]) connotes that he experiences only a wasted and mournful existence (Job 3:24; Pss. 42:3[4]; 80:5[6]). In the background "lies the ancient military practice of burning enemy cities, so that the association of ashes with death is common (Jer. 31:40; Ezek. 28:18; Mal. 4:34; 2 Pet. 2:6)."[63] *And mix* entails something is added to his drink to make it spicier, more potent and enjoyable (Song 8:2; cf. Isa. 5:22). The two other uses of *drink* (*šiqqûy*, Prov. 3:8 and Hos. 2:5[7]) suggest it means an elixir. Ironically, his "elixir" of intense and continual suffering is spiced up with "wailing" (Ps. 6:8[9]), a metonymy for *tears* (cf. Ps. 80:5[6]).

10[11] After the causal phrase *because of your indignation* (see Ps. 38:3[4]) *and anger* (Ps. 38:1[2]) *kî* is best glossed by *surely* or "indeed."[64] The precise meanings of the polyvalents *nāśā'* ("to bear/lift up") and *šālaḥ hiphil* ("to cast/throw") are determined by their collocation as opposites: *you have lifted me up* (Job 30:22) and *then threw me down* respectively. "I AM" lifted the afflicted to great heights to make his downfall greater, albeit the figure possibly implies the afflicted's former greatness.

11[12] *My days* (v. 3[4]) *are like a lengthened shadow,* a simile testifying to the passing of time, implying imminent night and symbolizing life's transient nature (Judg. 19:8; 2 Kgs. 20:10; Job 8:9; 14:2; Ps. 144:4) until it is lost in death (Ps. 109:23; cf. Jer. 6:4). The next simile, *I wither away like the vegetation* (v. 4[5]), explains and underscores the first simile.

---

63. Leland Ryken, James C. Wilhoit, and Tremper Longman III, eds., *Dictionary of Biblical Imagery* (Downers Grove, IL: IVP Academic, 1998), p. 50.

64. *IBHS*, P. 39.31d, p. 657.

C. A Prisoner's Vision of Hope (102:12-22[13-23])

1. "I AM" Restores His People to Favor in Zion (102:12-14[13-15])

"I AM's" grace to his covenant people initiates the new age. Verse 13[14] refers to God's grace and mercy at the appointed time as the Ultimate cause; verse 14[15], to God's slaves that cherish Zion's stones and rubble as the immediate cause (Neh. 4:2). The reference to God's enthronement (v. 12[13]) segues into Zion (v. 13[14]), the place of God's enthronement on earth (Ps. 132:13-14).

12[13] The vision of God's enthronement steadies the transient, gladdens the despairing, and reassures the perplexed. *But you,* "I AM" (vv. 1, 12[2, 13]), commonly marks a change of mood from complaint/lament to confidence. *Sit enthroned*[65] (Ps. 2:4[5]) speaks of God's transcendence, a transcendence that endures *forever* (Ps. 5:11[12]). The vivid anthropomorphism dramatically contrasts the fleeting mortal with God's eternal otherness. *And your renown* denotes the active cognitive occupation with God by retaining and reviving impressions of him and proclaiming them to others (Ps. 6:5[6]).[66] This remembrance continues forever by one *generation* proclaiming *to* the next *generation* his sublime person and works. *Generation* denotes a "cycle of time," "lifespan," which, after the patriarchal era (Gen. 15:16; cf. Ps. 90:10; Isa. 65:20), is calculated to be forty years.[67]

13[14] *You* is emphatic; victory is certain. *Will arise* is frequently used in martial contexts; sometimes it connotes anticipated or realized victory.[68] *Have compassion* signifies God's act, not merely his sentiment, to reinstall his parent-child relation to Zion (Hos. 1:6; 2:4, 23[6, 25]). "*Rḥm piel* stands in exclusive opposition to God's wrath or replaces it because wrath suspends the proper relationship of the people to God." This leads to its use in relation to sin. "Thus, in a few passages forgiveness, expressed by *rḥm piel,* constitutes the precondition for the reestablishment of the community with God that was lost through sin (Isa. 55:7; Mic. 7:19; cf. also 1 Kgs. 8:50)."[69] *On Zion* refers in the Psalms to "I AM's" city on earth, representing his heavenly city.[70] *For* explains the reason for this hope. *The time* (Ps. 32:6) *to show favor to her* entails three notions at one and the same time: (1) "Condescend to take note of someone" (Ruth 2:10).

---

65. Note the paronomasia of *ibaś* ("I wither") and *tēšēb* ("you sit enthroned").
66. H. Eising, *TDOT,* 4.66, s.v. *zākar.*
67. V. P. Hamilton, *NIDOTTE,* 1.931, s.v. II *dôr.*
68. L. J. Coppes, *TWOT,* 2.793, s.v. *qûm.*
69. H. J. Stoebe, *TLOT,* 3.1229, s.v. *rḥm.*
70. For "Zion," see Waltke and Houston, *PACW,* p. 168.

(2) "To feel goodwill," which precedes the actual doing of a generous deed (Gen. 32:5–33:10). (3) "To have mercy," because the person taking note with an attitude of goodwill has the capacity as a benefactor to meet the need of the favored beneficiary.[71] Mercy and grace are "entirely free and wholly undeserved"[72] and display God's glory (Exod. 34:6).[73] To clarify "the time," the appositional clause of verset Bb, signaled by repetition of *for*, is added to verset Ba. The eternal Sovereign has appointed fixed times on earth. *The appointed time (môʿēd)* derives from the verbal root that refers to "the announcement of a decree or a decision, whose execution is tied to a particular place or a fixed time." The parallel *time (ʿēt)* shows that a fixed time is in view (Gen. 1:14; Deut. 16:6; Ps. 75:2[3]). The Sovereign's fixed time for the salvation of Zion *is at hand* — that is to say, "it is here" (Isa. 40:2; 49:13).

14[15] *For* introduces the reason for the afflicted's confidence that the fixed time is at hand. The epithet *your slaves* connotes: (1) responsible obedience to the Lord whose norm gives slaves direction; (2) faithful dependence on God's care; (3) personal intimacy of trust in him, and (4) humility. The afflicted knows the appointed time has come because Israel is now ready to handle responsibly her mission to be a light to the Gentiles. They prove their conversion by their attitude toward Zion, the city of God. *They delight* has the basic meaning of "to accept"; its antonym is "to reject" (Gen. 33:10). *In her stones* probably refers to Zion's ruins (Neh. 3; Mic. 1:6; Ezek. 26:12). The Lord's slaves love her rubble because they recall the memory of a glorious past and they provide sustainable hope for future glory. *Show favor* or take pity denotes that they freely and actively accept the city (i.e., the kingdom of God) and do acts of kindness for it. *Her dust* refers to loose earth and a synecdoche for the ruined city's debris (1 Kgs. 20:10; Ezek. 26:4; 26:12). Dust connotes humiliation and/or punishment (Gen. 3:14; 2 Sam. 16:13; Job 4:19; Ps. 44:25[26]; Mic. 1:10). When God's slaves show favor to the debris of Zion, it implies that they extend pity, mercy, and generosity to it. "To be gracious means to aid the poor, feed the hungry, deliver those in distress from defeat and death."[74] In other words, God's forgiven people will again rebuild Zion.

---

71. L. Reed, *JBL* 432 (1954): 58f.

72. N. Snaith, *TWBOB*, 101.

73. "The quality of mercy is not strain'd, / It droppeth as the gentle rain from heaven / Upon the place beneath. It is twice blest; / it blesseth him that gives and him that takes" (*The Merchant of Venice*, Act 4, scene 1, 180-87).

74. D. Freedman and J. R. Lundbom, *TDOT*, 5.24-29, s.v. *ḥānan*.

2. Nations Worship "I AM" When He Rebuilds Zion (102:15-17[16-18])

Verses 15 and 16 are linked by "glory." The order of salvation is: The eternal "I AM" arises from his throne at his appointed time to start the new era; his people humble themselves as his slaves to rebuild Zion; and when the nations see Zion rebuilt and his glory appear, they will praise "I AM" (Isa. 52:10; 59:19).

15[16] *The nations* in the Psalms always refers to foreign nations. *Will fear . . .* "I AM" means the nations will learn and memorize his catechetical teachings out of their awe, love, and trust in Israel's patron deity (Ps. 5:7[8]). A person's *name* in the Bible "is based closely with a person's existence, representing and expressing his or her character and personality. To learn a person's name is to enter (into) a relationship with his very being."[75] *Kings* are in corporate solidarity with their subjects. Without exception, *all* of them, who before their conversion assumed they possessed the divine glory of their national deity and opposed God's rule (Ps. 2:1-3), will join Israel in their holy, covenantal relationship with "I AM" (Ps. 5:1[2]). *Your glory* refers to "I AM's" social weight, dignity, importance, honor. In sum, his restoration of Zion will be the prelude to the conversion of the world (Isa. 59:19; 60:3).

16[17] *For* introduces the cause why the kings will fear. "I AM" is the ultimate cause for the rebuilding of Zion, and his slaves who perform it are the immediate cause. Since the Lord's slaves now pity Zion's dust, *bānâ* ("build") means "rebuild" (Amos 9:11; Jer. 24:6; 31:4). *He will appear in his glory* may refer to the glory-cloud that overshadowed the tabernacle and appeared at the dedication of the temple (Exod. 16:10; 40:34-38; 1 Kgs. 8:11; Isa. 60:2). More probably, as Calvin thinks, it refers to the manifestation of his power and faithfulness when he restores Zion (i.e., true Israel) by raising it from death to life.[76]

17[18] *He will respond* glosses a woodenly literal "to turn to, look at," a figure that often connotes "to look at with favor" (Lev. 26:9; 2 Kgs. 13:23; Ps. 40:5; cf. Pss. 25:16; 69:17; 86:16; 119:132). To turn to/look at *prayer* (*t^epillâ*, see superscript) means "to respond," "to answer" (1 Kgs. 8:28). When God does not look at an offering, he rejects it (Num. 16:15; Mal. 2:13). The root of the lexeme for *destitute*

---

75. William Sanford LaSor, David A. Hubbard, and Frederick W. Bush, *Old Testament Survey: The Message, Form and Background of the Old Testament* (Grand Rapids: Eerdmans, 1992), p. 134.

76. John Calvin, *Commentary on the Book of Psalms*, translated from the original Latin, and collated with the author's French version by the Rev. James Anderson, vol. 4 (Grand Rapids: Baker, reprinted 2003), p. 114a.

means "to strip," "to lay bare." In other words, God has looked with favor on the prayer of the isolated, solitary "bird" in desolate places (vv. 1-11[2-12]). The B verset expesses the thought negatively for emphasis. *Despise* means to regard as worthless and vile, the antonym of "to regard with favor." *Their plea — (t^epillâ)* — is a rare parallel repetition for emphasis.

3. An Everlasting Proclamation to "I AM's" Glory (102:18-20[19-21])

18[19] That God saved his people from exile needs to be written down to ensure that future generations will know of his saving acts and proclaim his name. Historically, Israel sometimes failed to rehearse God's saving works from one generation to the next (Deut. 6:20-25; Judg. 2:10; but cf. Ps. 44:1-3[2-4]). *This* refers to the content of verses 19-20. *Let . . . be written* is to ensure its accuracy and permanence. This is *for* the benefit of *the following generation* (v. 12[13]; Deut. 29:21; Pss. 48:14[15]; 78:4, 6). *A people* has the fundamental notion of relationship. Its members understand themselves as related to each other in a group (familial, ethnic, judicial, political, and/or religious), and they find protection there. *To be created* refers exclusively to the divine activity of bringing something into existence (Gen. 2:4; Ps. 104:30). In parallel to "next generation" it refers to birth (Pss. 22:31[32]; 78:6; Ezek. 28:13; 28:15). *May praise* entails that in the people's adoration, they recognize, affirm, and confirm all that "I AM" is and does. To praise what is praiseworthy is a symptom of spiritual health; not to adore "I AM" is a sign of spiritual death. "If we do not admire [what is praiseworthy] we shall be stupid, insensible, and great losers."[77]

19[20] The inner frame of this chiastic parallel features "I AM's" heavenly transcendence, and its outer frame features his acute awareness of the earthling's situation. Corresponding to Isaiah's prayer (Isa. 63:15), "I AM" (v. 1[2]) *looked down from his holy place* (5:7[8]) *on high* (7:7[8]; 20:6[7]; Deut. 26:15), a metonymy for his heavenly residence where God sits enthroned (Ps. 93:4; Isa. 57:15; Mic. 6:6). *From heaven* may refer to everything above the earth, the phenomenal firmament that houses the sun, moon, and stars and/or the supernal waters held up by the firmament (Ps. 29:10). The metaphor connotes God's transcendence, including his omniscience, for God sees the world holistically, and so he sees clearly and absolutely. *Looks at* signifies the intentional act of looking at someone or something (Exod. 3:6; Num. 21:9). When God looks at someone or something he shows regard for it (Ps. 13:3[4]). When he refuses to

---

77. C. S. Lewis, *Reflections on the Psalms* (New York: Harcourt, Brace & World, 1958), p. 92.

look, he shows his rejection (Amos 5:22; Lam. 4:16). *Earth* is a metonymy for its mortals in their situations.

20[21] The written proclamation continues to explain why God looks down upon the mortal. His concern is for the prisoners. First, *to hear* (v. 1[2]) their *groans* (i.e., audible sounds of distress; Ps. 12:5[6]; Mal. 2:13). *Prisoners* refers to a confined person away from home (Gen. 39:22; Judg. 16:21, 25; Isa. 14:17). They are represented as needy (Ps. 69:33[34]); in misery and in chains (Ps. 107:10) and under a taskmaster (Job 3:18). Here God uses it as metaphor for the Babylonian exiles (Zech. 9:11). The parallel in 20B[21B] implies they have no future. Second, God looks down *to release* (lit., "to make open"). With reference to prisoners it means *to set free, release* (Ps. 105:20; Jer. 40:4). *Those condemned to death* (see notes 45, 46) glosses a phrase found elsewhere only in Psalm 79:11 in an identical context. In other words, they are condemned to die in prison, without hope. Zechariah, however, calls these exiles "prisoners of hope" (Zech. 9:11-12).

4. Nations Praise "I AM" in Zion (102:21-22[22-23])

21[22] *To proclaim* means literally "to count," "to recount," "to document" (Judg. 6:13; 7:13; Gen. 24:66). Elsewhere it is used of rehearsing God's glorious deeds (Pss. 44:1[2]; 73:28) and in that connection of rehearsing *the name of* "I AM" (i.e., *his praise* [Exod. 9:16; Ps. 9:14(15)]). God's name, *I AM WHO I AM,* entails that he will make himself known by his words and deeds in history. Hence his name encompasses his *magnalia dei. In Zion* (v. 13[14]) and *in Jerusalem* because "I AM's" temple is there (Pss. 68:29[30]; 79:1).

22[23] *When the peoples* (v. 18[19]) represents the groups of people as having distinct and different relationships from one another. Yet, though diverse, they *assemble themselves* in Jerusalem, which they formerly despised and reduced to rubble. *Together* modifies their state as a unity (2 Sam. 10:15; Isa. 11:11). "Assemble together" is gapped in the B verset, and "to worship 'I AM'" is gapped in the A verset. *And the kingdoms* represents the diverse peoples as each having an ethnic, social, economic, and political relationship under their kings (v. 15[16]; Deut. 3:21; Josh. 11:10; Ps. 135:11) who exercise sovereignty over realms (Deut. 3:10). These kings formerly served other gods and their idols (Isa. 10:10; 2 Chron 32:15) and held God's people captive (v. 20[21]; cf. 1 Sam. 10:18). Now they assemble together in Jerusalem *to worship* "I AM." "Worship," possibly a denominative of "slave" (v. 14[15]), fundamentally means "to work, labor" and can include "to work for another, serve them by labor" (Exod. 2:11; Gen. 29:15). "The question is never whether a person (or a group) serves a god; the only question is which god one serves. Since 'serving God' indicates one's relationship as a whole to God, it cannot mean 'to do god a service.' Instead it signifies acknowledgment of God as Lord, an acknowledgment that requires one's entire existence."[78]

D. Concluding Recapitulation (102:23-28[24-29])

The final stanza is framed by the radical contrast expressed in verses 23[24] and 28[29]. The afflicted's fragile and uncertain life may be cut short (v. 23[24]), but the physical and spiritual offspring of God's slaves will endure forever (v. 28[29]). The contrast serves to emphasize the urgency of the afflicted's situation to catch a glimpse of that certain future before he dies.

1. Psalmist Petitions Eternal Not to Cut Him Off in Midlife (102:23-24[24-25])

The contrast between the psalmist's few days and his changing circumstances versus "I AM's" unending years and unchanging state adds pathos to the mortal's plight, but at the same gives the faithful hope and meaning. The Eternal's determination that the posterity of his slaves will be established forever is his final word.

23[24] The gloss *in the course of my life* (*badderek*, see n. 47) *he broke my strength* (see n. 48) is probable though uncertain. The more common meaning of *badderek* ("in/on the way") is sensible when the psalm is read holistically. Verse 23[24] picks up where verses 11-12[12-13] left off. "My days are like a shadow" (v. 11[12]) is picked up by "you cut short my days" (v. 23[24]). Verse 10[11] ended "you lifted me up and threw me down." The story now continues "on the way." "My life" is added to facilitate making this connection. *He broke* glosses the root behind "the afflicted one" (see superscript). *Strength* refers to the vital power to produce. The B verset intensifies the A verset: *he cut short* (*qāṣar;* cf. Num. 11:23; Prov. 10:27) *my days* (vv. 3, 11[4, 12]; Isa. 38:10).

24[25] Though not indicated formally, verse 24[25] expresses the psalmist's response to his situation in verse 23[24]. Since God exists from generation to generation, why should God shorten a person's life prematurely? The combination *my God* unites God's transcendence with the personal intimacy of the covenant relationship. *In the midst* refers to half of anything (Exod. 38:4; 2 Sam. 10:4), or middle of something (Judg. 16:3; 2 Sam. 10:4). So the psalmist refers to his days

---

78. C. Westermann, *TLOT,* 2.829, s.v. *'ebed.*

(i.e., his life) as only half done. *Your years,* large countable time units, stand in marked contrast to "my days," the short time units (Prov. 3:2). *All generations* pertains to the past, present, and future generations as verses 25-26[26-27] imply.

2. God's Endurance Contrasted with Temporality of Cosmos (102:25-26[26-27])

25[26]   God's continuance through all generations is now traced back to a time *prior to that* (lit., "formerly" — that is to say, before cycles of time began). The metaphor, *you laid the foundations of the earth* (Job 38:4; Pss. 24:2; 78:69), depicts the earth as founded on a firm foundation for stability and permanence. *And the heavens* completes the merismus that represents all that the cosmos contains, as verse 26[27] assumes. *Are the work of your hand* continues the anthropomorphism of representing God as a laborer.

26[27]   Even the heavens, however, wear out. Pleonastic *they* contrasts the perishable heavens with imperishable "You." *Will perish* can mean "to ruin, destroy" (Ps. 31:12[13]; Jer. 9:11]) or "to be annihilated/exterminated" (Jonah 4:10; Jer. 48:36; Amos 3:13). *Remain* (Isa. 66:22) is in contrast to *perish. And all of them* refers to all the elements of the original heavens and earth, without exception. *They will all wear out* (Ps. 32:3) *like a garment (kabbegeḏ). Begeḏ* is made of cloth but otherwise unspecified. *Clothing* is the most common Hebrew word for apparel. *Change (ḥālap, hiphil)* implies the old cosmos will be replaced with a new heaven and earth; other texts specify the new cosmos will endure forever (Isa. 66:22; Jer. 32:14), for time will be no more. *And they will vanish (ḥālap, qal,* Job 9:26; Song 2:11).

3. Hope Eternal Will Establish Future Generations (102:27-28[28-29])

27[28]   Brown, Driver, and Briggs's lexicon defines the idiom *you are He who is* (Deut. 32:39; Isa. 41:4; 43:10, 13; 46:4; 48:12) thus: "as an emphatic predicate, of God, 'I am He,' i.e. I am He Who is (opposed to unreal gods, named in context, or to transitory world), the Unseen, yet Omni-present, and Self-consistent, Ruler of the world."[79] And your years (v. 24[25]) will never end *(lō' yittammû). Tāmmam* here has the nuance of "to come to an end" (Deut. 34:8; Lam. 3:22; 4:22; Isa. 18:5).

---

79. In Aristophanes, *Clouds* (line 218), Socrates is referred to as "the man himself," and in John's Gospel Jesus is referred to simply as "that one."

28[29] *The sons of your slaves* refers to the generations that descend from "I AM's" slaves who began the appointed time of salvation (vv. 13-14[14-15]). The reinforcing parallel *their seed* images their potential for life and generation. *Will dwell* by itself indicates the nature and/or duration of the stay. Its parallel, *will be established* or will be fixed (Ps. 38:17[18]), shows it means "to settle permanently *before you*," which is gapped in verset A. "Under the eye of, regard of" means and implies living under the blessing of He Who Is (Gen. 17:18; Ps. 61:6-7[7-8]). The promise assumes that the generations will have proclaimed from one to another the praise of "I AM" and that the generations keep covenant with God (Isa. 65:9; 66:22f.).

PART IV. CONCLUSION

The psalm contains a trove of theological treasures; here are several:

1. Moberly notes that "the predominance of laments at the very heart of Israel's prayers means that the problems that give rise to lament are not something marginal or unusual but rather are central to the life of faith. . . . Moreover they show that the experience of anguish and puzzlement in the life of faith is not a sign of deficient faith, something to be outgrown or put behind one, but rather is intrinsic to the very nature of faith."[80]

2. Although the reality of the rebuilding of Zion in the Persian era fell far short of the exilic prophets' visions and of the psalmist's expectation, the return was an essential part of salvation history; without it, that history would have reached a dead end. Its spiritual significance to God's slaves cannot be exaggerated, as can be seen in this psalm. Moreover, prophets combine in one vision both the near fulfillments and the remote consummation; they are generically the same.

3. God's saving acts bring salvation to his covenant partners when in distress, and praise to his name. The covenant relationship between God and his human partners serves the interest of both, for we live in a universe ("one verse"). Bur God's grace motivates his saving acts; his praise is the result.

4. The faithful remnant love Zion even when it is in ruin. The nations praise God when it is rebuilt.

5. When the individual members of God's people die off apart from their heavenly destiny, they lay hold of the certainty that God reigns forever and ever; that his name will continue from generation to generation until the end that outlasts all death when he clasps them in his bosom. God never falls prey to death, and in his appointed time in salvation history rebuilds and restores his kingdom.

80. R. W. L. Moberly, "Lament," *NIDOTTE*, IV, p. 879.

6. The church's continuance to a blessed future depends on God's mercy, not on her merits. God is *auctor primarius*. His mercy, however, works through his reviving his church so they love her "rubble" when she is humiliated.

7. The writer of Hebrews (1:10-12) refers verses 25-27 (LXX) to God's Son, for in the progress of revelation God revealed himself as a Trinity: what can be said of the Father can also be said of the Son.

8. The suffering of the afflicted psalmist and his vision of restored Zion in the metanarrative of salvation history prefigures the sufferings of Christ, his resurrection, and his glory in his church.

CHAPTER 10

Psalm 130: Lament of the Sinner
before the Triune God of Grace

PART I. VOICE OF THE CHURCH

I. Introduction

With its opening phrase, "Out of the depths have I cried unto thee, O Lord," the psalm has been titled traditionally *De Profundis*.[1] Throughout its history, theologians have reflected differently upon the psalm. Chrysostom associated the psalm with despair, whereas Leo the Great celebrated that "we cannot put limitations to the mercy of God or fix limits to times. With him there is no delaying of pardon when the conversion is genuine, as the Spirit of God says through the prophet: 'If being converted you lament, you will be saved'" (Isa. 30:15).[2] In the medieval penitential culture, Psalm 130 was associated with prayers for the dead in purgatory.[3] Martin Luther, with his acute sensibility to existential guilt as a sinner before God, considered this his favorite psalm, echoing as his central message verses 3-4, "If you, O Lord, kept a record of sins, O Lord, who could stand? But with you there is forgiveness."[4]

Out of these many differing reflections, we select two of the greatest pastoral theologians of the church: Hilary of Poitiers and John Owen. They reinforce comparable theological premises: the revelation of the triune God, humanity created in the image of God, the abyssal reality of sin, and how the sinner can be "justified," i.e., "put right with God" by divine grace alone. For Hilary and Owen,

1. Traditional title after its Latin incipit.
2. *Ancient Christian Commentary of Scripture*, vol. 8, *Psalms 51-150*, ed. Quentin F. Wesselschmidt (Downers Grove, IL: InterVarsity, 2007), p. 361.
3. Bernard W. Anderson with Steven Bishop, 3rd edition, *Out of the Depths: The Psalms Speak for Us Today* (Louisville: Westminster John Knox, 2000), p. 87.
4. Frank Lothar Hossfeld and Erich Zenger, *Psalms*, vol. 3, Hermeneia (Minneapolis: Fortress Press, 2011), pp. 441-42.

238

the primary context of such theological lament is not in human circumstances imposing human afflictions, but in the guilt of the sinner before a holy God. Both these Christian commentators strongly defended the doctrine of the Trinity against the denial of the divinity of Jesus Christ, whether by Arians or by their later successors the Socinians. Within the original Old Testament context, Psalm 130 parallels Jonah's psalm (Jonah 2:2-9), wherein the petitioner is threatened with chaos.

Permit me, if you will, to interrupt these historical reflections with my own. Being "in the depths as a guilty sinner" is not popular thinking today: "sin" has lost its meaning in secularism, and the role of the Holy Spirit has been misunderstood, as evidenced in the prevailing rivalry between the human spirit and the third person of the Trinity. Yet the emotional realm of "the depths of despair" remains overpopulated territory today with the global pandemic of human depression being viewed by the medical profession as clinically as serious as cancer and heart attacks. Yet to assume that guilt vanishes with medication and to dismiss religion is rather like treating a migraine by cutting off one's head. This psalm powerfully compels us all to reexamine our basic beliefs about God and sin. It is not about our social circumstances; it is about our primary existence as guilty sinners before the holy God.

II. Lament before the Triune God

Hilary of Poitiers (c. 310-367) is one of the least known of the early Church Fathers. There are hints he had a secular career, and was perhaps married, before becoming a bishop. His productivity as a writer was probably limited to his last fifteen years, near the end of which he wrote his commentaries on the Psalms.[5] What is autobiographical in them comes from Hilary's letters of defense responding to false accusations against him and other bishops such as Athanasius. He was sent into exile from France to Phrygia, although he was permitted to maintain his bishopric by delegation to his presbyters until his return. In the judiciary system of his society, not to defend one's case was deemed admission of guilt. But, as Hilary wrote to the Emperor Constantius, he is more concerned to defend Christian orthodoxy against "that poisonous, cunning and hidden plague of Arian dogma"[6] than to defend his own reputation. He notes that "dis

---

5. Hilary wrote about forty psalm commentaries, but of the penitential psalms, only those on Psalms 130 and 143 have survived.

6. Hilary of Poitiers, *Conflicts of Conscience and Law in the Fourth-Century Church*, trans. and introduced by Lionel R. Wickham (Liverpool: Liverpool University Press, 1997), "Letter of Liberias, bishop of Rome," p. 96.

pute about the Father, Son, and the Holy Ghost, into whom we are baptized, has led to a lamentable proliferation of creeds."[7] Four creeds were circulated that year (c. 360), "contradicting one another."[8] These four contradictory creeds all stemmed from a doctrine of monotheism, of one solitary god, that Arianism — and later Islam — asserted. Islam, according to John of Damascus, called Christians "associators" because Christ and the Holy Spirit were associated with God in his divinity.[9] The key role played by Hilary in the councils and debates concerning the three persons of the Trinity is beyond the scope of our topic, but we shall note how Hilary's commentary on Psalm 130 reflects upon his great work, *De Trinitate.* Following Origen, although in his own original way, Hilary's hermeneutic is that "the prophetic" originates in the past, anticipates the future, and is applicable to the present.[10] Hilary interprets the psalm primarily through the lens of the apostle Paul, for now "I AM" has been revealed as the Holy Trinity: Father, Son, and Holy Spirit. So he sweeps aside the Old Testament imagery of "the deep" as watery chaos, death, and decay, and replaces it with Paul's hymnal praise in Romans 11:33-36: "O the depths of the riches of the wisdom and knowledge of God." "To know this one thing only of God — that He is God — is a devout confession of human weakness"[11] and of human incapacity to explore both creation and the mysteries of his angelic servants. Praying "within the inner secret place of his heart," he also declares with the word of the apostle: "Out of the heart I have cried to you, Lord" (v. 1). Instead of being a place of the silence of death, argues Hilary, "since he is crying from the depths, he can say with confidence: 'Lord, hear my voice, let your ears be inclined to the voice of my prayer.'" The premise of Hilary, as with other of the early Fathers, was that only in the tension of *homoousion,* of one substance as God, yet also as two dis-

---

7. The root heresy was Monarchianism, which in the second century denied there were persons in God; Arianism then denied the full divinity of Christ; Adoptionists claimed Jesus was a mere man; Monarchianism accepted the Son of God in a lower sense than the Father; Modalists interpreted Father, Son, and Holy Spirit not as persons, but as modes, energies, or aspects of the one divine God. See Michael O'Carroll, C.S.Sp., *Trinitas: A Theological Encylopaedia of the Holy Trinity* (Collegeville, MN: Liturgical Press, 1987), pp. 17-28, 162-63, 186-89.

8. O'Carroll, *Trinitas,* p. 14.

9. Robert L. Wilken, *Remembering the Christian Past* (Grand Rapids: Eerdmans, 1995), p. 65.

10. Christoph Jacob, "The Reception of the Origenist Tradition in Latin Exegesis," in *Hebrew Bible / Old Testament: The History of Its Interpretation,* vol. 1, *From the Beginnings to the Middle Ages (Until 1300),* part 1, *Antiquity,* ed. Magne Saebo (Göttingen: Vandenhoeck & Ruprecht, 1996), p. 685.

11. Hilary of Poitiers, *CSEL,* vol. 22, 130 (VI129), Zingerle edition, translated for the author by Dr. Bongie, Professor Emeritus of Classics, University of British Columbia.

tinct persons, Father and Son, can God relate, as divine yet also human, to save humans from their fallen state.[12]

Hilary then observes that it is not a physical place nor is it the human facility of the ear that might obstruct God from hearing the psalmist's cry. It is because of the character of God, in his triune Being, that he has announced: "let *us* make man in *our* image *and* likeness" (italics mine). Moreover, "crying" and "being heard" are relational actions, expressive of the *imago Dei*. Again Hilary interprets verse 6 through the lens of the apostle, who confesses he is divided so that "through the outer man he is delighted by the law, but through the inner man he does what he does not want to [do]."[13] Again quoting the apostle, Hilary cites Colossians 3:9-10: "seeing that you have put off the old self with its practices and have put on the new self which is being renewed in knowledge after the image of its Creator."

In the next section (vv. 3-4) Hilary links Psalm 32:1, 5 with Romans 2:12, in an attempt to distinguish between "iniquities" and "sin," the one exposed and judged by infringements of the law, the other as the pervasive human fallen condition of ruin, yet with God's forgiveness and redemption. Hilary sees the advent of the Son of God as expressive of the incarnate Word of God, who now has replaced the Law of the Old Covenant (v. 5). He relates the last couplet of the psalm (vv. 7-8) with Jesus' parable of the laborers, some who worked from the third, sixth, ninth, or the eleventh hour. Israel might represent those working from dawn till night, Hilary argues. But the gospel is not determined by time, but by the assurance of the gospel. "The One in whom there is hope is good; and hope in Him must be maintained because there is mercy, full redemption is in Him, and He will redeem all peoples from their iniquities." He concludes: "Because the Lord is good, because He is merciful, let us hope in Him, so that although workers of the eleventh hour, we may obtain the denarius [given] for a full-day's labor through our Lord Jesus Christ, who is blessed forever and ever. Amen."[14] Throughout his commentary Hilary embraces the Pauline teaching of justification, forgiveness, and the assurance granted us in the triune being of God the Father, Son, and Holy Spirit.

John Owen (1616-1683). After the prolonged millennial period of ecclesial penance which distorted the truth of Psalm 130, John Owen voices the reformation of doctrine with his extensive commentary on *De Profundis*, "from the depths" of Christian orthodoxy. He explores "the psalmist's depths" as the basic

---

12. Hilary of Poitiers, 67-69, in Henry Bettenson, *The Later Christian Fathers* (Oxford: Oxford University Press, 1972), p. 48.

13. Rom. 7:22.

14. Bettenson, *The Later Christian Fathers*, p. 48.

issue of the guilty sinner being restored and made righteous before God. A false view of God falsifies one's understanding of the nature of human beings. But unlike Hilary's few pages of text, Owen composed a commentary on Psalm 130 of 325 pages in dense, "Latinized," stately prose![15]

Owen was perhaps the most influential Puritan theologian of the seventeenth century, rated as the greatest intellectual of England. During his time at Oxford (where he held the positions of Dean of Christ Church, Vice-Chancellor, and then Chancellor), his "junior colleague" also at Christ Church, John Locke, was wholly eclipsed. Locke, in reacting against the civil war as a voice of toleration, believed one only needed to cultivate a culture of sincerity to resolve the religious divisions. In contrast, Owen, with far more realism, explored the depths of the deceitfulness of sin within the "fallen" human condition.[16] Contemporary Christian literature likewise lives "in the shallows" if it does not explore "in the depths" with John Owen as a guide to the Christian life.[17] As in our age today, a vast amount of new knowledge was being pursued optimistically in Owen's time, but he was certain of one thing: no new knowledge could ever transcend knowing the status of humankind as sinners before God. Biblical lament was and is grounded upon the premise of the trustworthy assurance of justification by faith through grace.

Based on numerous homilies addressed to his congregation (during 1668), his exhaustive psalm commentary builds upon his previous published works: e.g., *Communion with God the Father, Son, and Holy Ghost* (1657); *Temptation* (1658); *Mortification* (1656, 1658); and *Indwelling Sin* (1667). He is perhaps the greatest pastoral theologian of "gospel assurance," expressed as the experience of being forgiven sinners, accepted in communion with the Father, through the Son, by the Holy Spirit.[18] In an age when the cultural quest for sincerity was strong,[19] he penetrated the intrinsic self-deception of being a sinner before God and of the continuance of "indwelling sin" within the heart of the Christian. An easygoing religious toleration was no solution for John Owen.

15. William H. Gould and Charles W. Quick, eds., *The Works of John Owen*, vol. 6 (Philadelphia: Leighton Publications, 1865), pp. 398-606.

16. For a helpful read on the life of Owen, see Peter Toon, *God's Statesman* (Exeter, UK: Paternoster, 1971).

17. Such is the valid claim of Sinclair Ferguson, *John B. Owen on the Christian Life* (Edinburgh: Banner of Truth Trust, 1987), p. x.

18. The author has paraphrased in shortened form these three treatises: see James M. Houston, *Sin and Temptation* (Portland, OR: Multnomah Press, 1983; reprinted Vancouver: Regent College Publishing, 2008).

19. Thomas Shepard, for example, writes on "The Sincere Convert." See Lionel Trilling, *Sincerity and Authenticity* (New York: Harcourt, Brace, Jovanovich, 1980).

Owen interprets Psalm 130 as a four-stanza description of the overall state of the soul before God. The focus of his commentary is on verse 4, "With Thee, there is forgiveness, that you may be feared." The assurance of Divine forgiveness fills two-thirds of his exposition. While reason should rule over the affections in the original state of the *imago Dei* before the Fall, Owen recognizes that sin's actions on the affections are primarily one of seduction from the truth; "they cloud and darken the mind, and fill it with strange dread, terror, sorrow, and all sorts of disconsolations."[20] These may also be: 1. pride and self-confidence; 2. the love of honor among one's contemporaries; 3. adherence to corrupt religious traditions and spiritual errors; 4. spiritual sloth in personal piety; and 5. a love of sin and hatred of the truth.[21] But the assurance of God's forgiveness, argues Owen, safeguards the Christian from the tyranny of his/her emotions, and is essential for stability in the life of faith. It is a remarkable exhortation on the richness of the Christian life.

In his comments on verses 1-2 Owen sets the whole context as his pastoral concern for Christians (not unbelievers) falling into sin. It is a development of his treatise on "Indwelling Sin in the Life of the Believer." This can result from a sense of divine abandonment, from having perplexing thoughts of one's relationship with God, feeling again the wrath of God, perhaps judging oneself rejected by God, indeed living wounded and in despair. Even members of the covenant of grace can exercise their free will, and Owen cites many causes for the distresses that sins induce within the free agent.[22]

Far worse, according to Owen, than the tyranny of our own negative emotions and responses, is the realization that we are all under the judgment of the Law of God (vv. 3-4);[23] by condemning sin, these verses condemn us all. This is a truer standard than our own conscience and self-condemnation could ever reveal. For only the Holy Spirit can disclose this.[24] Any other agent will mislead us into self-righteousness, or other false forms of assurance.

In verse 4, Owen, with Jerome, translates "forgiveness" as "propitiation," to express the mind of God as a merciful, forgiving God.[25] Nominal Christians assume God is forgiving, but it distressed Owen how few really enter "into the depths" of its profundity, as so great, holy, and mysterious. That is why many can become presumptuous, careless, and unaffected, in unchanged lives. For divine

20. Gould and Quick, eds., *The Works of John Owen*, vol. 6, pp. 57-59.
21. Steve Griffiths, *Redeem the Time: Sin in the Writings of John Owen* (Fearn, Ross-Shire, UK: Mentor, 2001), p. 82.
22. Gould and Quick, eds., *The Works of John Owen*, vol. 6, pp. 330-59.
23. Gould and Quick, eds., *The Works of John Owen*, vol. 6, p. 361.
24. Gould and Quick, eds., *The Works of John Owen*, vol. 6, pp. 368-76.
25. Gould and Quick, eds., *The Works of John Owen*, vol. 6, p. 380.

forgiveness communicates the love of the Father, the grace of the Son, and the fellowship of the Holy Spirit, in all their mystery: "They that know Thy name, will put their trust in Thee" (Ps. 9:10[11]). Assurance of such forgiveness unfolds the whole theo-drama of the incarnation and of the restoration of the *imago Dei* to commune eternally with God.[26] Like a mighty flood, Owen then pours out over two hundred pages on the statement: "there is forgiveness with God." It cannot be found anywhere else!

Verses 5-6 describe the deportment of the forgiven sinner: "I wait upon the Lord, my soul waits." He quotes from John Chrysostom that this is something we do throughout our life. Owen interprets four aspects of this vigilant watching: it is a duty the psalmist performs all through the dark night; but it is "I AM" that is the object of his watching; he is given support for the task by the word of promise; and so his manner of performance is with earnest diligence and perseverance.[27] Since it is God himself who is the motive, object, and sustenance of such "watching," Owen devotes the next thirty pages to expound on this way of "living-in-watchfulness."

In the final stanza (vv. 7-8) Israel likewise can only hope in the Lord. This is an admonition, the ground of encouragement, as well as a gracious promise that "He shall redeem Israel from all his sins, and out of all his troubles."[28] All this assurance of forgiveness is grounded wholly upon the character of God, in whose image we were created to be like Christ. With the psalmist, Owen concludes: "there is with God, mercy, redemption, plenteous redemption, redeeming from all iniquity; I have found it so, and so will every one that shall believe."[29]

PART II. VOICE OF THE PSALMIST: TRANSLATION

A[30] *song for*[31] *the ascents*[32]

1   Out of the depths[33] I cry to you,[34] "I AM";

---

26. Gould and Quick, eds., *The Works of John Owen*, vol. 6, pp. 398-606.

27. Gould and Quick, eds., *The Works of John Owen*, vol. 6, pp. 609-41.

28. Gould and Quick, eds., *The Works of John Owen*, vol. 6, pp. 643-48.

29. Gould and Quick, eds., *The Works of John Owen*, vol. 6, p. 348.

30. For the indefinite construct with definite absolute see *IBHS*, p. 241, P. 13.4c.

31. The parallel שִׁיר לַמַּעֲלוֹת ("a song for the ascents") in Ps. 121 superscript suggests the absolute is a genitive of a mediated object, i.e., "a song (composed for) the ascents" (*IBHS*, pp. 146f., P. 9.5.2d).

32. Or "steps." הַמַּעֲלוֹת could be glossed "ascent" (abstract pl. of a repeated series of actions [*IBHS*, p. 121, P. 7.4.2c]).

33. מַעֲמַקִּים is a plural of extension (*IBHS*, p. 120, P. 7.4.1c).

34. Construed as an instantaneous perfective (*IBHS*, p. 488, P. 309.5.1d; see "Form" below).

² Lord,[35] hear my voice.
   Let your ears be attentive to my cry for mercy.[36]
³ If you, "I AM," kept a close watch on iniquities,
   Lord, who could stand?
⁴ But forgiveness[37] is with you,
   so that you might be revered.[38]
⁵ I wait expectantly[39] for[40] "I AM," my whole being waits,
   and[41] for his[42] word I hope.[43]
⁶ My whole being[44]

---

35. The suffix signifies "Lord of all," not "my Master" (*IBHS*, p. 124, P. 7.4.3f).

36. Lit., "to the voice of my cry for mercy."

37. A generic article referring to an attribute (*IBHS*, p. 246, P. 13.5.1g).

38. Vulgate (not PIH), Symmachus, Theodotion, Sexta, and a Greco-Latin Greek text read
תוֹרָתֶךָ. LXX reads ἕνεκεν τοῦ ὀνόματος/νόμου σου ὑπέμεινά σε Κύριε, ὑπέμεινεν ἡ ψυχή μου εἰς
τὸν λόγον σου, linking תוֹרָתֶךָ with קוִּיתִי (v. 5). Variants *onomatou* and *nomou* is an inner Greek
problem (J. Ziegler, *Beiträge zur Jeremias-Septuaginta* [Göttingen: Vandenhoeck & Ruprecht, 1958],
p. 85). The Greek readings can be explained as due to: (1) unlike MT, its lack of an oral tradition (cf.
IBHS, pp. 26-28, P. 1.6.3i); (2) the unique form, *twr'* and its auricular similarity to *twrh*; (3) having
joined 4B with 5A, *twrh* made an excellent parallel to *dbrw*; (4) having joined *qiww^etâ napšî* with
ldbrw, the conjunction *waw* was obtrusive.

39. Frequentative *piel* (*IBHS*, pp. 414f., P. 24.5B). "Expectantly" is added to signify "wait"
does not denote "to linger," "to tarry."

40. For suffix cj. see n. 34. Verb can be related to its accusative directly or by prep. "for"
(see v. 6; BDB, p. 875, s.v. קָוָה).

41. Ancient versions and 11QPs omit "and," probably as part of their ad hoc solutions to
the problems encountered with *twr'* (see n. 38) and with inapposite syntax of הוֹחַלְתִּי נַפְשִׁי לַאדֹנָי
(vv. 5B-6A); see n. 44.

42. LXX glosses דְּבָרְךָ; see n. 38.

43. Internal *hiphil* (*IBHS*, pp. 439f., P. 27.2f.).

44. LXX reads ἤλπισεν ἡ ψυχή μου ἐπὶ τὸν κύριον, linking 5B with 6A, against the syntax
of MT and 11QPs^a, וְלִדְבָרוֹ׃הוֹחַלְתִּי, albeit 11QPs omits וְ. But the syntax of LXX created the grammatical anomaly of having a fem. noun as subject of a first common sing. masculine verb, and
so it probably dropped final *yodh* from הוֹחָלְתִּי (making it a third fem. sing.). N. Tromp ("The Text
of Psalm cxxx 5-6," *VT* 39 [1989]: 100-103) prefers the syntax of LXX. He thinks the fem. sing.
naphšî may be the subject of first common sing. verb הוֹחַלְתִּי, for the same grammatical anomaly
may occur in Ps. 57:4[5] and Isa. 26:9. He prefers, however, to follow Gunkel and read *naphšî*
as instrumental (= manner) accusative: "I hope with my soul for the LORD." Syriac and Jerome
follow the same syntax but omit נַפְשִׁי. Franz Sedlmeier ("Bei dir, das ist die Vergebung, damit du
gefürchtet werdest," *Bib* 73 [1992]: 473-95, esp. 477) rightly rejects Tromp's emendation because
the resulting v. 5 is too short. His objection, however, that one cannot appeal to Ps. 57:4[5] and
Isa. 26:9, because *naphšî* governs a third fem. sing. verb in 5a, is invalid. Grammatical variation
is to be expected in parallelisms. Štefan Porúbčan (Psalm cxxx 5-6," *VT* 9 [1959]: 322-23) further
emends LXX by removing the repetitions of v. 6B מִשֹּׁמְרִים לַבֹּקֶר שֹׁמְרִים לַבֹּקֶר. Duhm says that to
remove these repetitions would be like clipping the wings of a bird and making it walk on two feet

[waits for]⁴⁵ the Lord
more than watchmen for the morning,⁴⁶
more⁴⁷ than watchmen for the morning.

7   Israel, put your hope⁴⁸ in⁴⁹ "I AM,"
for with "I AM" is unfailing love
and the redemption with him is very great.⁵⁰

8   And⁵¹ he will redeem Israel from all their sins.

PART III. COMMENTARY

I. Introduction

A. Literary and Historical Contexts

Psalm 130 is the sixth of the traditional seven penitential psalms (6, 32, 38, 51, 102, 130, 143) and the eleventh of the fifteen songs for the ascents (120–134). Psalms 129 and 130 consists of two four-verse stanzas. But whereas Psalm 129 morphs from Israel's song of thanksgiving for salvation from the wicked (vv. 1-4) into maledictory petitions against them (vv. 5-8), Psalm 130 morphs from a

---

(cited approvingly by Robert C. Dentan in "An Exposition of an Old Testament Passage," *Journal of Bible and Religion* 15 [1947]: 158-61, esp. 159). The chiastic repetitions in 5A and 6B of the strophe support the more difficult syntax of 11QPsᵃ and MT. A. R. Ceresco ("The Chiastic Word Pattern in Hebrew," *CBQ* 38 [1975]: 303-11, esp. 308) defends MT by the chiastic structure linking 5-7: "my whole being hopes for the Lord more than watchmen . . .//more than watchmen . . . Israel, hope for 'I AM.'" Sedleir draws the conclusion: "MT ist beizubehalten."

45. 11QPs supplies *hwḥyly* (hiphil fem. impv. of *yḥl*) (= "My soul, hope in the LORD").

46. LXX (Vg) and Syr. read respectively ἀπὸ φυλακῆς πρωΐας μέχρι νυκτός ("from the morning watch till night watch") and ἀπὸ φυλακῆς πρωΐας μέχρι πρωΐας ("from morning watch to morning watch"). Probably the gapping of *min* with second שֹׁמְרִים led to their interpreting *min* as ablative, not as comparative. Tromp ("The Text of Psalm cxxx 5-6") connects שֹׁמְרִים לַבֹּקֶר (v. 6B) with יַחֵל יִשְׂרָאֵל אֶל-יְהֹוָה (v. 7): "Like watchmen for the morning, let Israel hope in the Lord!" His gratuitously emended syntax also demands adding inexplicably "like" to שֹׁמְרִים.

47. Comparative *min* is gapped.

48. See n. 45. Perhaps with this root, *piel* and *hiphil* stems are mixed forms. *Yḥl piel* impv. of this root occurs in 131:3, but its *Hiphil* impv. is unattested. Causative *hiphil* ("to cause something to act") and factitive *piel* ("to put something into a state of having been acted upon") can be interchanged readily.

49. Lit., "unto."

50. The fossilized inf. abs. הַרְבֵּה functions as a predicative (*HALOT*, 1.255, s.v. הַרְבֵּה; *BDB*, p. 915, hiphil. 1.e [4] s.v. רָבָה).

51. The conjunction militates against interpreting v. 8 as a congregational response.

petition from the depths into a song of trust that saves Israel. Psalms 130 and 131 are drawn to conclusion with the command: "Israel, put your hope in 'I AM'" (Pss. 130:7; 131:3).

The song neither identifies the religious leader whose song stirs up Israel's hope nor the historical circumstance that prompted its composition. The composition of the ascent psalms spans the history of Israel from the time of David (Psalms 122,[52] 124, 127, 131, 133) until the postexilic period (Psalm 126; cf. 137). The song's vocabulary points to its composition in the late exilic or postexilic period.[53] Like Daniel (9:4-19), Ezra (9:6-7), and Nehemiah (1:6), the faithful leader identifies himself with his people's sin and suffering.

B. Form

Identification of the psalm's form depends in part on the interpretation of the ambiguous suffix conjugation in verses 1 and 5. If it means "I called to 'I AM'" and "I waited for 'I AM,'" the psalm is a song of thanksgiving. In that case, verses 1 and 2 look back upon the poet's petition in time of need, and verses 3-4 are his testimony of salvation.[54] This interpretation, however, is unlikely, for atypically of thanksgiving psalms verse 1 lacks a summary statement of deliverance, and verses 3-4 do not clearly proclaim deliverance.[55]

Better then to interpret the ambiguous grammatical form as an instantaneous perfective (i.e., "I call" and "I wait" [see n. 34] and to identify the psalm provisionally as a lament, for it has the motifs of a lament: address with introductory petitions (vv. 1-2) and a confession of trust (vv. 3-4).[56] A penitential psalm is a subspecies of a lament psalm: a lament for sin. This traditional label is appropriate because the poet cries out for mercy and assumes he and all Israel are in need of God's forgiveness. Nevertheless, he neither confesses his sin (although he assumes it), nor asks for forgiveness, although he cries out for mercy. Atypically of lament psalms, there are no developed lament, petition, or praise motifs. The superscript identifies the psalm as a "song," and a song normally implies joy

---

52. Possibly David, the poet laureate of Israel, composed Psalm 122 for his future descendants, even as he composed the dedicatory prayer for Solomon's temple (30), knowing that "I AM" on oath had sworn to him, "One of your own descendants I will place on your throne" (132:11).

53. The following terms occur exclusively in postexilic literature (see exegesis): אָזְנֶיךָ קַשֻּׁבוֹת ("your ears attentive"), סְלִיחָה ("forgiveness"), עִמְּךָ ("with you," an idiom of possession).

54. So Artur Weiser, *The Psalms* (OTL; Philadelphia: Westminster, 1962), p. 773.

55. So also W. H. Schmidt, "Gott und Mensch in Ps. 130. Formgeschichtlich Erwägungen," *TZ* 22 (1966): 241-55, esp. 241.

56. Kraus, Westermann, Dahood, Allen, et al. identify it as a lament psalm.

and hope, not lament, or, as Gerstenberger would have it, protest. In sum, Psalm 130 transforms a lament psalm (vv. 1-2) into a song of trust.[57]

C. Rhetoric

The song has two stanzas of equal length (vv. 1-4; 5-8), each beginning with the suffix conjugation (see notes 34, 40) followed by other conjugations. Vocatives to "I AM" (v. 1) and to Israel (v. 7) and pronominal references to the divine person mark off the stanzas; namely, second person (vv. 1-4), and third person. Each stanza consists of two strophes, also of equal length. The first two strophes (vv. 1-2, 3-4) move from a cry for mercy (v. 2) to an argument that God is merciful (v. 3). The second and third strophes (vv. 3-4, 5-6) are linked by logic: God is forgiving (and so) I hope for his salvation. They are also linked by the catchword "watch" (שָׁמַר); "I AM" does not keep close watch on iniquities (v. 3), but the psalmist longs for salvation, like a watchman looking for the morning (v. 6). "Hope" links the third and fourth strophes (vv. 5-6, 7-8). The imperative to Israel, "hope in 'I AM'" (v. 7), matches the indicative, "I hope for his word" (v. 5). Inferentially, the psalm's hope is a paradigm for Israel.

Semantically, the psalm has the typical three parts of a composition:

I. Introduction: introductory petitions to hear cry for mercy	1-2
II. Body:	3-6
A. With God is forgiveness	3-4
B. Psalmist put his hopes in God	5-6
III. Conclusion: Israel, hope in God for he will redeem you	7-8

This outline can be morphed into a chiastic *(abb'a')* structure:

I. Address to God	1-4
A. Imperative: Hear me and show me grace	1-2
B. Indicative: Expression of passive confidence in God's grace, using *watch*	3-4
II. Address to Congregation	5-8
B'. Indicative: Expression of active confidence in God's grace, using *watch*	5-6
A'. Imperative: Israel, hope for God for he is gracious	7-8

---

57. Dentan ("An Exposition of an Old Testament Passage," p. 159) also labels it a psalm of trust.

This structure displays the psalm's unity: an outer frame encloses the psalmist's testimony of faith.

The psalm is also embroidered with an alternating *(aba'b')* structure:[58]

I. Address to God	1-4
A. I cry out to God for mercy	1-2
B. With God is forgiveness	3-4
II. Address to congregation	5-8
A'. I wait for God	5-6
B'. With God is complete redemption	7-8

The alternating structure displays the psalm's argument. The first and third strophes focus on the psalmist's posture before God, escalating from "I cry to 'I AM,'" to "I look expectantly to 'I AM.'" The second and fourth strophes focus on "I AM's" grace, escalating from God's attribute of being forgiving (v. 4) to his act of completely freeing his people from their sin and implicitly from punishment (v. 8). This outline will be followed in the exegesis below.

After the introductory petitions (vv. 1-2), the ensuing song of trust in God's forgiveness is framed by "iniquities": the first word of an enclitic in verse 3 and the last word of verse 8.

In contrast to the final strophe, which refers to the relationship of Israel to "I AM," the first three strophes feature the "I-Thou" of the psalmist to "I AM," thereby unifying the stanzas and escalating the whole from the individual to the community. In other words, the third strophe also functions as a janus.

The four strophes are also linked by referring to God in an alternating structure of ab (vv. 1, 2); a'b' (vv. 3, 4); a"b" (vv. 5, 6); a'''b''' (vv. 7, 8): *yhwh, 'ᵃdōnāy* (last word of v. 1; first word of v. 2); *yāh, 'ᵃdōnāy* (v. 3A, B); *yhwh* (v. 5); *'ᵃdōnāy* (v. 6); *yhwh* (v. 7B); *yhwh* (v. 7A).[59] The verses within the strophes are linked both semantically and formally by repetitions (see exegesis below).

D. Message

God's spirit, we may infer from 2 Timothy 3:16, fills our religious leader with hope and inspires him to compose this song to generate in Israel hope for God's salvation. The chaotic depths of guilt, like a tsunami wave, overwhelm the cove-

---

58. Beat Weber, "'Wenn du Vergehen aufbewahrest . . . ,'" *BN* 107-8 (2001): 146-60, esp. 147.

59. This pattern shows the superiority of the majority of medieval mss. against variants in some (see text notes in Bardtke *[BHS]*).

nant people. This song for over two and half millennia has buoyed the covenant people to survive the flood. Drowning in unspecified guilt, our inspired poet exemplifies saving faith in God's forgiveness. Forgiveness includes the cancelation of sin's punishment, but first and foremost it restores a relationship with God. His persevering faith in God's mercy is reasonable. History proves God is forgiving: "If you, 'I AM,' kept a close watch on iniquities, Lord of All, who could stand?" (v. 3). But humanity endures! The glory of the God of Israel is his attribute of mercy (Exod. 33:18–34:8). The psalm expands the penitent tax-collector's prayer, "God, have mercy on me, a sinner" (Luke 18:13), into a song of trust aimed to move God to reshape history. Full salvation depends solely on God's grace, not on human merit. Nevertheless, that grace operates in the spiritual realm of hope: "May your unfailing love be with us, 'I AM,' even as we put our hope in you" (Ps. 33:21; 1 Thess. 5:17). Like some other songs of trust, the poet turns a blind eye to the reality that before realizing complete redemption from the overwhelming flood the hopeful may feel "waterboarded." Job maximizes this reality: "Yet when I hoped for good, evil came; when I looked for light, then came darkness" (Job 30:26).

II. Exegesis

A. Superscript

Song (שִׁיר) refers to poetic words accompanied by vocal music (Ezek. 33:32); they may also be accompanied with instrumental music (Isa. 23:16; Amos 6:5). Songs aim to heighten feelings of joy, delight, merriment (Gen. 31:27; 2 Sam. 19:35[36]; Eccles. 2:8; 7:5-6; Isa. 24:9) and hope (Psalms 120–134). One can sing a lament (2 Chron. 35:25), but normally the noun "song" is not used in this way; songs are not for sorrow (Prov. 25:20; Ps. 137:3). The collection of fifteen psalms (120–134) bearing the superscription. *Šîr hammaʿªlôt* has the tone of joy and hope, not of lament. *Ascents*[60] glosses *maʿªlôt*, usually an appellative referring to the *step/stair* of a structure (Ezek. 40:6; Neh. 3:15; Amos 9:6). But it can also be used abstractly of *ascending* (from Babylon) (Ezra 7:9) or metaphorically of arising thoughts (Ezek. 11:5). The meaning of *šîr hammaʿªlôt* is debated. Putting aside arbitrary interpretations (e.g., Sadaʿadya Gaon, "a song sung to a high melody") and a silly aggadic story that David recited the Songs of Ascents

---

60. LXX glosses by ᾠδὴ τῶν ἀναβαθμῶν ("ode for stairs"); Vulgate, by *canticum graduum* ("gradual psalms"); Aquila and Symmachus, ᾠδὴ *eis tas anabaseis* ("ode for the ascents"); Theodotion, ᾄσμα *tōn anabaseōn* (song of the ascents).

in order to raise the waters of the abyss under the altar,[61] there remain three plausible interpretations:[62]

(1) Rashi, Lyra, Luther, et al. think the phrase refers to a liturgical processional on the fifteen wide, circular steps leading up from the temple's outer court to its inner court.[63] They base their theory on two Talmudic references to a liturgical processional on these steps.[64] The basis, however, is insecure. The Mishnah compares the fifteen steps to the fifteen psalms but does not specify that the Levites recited these songs on the steps. Moreover, the theory assumes that the superscriptions are later additions that pertain to the psalms' performance, not to their composition, for the songs were composed before Herod rebuilt the temple (see above). That may be, but the hard data from ancient Near Eastern hymns shows that superscriptions are part of the original composition, and a strong argument can be made that they pertain to composition, not to performance.[65]

(2) Delitzsch argues with erudition that the phrase signifies the psalms' stairlike parallelism, advancing by steps or degrees.[66] C. A. Briggs, however, objects: "But it is not used in them all, and in a thoroughgoing manner in any; and certainly not to such an extent as to give titles to the group. There are other Pss. which use this method of parallelism in a more thoroughgoing manner."[67]

(3) Most think the phrase refers to songs sung by the returnees who ascended from Babylon to the Land of Israel (Ezra 7:9; cf. 120, 124, 129, and esp. 126) and/or songs sung by pilgrims on their ascent to Jerusalem during the three feasts prescribed in the *Torah* (Psalm 122; Exod. 23:14-17; Deut. 16:16; cf. Psalms 42–43; 84: Mic. 4:2; Zech. 14:16; Isa. 30:29), especially the fall feast of Tabernacles. Both of these scenarios are plausible because: (1) The variant expression, "for the

61. The story gave rise to the Aramaic ṣ *shira' dᵉʿitʾammar ʿal massokyan ditHoma* ("A song recited on the steps of the abyss").

62. Amos Ḥakham, *The Psalms with the Jerusalem Commentary*, vol. 3, *Psalms 101-150* (Jerusalem: Mosad Harav Kook, 2003), p. 286.

63. "A Songs of Ascents" — that the Levites would recite on the fifteen steps that descended from the Israelite section to the women's section.

64. "And the Levites, with viols and lyres and cymbals and trumpets and innumerable musical instruments, are on fifteen steps that descend from the Israelite section to the women's section, corresponding to the fifteen Songs of Ascents in the Psalms, and the Levites stand on them with musical instruments and perform songs" (*Sukka*, [Mishnah 5:4]). "And fifteen steps lead up from it [the women's section] to the Israelite section, corresponding to the fifteen Ascents in Psalms, upon which the Levites perform songs" (*Middot* [Mishnah 2:5]).

65. Waltke and Houston, *PACW*, p. 88.

66. F. Delitzsch, *Psalms*, trans. Francis Bolton, vol. 5, Commentary on the Old Testament by C. F. Keil and F. Delitzsch (Peabody, MA: Hendrickson, 1996; reprinted from the English edition originally published by T. & T. Clark, Edinburgh, 1866-91), pp. 749-51.

67. Charles Augustus Briggs, *The Book of Psalms* (ICC; Edinburgh: T. & T. Clark, 1906), p. lxxix.

ascending," in the superscription to Ps. 122 clarifies its meaning, as Aquila and Symmachus recognized (see n. 32). (2) Eight of these psalms mention Jerusalem or Zion (Pss. 122:2, 3, 6; 125:1, 2; 126:1; 128:5; 129:5; 132:13; 133:3; 134:3).[68] (3) In the others their content also fits one or another, or both, of these situations. The psalmist laments his being held captive in Meshek (Central Asia Minor) and Kedar (in Arabia) and longs for salvation; expresses confidence that God will protect him as he lifts his eyes to the mountains (the vicinity of Jerusalem) (121); looks to God for his people's deliverance from the proud (123); is filled with praise for Israel's escape from its enemies (124); and encourages Israel to hope in "I AM" (130, 131). Only Psalms 127 and 128 do not necessarily assume an ascent to Jerusalem. (4) As Briggs notes, "these songs have a common social and patriotic character."[69]

B. Address to God (130:1b-4)

1. Cry for Mercy (130:1b-2)

Verse 1 contains the address and an introduction to the petition of verse 2. "I cry out" (v. 1) and "my voice" (v. 2) verbally unify the strophe.

1b The confession that God forgives iniquity (vv. 3, 8) infers that *out of the depths (mimma'ᵃmaqqîm)* is a metaphor for the total misery of iniquity, a holistic term for sin and its afflictions. Owen comments: "Sin is the disease, affliction only a symptom of it; and in effecting a cure, the disease itself is principally to be heeded, the symptom will follow, or depart of itself [cf. Prov. 16:7]."[70] *Ma'ᵃmaqqîm* occurs five times, four times qualified by "water" (Ps. 69:2, 14[3, 15]; Ezek. 27:34) or "sea" (Isa. 51:10), suggesting "depths" is an epithet for ocean depths, "which is an image of the realm of death."[71] Though metaphorically drowning in an unspecified flood of guilt, like Jonah (2:3) with full lung and loud voice (see "voice" [v. 2]) he prays, *I cry out to you, "I AM" (qᵉrā'tîkā yhwh)*. "Cry out" has the basic meaning of drawing oneself to the attention of someone by the voice. Our religious leader, notes Eugene Peterson, "does not look on suffering as something

68. They are also mentioned in two of the attachments to the songs of ascent, Psalms 135–37 (135:21; 137:1). In Jewish tradition 120–37 are labeled the "Great Hallel," in contrast to Egyptian Hallel (113–18).

69. Briggs, *The Book of Psalms*, I:lxxx.

70. John Owen, *The Forgiveness of Sin: A Practical Exposition of Psalm 130* (Grand Rapids: Baker, 1977), p. 14.

71. Robert Alter, *The Book of Psalms: A Translation with Commentary* (New York: W. W. Norton, 2007).

slightly embarrassing which must be hushed up and locked in a closet (where it finally becomes a skeleton) because this sort of thing shouldn't happen to a real person of faith. And [he] doesn't treat it as a puzzle that must be explained, and therefore turn it over to theologians or philosophers to work out an answer. Suffering is set squarely, openly, passionately before God. It is acknowledged and expressed. It is described and lived."[72] Human anguish and loud petitions to God for salvation are an integral part of shaping salvation history, for they move God to act. A prominent motto in my [Waltke's] boyhood home read: "Prayer changes things." If Israel had borne her distress in Egypt stoically or with a false optimism or with denial or with despair, she would still be in Egypt.

2   The A and B versets are connected by the repetition of "my voice" (see n. 36) and by the synonyms "hear" and "let your ear be attentive." The expansion to "my cry for mercy" is emphatic. The psalmist is not setting himself apart from the rest of humanity as a slave by using God's social title, *Lord ('adōnāy)*. The title identifies his God as Lord of all; no one and no thing is outside of his rule (see n. 35). *Hear my voice (šim'â bᵉqôlî)*, an imperative from an inferior to a superior, becomes an urgent request, not a command. שְׁמַע means to listen outwardly and consent inwardly (Ps. 5:1-2[2-3]; 5:3[4]). In a bold anthropomorphism he invokes, *Let your ears be attentive (tihyêynâ 'oznêkā qaššubōt)*. The collocation *'oznêkā qaššubōt* is found elsewhere only in 2 Chronicles 6:40; 7:15, and signifies being willfully and consciously attentive (Ps. 5:2[3]). *To my out-loud cry for mercy (lᵉqôl taḥᵃnûnay*, Ps. 143:1) implies that he throws himself on God's mercy, not on his own merits.

2. God Forgives (130:3-4)

The petition for mercy (v. 2) is based on the verity that God is forgiving (v. 3). If God punished sinners swiftly according to strict justice, the human race would cease to exist, "for there is not a just person upon the earth, who does good and does not sin" (Eccles. 7:2; Rom. 3:12). God is no Simon Legree. Verse 4 states the point. A medial "surely" links the argument with the assertion that God forgives.

3   The A and B versets are connected by the syntax of a conditional sentence. *If ('im)* introduces a contrary-to-fact conditional clause, *You kept a close watch (tišmār)* is one of two pertinent glosses for *šāmar*. The underlying idea of the root is "to pay careful attention," which spins off into many nuances. A pertinent

---

72. Eugene H. Peterson, *A Long Obedience in the Same Direction* (Downers Grove, IL: InterVarsity, 1980), p. 134.

nuance of "to pay attention to" is "to save, retain" something (e.g., food [Gen. 41:35; 1 Sam. 9:24], wrath [Amos 1:11], or memory [Gen. 37:11]). In Ecclesiastes 3:6 *šāmar* is the opposite of "to throw away." NIV, NJB, NLT gloss this nuance by "to keep a record of." Another pertinent nuance is a hostile one of paying attention in opposition to the interests of the person or thing under guard or observation (2 Sam. 11:16; cf. 1 Sam. 19:11; Job 10:14; 13:27). All the ancient versions opted for this nuance; English versions gloss this sense by "to mark" (KJV, ASV, NAB, NRSV, ESV). NET steers between the two by "to keep track of." The parallels in Job favor the ancient versions. For the short form of "I AM" *(yāh),* see Psalm 102:18(19). The holistic term *iniquities* (*'aōwnôt,* Ps. 32:1, 5) includes the act of sin and its guilt. As in 38:3(4) "guilt" functions as a metonym of cause for judicial punishment. *Could stand (ya'amōd)* connotes "to withstand" sin's speedy punishment (Mal. 3:2) and so continue to endure and not perish. *Who (mî)* functions as a rhetorical question, expecting the emphatic negative, "No one!" Inferentially, our religious leader convicts himself of being guilty. Calvin notes: "The psalmist aims to show the reality of God's mercy not to extenuate his own fault by thus involving others."[73]

4 *Surely* (כִּי) formally binds the inferred argument for God's mercy with the assertion, "there is forgiveness with 'I AM.'" *With you* (עִמְּךָ) is an idiomatic way of expressing possession of an ethical quality such as forgiveness (Neh. 9:17).[74] The root of *forgiveness* (*hassᵉlîḥâ,* see n. 37) has only "I AM" as its subject, for all sin is ultimately against God and so only he can forgive sin. הַסְּלִיחָה occurs only twice, both in late Hebrew (Neh. 9:17; Dan. 9:9). *Lᵉma'an* normally signifies purpose, not result.[75] *You might be worshiped* (*tiwwārē',* Ps. 5:7[8]; cf. Exod. 34:9-10; 1 Kgs. 8:39f.). *BDB* glosses this unique *niphal* of *yār'* by "inspire reverence, godly fear,"[76] and Fuhs glosses it by "worship"[77] (1 Pet. 1:17). "Gratitude for pardon," Spurgeon helpfully notes, "produces far more fear and reverence than all the dread of punishment" (Exod. 33:18–34:8).[78] Inferentially, without a consciousness of forgiveness a person does not truly worship — that is to say, worship with awe and reverence. The arrogant, however, treat God's grace with lassitude or con-

---

73. John Calvin, *Commentary on the Book of Psalms,* vol. 4 (Grand Rapids: Baker, 2003), p. 129.

74. *BDB,* p, 768, entry 2.3.b., s.v. '*m.*

75. H. A. Brongers, "Die Partikel *lema'an* in der biblisch-hebräischen Sprache," *OTS* 18 (1973): 84-96.

76. *BDB,* p. 431, s.v. *yr'.*

77. Fuhs, *TDOT,* VI.309, s.v. *yr'.*

78. Charles Haddon Spurgeon, *The Treasury of David,* updated by Roy H. Clarke (Nashville: Thomas Nelson, 1997), p. 1340.

tempt (Ps. 73:3-11; 2 Pet. 3:3-4).[79] But for those upon whom God chooses to show his mercy his grace leads to repentance (Exod. 33:18–34:8; Rom. 2:4; 9:15). Their worship includes loving, constant, faithful obedience to his word (Ps. 5:7[8]).

C. Address to Israel (130:5-8)

Confident of God's ability and willingness to forgive, the psalmist waits expectantly in hope for "I AM" to redeem him from his guilt (vv. 5-6). His posture serves as an example to Israel, for God will redeem not just him but all Israel (vv. 7-8, see "Rhetoric," above).

1. The Psalmist Put His Hope in "I AM" (130:5-6)

What more can the leader say to emphasize his hope for God to save him! Three times in verse 5 he repeats "I wait" or "I hope" for "I AM," and in verse 6 he compares himself to alert, albeit tired, watchmen who look eagerly for daylight. Chiastic repetitions in verses 5A and in 6B unify the strophe: "I wait expectantly for 'I AM,' my whole being waits" (2×) and "more than watchmen for the morning" (2×).

5 5A repeats "wait" but escalates "I" to "my whole being"; 5B clarifies that he waits in hope for God to fulfill his covenant promise of complete redemption (Ps. 25:5). The verb *I wait* (*qiwwîtî*, i.e., *I look expectantly*) — as seen in its related noun *qaw* ("tense string") — depicts expectation and hope as a tense attitude with reference to a specific goal; here *for* "I AM" (*yhwh*, see n. 44).[80] Weiser comments: "The true attitude of repentance, which differs from a merely transient mood of penitence, is a state of being according to which the believer lives in a constant inward tension . . . between hoping and possessing. . . ."[81] Emphatically, *my whole being* (NIV for *napšî*, see Ps. 6:3[4]) *waits* (*qiwwᵉtâ*). And *for his word* (*wᵉlidbārô*) refers to his covenant promises of salvation, not to a theorized priestly oracle of salvation.[82] Since God is

---

79. The dying poet Heinrich Heine mocked God's forgiveness: "It is God's business to forgive." Cited by Anderson, *Out of the Depths*, p. 98.

80. J. E. Hartley, *TWOT*, 2.791, s.v. *qwh*. Spurgeon (*Treasury of David*, p. 1340) comments: "Waiting is beneficial. It tries faith, exercises our patience, trains us in submission, and endears us to the blessing when it comes. The Lord's people have always been a waiting people. They waited for the First Advent, and now they wait for the Second."

81. Weiser, *The Psalms*, p. 775.

82. J. Begrich et al. ("Das priesterliche Heilsorakel," *ZAW* 52 [1934]: 81-92) detect in the Old Testament a "priestly oracle for salvation" "which promised the worshiper in the name of his God that God would hear his prayer." Although a normally cautious Leslie C. Allen (*Psalms 101–150*

merciful, he will put his willingness and ability into action as he promised. Israel's covenant relationship with "I AM" was conceived in love for "I AM" and brought forth through faith in him. The parallels, "I AM" and "his word," imply that God's person and word are inseparable. Unlike its English gloss, *dābār* refers to a full thought, not merely to a "word" within a statement. In Deuteronomy 4:2 *dābār* refers to the entire Book of the Law. Contexts may give more specific meanings than the general one of "word, speech"; e.g., "threat" (1 Kgs. 12:15), or as here, "promise" (1 Kgs. 2:4). Outside of Psalm 119, God's word occurs eighteen times with reference to his activity in nature (Pss. 33:6; 147:15, 18; cf. 103:2f.) or with reference to his covenant with Israel, especially its promises at work in the narratives of the people (Pss. 105:8, 42; 106:12, 24) and of the king (Pss. 56:4, 10[5, 11]; cf. 51:4[6]).[83] In Psalm 119 "word," along with *torah,* is one of many synonyms for God's covenant with Israel. Moreover, as in Psalm 130, its author is in distress and is looking expectantly for salvation in connection with his trust in God's covenant. Psalms 119:74, 114, 147; and 130:5 express hope for salvation in the same way: "I hope for his word." In sum, "his word" is his covenant promise to redeem Israel, and that promise is a metonym of cause for his objective act to completely save Israel. Verbs of trusting and hoping in the word of God extol its reliability (Pss. 56:4[5]; 106:12; 119:42, 81, 114, 147; cf. Isa. 66:2, 5).[84] The last word of the verse, *I hope* (הוֹחָלְתִּי), dynamically matches the first, *I wait (qiwwîtî),* which means to be in a state of painful expectation; it is probably related to *ḥûl,* "to be in labor." Both *yāḥal* and *qāwâ* have the psychological state of intense/painful waiting in the forefront. Both words belong and are used with others in the semantic realm of "trust," as C. Westermann notes.[85] P. R. Gilchrist says *yāḥal* ("hope") is a close synonym to *bāṭaḥ* ("trust").[86]

6 *My whole being (napšî,* v. 5*) [waits] for the Lord (la'ḏōnāy,* v. 2*) more than watchmen (miššōmᵉrîm,* see v. 3*) for the morning (labōqer,* Ps. 5:3[4]*).* G. Sauer notes: "in

[WBC 21; Waco, TX: Word, 1983], pp. 194, 196) without critical appraisal accepts this daring thesis, it goes beyond the evidence.

83. Psalm 107:19-20 is a textbook example of God's word at work in salvation history: "Then they cried to *I AM* in their trouble, and he saved them from their distress. He sent out his word (יִשְׁלַח דְּבָרוֹ) and healed them; he rescued them from the grave." H. Ringgren, *Word and Wisdom: Studies in the Hypostatization of Divine Qualities and Functions in the Ancient Near East* (1947), pp. 157ff., argues for a hypostatization of God's word in Isa. 9:7; 55:10f.; Ps. 107:20. This type of mythologization, considering God's word as autonomous and understanding it as an independent entity, fails to reckon with the poet's skill to trade in figures of speech. His word in these passages is a metonym of cause for his historical acts.

84. W. H. Schmidt, *TDOT,* 3.93-125, esp. 108, 118.

85. C. Westermann, "Das Hoffen im AT," *Theologia Viatorum* 4, 152/53: 19-70 = *Forschung am AT: Gesammelte Studien* (Munich: C. Kaiser, 1964-1974), pp. 219-65.

86. P. R. Gilchrist, *TWOT,* 1.374, s.v. *bṭḥ.*

addition to the usual watchfulness," שֹׁמְרִים indicates "an office that is bestowed. The result is an official title for court (and cult) officials: city watchmen (Isa. 21:11f.; 62:6, etc.), gatekeepers (1 Kgs. 14:27). . . ."[87] "Night watchmen" are in view (Ps. 127:1; Song 3:3; 5:7).[88] They were actively present, not idle observers (Gen. 16:13; 28:15; Isa. 27:3; Jer. 31:10). These alert, keen-eyed sentinels, among other duties (2 Sam. 13:34; 18:24-27), protected the city from danger (Ps. 121:7; Ezek. 3:17), giving themselves no rest (Isa. 62:6; cf. Ps. 121:3). Their duties were both tedious and dangerous, for wicked men wait for an opportunity to do evil (Job 24:15), and the night is their light (Job 38:15). The repetition of *more than watchmen wait for the morning* (*labōqer šōmᵉrîm*, see n. 46) serves both "to capture the tedium of the watchman's task (Isa. 21:11-12) and to heighten the urgency of his (the psalmist's) longing for a new relationship with the Lord."[89] Our poet feared God but "God was no more dreaded by [him] than light is dreaded by those engaged in a lawful calling."[90]

2. Israel, Put Your Hope in "I AM" (130:7-8)

7   God's unfailing kindness finds concrete expression in his act of liberating his covenant partner. *Israel (yiśrā'ēl)* means "striver with God," to which Genesis 32:28[29] adds "and with humankind and prevailed," and in that connection Hosea 12:4 adds "he wept and begged [the angel's] favor." In the Songs for the Ascent, Israel is a religious term for the whole nation.[91] The bearers of this honorific name were united by the covenants God made with them through the ancestors (i.e., Abraham, Isaac, Jacob), through Moses and David, and by their memory of God's mighty acts for them. Nominal Israel bore the honorific name but their hearts were far from "I AM." True Israel obeyed the command: *Put your hope in "I AM"* (*'el-yhwh . . . yaḥēl*, see n. 48); nominal Israel did not. Later, nominal Israel would not put their trust in the Lord Jesus Christ; true Israel did. They are to put their hope in the Lord *because (kî)* with "I AM" (*'im-yhwh*, v. 4) *is unfailing love* (5:7), *haḥes*, a co-referential term for "forgiveness" (v. 4). His unfailing love

---

87. G. Sauer, *TLOT*, 3.1381, s.v. *šmr*. It should not be confused with watches (= אַשְׁמֻרֹת) of the morning or of the evening (*pace* LXX and Targum).

88. A. Ḥakham (*Psalms*, p. 339) thinks "'those who watch for the morning'" may possibly refer to a group of God-fearing people who would rise early in the morning for prayer. Following this interpretation, the Sephardi custom is to recite this psalm after a *Siliḥot* service conducted in the early morning. Likewise, we find in many communities groups of people who rise early in the morning for prayer and Torah study, and who call themselves שֹׁמְרִים לַבֹּקֶר . . . "those who watch for the morning."

89. Leland Ryken, James C. Wilhoit, and Tremper Longman III, eds., *Dictionary of Biblical Imagery* (Downers Grove, IL: IVP Academic, 1998), p. 928.

90. Spurgeon, *Treasury of David*, p. 1341.

91. A. R. Hulst, "Der Name Israel," *OTS* 9 (1951): 65-106, esp. 103f.

finds expression in his liberating his people from guilt. *And the redemption with him is great (wᵉ harbēh ʿimmô pᵉḏût,* see n. 50), conceptualizing that redemption as an attribute God possesses.[92] *Pāḏâ* originally meant "to achieve the transfer of ownership from one to another through payment of a price or an equivalent substitute." In legal literature it commonly refers to redemption from slavery and in cultic law to the redemption of a human by an animal (Lev. 19:20; Exod. 4:23; 12:29; 21:30; 34:20; Num. 3:44-47; cf. Ps. 49:8[9]). In religious literature such as the Psalms, however, God is always the subject of *pdh,* and the term means "to set free, liberate" and no longer involves the exchange of something of equivalent value (1 Kgs. 1:29; Pss. 26:11; 44:26[27]; 69:18[19]).[93] Now its parallels are verbs "to deliver": *naṣal* (Jer. 15:21); *malaṭ* (Job 6:23).[94] A very great redemption refers to a complete salvation from a distressful situation.

8   *And he will redeem Israel from all their iniquities (wihū' yipdeh 'eṭ-yiśrā'ēl mikkōl ʿᵃwōnōṯāyw).* "And" joins his attributes of unfailing love and a willingness and ability to redeem with the fact he will redeem. "And this, of course," says Eugene Peterson, "is why we are able to face, acknowledge, accept and live through suffering, for we know that it can never be ultimate, it can never constitute the bottom line."[95]

PART IV. CONCLUSION

As Thornton Wilder noted, "Hope is a projection of the imagination; so is despair. Despair all too readily embraces the ills it foresees; hope is an energy and arouses the mind to explore every possibility to combat them."[96] Our inspired poet, gifted with hope that God will redeem his people, arouses Israel to survive the flood through hope. He points them to history — sinful humans endure — and to God's inherent inclination to forgive and to keep his covenant promises. Placed within the canon of Scripture, the song is based on the New Covenant enacted through the suffering and blood of Jesus Christ. "His oath, His covenant, His blood, / Support me in the whelming flood. / When all around my soul gives way, / He then is all my Hope and Stay."[97]

---

92. "Our comfort does not lie in what is with us but in that which is with our God. Let us look out of self and its poverty to Jehovah and His riches" (Spurgeon, *Treasury of David,* p. 1341).

93. J. J. Stamm, *TLOT,* 2.969.

94. W. B. Coker, *TWOT,* 2.716f.

95. Peterson, *A Long Obedience,* 137.

96. Cited by Peterson, *A Long Obedience,* p. 132.

97. Edward Mote (c. 1834).

CHAPTER 11

Psalm 143: The Lament of the Justified

PART I. VOICE OF THE CHURCH

I. Introduction

For the concluding of the seven penitential psalms, we shall summarize three of the significant historical periods of penitential formation and re-formation in the commentaries on Psalm 143 of Augustine, Denys the Carthusian, and John Calvin. Each of these commentaries is shadowed by three great classics of the church: Augustine's *City of God*, Thomas à Kempis's *Imitation of Christ*, and Calvin's *Institutes*.

II. The Voice of *Totius Christi* According to Augustine (354-430)

Augustine devoted some twenty-six years of pastoral ministry (392-418) to reflecting and preaching weekly sermons on the Psalms. His rhetorical exposition of Psalm 143 was preached on September 15, somewhere between 412 and 416.[1] Approaching the last book of the Psalter (Psalms 107-150) with its echoes of Zion, he began the compilation of his book *The City of God* between 413 and 427.

These works should be understood in their historical context. The sack of Rome by the Goths in 410 was a prelude to them. The pagans promptly blamed the Christians for this disaster, which they superstitiously attributed to the anger of Jove for the Christians' forsaking the gods, which the Roman elite had already done. The elite more realistically blamed the loss of the Roman public spirit to the rapid spread of Christianity. This blaming of Christians for the loss of Rome

---

1. Saint Augustine, *Expositions of the Psalms,* vol. 6, trans. Maria Boulding, O.S.B. (Hyde Park, NY: New City Press, 1990), p. 344.

prompted Augustine to reinforce his doctrine of *totius Christi*. According to this doctrine, which assumes the psalms are prophetic, the voice of the whole Christ, head and body, is the one voice of the incarnate Word speaking to, with, and within the church as a spiritual citizenship. Through this Christological lens Augustine interpreted the Psalter. It is what Roman Catholicism has validated ever since. Roman civic patriotism was replaced by the robust ecclesiology of *The City of God*.[2]

Having sung Psalm 143 in the church service, Augustine now expounds it within the historical context of 2 Samuel 15–18. Lamenting over his son Absalom's usurpation, which David believed was due to his adultery with Bathsheba, at the Lord's judicial court David is himself judged guilty before he can even condemn Absalom for his political insurrection. Augustine took this context from the Vulgate heading of the Psalm, found also in some editions of the Septuagint: "a psalm of David when his son pursued him." Waltke (see below pp. 269-70) suggests this background from the internal evidence of the psalm, not from this most likely later scribal addition. Throughout subsequent medieval commentaries this Augustinian adaptation was repeated consistently, to explain verse 2: *"Do not contend in judgment with your servant, for no living person will be found righteous in your sight."*

In verses 3 and 4 of the psalm, Augustine hears the voice of the suffering Christ in his humanity, and of the church too, in an allegorical reach that speaks of the devil's attacks and of "places." In verse 5, the whole body of Christ is made to respond, tracing "in days of old," the work of divine grace, yet also divine wrath, as the work of salvation. He reminds his audience to be "in fear and trembling," as we listen to Paul's words: "For it is God who is at work in you, inspiring both your will and work, for his good purpose" (Phil. 2:13). "As I contemplated your works, what I saw was this: that there can be nothing good in us, unless it comes from you who made us."[3]

In verses 6-7, Augustine sees himself with the psalmist in a waterless place, botching God's work of grace with his own independent spirit. Does God delay in order to deepen our desires for his Spirit within us? Does God turn away his face from our pride? Is that why I am still in the night? So don't destroy me, for the dead cannot confess to you. Then Augustine reflects with the psalmist on verse 8, "mercy in the morning; while night lasts, walk towards the lamp of the divine scriptures." "The night demands patience, the day will give us joy . . . we must seek the Lord in the night with open hands . . . by performing good works."[4] In verse

---

2. Ernest L. Fortin, "Civitate Dei, De," in *Augustine through the Ages: An Encyclopaedia*, ed. Allan D. Fitzgerald, O.S.A. (Grand Rapids: Eerdmans, 1999), pp. 196-202.

3. Saint Augustine, *Expositions*, vol. 6, p. 353.

4. Saint Augustine, *Expositions*, vol. 6, p. 356.

9, Augustine exhorts his audience to "flee from principalities and powers and rulers of this world" — these are their enemies — and seek refuge in God alone.[5]

In a hurried conclusion to complete the sermon, he then summarizes verses 10-12: "teach me, that I may do your will, for you are my God." "What a magnificent confession! What a comprehensive rule of life! . . . if you do not teach me [O Lord], I shall do my own will . . . [for] my own bad spirit has led me in a crooked way, into the wrong place. . . . If I were to put forward any merits of my own, I would be proved to deserve nothing from you except punishment. But you have torn out my demerits and engrafted your gifts. For the glory of your name, O Lord, you will give me life in accordance with your justice. . . ."[6]

III. Late Medieval Penitence and Denys the Carthusian

Denys the Carthusian (1402-1471) wrote his commentary on the Psalms in the context of late-medieval penitence. The monastic movement from its beginning, as the ascetic John Cassian (360-435) recognized, was always going to be, by its liturgical routine and by its enclosed life, subject to acedia or moral sloth. He described it in the early fifth century as moral sadness, a disease of the heart, a lament indeed. Quoting 2 Corinthians 7:10, Cassian affirms that the sadness that "works repentance unto a lasting salvation" is, in contrast to acedia, "obedient, humble, mild, gracious, and patient, inasmuch as it comes from the love of God . . . it retains all its gracious courtesy, and forbearance, having in itself all the fruits of the Holy Spirit" (as spelled out in Gal. 5:22-23).[7] Seeking to revive monastic vitality, the conciliar reform of writers such as Pierre d'Ailly (1350-1420) appropriated this seventh penitential psalm to challenge moral sloth, as the seventh deadly sin.

The complete commentary on the Psalms by Denys the Carthusian, in the reform movement of *Devotio Moderna*,[8] seeks to make the monastic liturgical use of the Psalms once more spiritually alive. This is linked with such works as *The Life of Christ* by Ludolph the Cartesian (d. 1370) and Thomas à Kempis's *Imitation of Christ*, in the renewal of penitential devotion.

Denys's "exposition" on Psalm 143 begins with the Vulgate reading, which sets the psalm in the context of David's flight from Absalom.[9] "In the High Mid-

5. Saint Augustine, *Expositions*, vol. 6, p. 357.

6. Saint Augustine, *Expositions*, vol. 6, pp. 358-59.

7. Ancient Christian Writers, John Cassian, *The Institutes*, trans. and ed. Boniface Ramsey, O.P. (New York/Mahwah, NJ: Newman, 2000), pp. 213-14.

8. See Bruce K. Waltke and James M. Houston with Erika Moore, *The Psalms as Christian Worship* (Grand Rapids: Eerdmans, 2010), pp. 286-87, 314-15, 390-91 (hereafter *PACW*).

9. I am indebted to my former student and friend, Ken Pearson, for the translation from

dle Ages, David was viewed as a virtuous example of a good and holy man, but later in the sixteenth century Jacques Lefèvre d'Étaples condemned David as in need of renovation — like the contemporary monks he associated with — while later in the century Theodore Beza interpreted David as the reformed model of repentance. It is a shift from a historical view of David to a more 'spiritual' hermeneutic."[10] David's persecution by Absalom was increasingly emphasized in the later period of the Renaissance, forming the cause for all seven of the penitential psalms[11] and eclipsing any reference to Paul's indictments in the Roman epistle about "justification by faith." But in the context of Denys's period, "the David of repentance" is depicted iconographically as buried halfway into the ground, needing rescue from the psalmist's "pit," as in Psalms 131:1 and 143:3. Here David himself is being judged; another penitential scene depicts David going out into the wilderness, no longer in the victorious context as a military hero, but as a penitent, bewildered and without proper orientation, awaiting the Lord's mercy to save him from the inner tempest of his own deep distress. Petrarch depicts this locale as a desert cave, symbolic of the inner recesses of one's soul.[12]

Denys follows Augustine's explanation of the "hearing of the Lord" as expressive of his mercy. In repetitive refrain, as a device to deepen "the good desire" (*affectus*), Denys quotes Hezekiah's exemplary prayer: "I beseech you, O Lord, remember how I have walked before you in truth and with a perfect heart" (Isa. 38:3).[13] He then repeats Augustine's argument that David confesses his sin with Bathsheba, as evidence he is in no moral condition to be a judge of others. Verse 2 he interprets as: "no man living in this world is just before your perfect justice, as if he would have nothing of injustice of sin for the sake of which he ought to ask that God not enter into judgment with him."[14] Following Gregory the Great's *Pastoralia,* much stress is placed on the vital role of humility for penitence, as the psalmist demonstrates in verse 3. Much of the textual explanation follows Augustine's homily.

Verse 4 he links with the sufferings and death of Christ, a common peniten-

---

the medieval Latin, of Denys the Carthusian's text: *D. Dionysii Cartusiani insigne opus commentariorum, in psalmos omnes Davidicos,* in *Doctoris Ecstatici D. Cartusiani Opera Omnia* (Monstroli: Typis Cartusiae S. M. De Pratis, 1898), vol. 6, pp. 45-48, 659-63.

10. Edward A. Gosselin, "Two Views of the Evangelical David: Lefèvre d'Etaples and Theodore Beza," in *The David Myth in Western Literature,* ed. Raymond-Jean Frontain and Jan Wojcik (West Lafayette, IN: Purdue University Press, 1980), pp. 58-59.

11. Clare L. Costley, "David and Bathsheba, and the Penitential Psalms," *Renaissance Quarterly* 57 (Winter 2004): 1235-77.

12. Charles A. Huttar, "Frail Grass and Firm Tree: David as the Model of Repentance," in Frontain and Wojcik, eds., *The David Myth,* p. 47.

13. Denys the Carthusian, *D. Dionysii Cartusiani,* vol. 6, p. 660.

14. Denys the Carthusian, *D. Dionysii Cartusiani,* vol. 6, p. 660.

tial theme, reflecting on Jesus' words in Gethsemane, "now is my soul sorrowful, even to the point of death" (Matt. 26:38; John 12:27).

Remembering "the days of old" he explains as reference to the Fall of Adam when original righteousness was lost, and to the days of Noah, with further divine judgment. For God to avert his face in verse 7 is for Denys the denial of God's gracious presence, and "descending into the pit of hell. Indeed, I will be made like them in this life through guilt [*culpam*], but in the future through punishment [*poenam*]."

In verse 11, in being delivered from one's enemies, "visible and invisible," Denys then enjoins: "let us also so make an effort to be united with, and to cling to God, so that we might worthily and truthfully say to him 'you are my God.' For the almighty God, who is the God of all, is especially God of those who offer themselves wholly to God and totally deliver themselves up to the worship of him; they desire nothing else but God and they always honour God in such a way that they are unhesitatingly diligent."

Denys concludes his homily: "See, for we have clearly heard this virtuous and affective psalm, the last of the penitential psalms, in which the penitent most ardently beseeches God. And at the end of the psalm he confidently speaks, saying: 'Your good spirit will lead me . . . into the land of the living where all are just and right [quoting Isa. 60:21].' . . . The Holy Spirit will lead us into this land through good works and holy desires. . . . Such words are also virtually a prayer. Therefore, let us endeavour to sing this psalm with heartfelt contrition and true devotion, and with desire to express all the prayers contained in it."[15]

Similar to Augustine, Denys is still using the penitential psalm within a sung liturgy.

IV. The Reformation Commentary of John Calvin

Entering the commentary of John Calvin (1509-1564) is like entering a different world of faith and culture.[16] Composed in his mature years (1553-57), his Psalms commentary was a source of his preaching from 1549 until 1554. More than any of his other writings, his commentary on the Psalms mirrors his inner life, as he identifies so intimately with David in all his afflictions. Contemporaneously, he is writing the final edition of his *Institutes* (completed in 1559), which is not a textbook of systematic theology, but rather a glossary for all his biblical com-

---

15. Denys the Carthusian, *D. Dionysii Cartusiani,* vol. 6, p. 663.

16. See previous studies of Calvin's use of the Psalms, in Waltke and Houston, *PACW,* pp. 62-64, 123-27, 252-53, 288, 315-17, 346-48, 429-31, 493-96, 529-331.

mentaries. He refers to 113 psalms in the *Institutes,* with 414 references.[17] Many scholars make the mistake of ignoring his existential Psalms commentary in favor of their abstract study of the *Institutes.* Although he pays tribute to Augustine's anti-Pelagian stand, Calvin judges him mistaken in interpreting God's righteousness as evidence against the merit of "works." Rather, from the Psalms, Calvin interprets God's righteousness dynamically as his active faithfulness to protect his people and to set them free.[18]

We have expressed our desire to reference the biblical God as the "I AM," existing in himself, and uniquely in his own power. Likewise, Calvin's "theology" emphasizes God's essential character, his "being-God." He sees the mercy of God and his faithfulness to David as the only basis for the divine response to human lament. Identifying with David's affliction, yet trusting likewise in God, Calvin shares with us the same redemptive personal and dynamic experiences of divine mercy.

Calvin's mature commentary on Psalm 143 reflects a contrasted religious and cultural context from that of medieval penance. The monastic model has now been demolished, so that singing the Psalms has taken on a congregational character, more like Augustine's setting. But the Turks had been defeated at the gates of Vienna (1683), unlike the Goths at Rome. Calvin appreciates Augustine's stand against the Pelagians, as he needed to guard against similar tendencies of self-righteousness. Calvin too, wished to demonstrate the Reformers were in continuity with the early Church Fathers. His context is much more as a pastor than as a philosophical theologian, so his priority is to communicate the mercy of God through the Psalms, rather than to focus upon the *Institutes, per se* — the converse of much "Calvinism," past and present.

We may paraphrase Calvin's commentary as follows. First, he reckons David must be in severe trouble to pray as he does, in such psalms of lament. But his prayers of lament are always based upon the character of God, as true, faithful, and merciful. We can follow David in seeking help in adversity, but behind it all is the reality we are all sinners, so that seeking forgiveness is more basic than asking for help. For at God's tribunal all human righteousness avails nothing, as we all have sinned.[19]

In the second stanza of the psalm (vv. 4-7), the external and circumstantial

---

17. Based on the author's (J. M. H.) calculations of Psalm references listed in Calvin's *Institutes.*

18. Herman J. Selderhuis, *Calvin's Theology of the Psalms* (Grand Rapids: Baker Academic, 2007), pp. 157-58.

19. Significantly, in German Lutheran culture the word for "lament" *(Klage)* is a legal term connoting taking legal action. See Eva Harasta and Brian Brock, eds., *Evoking Lament: A Theological Discussion* (London: T. & T. Clark, 2009), p. 4, n. 4.

trials cannot compare with the internal and spiritual condition of our hearts before God. Our own narrative may comfort us as we reflect on how God has helped us before, but we must also have the bigger picture of God's past dealings of mercy with all his people. We may not find relief just contemplating our personal experience of God; reviewing the grand sweep of the biblical narrative will always bring solace. This requires deep meditation, for even if we experience intensely dry "desert experiences," becoming so weak as to be ready to sink into the grave, all such causes for lament are used by God to intensify our desire for God alone. This ultimate necessity becomes like a chariot that takes the psalmist upwards, to be alone with God.

In the third stanza (vv. 8-12), the psalmist seeks existentially to actually experience God's goodness. For theoretical knowledge of doctrine is not enough. But the psalmist perhaps is impatient to experience this as soon as possible, i.e., "in the morning," for he is still anxious and perplexed, even dismayed. The fact, too, that his enemies are so bent on further destruction deepens the pray-er's trust in God.

Praying now ever more deeply, "teach me that I may do your will" (v. 10), the psalmist desires more than external help; he needs to be kept in the way of rectitude, by the guidance of God's Spirit. For all sorts of false emotions — anxiety, fear, languor, even disease and pain — as well as temptations that go with them — can make us impulsive, to react wrongly. Thus God must teach us much more than theology as an abstraction, but by his Spirit so enlighten our minds and engrave his instruction upon our willing and obedient hearts, that we live out his truth, in the most intimate way. As the apostle expresses it: "for it is God who works in you to will and to act according to his good pleasure" (Phil. 2:13). So when David adds "for you are my God" (v. 10), he shows that his confidence lies in God alone.

Making it still more emphatic, "For your name's sake" (v. 11), David confesses that it is entirely of God's free mercy that he has looked for deliverance, finding nothing in us that would conciliate God's favor.

Medieval penitence might invoke plea-bargaining with the Almighty, but not Calvin, who makes no mention whatever that this is the seventh penitential psalm! For God's righteousness to be invoked, this can only be freely given by God himself, as he reveals his character of grace. It can have no human basis of "merit" to receive it. Only God, who has the issues of life, can provide a kind of resurrection, in the extremity of human need.

Finally, in the last verse (v. 12) Calvin notes that the psalmist repeats for the fifth or sixth time that he can only look for God's mercy; nothing else will do! However severe God's wrath on the wicked may appear, the other side is his divine goodness, as Isaiah 63:4 conjoins God's character: "The day of vengeance is in my heart, and this is the day of redemption." Because it is all God's unmerited favor, the psalmist commits his whole life under God's protection. In calling himself God's servant, he can have no boast about "my ministry" but only praise "our God" for all his unmerited mercy.[20]

PART II. VOICE OF THE PSALMIST: TRANSLATION

A psalm by David.

1   "I AM," hear my prayer! Listen to my cry for mercy![21]
       in your faithfulness[22] answer me;
       [answer me] in your righteousness!

2   And[23] do not enter[24] into judgment with your "slave,"
       for no one living is righteous[25] before you.

3   Surely, the enemy[26] pursues[27] me; he crushes me to the ground;
       he makes me dwell in a dark place[28] like those long[29] dead.[30]

20. For an alternative paraphrase, see Sinclair B. Ferguson, *John Calvin: Heart Aflame: Daily Readings from Calvin on the Psalms* (Phillipsburg, NJ: P. & R. Publishing, 1999), p. 359.

21. Always as an abstract plural (*IBHS*, p. 120f., P. 7.4.2a).

22. Syriac inexplicably reads *b'mrk* ("with your word"). MT's accents connect בְּצִדְקָתֶךָ with עֲנֵנִי. LXX probably connects בְּצִדְקָתֶךָ with הַאֲזִינָה, yielding the felicitous parallel syntax of a threefold: imperative + "my" [prayer] + "your" [virtue]. Nevertheless, with regard to external evidence MT is normally the preferred reading (*IBHS*, pp. 24-28, P. 1.6.3), and as for internal evidence linking the virtue "in your faithfulness" with the virtue "mercy" is not as felicitous as linking "in your faithfulness" with "answer me."

23. Conjunctive *waw* joins this overlapping injunction with the preceding three injunctions (*IBHS*, p. 653, P. 39.2b).

24. H. Bardtke *(BHS)* prefers with Syr to read *hiphil*, citing Job 14:3, but fails to note that with the phrase בְמִשְׁפָט the three instances of *bo' hiphil* occur with direct object (Job 14:3; Eccles. 11:9, 12) and the four instances of *bo' qal* occur without direct object (Isa. 3:14; Job 22:4; Ps. 143:2; Job 9:32).

25. Lit., "every living thing is not righteous."

26. The anarthrous construction is probably due to the stricture of poetic rhythm.

27. Construed as a persistent perfective (*IBHS*, p. 487, P. 30.5.1c).

28. Since three of the seven occurrences of מַחְשַׁךְ are singular and the reference is to the grave, a place with many chambers (Prov. 7:27), the plural is best construed as a complex inanimate noun (*IBHS*, p. 120, P. 7.4.1c).

29. Genitive of the measure (*IBHS*, p. 152, P. 9.5.3d).

30. The acrostic and rhythm show beyond reasonable doubt that בְּמַחֲשַׁכִּים הוֹשִׁיבַנִי כְּמֵתֵי עוֹלָם in Lam. 3:6 is original in Lamentations, suggesting the parallel Ps. 143:3 is a later scribal gloss. Possibly both poets are borrowing a known phrase.

4   So[31] my spirit[32] grows faint[33] within[34] me;
    my heart is dismayed[35] within me.

5   I remember[36] the days of long ago;
    I meditate[37] on all your deeds;
    I consider[38] what your hands[39] have done.

6   I spread out[40] my hands to you;
    I[41] thirst[42] for you like a parched land.

7   Answer me quickly,[43] "I AM," my spirit fails.
    Do not hide your face from me
    for I am like[44] those who go down to the pit.

8   Let me hear[45] in the morning of your unfailing love,
    for I have put my trust in you.
    Show me[46] the way I should go, for I entrust my life to you.

9   Rescue me from my enemies, "I AM,"

31. *Waw* consecutive denotes a correlative situation, either a chronological and/or logical consequence (*IBHS*, p. 547, P. 33.2a).

32. נַפְשִׁי may be a facilitating reading from verse 3. The more difficult reading רוּחִי finds support in 142:3[4].

33. Durative *hithpael* (*IBHS*, pp. 426-28, P. 26.1.2); see E. A. Speiser, "The Durative Hithpa'el: A *tan* Form," *Journal of the American Oriental Society* 75 (1955): 118-21.

34. Lit., "upon me" (see exegesis).

35. Durative *hithpael* (*IBHS*, pp. 426-28, P. 26.1.2).

36. Construing the quasi-fientive stative verb in suffix conjugation as representing a situation in present time (*IBHS*, pp. 491f., P. 30.5.3c).

37. See n. 36.

38. Construed as a progressive nonperfective (*IBHS*, p. 504, P. 31.3b).

39. יָד: ("hand") is the body part from the elbow to the fingertip.

40. A resultative *Piel* ("make spread out") construed as an instantaneous perfective (*IBHS*, p. 588, P. 30.5.1d).

41. The original meaning of נֶפֶשׁ, "throat," may still be felt in this context. If so, "throat" is parallel to "hands."

42. The pregnant prepositional phrase לְךָ demands that a verb such as thirst has been elided (*IBHS*, p. 224, P. 11.4.3d).

43. מַהֵר is an inf. abs. used adverbially following a verb. Before עֲנֵנִי it functions as an adverbial imperative (Pss. 69:18, 79:8, 102:2[3]; see GKC, P. 110h; cf. 120d).

44. Since the accent did not shift, the form is a *waw* conjunctive with suffix conjugation, not *waw* consecutive (i.e., "lest I become"; see *IBHS*, pp. 520f., P. 32.1.1b,c).

45. Permissive *hiphil* (*IBHS*, p. 445, P. 27.5).

46. LXX (cf. Syriac) reads κύριε ὁδὸν ἐν ᾗ πορεύσομαι, breaking the pattern of vocative "Lord" in the odd verses of petition (see below, "Rhetoric").

for[47] I flee[48] to you.

10   Teach me[49] to do your will, for you are my God;
    may your good Spirit lead me[50] on level ground.

11   For your name's sake, "I AM," preserve me;[51]
    in your righteousness, bring me out of trouble.[52]

12   In your unfailing love, silence my enemies;
    And destroy[53] all my foes, for I am your "slave."

PART III. COMMENTARY

I. Introduction

A. *Literary Context*

This is the sixth of an octave of Davidic — and so royal — psalms (138–145) before the Psalter's concluding praise psalms, which have the introit הַלְלוּ-יָהּ. The

47. The majority of medieval mss. assume an ad sensum logical connection between 9B and A; a few formally express it by כִּי.

48. MT כִסִּתִי ("I cover/hide myself") faces four objections: (1) defective reading or כָּסָה *piel* occurs only 1× out of 16× with this form; (2) normally כָּסָה *piel* takes an object, though a reflexive sense is attested in Gen. 38:14; Deut. 22:12; (3) כָּסָה means "to cover over [so as not to be seen]," not "to seek protective covering"; and (4) one expects the preposition בְּ or עַל, not אֵלֶיךָ. Even if one grants the reflexive sense, "I cover myself," it signifies "not to be seen," not to hide myself protectively. Syriac did (could?) not translate the clause. The rabbinic interpretations are ad hoc (cf. Ḥakkam, *The Psalms*, 436, n. 12). Ibn Ezra argues "to hide from a person" is the opposite of "to hide to a person"; Rashi paraphrases "I conceal my troubles from other people to tell them to you." The Targum renders "I was appointed as the one who redeems," assuming the root is כָּסַס ("to compute," Exod. 12:4). With more probability *Psalmi Iuxta Hebraeos* reads *"a te protectus sum"* (*kussᵉ ṭi*), but with that construal of כָּסָה one expects either an adverbial accusative or the preposition בְּ. The best solution is to read נַסְתִּי, found in 1 MS and the Vorlage of LXX, which reads κατέφυγον. Scribes commonly confuse *k/n* (see Waltke, *NIDOTTE*, 1.63).

49. Factive *Piel* ("make me accustomed," *IBHS*, p. 401, P. 24.2c).

50. The syntax of רוּחֲךָ טוֹבָה תַנְחֵנִי is ambiguous. If תַנְחֵנִי is 2nd pers. impf. ("may you lead me," רוּחֲךָ טוֹבָה is either a nominal clause ("your spirit is good") or an adverbial accusative ("lead me by your good spirit"). If תִנְחֵנִי is 3rd fem. jussive, רוּחֲךָ is subject and טוֹבָה is either a predicate or attributive adjective. Neh. 9:20 favors the last interpretation. The suffix of רוּחֲךָ may weaken the connection, allowing anarthrous טוֹבָה (GKC, 126z).

51. Lit., "make me alive"; imperfect of injunction (*IBHS*, p. 509, P. 31.5b).

52. Ḥakkam (*The Bible/Psalms*, III. 438) notes the assonance with the Hebrew consonant *tzadi*: בְּצִדְקָתְךָ תוֹצִיא מִצָּרָה.

53. *Waw* consecutive with suffix conjugation (see n. 44).

Davidic collection begins with a confession of thanksgiving (138) and concludes with a hymn of praise (145). Psalms 139 and 144 are a mixture of praise and petition; 140–143 are petition psalms. 143 is joined with 142 by more or less salient catch-terms: "cry for mercy" (*taḥᵃnūnay,* Ps. 143:1, and *'etḥannān,* Ps. 142:1[2]); enemy "pursues" me (Ps. 143:3, *rādaph 'ōyēb;* Ps. 142:6[7], *mirōdᵉpî*); "my spirit faints" (Ps. 143:4, *watiṭ'aṭōph 'ālay rūḥî;* Ps. 142:3[4], *bᵉhiṭ'aṭṭēp 'ālay rūḥî*); "the way I should go" (Ps. 143:8, *derek-zū 'ēlēk;* Ps. 142:3[4], *bᵉ'ōraḥ-zū 'ᵃhallēk*); "save me" (Pss. 142:6[7]; 143:9, *haṣṣîlēnî*); "your name" (Ps. 143:11, *lᵉma'an-šimkā;* Ps. 142:7[8], *'eṭ-šᵉᵉmekā*). Psalm 143 is also linked with Psalm 144 by the king's labeling himself a "slave" (143:2, 12; 144:10). He depends on God's covenant love *(ḥesed)* in 138:2; 141:5; 143:12; 144:2; 145:8 (cf. 2 Sam. 7:16), and cries out for mercy in 140:6[7]; 142:1[2]; 143:1.

B. Historical Context

The superscript (see below) does not specify the historical circumstance that prompted David to compose this psalm. Commentators speculate on the historical significance of "in the morning" (v. 8);[54] probably there is none. Nevertheless, comparing this psalm with those whose superscripts identify them with David's flight from Saul and with those whose superscripts associate with his flight from Absalom is theologically instructive. On the one hand, the language of 143 favors the former situation. As in the "Saulide" Psalm 7, David identifies his enemy in 143 as an individual (v. 3) and a group (v. 9), and in both psalms he depicts his enemy as crushing his life into the ground (Pss. 7:5[6]; 143:3). Moreover, striking verbal similarities (see above) link 143 with 142, whose superscript dates that psalm to David's flight from Saul. On the other hand, David's psychology in 143 differs radically from that of Psalms 7 and 142. In Psalm 7 he asks God to judge him according to his righteousness in comparison to his enemies (7:8[9]), and in 142 he asks for mercy for God to preserve his life delivered from his enemy. In 143, by contrast, he asks God not to put him on trial, for none is righteous in God's estimation (143:2), and so he seeks spiritual salvation in connection with physical salvation. This more mature theology fits the psychology expressed in the penitential psalm 51 for his sin against God when he took Bathsheba.[55] After

---

54. See Leslie C. Allen, *Psalms 101–150* (Word Biblical Commentary, 21; Waco, TX: Word, 1983), p. 282.

55. Some Greek codices, followed by Syriac and the Vulgate (not PIH), explicitly identify the enemy as Absalom, but these superscripts are better understood as conjectural expansions, inferred from the psalm's content, in the Greek textual tradition. Codex Vaticanus reads: ψαλμὸς τῷ Δαυιδ ὅτε αὐτὸν ὁ υἱὸς καταδιώκει.

that debacle David realized his need of God's mercy to forgive him and of God's spirit to empower him to do the divine will (Pss. 51:9-11[10-12]; 143:10). Though convinced of the rectitude of his cause, he also knows none is without guilt and so all are worthy of God's discipline; self-righteousness is excluded. By placing Psalms 142 and 143 back to back, the editors of the Psalter give the church the opportunity to taste mature theological wine — from the young wine of David's cry for mercy and political salvation based on his legitimate protest of innocence in a comparison to his enemy, to the rich wine of a mature David's cry for mercy, both political and spiritual, by his comparison of humankind to God.

C. Form

The statement for "no one living is righteous before you" led the church to include the psalm among the seven penitential psalms (6, 32, 38, 51, 102, 130, 143)[56] and to recite it on Ash Wednesday, although David makes that assertion as dogma (Job 9:2; 4:17-18; 15:14-15; 25:4), not as a penitential *cri de coeur*. The typical motifs of lament psalms help shape this petition:[57] address to "I AM" with introductory petitions (vv. 1-2), lament (vv. 3-4), confidence (vv. 5-6), and petitions proper (vv. 7-12). The notion of praise surfaces in verse 11A: "For the sake of your name preserve me" — that is to say, your name will be praised, not defamed. Though the psalm is more martial than penitential, it is more devotional than martial. "I AM's" "slave" is being buried alive by enemies of God's kingdom, but the "slave"-king's memory of salvation history and his faith in God's covenant attributes raise him from the grave to vanquish his enemies.

D. Rhetoric

The psalm consists of two stanzas: I. Introduction to petitions (vv. 1-6) and II. Petitions (vv. 7-12).[58] Form and rhetorical criteria combine to analyze the stanzas as each consisting of three strophes, here labeled as A, B, C, etc. In stanza I, strophe A, addressed to God, contains introductory petitions to be heard (vv. 1-2); B, with a focus on the enemy, presents his lament (vv. 3-4); and C, which focuses on the worshiper, expresses his confidence prompting him to pray (vv. 5-6). Medial particle *kî* ("I say this because") formally links B to A. His

---

56. N. H. Snaith, *The Seven Penitential Psalms* (London: Epworth, 1964), pp. 9-10.

57. Waltke and Houston, *PACW*, p. 95.

58. Perhaps סֶלָה helps mark this division.

lament narrates his enemies' persecution (v. 3) and his inner turmoil (v. 4). This interiority segues into his meditation on "I AM's" historical track record, giving him confidence to spread out his prayerful hands to God. In stanza II, strophe A' consists of six or seven imperatives focusing on his urgent need to be heard and answered (vv. 7-8), and B' presents his plea to be delivered from his enemies (vv. 9-10). C', now using imperfects of volition, reprises the psalm. The volitional imperfect of 10B assists the transition from B' to C'. Catchwords unify the strophes: A by "righteousness" (*ṣedeq*, vv. 1, 2); B by overlapping anthropological terms "soul" and "spirit"/"life" and "heart" (*napšî* and *ḥayyātî/rûḥî* and *libî*, vv. 3, 4); "hand" *yād* ("yours," v. 5 and "my," v. 6); complementary "answer me" and "make me hear" *ʿănanî* and *hašmîʿnî* (vv. 7, 8); statements of trust (vv. 9-10), and traditionally "soul" (*napšî*, vv. 11-12). Vocative יְהוָה occur in the first verset of the petition strophes (vv. 1, 7, 9, and 11). Also, references to *napšî* punctuate, and so unify, the psalm (vv. 3, 6, 8, 11, 12).

The strophes are arranged in a concentric pattern:[59]

A. Focus on king: petitions to be heard   1-2
    B. Focus on "enemy": lament of persecution   3-4
        C. Focus on God: God's deeds — basis for trust   5-6
        C'. Focus on God: prays on basis of trust   7-8
    B'. Focus on "enemy/enemies": petition to be delivered   9-10
A'. Focus on king: petitions to preserve his life and punish enemy   11-12

Catchwords form the frame: *yhwh* (vv. 1, 11), "slave" (vv. 2, 12); "righteousness" (vv. 1, 11; cf. v. 2); word pair "faithfulness" and "unfailing love"; and "life" (vv. 2, 11). The last strophe also reprises the lament strophe by referring to his enemy/enemies (vv. 3, 12) and "my life" (vv. 3 and 11).

Verse 7 also functions as a janus, uniting the two halves by repeating from stanza I "answer me" (v. 1), "my spirit" [is faint] (v. 4), and "I am like" [the dead and dying] (v. 3). The closure of stanza I, "I spread out my hands to you," and the introduction of stanza II, "Answer me quickly," tightly sew the stanzas together into a unified poem. In that light, "do not hide your face" is probably to be associated with "do not enter into judgment with your 'slave'" (v. 2), the reason God would hide his face from him.

59. Cf. Robert Alden, "Chiastic Psalms (III): A Study in the Mechanics of Semitic Poetry: Psalms 101–150," *JETS* 21, no. 3 (1978): 199-210; Samuel Terrien (*The Psalms: Strophic Structure and Theological Commentary* [Cambridge and Grand Rapids: Eerdmans, 2003], p. 892) sees a chiastic structure with a focus on v. 7.

E. Message

This cold analysis of the psalm's form and rhetoric conceals the extreme sufferings of the dying king and his earnest desire for full salvation. The psalm has many theological similarities to other lament psalms. As in those psalms, the psalmist, standing on the edge of descending into the grave, petitions his heretofore silent God to deliver him from his enemies. Moreover, as in other laments, the king bases his appeal for salvation on "I AM's" sublime covenant attributes of mercy and righteousness. As in other laments, memory of the *magnalia dei* revitalizes faith (Ps. 22:4-5[5-6]). The reminder that God's name is at stake in this fight-to-the finish between the king and his enemies (v. 11) is rare, but does not distinguish the psalm (Pss. 23:3; 109:21). (The king petitions God to preserve his life for God's name, and his faithfulness to keep his covenant promises is at stake, not because the king fears death *per se*.) The psalm closely resembles the elevated theology of Psalm 51; namely, his recognition of his original sin (v. 2) and so his need of God's spirit to empower him. Psalm 130 also implies the covenant relationship can be maintained only by divine forgiveness of original sin (esp. Ps. 130:3-4).

Psalm 143, however, uniquely intermingles his request for physical salvation (vv. 7, 8A, 9A) with his request for spiritual salvation. The enemy's crushing him into the realm of the dead (vv. 3, 7A) lifts his theological reflections to Pauline heights (see conclusion). As for the divine covenant partner, the king's salvation depends on God's kindness, righteousness, and reliability. As for the human partner, the king's salvation depends on his enjoying intimacy with "I AM." This intimacy is nurtured in two interrelated ways. First, the king petitions God to empower him to keep covenant — to show him the way that he should go (v. 8B), to teach him *to do* his will (v. 10A), and to impart God's good spirit to lead him (v. 10B). David's zeal to keep his covenant obligations is that of a humble, chastened, mature saint, not that of an immature idealist or proud legalist. Second, God's "slave" asserts his trust in "I AM" (vv. 8A, B, 9B; 10A). In spite of his depravity, and though as good as dead (v. 7), having reflected on Israel's and his own salvation history (v. 5), the "slave" flees upward to God and obstinately trusts him (vv. 8-9), a trust the reliable covenant Partner will not disappoint (Rom. 5:5). The trusting "slave" fights to the finish, for as long as the enemy endures there will be no peace (v. 12).

II. Exegesis

A. Superscript

Many critics reject the psalm's claim "by David" because of its several direct quotations and allusions to other psalms[60] and its advanced theology. Its citations mostly derive from psalms also attributed to David and so in fact may reinforce Davidic authorship, although they and others may be due to the liturgical style. Its so-called advanced theology — the generality of sin and need of God's spirit — can be explained by David's fall (2 Samuel 11–20). The psalm's content suggests the author is a king, for he: (1) calls himself by the royal title, "slave" (2 Sam. 3:18; 7:8; 7:26 + 27 times);[61] (2) petitions God to eliminate enemy (vv. 2, 12); (3) appeals to God's covenant attributes, unfailing love and righteousness (vv. 1, 8, 12); and (4) prays for his own covenant fidelity (vv. 8, 9, 10). The adjoining psalm, 144, has many royal benchmarks. "All in all," says Eaton, "there is sufficient reason to see the singer of this *leḏāwiḏ* psalm as the king."[62]

B. Introduction to Petitions (143:1-6)

1. Introductory Petitions (143:1-2)

Three imperatives aim to rouse heretofore silent "I AM" to deal with his king in righteousness in the sense that he do right by his "slave" in saving him, not in the sense of bringing him to trial.

a. To Be Given a Hearing (143:1)

The typical direct address to "I AM" must not be regarded as a *pro forma* to petition psalms, like the perfunctory playing of the national anthem before a ballgame, but as incorporating the psalm into the salvation history that gives

---

60. Herman Gunkel, *Die Psalmen* (Göttingen: Vandenhoeck & Ruprecht, 1926), p. 603; H. E. Leupold, *Exposition of the Psalms* (Grand Rapids: Baker, 1959), p. 966; Amos Ḥakkam, *The Bible/Psalms with the Jerusalem Commentary,* vol. 3 (Jerusalem: Mosad Harav Kook, 2003), p. 430 Leupold, who accepts Davidic authorship, compares with vv. 8A, 69:17; 27:9; 102:2; and with the second part Pss. 28:1; 88:4. In like manner on v. 8 we might compare Pss. 90:14; 25:2; 25:4; 142:3; 25:1; 86:4. "Here particularly the mosaic character of the psalm becomes apparent."

61. *BDB*, p. 714, entry 3, s.v. *ʿebed*. See John H. Eaton, *Kingship and the Psalms* (SBT, second series, 32; Naperville, IL: Allenson, 1976), pp. 149-52.

62. Eaton, *Kingship and the Psalms*, p. 64.

meaning to God's name (v. 12; cf. Pss. 5:1[2]; 6:1[2]; 7:1[2]; 38:1[2]; 102:1[2]). His only hope is in God. "He dismisses all other hopes from his mind, and makes a chariot for himself of the extreme necessity of his case, in which he ascends upwards to God."[63] The blunt threefold imperatives — "hear" (*š*ᵉ*ma‘*, Ps. 102:1[2]), "listen" (*ha'ᵃzînā*, etymologically "give ear," Ps. 5:1[2]) and "answer me" (*'ᵃnēnî*, Pss. 38:15[16]; 102:1, 2[2, 3]) — underscore the psalmist's intimacy with God, the urgency of his situation, and his zeal (Ps. 5:1-2[2-3]). By identifying his psalm as "my prayer" (*t*ᵉ*phillātî*, Ps. 102: superscript, 17[1, 18]) and as "my cry for mercy" (*taḥᵃnûnay*, traditionally "supplication"; see n. 21; Ps. 6:9[10]), he throws himself on God's grace, not on his own merits. In addition to God's mercy, he hopes in "your faithfulness" (*be'ᵉmûnāt*ᵉ*kā*) and in "your righteousness" (*b*ᵉ*ṣidqāt*ᵉ*kā*, Ps. 5:8[9]). Faithfulness designates God's conscientious character and conduct. "Faithfulness," "reliability," "trustworthiness," signify ways of acting that grow out of a person's inner stability.[64] If we were rappelling off a cliff, we would want this sort of person to hold the rope. "If we confess our sins, he is faithful and just (true to his promise and true to his revealed character) to forgive us our sin." God is faithful.

b. Not to Be Put on Trial (143:2)

In appealing to God's righteousness, God's humble "slave" does not claim that his sufferings are undeserved. Unlike a proud Job he does not ask for a trial, for no one, not even the most godly among mortals, is without sin, apart from our blessed Lord Jesus Christ (1 Kgs. 8:46; Eccles. 7:20). "All living things" probably includes animals (Gen. 9:5) and angels (Job 4:18; 15:15). David "comes before God," says Weiser, "as a suppliant, not as one who makes demands of him."[65] Spurgeon put it this way: "David pleaded for an audience at the mercy seat, but he had no wish to appear before the judgment seat."[66] In light of universal depravity, the only way open to mortals for salvation is to throw themselves entirely upon God's covenant grace, a covenant enacted by the blood of Christ. *And do not enter* (*w*ᵉ*'al-tābō'*, see n. 24) *into judgment* pictures God as the prosecutor accusing the psalmist of crimes deserving his suffering, and treating him as a defendant in court litigation. "Do not come" is a metonym for "do not confront" (Job 9:32), and "judgment" is a metonym for the place of judgment (i.e., the court; Job 14:3; Eccles. 11:9) and for the process of judgment (i.e., litigation, the process of judg-

---

63. Calvin, *Psalms*, vol. 4 (Grand Rapids: Baker, 2003), p. 254.

64. A. Jepsen, *TDOT*, 317, s.v. *'aman*.

65. Artur Weiser, *The Psalms*, OTL (Philadelphia: Westminster, 1962), p. 819.

66. Charles Haddon Spurgeon, *The Treasury of David*, updated by Roy H. Clarke (Nashville: Thomas Nelson, 1997), p. 1459.

ment; Isa. 3:14 and Job 22:4). In short, he prays, "do not treat me as a criminal on trial."[67] The metaphor *with your "slave"* (*'eṯ-'aḇdeḵā*, Ps. 116:16) denotes his: (1) high calling and paradoxically his (2) humility, (3) responsible obedience to God's direction, (4) faithful dependence on God's care, and (5) personal intimacy of mutual trust.[68] His reason [*because*] for petitioning God not to bring him to trial is that *every living thing (ḵol-ḥāy)*, humankind and/or animals (Gen. 3:20; 6:19; 8:21; Job 12:10; 28:21; 30:23; Pss. 143:2; 145:16), himself included, cannot be in the right or proved right and so acquitted (Gen. 38:26: Job 9:15; 9:20; 11:12; 13:18; 33:12; 34:5; Isa. 43:9, 26; 45:25). *Before you* ("in your sight") means "in your estimation."[69] Although the "slave" is unaware of apostasy, he may be guilty of sins of ignorance or inadvertence (Ps. 139:24). He asserts the doctrine of universal sin, not to reduce his guilt, but to stress the universal need of God's covenant grace. Eternal life depends on God's mercy, not on human merit.

2. Lament (143:3-4)

a. The Enemy Pursues Him to the Grave (143:3)

The three introductory imperatives of verse 1 give way to three narrative indicatives of verse 3. Verse 3 represents the actions of the enemy without; verse 4, his feelings within. The two are related by reference to his essential being: "my *nephesh*" (v. 3A), "my life" (v. 3B), "my spirit" (v. 4A), "my heart" (v. 4B). At the dark center of verse 3, he links himself with the long dead. *Surely (kî)* formally introduces the reason for the petitions. The reason is given in three clauses that are semantically sequential. First, *the* (or *an*, see n. 26) *enemy* (*'ōyēḇ*, Ps. 6:10[11]) *pursues* (*rāḏap*, see n. 27; Ps. 7:1[2]) *me* (*napšî*, Pss. 6:3[4]; 38:12[13]). Second, *he crushes (dikkā'),*[70] as with a mace, *my life (ḥayyāh)*. *Ḥayyāṯ* derives from a verbal root meaning "to be/remain alive"; "the contrary, 'to be dead, to die' is always involved somehow" (v. 2B).[71] As a feminine adjective, *ḥayyâ* usually denotes free-living, untamed land animals in distinction from domesticated animals, but in its eleven uses as an abstract noun — always in poetry — it means "life." Here,

---

67. A. R. Johnson, *The Cultic Prophet and Israel's Psalmody* (Cardiff: University of Wales Press, 1979), p. 267.

68. Bruce K. Waltke with Charles Yu, *An Old Testament Theology* (Grand Rapids; Zondervan, 2007), p. 660.

69. BDB, p. 811, entry 4 (g), s.v. *pāneh.*

70. כָּא occurs eighteen times in the Bible. It is found only in poetry and only in the factitive D stems, except for the *niphal* ptcp. in Isa. 57:15, and only figuratively. For its parallels such as "grind," "break in pieces," "smite and injure," etc. see Fuhs, *TDOT,* 3.204.

71. G. Gerleman, *TLOT,* 1:413, s.v. *ḥyh.*

as in Job 33:18, 20, 22, 28; 36:14 (LXX), it occurs as a parallel and as an equivalent of *napšî*. After "crush," semantic pertinence demands that *'ereṣ* has its physical sense, *"to the ground (lā'āreṣ)."*[72] The phrase adds the vivid scene and pathos of his enemy so overpowering him that his knees buckle. Defeated and humiliated, his life swoons away under the deadly blows. Third, in that connection, *he* [the enemy] *causes me to dwell (hôšîḇanî) in a dark place (ḇᵉmaḥᵃšakkîm,* see n. 28; Ps. 88:6[7]). The analogy with those long dead shows that *yāšaḇ* has the meaning "to dwell," derived from its original sense "to sit," with the extended sense to "dwell in a place, emphasizing the stability and duration of residence."[73] The poetic metonym, "in a dark place," refers to the underworld (Ps. 88:18),[74] as inferred by the comparative *like those long dead (kᵉmētê 'ôlām).* The grave is a realm of gloom and darkness where the light of the sun cannot penetrate. Death "conjures up feelings of terror (Ps. 55:4[5]), panic (1 Sam. 5:11), and bitterness (1 Sam. 15:32; Eccles. 7:26)."[75] *'ôlām* ("long," see n. 29) means "the most distant time," a relative concept according to the temporal horizon assumed in the context.[76] If the phrase is original (see n. 30), the simile signifies that he whose name God promised to make famous is already reckoned among the forgotten (2 Sam. 7:9) and that God can raise the forgotten dead from the most remote times.

b. His Spirit Faints (143:4)

Narrative *waw (watitt'aṭṭēp), and so,* represents his subordinate consequential feelings, not a chronologically subsequent situation.[77] As the "slave's" life ebbs away into death, he says, *my spirit (rûḥî,* see 32:2) *grows faint (wattit'aṭṭēp,* see n. 33). As the body loses its vigor without food and drink (Ps. 107:5) and as starving children faint in the streets like a wounded man (Lam. 2:12), so the king's psychic, dynamic vitality loses boldness and courage to fight on (Isa. 57:16). *Within me ('ālay,* lit., "upon me") glosses reflexive *'al,* wherein the subject feels the pathos "upon himself."[78] *Within me (bᵉṭôḵî),* parallel to "upon me," underscores the interiority of his situation in contrast to the outward violence being done to him. *My heart (libê)* notes the inner forum where a person decides one's conduct on the

---

72. אֶרֶץ can also designate the cosmological earth in contrast to heaven and sea, a geographical portion of the earth or a political district of it.

73. Gerald H. Wilson, *NIDOTTE,* 2.550, s.v. *yāšaḇ.*

74. BDB, p. 365, s.v. מַחְשָׁךְ.

75. Eugene H. Merrill, *NIDOTTE,* 2.887, s.v. *môt.*

76. Ernst Jenni, *THAT,* 2.229-31, s.v. *'ôlām.*

77. *IBHS,* pp. 547, 550, P. 33.2a; 33.2.1d.

78. *IBHS,* p. 217, P. 11.2.13c.

interplay of thoughts, feelings, desires, and religious affections.[79] In the face of terror it *is dismayed* (*yištômēm*, see n. 35) — that is to say, it feels lifeless, becomes stiff and numb and so can no longer direct the body's functions.[80] The king is no rock-like stoic or one who wills to be happy; his pathos makes him yearn for God and a tangible level plateau (2 Cor. 4:7-9).

3. Confidence (143:5-6)

Nevertheless, in his enclosed darkness his memory and faith see the light of salvation beyond his immediate, visible horizon. His memory sees that light in the unseen remote past and his faith sees it in the unseen future of the morning (Pss. 22:3-5[5-7]; cf. 77:5, 11[6, 12]). Paraphrasing Spurgeon, sacred memory is the flower the bees of faith visit to make honey for their present distress.[81]

a. Recollection of Salvation History (143:5)

First, his memory serves as a handmaid to his faith (v. 5), prompting him to pray the manifold petitions of stanza II. *I remember (zāḵartî)* "pertains to past events that the memory awakens to realization because of their present significance."[82] *The days (yāmîm) from* [i.e., the beginning point of] *long ago (miqqeḏem)* have a formative character in the king's existential moment. The formative days in view may be the days God created the earth (Prov. 8:22), but more probably are the epoch when God founded the nation of Israel — the exodus, the wilderness wanderings, the conquest and settlement of the land (Pss. 44:1[2]; 74:12; Lam. 1:7; Isa. 51:9; Mic. 7:12). *I meditate (hāḡîṯî*, see 38:12[13]) *on all your deeds (bᵉḵol-poʿ°leḵā).* "All" includes as well those in his own experience (Ps. 22:4-5; 9-10[5-6; 10-11]). Poetic *pōʿal* (Ps. 5:5[6]) can be glossed "work" or "doing/deed"; the latter better connotes God's deeds in history (Pss. 44:1[2]; 77:12[13]); the former, his works of creation (Job 36:24) or both (Isa. 5:12; Ps. 64:9[10]). *Pōʿal* is a stock-in-trade parallel of the prosaic *maʿᵃśeh* (Isa. 5:12; 45:9; Ps. 64:9[10]). *What your hands have done* glosses "the work of your hands" (*bᵉmaʿᵃśēh yāḏîḵā*, Ps. 102:25[26]). Both *pōʿal* and *maʿᵃśeh* refer to what is accomplished by the action of their verbal root. *Maʿᵃśeh* can also refer to the *magnalia dei* (Exod. 34:10; Josh. 24:31; Judg. 2:7; Ps. 111:2) or to creation (Pss. 8:6[7]; 103:22; 104:24, 31). By reflecting on God's mighty acts in the past, David invigorates his faith and by mentioning them motivates the Lord

---

79. Waltke and Houston, *PACW*, p. 236.

80. F. Stolz, *TLOT*, pp. 1372-74, s.v. *šāmēm*.

81. Spurgeon, *Treasury of David*, p. 1460.

82. W. Schottroff, *TLOT*, p. 383, s.v. *zāḵar*.

to intervene in his present distress. The qualifying phrase *of your hands (yāḏîḵā)* adds the notions of power, care, and authority. The parallels "I remember" and "meditate" suggest the gloss *I consider (ʾăśôḥēḥ)* with thanks and praise, not the other meaning of *śîḥ*, namely, "loud, enthusiastic, emotionally laden speech."[83] In sum, "memory, meditation and musing are set together as three graces ministering to a depressed mind."[84]

b. Yearns for God in Prayer (143:6)

Having aroused his spiritual strength — that is to say, his faith and hope — he adds, *I spread out (pēraśtî)*[85] *my hands (yāḏay)*, as in swimming (Isa. 25:11), but upwards, *to you (ʾēleḵā)*. The context suggests the gesture pertains to prayerful petitions (Ps. 28:2; 1 Kgs. 8:38; Lam. 2:19; cf. Isa. 65:2; Lam. 1:17). His raised, spread-apart, and open hands (1 Kgs. 8:54; Ps. 141:2; Isa. 1:15; 1 Tim. 2:8) may symbolize wafting the prayer upward (Ps. 141:2) or lifting the heart toward heaven (Lam. 3:41).

The B verset underscores "to you." *My soul (napšî,* see n. 41) — his spiritual drive and appetite — *is like a thirsty (ʿăyēp̄â) land (ʾereṣ,* v. 3). עָיֵף signifies "to be faint/weary" as from exertion and hunger (Gen. 25:30) and specifically from thirst (Isa. 29:8; Prov. 25:25). Psalm 63:1(2) speaks of a "dry and thirsty land" *(ʾereṣ ṣiyyâ wᵉʿāyēp̄).* The poetic ellipsis stands for "as a dry and thirsty land [yearns for water] so my soul *yearns for you" (lᵉḵā,* see n. 42).

C. Petitions (143:7-12)

Urgent imperatives for help introduce both versets of 7 and 8 and also the A versets of verses 9 and 10. All the imperatives have the /ny/ suffix or its equivalent, and the three imperatives of verses 8 and 9 feature the *hiphil.* The compounding of these features yields an anaphoric effect.

1. Answer Me Quickly and Show Me the Way (143:7-8)

a. Answer Me Quickly and Show Me the Way (143:7)

The king's glimpse of his fountain of life is quickly fading away as he swoons into death. And so he prays, *answer me quickly (mahēr ʿᵃnēnî,* Ps. 102:2[3]), "I

---

83. *HALOT,* 3.1230, s.v. *śîḥ.*

84. Spurgeon, *Treasury of David,* p. 1460.

85. Verb is used of spreading out a garment (Judg. 8:25), wings (Deut. 32:11), sail (Isa. 33:23), etc.

AM" *(yhwh)*. Though not stated grammatically, the reason for his urgency is *my spirit (rûḥî,* v. 4) *is faint (kāleṭâ,* Ps. 102:3[4]) — that is to say, "my spirit to fight on fails." *Do not hide your face from me ('al-tastēr pānêkā,* Ps. 102:2[3]) — that is to say, "do not deal with me in anger." *For I am like* [or equal to] *(weʾnimšaltî,* see n. 44) *those who go down to the pit ('im-yōrḏê ḇôr). Ḇôr* denotes specifically the entrance hole into the grave. The phrase represents people facing imminent death (Ps. 22:29[30]). Unless God saves him now, all hope is gone.

b. Act According to Covenant (143:8)

Verse 8 applies the covenant relationship between "I AM" and his king to the crisis. The king looks to God to keep חֶסֶד, and he has the obligation to keep God's word, and so he asks: "Show me the way in which I should walk." Both sides of the covenant coin entail faith in "I AM," as the B versets note.

Cause me to hear (hašmîʿēnî) your kindness (ḥasdekā, Ps. 138:7[8]) by its inapposite juxtaposition of a physical activity, "hearing," with the spiritual attribute, signals "kindness" is a metonym of cause for deliverance (Ps. 51:8[10]). *Ḥeseḏ* essentially means "help to the needy" and has no precise English equivalent. It refers to a situation where a needy partner depends on another for deliverance, and the deliverer does so freely from his finer sensitivities of mercy, kindness, and loyalty. *In the morning (baḇōqer,* Ps. 5:3[4], see above) contrasts the darkness of the underworld with the morning light of salvation, points to the immediacy ("quickly," v. 7) of his salvation, and signifies the temporal shortness of his dark night in comparison to the duration of his salvation. His thought is similar to that of "weeping may remain for a night, but rejoicing comes in the morning" (Ps. 30:5[6]; so also Ps. 90:14). He puts God under obligation and so motivates God to be reliable by noting *because I trust in you (kî-ḇekā ḇāṭāḥtî).* His trust, his sense of security in the face of danger, comes from his knowledge of God's *ḥeseḏ* (Ps. 23:6). The king's responsibility is to be a faithful "slave" of Israel's Sovereign, and so he petitions: *Show me (hôḏîʿēnî,* see n. 46; Ps. 32:5) *the way [in which] I should walk (derek-zû ʾēlēk).* He needs to walk on the way that leads to life. He asks this, he explains, *for I entrust my life to you (kî-ʾēlêkā nāśāʾṭî nap̄šî).*[86]

---

86. נֶפֶשׁ נָשָׂא means "to be occupied with" and that in turn is nuanced by that toward which the נֶפֶשׁ is raised (e.g., wages [Deut. 24:15]; death [Prov. 19:18]; iniquity [Hos. 4:8], or falsehood [Ps. 24:4]). With "to 'I AM'" and its equivalents נֶפֶשׁ נָשָׂא means "I entrust my life to you" (Pss. 25:1; 86:4), a synonymous parallel with verse 8A.

2. Deliver Me from Enemies and Teach Me (143:9-10)

In this penultimate strophe David applies his expectations of his covenant relationship with "I AM" to his enemies.

a. Deliver Me from Enemies (143:9)

Verse 9A states his petition to be delivered from them and 9B affirms his dependence on his Covenant Partner. On God's part he asks: *Rescue me* (*haṣṣîlēnî*, Ps. 6:4[5]; 7:1[2]) *from my enemies* (*mē'ōy'ḇay*, see v. 3), "I AM" (*yhwh*, vv. 1, 7). A few manuscripts and LXX add the logical particle "because." *I flee to you* (see n. 48) expresses in yet another way his covenant trust in "I AM." "It may be an ill wind that makes us flee to God for shelter, but it blows us in the right direction."[87]

b. Teach Me and May Your Good Spirit Lead Me (143:10)

Verse 10 matches the king's covenant responsibility with that of "I AM" (v. 9) in the same way that 8B complements 8A. As in 8B he does not claim he merits deliverance but only asks: *Teach me* (*lamm'ḏēnî*, see n. 49) *to do* (*la'ᵃśôṭ*, Ps. 7:3[4]) *your will* (*r'ṣôneḵā*, Rom. 7:15–8:15). God must teach him to do what pleases God (v. 10A), and that entails that his "good spirit" lead him into right behavior (v. 10B). The common English gloss, "teach," conceals that לָמַד *piel* means "to habituate," not merely to signify intellectual learning. Unlike its synonym יָרָה *hiphil* (Ps. 32:8), לָמַד also occurs in reference to animals. The verb belongs surprisingly not in wisdom literature or in the prophets but "in Deuteronomy and in Psalm 119 in the series of the typical verbs for observing the law,"[88] and that is probably its use here. His prayer "to teach him" and his motivation *because you are my God* (*kî-'attâ 'ᵉlôhāy*, Ps. 5:2[3]) show that he keeps covenant out of desire, not out of reluctant compliance (Ps. 1:1, 2). He desires to do what is good but he cannot carry it out. So he prays for God's enablement: *may your good spirit* (*rûḥᵃḵā ṭôḇā*, Ps. 38:20[21]). God's spirit in the Old Testament, unlike in the New Testament, is a *qualitative* (i.e., superhuman power) aspect of his person, not *quantitative* (i.e., a separate person). Christ and his apostle reveal the Trinity, wherein God's Spirit is a separate person. As a spiritual living Being, God can impart his spirit to human beings. "Good" qualifies that spirit as aesthetically beautiful and functionally beneficial to enhance life and so desirable. God said to Moses, "I will cause all my goodness to pass in front of you" (Exod. 33:9-20). Subsequently he passes

---

87. Spurgeon, *Treasury of David*, p. 1462.
88. E. Jenni, *TLOT*, 2.647, s.v. *lmd*.

by, proclaiming his gracious attributes including his abounding love *(ḥeseḏ)*. In other words, the king is asking that God's spirit empower him with the same attribute that enables "I AM" to keep covenant. The verb "lead me" *(tanḥēnî)* originated in the shepherd's life and is commonly used in situations of leading one safely through snares and triumphantly to a desire and promised destiny,[89] here depicted as *on level ground (bᵉʾereṣ mîšôr)*, a place free of obstacles so that he can walk and run freely without fear of being tripped up. The metaphor signifies a place of safety, comfort, and prosperity and possibly of ethical, upright behavior (Isa. 11:4; 42:10; so also Ps. 26:12; 27:1). God upholds this deed (ethical behavior)–consequence (prosperity) nexus.

3. Reprise of Psalm (143:11-12)

Finally, David again asks God to preserve his life, to deliver him from his distress and destroy his enemies because of his covenant relationship with God.

a. Preserve Me (143:11)

For your name's sake (lᵉmaʿan-šimḵā, see Ps. 5:11[12]), "I AM" *(yhwh,* see Introduction, D. Rhetoric, above), *preserve my life (tᵉḥayyēnî,* see n. 51) adds the climactic motivation for "I AM" to show covenant fidelity. A. S. van der Woude notes: "Because names represent the personality, bearers must be concerned with their names, i.e., their good reputations."[90] Acting "for your name's sake" here means acting to uphold this reputation by keeping covenant. Since name and person are inseparable, if one loses one's name, one fades from memory and ceases to exist epistemologically.[91] On the other hand, by covenant faithfulness his name increases in honor and in fame.[92] *In your righteousness (bᵉṣidqāṯᵉḵā, v. 1) bring . . . out (ṯôṣîʾ, Pss. 25:17; 68:6[7]; 107:14, 28; 142:7[8]) me (napšî, v. 3) from distress (miṣṣārâ),* "the strong emotional response that one experiences when pressed externally by enemies."[93]

---

89. E. Jenni, *TLOT*, 2.730, s.v. *nḥḥ*.

90. A. S. van der Woude, *TLOT*, 3.1351.

91. Someone or something may exist as a reality known only by God alone but if that person or thing is unknown in human experience it is in practice nonexistent. So also God may exist in reality but not exist in human experience.

92. Waltke and Houston, *PACW*, p. 440.

93. J. Hartley, *TWOT*, 2.778, s.v. I. *ṣārāh*.

b. Eliminate My Enemies (143:12)

The psalm climactically concludes with a petition that "I AM," in connection with preserving his life, also eliminate his enemies, who by their opposition to "I AM's" king show their opposition to the righteous kingdom of God. *And in your unfailing love* (*ûbeḥasdekā*, v. 8) *silence (taṣmît) my enemies* (*'ōyebay*, v. 9). Concerning *ṣāmat* Hartley comments: "The verb is a very strong word for destruction or for completely silencing someone (KB; Job 23:17); e.g., friends vanish under stress like snow before the heat (Job 6:15ff.)."[94] *And so destroy* (*wiha'abadtā*, see n. 53; Ps. 5:6[7]) *all my foes* (*kol-ṣōra rê*, Pss. 6:7[8]; 7:4, 6[5, 7]; 23:5). *For I am your "slave"* (*kî 'anî 'abdekā*, v. 2).

PART IV. CONCLUSION

Like David's other lament psalms, the king's extreme grief — yes "burial" — and his buoyant, triumphant faith typify the sufferings and glory of Christ Jesus. In addition to this Christology, Psalm 143 also anticipates Paul's soteriology.[95] They both teach: (1) the universal deformity of human nature (v. 2; Rom. 3:20; Gal. 2:16); (2) God's election of his covenant partner out of this obnoxious humanity (his "slave," vv. 2, 12; Rom. 8:28-39; Eph. 1:3-14; 2 Thess. 2:13, 14; 2 Tim. 1:9, 10); (3) the covenant "slave's" devotion to God (vv. 6-10; Rom. 1:17; 3:21; Col. 3:20; 2 Tim. 2:4); (4) his need for God's Spirit to fulfill their spiritual yearnings (v. 10; Rom. 7:15–8:15); and (5) the elimination of the reprobate (v. 12; Rom. 2:5). The psalmist's intimacy with God is expressed as union with Christ in the mature theology of the New Testament. Christ's blood of the New Covenant makes this soteriology possible.

---

94. J. E. Hartley, *TWOT*, 2.770, s.v. *ṣāmat*.
95. Luther called 32, 51, 130, and 143 Pauline psalms.

Glossary

acedia: from the Greek *akēdeia,* "indifference"; state of indifference or apathy, especially in spiritual matters, which leads to becoming prey to temptation and pride. The Desert Fathers* saw it as highly contagious.

allegory: from the Greek *allegoria,* "speaking otherwise," by which another level of meaning is concealed within what is usually a story of some kind. Since its Greek origin is related to myth and fable, we have strongly distinguished this literary device from typology*.

anagogic: "elevation," that is, seeking symbolic meaning in the text.

analogy: closely linked with the theory of participation, analogy justifies our knowledge of God. This is controlled by the distinctives of the analogy of attribution and the analogy of proportionality, to avoid distorting the unique revelation of God, the "I AM," from anthropomorphism*. Thus analogy does not give us exhaustive knowledge of God nor remove the mystery of his divine being.

anthropomorphism: a figure of speech in which God is referred to as having human characteristics and/or functions.

Antiochene commentators: Christian commentators influenced by Semitic culture from Syria, who read the Scriptures in a rather literal and historical way that was self-consciously opposed to the excesses of allegory*.

aposiopesis: figure of speech in which a thought is deliberately and suddenly broken off in the midst of a sentence and left incomplete owing to either inability or unwillingness to finish the thought.

apostrophe: rhetorical device in which a speaker redirects comments to an absent or nonexistent third party.

arete: pursuit of excellence.

Arianism: possibly the most dangerous heresy of the church; following on the teaching of Lucian of Antioch, and later of Arius of Alexandria, it denied the divinity of Christ and was condemned by the Councils of Nicea (325), Constantinople (381)*, and Chalcedon (451).

Cappadocian Fathers: a collective term referring to the three Fathers of the Eastern church, Basil the Great of Caesarea (d. 379), his younger brother Gregory of Nyssa (d. c. 395), and their friend Gregory of Nazianzus (d. 389/90). Sometimes Amphilochius of Iconium (d. 395) is included in the group. Their key contributions to Trinitarian doctrine included the teaching that the Holy Spirit, as the third person of the Trinity, was *homoousios* with the Father and the Son, and how the *homoousia* between the Father, the Son, and the Holy Spirit relates to their distinctiveness. The terms *ousia* (oneness) and *hypostasis* (threeness) of God were now distinguished and no longer viewed synonymously.

Carolingian renaissance: the cultural renewal associated with the Frankish king Charlemagne and his successors in the eighth and ninth centuries.

chiasm: a literary device in which two or more words, phrases, or concepts are arranged in an inverted order.

Cistercian order: a Benedictine reform movement established in 1098 by St. Robert of Molesme; it emphasized solitude, recruitment of adult monks, and a return to manual labor.

compunction: from the Latin *compunctio,* a medical term for being pricked as by a thorn; first used in the audience's response to Peter's address in Acts 2:37, as "cut to the heart." Thereafter it referred to the sorrow over sin, and a state of being in the process of conviction, repentance, and conversion.

contrition: an expression of godly sorrow for one's sinful condition, reflected in the psalmist's experience of a "broken and a contrite heart" (Ps. 51:17). From the Latin *contritus,* it reflects on the Hebrew *daka',* or "bruised" (Isa. 57:15). For the Fathers, contrition — like compunction* — was fundamental to a biblical view of the relations of God and humanity.

Council of Constantinople (381 CE): repudiated Arianism.

Desert Fathers: early Christian hermits who, beginning in the third century, lived a life of asceticism in the Egyptian desert.

Devotio Moderna*: the Rheno-Flemish spiritual movement of reform that flourished in the Rhineland and Belgium in the thirteenth to early fifteenth centuries. This spontaneous lay movement was strongly influenced by women, the Beguines, who, with their male counterparts, the Beghards, led a communal movement of piety and charity from their homes. There are still Belgian Beguine communities today.

Dominican: name of the order founded by St. Dominic in the early thirteenth century to combat heretical teaching (such as that of the Albigensians); primarily concerned with preaching.

exegesis ("drawing out"): the attempt to determine the meaning of a text intended by the author(s) and warranted to be understood by the original audience.

form criticism: a development from historical criticism, an interpretive approach that seeks to identify the literary genre of a text and provide a classification of diverse literary expressions.

Fourth Lateran Council: the twelfth ecumenical council convened by Pope Innocent III in 1215, with the intent of clerical reform, especially of the revival of the Dominican and Franciscan orders.

gematria: system of Jewish numerology in which the numerical value of letters, words, and phrases is calculated in order to explore the significance of the interrelationships between those with identical numerical value.

Gnostics: adherents of Gnosticism, the heretical movement popular in the second century that based salvation upon acquiring inner knowledge.

hapax legomenon ("spoken once"): a word that appears only once in a defined corpus of literature.

haplography: accidental omission by a copyist of a letter, word, or lines due to the similarity and close proximity of letters, words, or lines.

Heilsgeschichte: German for "salvation history," reading the story of Scripture as God's saving work in history.

hermeneutics: the study of the theory, principles, and methods of interpretation, especially pertaining to ancient texts such as the Scriptures.

hexapla: following the innovation of "the paged book," Origen created a six-columned text of various Hebrew and Greek versions of the Old Testament, in the attempt to standardize Greek translations of the Hebrew original. It was a remarkable breakthrough in reducing a vast armarium of scrolls into one text.

inclusio: a literary device used in Hebrew poetry in which key words or phrases are repeated at the beginning and end of a poem as a means of achieving closure.

Janus: a literary device deriving its name from the two-headed Roman god, perched on the door simultaneously looking forward and backward. In literature, it refers to a transitional passage that hearkens back to what precedes it as well as hearkening ahead to what follows, thus linking the passages together.

literary criticism: as old as literature itself have been the explication and evaluation of works of literature. The early Fathers adopted various principles of criticism from the classical culture, just as contemporary biblical criticism applies contemporary literary theories, both conservatively and more radically.

litotes: a form of understatement in which something is affirmed by denying its opposite.

Lollards: late medieval reformers in England, who as a lay movement emphasized the authority of Scripture over the clergy, and were engaged also in the reform of morals.

LXX: Roman numerals for seventy, denoting the Septuagint, the oldest known Greek version of the Hebrew Bible, translated between the third and first centuries BCE in Alexandria. "Seventy" is a reference to the claims of the apocryphal "Letter of Aristeas" that 72 scribes took 72 days to complete the translation of the Torah; in common usage the term LXX has been extended to refer to the whole Old Testament.

Manichaeanism/Manichees: the doctrine and followers of the Persian Mani (216-276/277), who promoted a Gnostic-type dualistic religion whose purpose was a world mission to release the light enclosed potentially in humanity. Mani claimed to be the transcendent successor of Jesus and produced an extensive literature in his claims to supersede Christianity.

Marcionites: followers of Marcion, the heretical second-century bishop who rejected the Old Testament Scriptures and the God described in them as a sub-deity in favor of the Jesus portrayed in selected portions of the New Testament.

Masoretic Text (MT): the authoritative text of the Hebrew Bible; in the seventh to tenth centuries CE, Jewish traditionalists (Masoretes) added vowel points, textual markers, and annotations in an attempt to preserve how the text was read; the oldest extant manuscript dates to c. 895 CE.

merismus: from the Greek *merismos,* "distribution"; a literary device in which totality is expressed by referring to opposites or extremes; an example would be Genesis 1:1 in which "heaven and earth" are used to represent the entire cosmos.

metaphor: a figure of speech in which an implicit comparison is made between two seemingly unfamiliar objects/things.

metonymy: a figure of speech in which a part is used to refer to the whole of something to which it is closely related.

Mishnah: from the Hebrew *shnh,* meaning "to repeat, to learn"; it is the first record of rabbinical oral law, from about 200 CE, in six main categories of laws for daily life.

missal: a liturgical book containing instructions for the celebration of Mass throughout the year. It includes prayers, psalms, other biblical readings, and ceremonial and singing directions.

Monarchianism: the name given to second- and third-century heretical writers who denied the separate persons in God. Differing names were given according to their bias: the Adoptionists held Jesus to be a mere man; the Modalists identified the divine persons as mere modes of being for the one God; eastern modalists were known as Sabellians.

Montanists: a second-century apocalyptic movement originating in Phrygia and spreading later through North Africa, which valued contemporary outpourings of the Spirit over ancient biblical prophecy.

Pelagianism: the fourth-century heresy of Pelagius, a Roman lawyer, who taught that humans have responsibility for their own salvation, thus minimizing the role of the grace of God in human redemption.

penance: from the Latin *poena,* "punishment"; it reflects upon both the inner turning towards God as a sinner and the outward discipline of the church in appropriate punishment, in order to reinforce repentance of heart by outward deeds. Later, for the Reformers, more emphasis was given to divine mercy than to the pursuit of a penitential way of life.

penitence/penitential: the act and result of penance* were celebrated from the early Middle Ages in the recitation of the seven penitential psalms (Pss. 6, 32, 38, 51 [*Miserere*], 102, 130 [*De Profundis*], and 143). They were regularly recited by the Western church on Fridays during Lent. Many vernacular rhyming versions were made of these psalms. For catechetical purposes these psalms were appropriated to "the Seven Deadly Sins": Ps. 6 against wrath; Ps. 32 against pride; Ps. 38 against gluttony; Ps. 51 against lechery; Ps. 102 against avarice; Ps. 130 against envy; Ps. 143 against sloth.

postexilic: the period initiated by the Persian liberation of the Jews from Babylonian exile under Cyrus beginning in 538 BCE.

Qumran: ascetic Jewish sect living near the Dead Sea from the second century BCE to the first century CE, which produced the Dead Sea Scrolls.

scholia: grammatical, critical, and explanatory comments inserted in texts used for teaching.

Talmud (derived from the Hebrew *lmd,* "to study or learn"): rabbinic commentary and interpretative writings viewed by Jewish scholars as second in authority only to the Old Testament text; it includes both the Mishnah (the oral law put to writing) and the Gemarah (commentary on the Mishnah). The Jerusalem Talud is also known as the Palestinian Talmud. The word "Talmud," when used without qualification, usually refers to the Babylonian Talmud.

targum: an Aramaic paraphrase or loose translation of the Hebrew Scriptures that was given after the reading of the Hebrew Scriptures as an accommodation for Jews who were unfamiliar with Hebrew.

Tell Fekherye inscription: a life-sized statue of a man discovered in northern Syria in 1979; the statue contains an engraved bilingual (Assyrian and Aramaic) inscription on both sides of the man's skirt.

Tetragrammaton (Greek, "four letters"): referring to God's name in Hebrew, YHWH, usually translated in English as Lord, and in this commentary as "I AM."

theodicy: the vindication of divine goodness in light of the presence of evil in the world.

tropological reading: a mode or turn of speech; at first it meant no more than allegory*. But for Origen, the "third exposition" of Scripture, after the "literal" and the "allegorical" (as the "edification of faith"), was the "tropological" (for the "edification of morals"). What had been written prophetically ought to be explained morally as well, the medieval commentators argued. In broad terms, this meant that what was understood should be applied in moral behavior.

typology: a unique specie of promise and fulfillment. Whereas prophecy is concerned with prospective words and their fulfillment, typology is concerned with comparative historical events, persons, and institutions recorded in the Bible. Unlike allegory*, which is a loose, literary device, typology is fixed by the biblical canon.

Ugaritic: ancient language of north Syria, discovered in 1928 in the Ras Shamra texts, which illumine cultural ways the Old Testament writers borrowed from the surrounding cultures.

Unitarian: believer in one God who denies the Trinity and thence the divinity of Christ.

Vulgate (from the Latin *editio vulgata,* meaning "the common version"): this version of the Bible was primarily translated by Jerome, c. 383. From the sixth century it became the accepted version of the Western church. In 1546, the Council of Trent decreed it was the exclusive authority for the Bible.

Index of Authors

COMMENTATORS ON THE PSALMS
(up to the end of the sixteenth century)

Alcuin of York, 14, 15, 71, 77-79, 128, 129

Alfred the Great, 71, 77-79

Ambrose, 99, 101, 122-24, 216

Aquinas, Thomas, 175, 177-78, 187

Athanasius, 14, 45, 239

Augustine of Hippo, 14, 15, 18, 25, 77, 79, 98-104, 119, 122, 124-26, 128, 129, 153, 155, 173, 259-64

Basil the Great, 43, 45, 46, 73-74

Bucer, Martin, 212, 215

Calvin, John, 1, 93, 120, 164, 166, 167, 169, 170, 172, 175, 180-82, 187, 188, 190, 196, 212-13, 215, 231, 254, 259, 263-65

Cassiodorus, 14, 15, 122, 126-29

Charlemagne, 71, 77-79, 128

Chrysostom, John, 71, 73-77, 125, 153, 238, 244

Cyprian, 153

Denys the Carthusian (or Dionysius the Carthusian), 130, 259, 261-63

Desert Fathers, 15, 16, 19, 211

Didymus, 45

Erasmus, 149-55, 213

Eusebius, 19, 45

Evagrius Ponticus, 16, 19, 49, 211

Fisher, John, 210-12

Gregory Nazianzen, 43, 45

Gregory of Nyssa, 43-50, 73-74, 101, 151, 152

Gregory the Great, 16, 79, 128, 262

Hilary of Poitiers, 20, 153, 238-42

Hippolytus of Rome, 18

Irenaeus of Lyons, 45

Jerome, 18-23, 25, 31, 43, 101, 125, 150, 152, 153, 155, 243

Lefèvre D'Étaples, Jacques, 212-16, 262

Luther, Martin, 8, 15, 87, 119, 149, 153, 175, 178-80, 212, 238, 251

Origen, 15, 19, 20, 43-45, 101, 153, 175-77, 213, 240

Rolle, Richard, 122, 123, 130, 149

Tertullian, 128

Theodore of Mopsuestia, 125

Theodoret of Cyrrhus, 19, 125-26

Thomas à Kempis, 213, 259, 261

Tyndale, William, 216

Vermigi, Peter Martyr, 215-16

Wyatt, Sir Thomas, 217-18

MODERN AUTHORS
(since the seventeenth century)

Index of Subjects

Abram, Abraham, 9, 11, 171, 181, 257; faith of, 103

Adam, 9, 12, 41, 257; fall of, 263; as human, 112

Affliction, afflicts, afflicted, 154, 160, 164, 165, 168, 169-70, 182, 186, 206, 212, 221, 227, 228, 230, 234, 237; cause of, 58-59, 144, 181, 239; of Christ, 124, 147, 173; of David, 42, 56, 61, 152, 263-64; emotional, 122; justness of, 128, 178-79, 181; and lament, 175; length of, 166; physical, 118, 126-27, 130, 134, 136-39, 204, 237, 252; prayers of, 78, 210, 214, 218, 223-25; psychological, 118, 153, 204

Agony, agonies, 92, 113, 127

Alienation, 173-74

Allegory, 20, 44, 155; allegorical, 46, 101, 178, 216, 260

Anagogy, 44, 152; anagogical, 44-45, 178, 216

Anger, angry, 8, 30, 65, 259; of Absalom, 75; against, 15, 16; of God, 48, 50, 54-57, 59, 60, 80, 91, 115, 219, 221, 228, 279; of Holy One, 112; of "I AM," 47, 63, 131, 137-38; of Israel, 205

Anguish, 1, 172, 236, 253; of Christ, 148, 163, 165, 172, 226, 236, 253; of David, 63, 64, 113, 148, 163, 165; physical, 226

Anxiety, 5, 165, 265; anxious, 167, 214, 265

Baptism, 13, 15, 98, 124

Blessing, 177, 180, 181, 213; blessed, 44, 74, 102, 104, 109, 111, 121, 127, 154, 176, 236, 241, 274; blessedness, 110, 121; and Christ, 241, 274; covenantal, 5, 187, 190, 199, 209, 236; and forgiveness, 104, 109-11, 121; of God, 24, 41, 61; and memory of the deceased, 13; to the nations, 10; spiritual, 42, 60, 146, 154, 213

Chastisement, 56, 64, 129, 130, 169

Chiasm, 27, 53, 64, 109, 113, 190, 222, 225; chiastic structure, 27, 31, 35, 40, 188, 192

Christ, 20, 22, 45, 99-100, 149, 209, 242, 280; and church, 14, 18, 21, 25, 129, 174, 179, 181-82, 214-16; and covenant, 257-58, 274, 282; David as type of, 42, 74, 77, 87, 97, 102, 147-48; divinity of, 239-41; friends of, 5; grace of, 12-13; imitation of, 50, 73, 76, 213, 244, 259-60; mediatorial work of, 98; resurrection of, 14, 36, 69-70, 180, 208; righteousness of, 173; sacrifice of, 121; Second Coming, 76, 171; sufferings of, 79, 122, 129-30, 147-48, 152, 176-77, 180, 202, 237, 258, 262, 282; *totius Christi* (the whole Christ), 101, 104, 124-26, 129, 174, 259-60. *See also* Jesus

Church Fathers, 19, 46, 47, 77, 153, 239, 264

Compassion, appeals for, 64, 171, 139; and "I AM," 54, 63, 66, 161, 219, 221, 229; compassionate, 221

Complaint, 4, 7, 59, 164, 165, 181, 229; God-directed, 10, 12, 134, 135, 161, 186, 218, 221, 225

INDEX OF SCRIPTURE REFERENCES

5:11	88, 96, 198, 228, 281	12:6-7	6	23:1-6	66
6	6, 7, 14, 83, 88, 93, 97, 126, 133, 151, 222, 246, 270	13:2-3	59	23:3	36, 37, 272
		13:3	62, 141, 232	23:5	282
		15	33	23:6	279
		15:1	33	24:2	235
6:1	17, 55, 137, 225, 274	15:3	34, 145	25	38, 160
6:1-8	91	16:9-11	12	25:5	255
6:2	113, 138, 226	17	38	25:7	136
6:3	141, 255, 275	17:1	67	25:16	231
6:4	88, 89, 280	17:6	225	25:17	281
6:5	12, 96, 198, 229	17:6-7	89	25:18	136
6:6	226	18:2	93, 197	26	137
6:7	282	18:6	30, 225	26:11	258
6:8	95, 226, 228	18:13	96	26:12	281
6:9	224, 225, 274	18:14	94	27–28	38
6:10	88, 198, 227, 275	18:25	34	27:1	281
7-9	83	18:26	115	27:1-6	66
7	7, 137, 269	18:30	93	27:5	116
7:1	146, 274, 275, 280	18:35	93	27:8	56
7:3	280	18:37-45	197	27:11-12	37
7:4	282	18:41	30	28:2	278
7:5	146, 206, 269	19	9	28:8	61
7:6	197, 205, 207, 282	19:6	206	29	9
7:7	116	20:1-4	226	29:10	232
7:8	202, 269	20:6	147	30:2	30
7:9	118, 140, 203, 226	20:7	197	30:3	58
7:12	198	20:9	147	30:5	56, 279
7:15	145	21:1	61	31	38, 107
8	9, 83	21:7	96	31:1	61
8:2	203	21:9	194	31:2	225
8:4	217	21:13	94	31:9-13	106
8:6	277	22	124, 150, 208	31:12	6, 235
9	107	22:2	6	31:14	106
9:1-2	83	22:2-3	29	31:20	116
9:2-3	41	22:3-5	277	31:22	106
9:6	61	22:4-5	272, 277	31:23	107, 145
9:10	244	22:7	6, 202	32	7, 14, 15, 54, 133, 160, 222, 246, 270
9:14	233	22:8-9	6		
9:15	95	22:9	6	32:1	138, 241, 254
10	107	22:9-10	277	32:2	138, 205, 225
10:2	225	22:12	6	32:3	137, 235
10:10	140	22:14	6	32:4	138
11:2	94	22:15	90	32:5	17, 241, 254, 279
12	6, 14, 26, 44, 45	22:22	198	32:6	229
12:1	92	22:24	206	32:8	280
12:4	6	22:28	279	32:10	145
12:5	233	22:31	232	33	107, 150

CPSIA information can be obtained
at www.ICGtesting.com
Printed in the USA
LVHW110612130520
653793LV00003B/28